Williamson County Tennessee

VOLUME 1

WILLS, INVENTORIES AND ADMINISTRATIONS

1800–1812

WPA RECORDS

Heritage Books
2024

HERITAGE BOOKS

AN IMPRINT OF HERITAGE BOOKS, INC.

Books, CDs, and more—Worldwide

For our listing of thousands of titles see our website
at
www.HeritageBooks.com

A Facsimile Reprint
Published 2024 by
HERITAGE BOOKS, INC.
Publishing Division
5810 Ruatan Street
Berwyn Heights, MD 20740

International Standard Book Number
Paperbound: 978-0-7884-8537-4

Williamson County

Vol. 1 - Wills, Inventories, Adm., Acc., ect.,
1800-1812
Office of County Court Clerk

Page
(1)
James Hopkins Will-July 18, 1800. In the name of God, Amen
I James Hopkins of the County of Williamson and State of Tennessee
being sick and weak in body but sound in mind and memory do make
and ordain this my last will and testament as follows (viz.0
Item. I give my body to the dust and my soul to God that gave
it hoping for a happy resurrection at the great day of Judgment
only through the righteousness of Jesus Christ imputed to my
soul.
Item. My will and desire is, that my Executors pay all my just
debts and to enable them to do this that they collect a bond I
have on John Blackamore and likewise they sell a young stud horse
named Hyderalle to the best advantage for the defraying the same.
Item. I lend to my beloved wife Elizabeth the house and plantation
I now live on during her widowhood and at her marriage or death
all my household furniture, stocks of all kinds, tools of every
sort be equally divided between my children that now live with
me (viz.) John, Elizabeth, Jonathan, Hannah, Jason, Winifred,
Heziah, Bitha, and James Pickering to them and their heirs forever.
Item. I give my daughter Lucy sundry matters of household furniture and stock in my lifetime as her full share of my property
to her and her heirs forever.
Item. I give the tract of land and plantation I now live on containing one hundred and forty acres to my son Jason to him and
his heirs forever my will and desire is that as my sons, Jonathan,
Jason and James Pickering come of age that my executors furnigh
them with a riding creature, cow and calf to be given to them
out of the estate to them and their heirs forever.
Item. I give to my wife Elizabeth one mare called Blaze with
saddle and bridle to her during her natural life. And whereas
I have received fifty dollars of John Pickering in part pay for
one hundred acres of land being a part of my tract on Stone's
river, there being a balance due me of one Hundred Dollars, my
will and desire is that if said John Pickering does not within
twelve months from this date pay to my Executors the said balance
of one Hundred Dollars, they then proceed to sell said Hundred
Acres and after paying back the before mentioned fifty Dollars to
the said James Pickering the remains be equally divided between
my Daughters living with me Viz. Elizabeth, Hannah, Winifred,
Heziah and Bitha. My desire is that if my Executors at any time
shall think it most for the good of my sons or Expedient for
them to be bound to a trade that they do agree thereto I do
constitute my beloved wife Elizabeth and Brother Joseph Hopkins
my Executors to this my last will and Testament. Given under my
hand this ninth day of February 1800.
                    Signed James Hopkins.
    The Execution of which will and Testament as before recited
was in Open Court held for the County of Williamson May Session
1800 proved to be the Act and Deed of the said James Hopkins,

Page
(2)

dec.d by the Oath of John Pickering a subscribing witness thereto
at which time Elizabeth Hopkins and Joseph Hopkins qualified as
Executors and Executress and Received Letters Testamentary.

Page
(3)   James Hopkins Inventory and Valuation as made and returned into
Court Aug. Session 1800 by Elizabeth Hopkins Exctrs. (to wit) one
cow, calf and Bell, 9 Doll. 50 cents, one ditto, 12 doll. one
ditto 12 Doll., one ditto, 9 Doll., one ditto., 10 dollars, one
ditto. 11 Doll., one Heifer, 5 Doll., Four yearlings 18 Dollars,
one Steer 9 Dollars, one Horse and Bell 10 Dollars, one mare 60
Dollars, one ditto 55 Dollars, Two Coalts 40 Dollars, Fifty two
head of hoggs 52 Dollars, one Grindstone 50 cents, four pole axes
7 Dollars 50 cents, one Broad Axe 4 Dollars, four Hoes 3 Doll. 50
cents, one plough 3 Dollars, Iron tools to the amt. of 6 Dolls. 75
cents, one trowel 1 Dollar, one bell 50 cents, one Gun 2 Dollars,
one Sickle 50 cents, Pewter 16 Dollars 50 cents, Crockery ware 3
Dolls. 75 cents, Tins I Doll 50 cts., one Lamp 25 cents, clevises
75 cents, cooper ware 2 Dollars 50 cents, one crock, 50 cents, one
Auger 50 cents, Carter heels and harness 8 Dollars, one plough 2
Dollars 50 cents, Barrels 2 Dollars, Castings potts ovons 23 Dolls.
50 cts., Loom and harness 11 Dolls., two Saddles 12 Dollars, Mounting
for a cupboard 3 Dolls., one chest 4 Dollars, three beads and furniture 55 Dollars, one Table 1 Doll. 50 cents, Six chairs 3 Dollars,
Books 2 Dollars 33 1/3 cents, Razor and Box 1 Doll.50 cents, two
flatirons 1 Doll. 75 cents,Wheels, reel and cards 5 Dolls, knives
and forks 50 cents, one Looking-glass 50 cents, one pair of Scissors
33 1/3 cents, one Sugar tub 25 cents, two Baskets Spools, 1 Doll.,
thirteen Geer 12 Dolls., one slate 50 cents, and one frow 75 cents.
                    Signed Sam.l McCutchen
                           Sam.l Edmeston

Page
(4)   JOHN STEWART, Inventory of Appraisement as made and returned
into Court Nov. Session 1800 by Thomas Stewart Adm. to wit.
    A motled fac'd. heifer 7 Dolls. a white Dunish heifer 7 dolls,
a red cow and yearling 10 Dolls, a black crommy cow 7 Dolls., a
Dun bull yearling 4 Dolls., a red bull yearling 2 Dolls 50 cents, one
old dun cow and heifer calf 12 Dolls, a white spotted heifer with
a heifer calf 8 Dolls, a brown white fac'd. cow and bull yearling
12 Dolls, a young dun cow and heifer calf 12 Dollars, one brown
yearling heifer with a star 4 Dolls., a Brown crommy cow with a
bull calf 11 Dolls, one white heifer with five red spots in the side
5 Dollars, ten large hogs sows and Barrows 23 Dollars, ten small shoats
10 Dollars, one old Grey and mare colt 25 Dolls., a large grey mare
thirteen years old 40 Dolls., a mare call'd Irish grey (since dead)
35 Dollars, a grey two year old colt 80 Dollars, a bay yearling filly 80 dolls.,a black horse colt 15 Dolls., one big pot 2 Dolls., a
large Dutch oven 3 Dolls. 33 1/3 cents, an Iron Kettle 7 Dolls.,
one handsaw 1 Doll 50 cents, Drawing knife 33 1/3 cents, two wedges
1 Doll 50 cents, four Sickles 1 Doll. 50 cents, a Barrel 50 cents,
a tub 25 cents, a leather collar hems and chains and a husk collar
traces and hems 4 Dolls., one lock chain 2 Dolls. a mans saddle
2 Dolls.,50 cents, a womans saddle 2 Dolls 50 cents, one old saddle 50 cents, a trowel 25 cents, a swingletree for one horse 50
cents, four old Bridles some old iron and curry comb 3 Dolls 25

a plow and irons, clevis swingle tree and screw of another, 7 Dolls.,
a grubing how 1 Dollar 25 cents, an ax 2 Dolls, a large hoe and
small one 25 cents, a mattock 2 Dolls. 25 cents, a spade 2 Dolls, a her
horse brush 6½ cents, a frying pan 1 Doll., a tea kettle 25 cents,
two brass candlesticks 3 Dollars, a tin coffee pot funnel and candlemoulds 50 cents, a coffee mill 1 Doll., one large pewter plate
2 Dolls., one ditto 2 dolls., one ditton 2 Dolls, five small pewter plates and two broken ones 2 Dolls, five pewter basons, 1 Doll
50 cents, one large looking glass and one small 2 Dolls, a bucket
Page   25 cents, a small vessel 12½ cents, a gun powder horn, shot bag and
(5)   moulds 10 Dolls. 7 Spoons and a tin cup 50 cts. a large Bible 2
Dolls., Allins Alarm 2 Vol. 2 Dolls, Josephus' works 4 Vol. 4 Dolls.,
Nesbit on ecleseastes, confession of faith and Psalm books 2 Dolls..,
50 cents, shema sacrum gospel sonnets come and welcome 2 Dolls,
Satans invisible world, due priviledge of Scots goverment, Robert M.
Ward and two pamphlets 1 Doll 50 cents, pamphlets 50 cents five old
bibles 2 Dolls, three old sermon books and history of William 3 1 Dpl.
a brush 12½ cents, thirteen knives and ten forks 1 Doll., a brush
12½ cents, thirteen knives and ten forks 1 Doll 50 cts., a reel 1 Dol.
a Spining Wheel 2 Dolls., a feather bed, 2 sheets a pair double blankets, a coverlet bolster and pillows 18 Dolls, one ditto with under
bed 18 Dolls., a great coat, small coat, jacket, leather breeches,
three shirts, boots, etc., 10 Dolls, two screw Augers and a barrel
auger 1 Dol 50 cents, a lantern 12½ cents, a trunk 2 Dolls, a large
trunk 1 Dol., a trunk 2 Doll. a chest 1 Dol, a pair saddlebags 25
cents, three small shawls 2 dolls 50 cents, two large shawls 2
Dolls, one large shawl 1 Doll. 7 shawls 7 Dolls, two shawls 2 Dolls.
1 black spotted shawl 75 cents, seven black spotted shawls 5 Dolls.
25 cents, 4 yellow spotted handkerchiefs 4 Dolls, five 4½ yds. of
large spotted callico 5 Dolls., 4½ yds of green spotted callico 3
dolls 83 1/3 cents, 2½ yards white spotted callico 1 Dol 87½ cents,
3 yards spotted callico 3 Dolls, 14¼yds spotted callico 14 Dolls.
25 cents, 11 3/4 yard blue spotted callico 8 Dolls. 81 ½ cents, 1 3/4
yards of callico 1 Doll 31½ cents, 11½ yds. callico 8 Dolls. 62½ cents
3/8 yd. of callico 25 cents, 13 yds. blue ribbon 3 Dolls, 25 cents,
1½ yards blue ribbon37½ cents 4 yards of purple ribbon 37½ cents,
5 ½ yards blue ribbon 1 Doll 37½ cents, 14 yards of striped ribbon
1 Doll 25 cents, 11 yards of striped ribbon 1 Dol 83 1/3 cents, 7
yards purple ribbon, 1 Doll 16 2/3 cents, 1/3 yards blue ribbon 43
cents, 10½ yards striped ribbon at ₺ 1, 13½ yds Hupedril bags 1 Dol.
80 cents, 2 bags 75 cents, 22 Spools of leather 3 Dolls, a cask with
flaxseed 16 cents, a tin cup with some pewter 25½ cents, a set of
shoemakers tools whetstones and lasts 1 Doll. 50 cents, a bottle 25
cents, a large hemp hackle 2 Dolls, a smaller heckle 2 Dolls, two
gimblets 12½ cents, a fine brass heckle 2 Dolls, two shawls 1 Doll.
50 cents, 1 Tacket, one pair of stockings, i crevat, a quantity of
corn, one sow 2 Dolls. 50 cents, 4 pigs 4 Dolls, six chairs 3 Dolls.
The above is a true copy of the property and prices appraised Sept.
6th, 1800, by John Johnson, Dan.l Perkins and Sam.l McCutchen to
which they gave the following certificate. We the subscribers appraised the above property 6th September 1800. Signed John Johnson, Dan.l
Perking, Sam.l McCutchen, Underneath of which was wrote, since found.
Page   One grind stone, one hair sifter, one razr, hone, razor, case
(6)

and shaving box, 30 chicken fowls, six ducks, Christopher Mosers
note dated Dec. 4th, 1798 for ₤-1. 19Vorg. currency payable 10
days after date 6 Dolls 50 cents, Frederic Fisher's note dated Dec.
4th 1798 for ₤1:4½ currency payable ten days after date 3 Dolls
56¼ cents, John Carpenters note for ₤2-14-6 date 13th Feby 1798
payable March 2nd next 9 Dolls 8 1/3 cents, Noel Watkins note for
8 Dolls. 16 2/3 cents, John Weakleys note for $11.7 pence paid
$10, 1 Doll. 10 cents, Alexander Gower on acct. 17/11, 2 Doll.
88 cents William McDowels note for ₤11-17 Pennsylvania money dated
Oct. 24th 1767 31 Dolls. 60 cents, Frederick Hebel by Acct. Dr.
₤4,16 Pennsylvania currency 12 Dolls 90 cents, Elisha Gowers acct.₤
12- sd. V. cury 1 Doll. 61 cents, Thomas Molloys bond for 274 acres
land which if not completed with may belong to the administrator
411 Dolls 10 cents, Thos. Weakley's acct. 10/6. 1 Doll. 75 cents.
Thomas Holemane acct ₤10-4-34 Dolls, Moses Moody Acct. ₤3-11-3 11
Doll 87½ cents, Hannah Denton ₤ 1-19-6 Dolls95 cents, Adam Binckley's
note 13 Dolls 75 cents, Holme note ₤2-4-8¼ 7 Dollars 30 cents, John
Nash note dated 13th Oct. 1798 payable last March next after for
15 Dollars.
        The above is a true inventory of the goods and chattles rights
and credits of John Stewart dec.d so far as they have come to my Possession or knowledge 4th Nov. 1800.
                        Signed Thos. Stuart, adm.
        The foregoing Inventory as above recited was in Open Court held
for the County of Williamson November Session 1800 proven by the Oath
of Thomas Stuart Admr. to be just and true so far as they have come to
Page   his knowledge or Possession.
(7)

        JOHN HIGHTOWER inventory as made and returned to Court May Ses-
sion 1801 by Polly Hightower Administratrix (to wit).
        Eight negrows, one feather bed and furniture, two blankets,
two sheets, one counterpane, one bed quilt, one stand of curtain,
eight volumes of Sterns works, three volumes of the Laws of the
United States, Gordons History of America in three volumes, Wilsons
reports, in three volumes Bullards one volume, one Small Dictionary,
Thondan s Dictionary in full, one flax wheel, one womans Saddle,
two Dozen Pewter plates, five dishes three Basons, half Doz Spoons,
two glass Salt Cellars, one small iron kettle, one dutch oven, one
copper tea kettle, one weding hoe, one ax, two carpenters augers, two
trunks one pair cotton cards, three small servers, one stock of
glass, one Decanter and one pair of pot Hooks.
        John Hightower Acct. sales ret.d by Polly Hightower admrx. May
Session 1802 property sold 25th March 1802, to wit.
        Polly Hightower one feather bead and furniture thirty dollar,
one stand of curtens fourteen Dollars, one counterpin Dolls. (2)
50 cents, one bead quilt 3 Dolls, 20 cents, one rose Blanket 3
Dolls. pme rose blanket 3 Dolls., three pewter Dishes 5 Dolls,
six pewter plates 3 Dolls. 80 cents, six pewter plates 3 Dolls. 90
cents, one pewter dish 3 Dolls 10 cents, two pewter basons 4 Dolls
55 cents, one pewter bason and dish 3 Dolls, 65 cents, one pewter
bason 3 Dolls 5 cents six pewter plates 3 Dolls., 28 cents, five
pewter plates 3 Dolls, 15 cwnts, two brass candlesticks 3 dolls.
two salt cellars 4 Dolls. 26 cents, one volume Coopers reports 2
Dolls. 30 cents. Sheredans Dictionary in full 8 Dolls. 25 cents,

two waiters and bread dish 2 dolls., 2 cents, one kea kettle
2 Dolls., one pepp er mill 1 Doll, one Decanter 35 cents, one t
trunk, 6 dolls., 10 cents, one small trunk 2 Dolls., one pole ax
2 Dolls. 10 cents, one small trunk 2 Dolls., one pole ax 2 Dolls.,
2 cents, one small trunk 2 Dolls., one pole ax 2 Dolls., 2 cents,
one small trunk 2 Dolls., one pole ax 2 Dolls 2 cents, one bake
oven 2 Dolls 26 cents, one kettle and hooks 2 Dolls 26 cents,
richard Hightower three Volls. Laws of the United States 10 Dolls,
three Vol. of Gordons History of America 8 Vols. Wilson Reports
6 Dol. 55 cents William Sanders Enticks Dictionary 85 cents, one
5 gr Auger 1 Doll. 25 cents James McCuiston eight Volls. Sterns
works 11 Dolls, William Orton one hoed Auger 1 Doll., Alexander
Smith one womans Saddle 6 Doll. 27 cents.

Page
(8)

        WILLIAM BELL, JNr. Will 5th 6ct., 1803.
        In the name of God amen I William Bell Jnr. of Williamson
County and state of Tennessee being in my perfect sences do make
my last will and testament in the following manner, that is to
say,
        I give and bequeath to my Father William Bell, Senr. one sor-
rel mare about six years old, namely Poll, I give and bequeath to my
sister Elizabeth Bell one black mare two years old, namely Madam,
I give and bequeath to my Brother James Bell one year old horse
colt namely Jack also one handsaw, one keesaw, one falling ax and
four plain belts, I give and bequeath to my sister Sally Bell one
bay mare two years old namely Cate, I give and bequeath to my
Brother Thomas Bell one sorrel mare about four years old namely
Winn I give and bequeath to my brother Stinson Bell one bay mare
two years old namely Jewel I give and bequeath to my brother John
Bell one Rifle gun one cow and calf namely Wylie one year old steer
and one year old heifer, I give and bequeath to my brother in law
Matthew Cunningham four hoggs, I give and bequeath to my brother in
law Joseph Payton four hoggs, all of the wether property named
to the different persons I give and bequeath to them and their
heirs forever. In witness whereof I have hereunto set my hand a
and seal this sixth day of October in the year of our Lord
one thousand eight hundred and two. Test. H. Childress and James
Love.
                                signed William Bell.
        The execution of which will as above recited was proven by the
Oath of Henry Childress and James and James Love in open court
February Session 1803, to be the Act anddeed of William Bell, dec.d

        GILES PARMELY will   5th October 1803

        February 26th 1803. In the name of God amen I Giles Parmely
of the State of Tennessee and county of Williamson being weak in
body yet in sound memory thanks be to almighty God, and well knowing the mutability of all erthly enjoyments and by all appearances
drawing nigh my disalution do make and constitute and by these
presents has made and constituted and conformed before a sufficient
number of evidence, do make null and used all former wills, or
testaments, this to be my last will and testament by me signed
as compleatly as if they had never been, and first I leave my
soul to almighty as a merciful Creator supremely good

and my body I resign to the dust of the earth from whince I came
and my worldly goods and effects shall be left in the following
manner, that I give a certain brown mare that I had of Samuel
Bruton and a certain sorrel horse that I had of Henry Skidmore
which was stolen from me likewise all my goods and chattles bills,
bonds and notes this shall be to the use of my older son Ephraim
Parmely of the state and county aforesaid my lawful executor to
see this my last will and testament faithfully executed, I witness
whereof I have hereunto set my hand and affixed my seal the day
and year above written signed sealed and delivered in the presents
of Edward Elam and Sam Parmley.
                         Signed Giles Parmley.
Which will and testament as recited was in Open Court Augt. Session 1803 proven by the Oath of Saml. Parmly to be the Act and deed
of Giles Parmly dec.d and the Executor therein named ex.d Letters
and qualified.

Page
(9)

        BENJAMIN LEE Will   11th October 1803
     In the name of God amen I Benjamen Lee of Williamson County and
State of Tennessee being low in body but of sound mind and memory
do make and ordain this my last will and testement in manner following, Viz I resign my soul and body to almighty God who gave it
me hoping for eternal life through Jesus Christ my redeemer.
Item. I give unto my nephew Braxton Lee the tract of land whereon
he now lives on marrow bone creek frely to enjoy to him and his
heirs forever, which said tract of land contains six hundred and
forty acres but under the express reservation herein next made.
Item I give unto my nephew John Lee and his wife Jenny Lee during
thrif natural life or lives fifty acres of the above recited
tract of land in two separate parcels (as follo with) twenty
acres to include the houses and other improvements whereon they
now live and thirty acres on the west boundary line of the first
mentioned tract to include the improvement made by said John Lee
freely to enjoy the same during their natural life or lives it
being the reservation above intended to be made. Item I give
unto my nephew Braxton Lee three negroe slaves (viz) Anthony, Lucy,
and Ben to him and his heirs forever and desire he may have possession of them on the twenty fifth day of December next. Item
I give unto my nephew Braxton my old yoke of oxen (viz.) the Bull and
pide, black and white steer also my whip and x cut saws. After
December next also the small waggon wheels and half the body and
Irons pertaining to said waggon freely to enjoy the same.
Item I give unto my relation Benjamin Lee son of Braxton my saddle
and Bridle. Item. I give unto my friend Chapman White at the death
of my wife Mary three negro slaves, Viz., Tom, James and Lucy to
him and his heirs forever. Item, I also give to my friend Chapman
White my young yoke of steers (Viz.) one black and one white face
steer also my large waggon wheels and half the body and irons
pertaining to said waggon freely to enjoy the same. Item, I give
to my beloved wife Mary Lee three negroes during her natural life
namely Tom, James and Lucy frely to enjoy the same during her natural
life and at her death to revert to my said friend Chapman White
as above recited. Item. I also give to my beloved wife Mary all
my household and kitchen furniture stock of all kinds, as also all
things whatsoever belonging or in any wise appertaining to my es-

tate not herein before enumerated freely to possess dispose of
or enjoy forever. I do hereby constitute and appoint my friend
Chapman White Executor of this my last will and Testament. In
witness whereof I have hereunto set my hand and seal this 18th
day of August 1802.
Test. John P. Neal, Caleb Mandley.
                    Signed Benjamin Lee
    The execution of the above recited Will was duly proven in Open
Court November Session 1802 by the oaths of John P. Neal and Caleb
Mandly to be the Act and deed of Benjamin Lee Dec.d.
    Inventory of the Estate of Benj. Lee Dec.d. 6 slaves, to wit,
Tom, James, Anthony, Ben, Henry, and Lucy- 1 Bay mare, one waggon,
one yoke of oxen, one young do., six head of cattle, thirty head
of hogs little and big one plough shear and four weeding hoes, three
grubing hoes, three feather beds and furniture and steads, 1 pine
chest, one hair trunk, 2 kettles, 2 potts and 2 dutch ovens, 1 x
legged table, one corner cupboard, 1 small shott gun, 2 pole axes,
one Broad ax.
                        signed Chapman White, Feby. 7, 1803, Excr.

Page
(10)   of Benj. Lee dec.d.

    YOUNG MCLEMORES Will
    In the name of God amen I Young McLemore of the State of Tennessee
and County of Williamson being low of body but of sound disposing
mind and calling to mind that it's appointed for all men to die
do make constitute and ordain this my last will and testament in
the following manner.
    First I give and bequeath unto my beloved Daughter Sukey
            Gray the following negros (viz) James, Nan, Essex,
            Joyce, Sydia, and Stephen. Also my Smith's tools
            to her and her heirs forever.
    Second. I give and bequeath unto my Grandson Young A. Gray
            the land whereon I now live. One negro named Benjamin, two
            cows and calves, two feather beds and furniture one
            horse Dick, three sows and piggs, my household and kit-
            chen furniture except my bed, fifteen Barrels of corn
            to him and his heirs forever.
    3rd I give and bequeath to my Grand-daughter Polly W. Dickson
two cows and calves and one hundred dollars to her and her heirs
forever.
    4. I give and bequeath unto my Grand daughter Sukey M.L. Gray
the following negros viz., Jack, Beck, Effey and Davy to her and
her heirs forever.
    5th. I give and bequeath unto my Grand son James McK. Gray
the following negros Viz. Furry and Abram to him and his heirs
forever.
    6. I give and bequeath unto my Grand daughter Sally S. Gray
the following negros viz., Harper, Dudley and Lucy to her and her
Page   heirs forever.
(11)   7. I give and bequeath unto my Grand-Son Henry K. Gray the
following negros viz., Hardy, Jinney and Hester to him and his
heirs forever.
    8 I desire one thousand dollars to be paid out of my estate
towards the payment of the large tract of land that James Gray
bought of Gene Robertson provided the said Gray divide the same

eq ually between his two sons James M. K. Gray and Henry K. Gray reserving to himself and wife a life estate in the said land.

9-It is my further will and desire that James Gray his wife and all their children shall each have a suit of mourning furnished out of my estate.

10-I furthermore give and bequeath unto my beloved daughter Sukey Gray all the residue of my estate of what kind soever to her and her heirs forever.

Lastly I do hereby nominate and appoint my trusty and beloved friends James Gray, William Dickson and Young A. Gray Executors to this my last will and Testament revoking all former wills whatsoever. In Witness whereof I have hereunto set my hand and seal this thirty first day of December on thousand eight hundred and three.

Signed Sealed and Acknowledged and Signed in presence of
Young McLemore   (Seal)

Thos. Masterson, Abraham Maury Invt., A. Maury Degraffenreid, Nathan Farmer.

The Execution of the foregoing recited will and Testament was duly proven in open court April Session 1804 by the oaths of Abraham Maury Invt. and Nathan Farmer two of the subscribing witnesses thereto to be the Act and deed of Young McLemore for the use and purposes therein contained and the same was ordered to be recorded.

Page (12)   An Inventory of the Estate of Young McLemore dec'd. April 9th 1804, viz

Eighteen negros, 9 head of horses, about fifty head of Hogs, twenty-eight head of cattle, twenty three head of Sheep, a parcel of corn, supposed, 2 Hundred Barrels, a parcel of fodder, one sett Smiths tools, one Waggon and gear, one half of a cart, 4 grubing hoes, 4 plough hoes, six weeding hoes, one pitt saw, one x cutsaw, one hand saw, two augers, one broad ax, six narrow axes, one adze, one grindstone, one broken sett of China, one castor, three decanters, four flask bottles, one glass can, 14 Earthen plates, four dishes, one mug, three Salt sellers, one sugar box, two Butter potts, 9 pewter plates, one looking glass, one copper kettle, two Iron pots, one oven, one frying pan, one griddle, 4 piggins, one tub, two trays, one teaboard, two waiters, one quart Bottle, one table, one tea kettle, two coppee pots, three candlesticks, one pair tongs, one churn, one Beaver trap, four feather beds and furniture.
Bonds, viz. Abraham Maury's note for thirty one dollars twenty five cents, Elizah Williams note for fifty Dollars, Henry Walker balance of Sixty Dollars, Henry G. Kearny Settlement Eighty two Dollars ninety cents, Robert Johnston balance of four Dollars, John Farmer balance of eighty three dollars, Cash on hand two hundred and thirty seven Dollars twenty six cents, one pr. fire dogs, one pr. Sad Irons, two guns, a small parcel of books, one pair Snuffers, one Dozen knives and forks, three spinning wheels, one flax wheel.
Signed J. Gray.

Page (13)   ELIJAH OWENS Will
In the name of God amen I Elijah Owens of Williamson County

and State of Tennessee being weak in body but of disposing and sound mind and memory do by this my last will and testament devise dispose and bequeath all my worldly Estate real and personal as follows.

Item. My will and desire is that my Executrix hereafter to be named shall sell one hundred acres of my land on Harpeth which contains in the whole three hundred and eighty acres for the purpose of paying my debts, said one hundred acres is to be in the South West corner of said tract to be laid off in an oblong runing north and south the oblong to be double as long as wide and not to include my mill on said tract. Item. my will is that my wife Nancy Owens shall have during her natural life one hundred and fifty acres of said tract including the mill and runing from the north east to the north west corner of said tract and south for complement and that after the death of my said wife the said one hundred and fifty acres shall go to my daughter Amelia and her heirs. Item my will is that the remaining one hundred and thirty acres of said tract shall go to my Daughter Amelia and her heirs.

Item. My will is that all my personal property and debts due shall go to my wife absolutely and be disposed of by her as she in her discretion may think fit. Item, my will is that my beloved wife Nancy Owens shall be sole Executrix of this my last will and testament. In testimony whereof I have hereunto set my hand and affixed my seal this second day of March 1804.

Signed, Sealed, Published and declared in presence of Thos. Stuart, Ann Hay, Thomas Rand. Signed Elijah Owens.

The Execution of the foregoing recited Will and Testament was duly proven in open Court April Session 1804 by the oath of Thomas Stuart to be the Act and Deed of Elijah Owens for the use of purposes therein expressed and the same was ordered to be recorded.

Inventory the Estate of Elijah Owens dec'd. June 28th day 1804.

One mare and colt and four two year old horses, 6 head of cattle, 1 bed and furniture, 2 Bedsteads, 1 chest, 7 chairs, 2 tables and some table furniture, 1 linen wheel, 1 pail and 2 fat stands, 1 piggin, 1 churn, 1 Bucket, 1 Barrel, 1 Tub, 1 pot and 2 pair pot hooks, 1 Dutch oven, 1 Kettle, 1 Smoothing iron, 2 Axes and 2 mattocks, 1 plow and two pair of drawing chains, 1 pair saddle bags and 2 books, 2 bottles and one crowbar and one s pade, one log chain and three bridles.
Signed Nancy Owens, Extrix.

JESSE EVANS Will. In the name of God amen I Jesse Evans of the State of Tennessee and County of Williamson being very sick and weak of body but of perfect mind and memory thanks be to God calling unto mind the mortality of my body and knowing that it is appointed for all men oce to die do make and ordain this my last will and Testament that is to say principally and first of all I give and recomend my Soul into the hand of Almighty God that gave it, and my body I recommend to the earth to be buried in decent Christian burial at the discretion of my Executors; nothing doubting but at the general resurrection

I shall receive the same again by the mighty power of God and as touching such worldly estate wherewith it has pleased God to bless me in this life I give dismiss and dispose of the same in the following manner and form.

First. I give and bequeath to Mary Evans my beloved wife my land and plantation whereon I now live with all my plantation tools with all my household furniture together with all my Stock which is to say Horses, cattle, Hogs and sheep and my man Minie which I give and bequeath unto my wife during her widowhood or life - Except one bed and furniture, one side saddle, one cow and calf I give unto my daughter Rachel Evans one bed and furniture, one side saddle, one cow and calf at the arrival of age or marriage. Also I give and bequeath unto my son John Evans my land and plantation whereon I now live at the marriage or death of my wife to him and his heirs forever. And I do hereby name my two sons Daniel Evans and Robin Evans Executors to my last will and testament, and the remains and residue of my estate to be sold and equally divided at the death of my wife Mary Evans, that is to say Daniel Evans, Robin Evans, Patsy Nash, Sarah Jackson, Rebeckah Evans, Rachel Evans and John Evans.

                    Excepted November 21st 1804
                    Signed Jesse Evans
Test.
Burwell Temple
Saml. Jackson.

The Execution of the above recated will was duly proven in open Court Jan'y. Session 1805 by the oaths of Burwell Temple and Saml. Jackson to be the act and deed of Jesse Evans, for the use and purposes therein expressed and the same was ordered to be recorded.

Page
(16)

Inventory of the estate of Jesse Evans, ded'd. January 14,1805.

To 100 acres of land, 1 negro man, 4 head of horses, 27 head of cattle, 6 head of sheep, 26 horses, 26 head of hogs, 6 geece, 18 Ducks, 2 plows, 2 axes, 1 hand saw, 2 Drawing knives, 2 chissels 3 hoes, 2 cleves, 3 beds and furniture, 2 Saddles, 2 Bridles, 3 Wheels, 1 reel, 1 loom, 5 Slays, 5 pair harness, 9 pewter plates, 1 pewter Dish, 3 pewter basons, 1 tin pan, 6 spoons, 6 tin cups, 1 coffeepot, 12 Earthen plates, 6 punch bowls, 9 cups and saucers, 1 tea pot, 2 Salt cellers, 1 milk pot, 6 tea spoons, 1 Glass pitcher, 3 tumblers, 4 bottles, 1 pepper box, 1 coffee mill, 6 knives, and forks, 2 potts, 2 ovens, 1 laddle, 1 flesh fork, 7 chairs, 3 bedsteads, 4 books, 1 slate, 4 pails, 1 washing tub, 2 barrels, 1 churn, candlestick, 1 glass, 3 towels, 1 knife box, 1 table, 1 round shave, 1 Halter, a parcel of corn and bacon, 1 trunk, 1 chest, 441-8 feet of plank, 1 hone, 2 pr. pot hooks, 1 pair flat irons, 1 inkstand, 1 pair cards, 1 Iron Wedge, 1 pair Shears, 1 Tommehawk, 1 pipe, 1 raw hide, 1 Sewel, 2 Bells, 2 cealean, 1 Brass Kettle, 19 Spools, 1 dye tub, 1 Salt barrel, 1 gun and shot pouch, 1 Bond for two Hundred and fifty acres land. 1 round shave.

                    Signed   Daniel Evans   Exrs.
                    Robert Evans.

WILLIAM WILKINS Will
I William Wilkins in the name of God do make this my last Will and testament being weak in body but of sound memory htat is to say I will and bequeath that those my executors do pay all my

Page
(17)
just debts out of my money and I give to my wife one mare and half
her increase, Saddle and bridle during life and the rest of my
stock horses cattle and hogs to be for the support of my wife
and children with all the rest of my household furniture during
my wifes widowhood and if anything remains then to be equally
divided with my children except my Stud colt, and my Will is that
he should be sold to the highest bidder at weelve month credit
and the money with the rest of my money to buy a piece of land
with for my sons John and James. And if the child that my wife
is now with is a Son and my will is that my three negroes Judy
and Milly and Conkard with their increase be equally divided between my sons and daughters when they all arrive to age and my
Will is that my wife or Ececutors school my children well and
my Will that James Wilkins should be executor to this my last
Will and he should hire out either of my negros for the support
of my family and he should sell my part of my lease and apply
the money to the use of building and clearing of ground when he
buys a piece of land for my family to live upon.
     Signed and Sealed this twenty third day of August 1805.
Elijah Hunter   Signed William Wilkins   (Seal)
Jean Powell
     The Execution of the above recited will and Testament was
duly proven in open Court January Session 1806 by the Oaths of
Elijah Hunter and Jean Powell to be the Act and Deed of William

Page
(18)
Wilkins for the use and purposes therein expressed and the same
was ordered to be recorded.
     Inventory of the Goods, Chattels rights and Credits of Wil-
liam Wilkins Dec'd. Jany 31st, 1806. Robert Wilkins Dr. to 1
hoe 8/1 Rebukah Wilkins 2 hoes 9/- Robert Wilkins 2 hoes 3/-
William Kindrake 2 chissels 4/6- James Wilkins 1 Drawing Knive
6/- Robert Wilkins 1 Auger 2/- James Wilkins 1 foot adze 9/-
ditto for 2 augers9/4 ditto for 1 broad ax 17/- dittonfor 1
plough 21/-ditto Frissens and clevice 11 d. Augustia Willis 1
Shovel, 1 Slough 13/2 James Wilkins 1 Iron Wedge 6/5½- William
Nully 1 Grindstone 24/- James Wilkins one third part of Waggon
and gears L5- 14 Ditto, 1 Blind Bridle 3/- Robert Wilkins 1 Stud
Horse L36-0-0, Grindstones sold to different people for L3-19-3¼.
     The above mentioned property has been sold for the purpose of
raising a fund for the payment of debts, Leganis, etc. as by
Will directed. Property remaining and reserved for leganis, etc.-
A negro wench Jude and child and girl Milley, one mare and one
horse, eight head of cattle, nine head of Hogs, Household and
Kitchen furnityre consisting one pot, one kettle, one oven, one
skillet, two beds and furniture, 2 smoothing irons, half a dozen
knives and forks, and one pair Steelyards, three dishes, 5 pewter
plates, 5 earthen plates, half a dozen tea cups and saucers, one
chest, one pot rack, one candlestick on Decanters, one looking
Glass, two bedsteads, one Washingtub, one spice mortar, the above
is an Inventory in full of all the Goods Chattels rights and credits of William Wilkins dec.d that has come into my hands to this
date April 14th. 1806.
     N.B. Beside the above there is a judgment against Thomas
due for L1-6 also in the hands of Rus Porter L1-2- Likewise one
Spining wheel and two old barrels, three water pails and one
Page
(19)
Keeler.   Signed James Wilkins Exr.

WILLIAM GARDNER'S Will. In the name of God amen I William Gardner of Williamson County being sick and weak tho in perfect mind
and memory blessed be God, do this 13th day of February in the
year of our Lord 1805 make and ordain this my last Will and Testament in manner and form following that is to say.
First, I give and bequeath to my beloved wife Jane Gardner during
her natural life the land and Stock and negros and everything else
that I now possess and a Negro boy named Simon I give and bequeath
to her and at her disposal forever.
Item. I give and bequeath to my beloved Sons Richey and William
the land where I now live to be equally divided between them agreeable to quantity and quality as they may agree when they come to be
grown. Item. I give and bequeath also to my son William one negro
boy named Philiss to him and his heirs forever. Item. My desire
is that my two sons Richey and william shall when convenient to
raise and pay to my two daughters Jane and Hannah in cash or
property, Richey to pay one hundred Dollars and William three Hundred Dollars. Item I give and bequeath to my beloved son Thomas
two hundred dollars which is to be raised out of the Sale of the
Stock. Item. I give and bequeathto my beloved son John one sorrel
mare which he has in pession and one hundred dollars to be raised
out of the sale of the stock. Item I give and bequeath unto my be-

Page
(20)

loved daughter Ann as much property and as well fixt as the rest
of my daughters that is married had.-Item. My advice is that my
two sons Richey and William when convenient without distressing
themselves shall give to my children that are married ten dollars
to each of them. Item, I desire at the death of my wife that Dolly
shall live where she pleases, so as she lives in the family and
if my wife should die before all the children are grown, then to
take care of the children. Item, I desire that my Executrix shall
pay all my just debts be paid out of the Sale of the Stock. Item, I
consttute and appoint my beloved wife Jane Gardner wholeand sole
Executrix of this my last will and Testament revoking all other
wills by me made. In witness whereof I have hereunto set my hand
and seal this day and date above written.
                    Signed William Gardner   Beal
      Signed Sealed and Acknowledged in presence of us, Nicholas
Scales, William W. Knight, Joseph Sumners. The Execution of the
foregoing recited will was duly proven in open Court April Session
1806 by the oaths of Nicholas Scales and William W. Knight to be the
act and deed of William Gardner for the use and purposes therein
contained and the same was ordered to be recorded.

Page
(21)

HANNAH MONTGOMERY'S Will - In the name of God amen I Hannah Montgomery of the County of Williamson and State of Tennessee being
weak in body but sound in mind and memory, blessed be God, do make
and constitute this my last will and Testament, disannulling and
revoking all others. Item, I give my body to the earth from whence
it was taken in sure and certain hope of the resurrection thereof
again at the last day through our Lord Jesus Christ. I will and
positively order that all my just debts be paid. Item. I give

to my daughter Mary Montgomery one large Bible, one pair fire
tongs, one flax hackle, and one Iron pot rack. Item, I give to my
daughter Elizabeth Bailey one shilling. Item. I give to my grand-
daughter Jane Montgomery the balance of one Hundred and Sixteen
Dollars after paying my just debts now in the hands of my son
David Montgomery also I give the rest and residue of all my Estate
to said Jane Montgomery. And I do hereby appoint and ordain my
son in law Thomas Aydelott and Mary Montgomery my whole and sole
Executors of this my last Will and Testament. In testimony whereof
I have put my hand and seal this 21st day of February 1806.

Signed Hannah Montgomery

x - her mark

Signed in presence of us - J. Pope J. Neelly.
The Execution of the above recited will and Testament was duly
proven in open Court July Session 1806 by the oaths of John Pope
and James Neelly to be the Act and deed of Hannah Montgomery for
Page   the use and purposes therein expressed and the same was ordered
(22)   to be recorded.
Inventory of the Estate of Hannah Montgomery Dec'd. A memorandum
of accounts left in my hands as an Executor of the Estate of Hannah
Montgomery this 13th April 1807. One note on David Montgomery for
$115. An account on William Bailey for $14.75. An account on
Greenham Taylor for $2. left in my hands one bed and furniture, one
pot, one ax, one pair fire tongs, one pot rack, one flax Hackle,
one Iron Wedge, four small dishes, six small plates, three knives
and forks, one foot adze, one shovel, and two chairs, one barrel.

Signed Thomas Aydelott

WELCOM HODGE'S Will - In the name of God amen I Welcom Hodges of
Williamson County and State of Tennessee farmer being in perfect
sound mind and disposing memory thanks be to God calling to mind the
mortality of my body and knowing that it is appointed for all men
once to die do make and ordain this my last will and Testament that is
to say, principally and first of all I recommend my Soul into the
hands of God who gave it and my body I recommend to the Earth to be
buried in a deasent Christian manner, at the deseition of my Executor nothing doubting but at the general resurrection I shall re-
sume the same again by the mighty power of God and touching such
Page   worldly estate as it hath pleased God to bless me with herein this
(23)   life I give and demise and dispose of in the manner and form following that is to say after my funeral expences are taken out and
all my lawful debts paid first of all I give and bequeath unto my
beloved Son Philip Hodges the one fourth of all my landed property
Also I do give and bequeath unto my beloved Daughter Elizabeth also
one fourth part of my landed property. I also give and bequeath
unto my beloved son James one fourth part of all my landed property.
I give and bequeath unto my beloved daughter Lydda the remaining one
fourth part of all my landed property and last of all I do give and
bequeath unto Betsey Cottingim all the rest of my estate both real
and personal to be her own right and property and lastly I do make
constitute and appoint Burton Jordan and Samuel Shields executors
of this my last will and Testament. And do hereby utterly disallow
revoke and disannul all and every other forms, Testaments, Wills,
bequeaths and Executors by me in any wise before named willed bequeathed ratifying and confirming in this and no other to be my last

will and Testament. In witness whereof I have hereunto set my
hand and Seal this Sixth Day of June in the year one Thousand
Eight Hundred and Seven. Signed Welcom Hodges   (Seal)
   Signed Sealed published pronounced and delivered by the said
Welcom Hodges to be his last will and Testament in the presence
of us who in his presence and in the presence of each other have
hereunto inserted our names.
David Floyd, John Keeth (his mark), Elizabeth Beaver (her mark)

Page (24)

   The foregoing recited Will and Testament was duly proven in
open Court July Session 1807 by the oaths of David Floyd and John
Keeth to be the Act and deed of Welcom Hodges for the use and
purposes therein expressed and the same was ordered to be recorded.

RICHARD WINDROW Will - In the name of God amen I Richard Windrow
of Williamson County in the State of Tennesseee being in health
of body but considering the shortness of life and my advanced
age do make this my last will and Testament revoking all others
that is to say first I command my Soul to Almighty God who gave
it in sure and certain hope of a blessed resurrection from the
dead unto eternal life through our Lord and Saviour Jesus Christ
and my body to be decently buried at the discretion of my sur-
viving friends, and with respect to my worldly goods with which
it hath pleased God to bless me with I dispose of in the following
manner to wit, first my will and desire is that all my just
debts be paid and then I give to my daughter Elizabeth Windrow one
feather bed and furniture to her and her heirs forever. Item, I

Page (25)

give to my daughter Millender Windrow one feather bed and furniture
to her and her heirs forever. Item. My will and desire is that
my two sons John Windrow and Henry Windrow have and enjoy all my
lands equally but that being an over proportion of my estate I
give to each of my Daughters (to wit) Jane Sea, Elizabeth Windrow, Nancy Brown, Sally Windrow, and Millender Windrow twenty
Dollars to be paid jointly by my two sons John and Henry and then
on condition that they that is to say John Windrow pays fifty
dollars to his five sisters to be equally divided and Henry Windrow pays fifty Dollars to his five Sisters to be equally divided
then I give devise and bequeath to my son John Windrow one Hundred and sixty acres of land joining his and the land be sold
to Roswell. The same to him and his heirs forever - as also I
give devise and bequeath to my Son Henry Windrow one Hundred and
sixty acres of land including the plantation whereon I now live
the same to him and his heirs forever. Item my Will and desire
is that my well beloved wife Millender Windrow have the use of
my land and plantation whereon I now live with all my household
and kitchen furniture not other ways dispond of my cart and
gears, grindstone, and plantation tools, one mare and colt
(her choice) with all my stock of cattle and Hogs and corn during her natural life or widowhood and at her marriage or death
my will and desire is that all my estate left to the use of my
wife be equally divided betixt all my daughters (to wit) Jane,
Betsy, Nancy, Sally and Millender as also one mare and colt (or

Page (26)

filly) to them and their heirs forever--finally I constitute and
appoint my sons John Windrow and John Sea Executors of this my
last will and Testament. In witness whereof Ihave hereunto set
my hand and seal this 21st day of November 1805.
                    Signed Richard Windrew Seal

Signed Sealed Published
declared in presence of G. Hill, A. Maury, De Graffenreid,
William Hill. The foregoing recited Will and Testament was
duly proven in open Court July Session 1806 by the Oaths of
Green Hill and Abram Maury De Graffenreid to be the act and
deed of Richard Windrow for the use and purposes therein expressed and the same was ordered to be recorded.
    Inventory of the Estate of Richard Windrow, Deceased, vizt.
    State of Tennessee) A just and true inventory of the Estate
    Williamson County) of Richard Windrow as far as hath come to
the knowledge of the Executor (to wit) two mares, two yearling
colts, sixteen head of cattle, eight sowsans pigs, thirty nine
dry hogs, two kettles, two pots, one dutch oven, and a spider,
dour weeding hoes, three grubing hoes, two plows, two set of
plow harness, one grindstone, two axes, two iron wedges, one
cart, one loom, four feather beds and furniture, one table, two
trunks, eight chairs, six pewter basons, eleven pewter plates,
four spoons, one sett of knives and forks, six Earthen plates,
three spinning wheels, one cut reel, two coffee pots, one sett
cups and saucers, three pair of pot hooks, five water vessels,
two butter p ots, four pewter dishes, one pair fire tongs, one
mans saddle, one womans saddle, one rifle gun, and one shot gun,
one small trunk.   Signed John Windrow.

Page
(27) AMMON DAVIS Will - In the name of God amen I Ammon Davis being
sick and weak of body but of perfect mind and memory thanks to
Almighty God do give and dispose my worldly goods and Estate in
manner and form following. Imprimes, first of all I appoint my
beloved brother James Davis Executor to my last will and Testament, that after my possession the whole of my Estate real and
personal and settle the whole of my worldly business that after
all my debts is settled then the balance that may remain I give
and bequeath unto my beloved Daughter Sally Davis if she lives
to arrive to the years of maturity and if she should die before
she has an heir the profits arising from my land and plantation
on Mill Creek is to return unto my beloved brother John Davis
his heirs and Assigns. Acknowledging this to be and remain my
last Will and Testament this 23rd day of December 1806.
                            Signed Ammon Davis
Declared in presence of A. Pearee, P. H. Pinkston, George Shannon.
    The foregoing recited Will and Testament was duly proven in
Open Court April Session 1807 by the oaths of Arthur Pearee,
Peter Pinkston and George Shannon to be the Act and Deed of
Ammon Davis for the use and purposes therein expressed and the
same was ordered to be recorded.
    An Inventory of the personal property of Ammon Davis, De-
ceased. Supposed to be 9 head of Horses, do. to be 18 heads
of cattle, 14 head of Sheep, 1 feather bed and furniture, 2 chests,
Page
(28) 1 large Iron Kettle, 1 pot, 1 stew pot, 1 Dutch oven, 1 Sett of
plow irons, 1 case of Holster pistols, 1 silver watch, 1 Morocco
pocket book, 1 Bible, 1 arithmetick, 1 ax, 1 Hatchet, 2 screw
augers, 2 hoes, 1 iron wedge, 1 foot adze, 1 pair of compasses,
1 claw hammer, 1 piece of steel, 1 gimblet, one 2 foot rule,
1 pair of table batts, one bridle bitt, one handsaw, 2 files,
1 drawing knife, one pair of pot Hooks, 1 mans saddle, ½ dozen
earthen plates, ½ dozen cups and saucers, 1 pepper box, 1 iron

candlestick, 1 case of razors, 1 pewter dish, 4 pewter plates, 1 coffee pot, 1 Butcher knife, 1 looking glass, 1 pair of boots, one cappo.

NANCY BENTON'S Will - In the name of God amen I Nancy Benton daughter and one of the heirs of Jesse Benton, late of No. Carolina, dec.d do make and ordain this my last Will and Testament - as one of the heirs and devisus of my aforesaid father I am entitled with the rest of his children to an equal proportion of all the property that may remain in his Estate after the payment of his debts and the leganes granted by his will to my mother. And whereas the aforesaid property does at this time consist of negros in the State of Tennessee and various lands lying on Harpeth and Duck rivers, Cumberland river, Tennessee river, and other rivers emptying into the Mississippi. It is my will and desire that all and every particle of property that I may be entitled to lands and negros, in the event of my death descend to my two sisters Polly Benton and Susannah Benton. And whereas on the death of my Sister Peggy Benton, one of the heirs and divisers of Jesse Benton, I became entitled as one of her heirs at law, to an equal division with the rest of my brothers and sisters to all and every species of property that was in her possession or to which she had any right. It is my further will that whatever my Executor shall hereafter receive on my account as heir at law of my aforesaid Sister shall descend and go to my two sisters Polly and Susannah Benton; to be divided between them in equal proportions, their heirs and assigns forever. And I constitute and appoint Thomas H. Benton my Executor of this my only Will this 19th Jany. one thousand eight hundred and seven.

Page (29)

    Signed in the   Signed Nancy Benton   Seal
presence of Thomas H. Benton,
John Record, Samuel Benton

    The foregoing recited Will and Testament was duly proven in open Court April Session 1807 by the oaths of Thomas H. Benton and John Record to be the act and deed of Nancy Benton dec.d for the use and purposes therein expressed and the same was ordered to be recorded.

    SUSAN LOVE'S Nuncupative Will - State of Tennessee, Williamson County - June 10, 1807
    Whereas on the fourteenth day of December in the year one thousand eight hundred and Six Susan Love departed this life at Franklin in the County aforesaid; a few hours before her death on the same she expressed it as her will that the whole of her estate in the event of her death should descend to the eldest daughter of her brother William, that is, to Peggy Love.

Page (30)

    And whereas the said Susan Love having died as aforesaid, the declarations made in her last moments, according to the act of assembly in such cases made and provided were this day proved before me; by virtue of which the declaration made as aforesaid have acquired the force of a nuncupative Will.
    Provide by the Oaths of Harrison Boyd and Rhoda Boyd in the presence of (H. Boyd   Signed
               (Rhoda Boyd Sworn to and subscribed before me this
               (J. Hicks   Eleventh day of June 1807

At the same time, to wit, on the day and year last mentioned, Thomas H. Benton, Charles Boyles, Jenny Bright, Mary Williamson made oath that they were present on the fourteenth day of December in the year one Thousand Eight Hundred and Six when Susan Love expressed it as her will that her estate should decend to one of the Daughters of her brother William and that they believe that Peggy Love the eldest daughter of her aforesaid brother was the one she mentioned on that occasion.

Sworn to and subscribed   Signed
before me this eleventh   (Thos. H. Benton
day of June One Thousand   (Charles Boyles
Eight Hundred and Seven   (Jenny Bright
                        (Mary Williamson

        J. Hicks, J.P.

Which nuncupative will as above recited was duly proven in Open Court July Session 1807 by the oaths of Harrison Boyd and Charles Boyles to be the nuncupative will of Susan Love and the same was ordered to be recorded.

JOHN DICKEY'S Will - In the name of God amen I John Dickey of the County of Williamson and State of Tennessee being weak and low in body, but of sound mind and memory and calling to mind that it is appointed for all men once to die do make and constitute this my last will and Testament in manner and form following viz, Item; I give and bequeath to my beloved wife Mary Dickey during her natural life and no longer, Sixty Acres of my land purchased of Ray Sands as agent of the heirs of Nathaniel Green to include the improvements already erected thereon with a free and unmolested use of my portion of the Spring. I also give to my daid wife Mary during the term aforesaid five negroes, as follows, viz, Friday, Nanny, Old/Lena, Ned and Labina, also two horses, one known by the name of old Sorrel with the chair and harness, one cow and calf, two two year old heifers, one bed and furniture, a proportional share of my stock of hogs, household and kitchen furniture and plantation utensels, with a plentiful share of corn and meat for the following year. Item, it is my Will and desire that my friends Moses G. Brierson and David Frierson do pay to my daughter Sarah Blakely the value of three cows and calves and to my Grandson Isaac Edwin Frierson the value of one cow and calf out of the money due me from David Frierson, Item, I give unto my Son Benona all the rest and residue of my Estate both real and personal together with the revertion of the estate above limited to my said beloved wife at the expiration of her natural life freely to enjoy the same to him and his heirs forever; and whereas a possibility exists that the title to the lands purchased of Ray Lands agent of the heirs of Genl. Nathaniel Green alluded to in the foregoing part of this my last will and Testament may not be finally compleated and being prompted by an ardent desire to provide a mansion for my beloved wife, in case of failure in the same in the event of a non execution of proper Deeds of conveyance by the proper representatives of the said late Nathaniel Green as aforesaid, I do hereby constitute and appoint my trusty friends Moses G. Frierson, David Frierson and my son Benona trustees with efficient power and authority to apply the money stipulated to be paid for the aforesaid tract of land, viz. Six hundred and thirty dollars to the purpose of purchasing one other tract of land for the use and

Page (31)

Page (32)

benefit of my said wife Mary and my son Benona under the same
restrictions and limitations as aforesaid, that is to say,
giving my beloved wife a life estate in the same in a proportion
as sixty is to two hundred with the reversion as aforesaid and
all the residue thereof to my said son Benona his heirs and assigns forever - I do hereby constitute and appoint my friends
Moses G. Frierson, David Frierson and my beloved son Benona
Dickey Executors to this my last Will and Testament and do further empower them to execute and perform all contracts entered
into on my part relating to the purchase of the five thousand
acres of land in copartnership with sundry others of the said
Ray Lands agent as aforesaid. In testimony whereof I have here-
unto set my hand and affixed my seal this fifth day of December
in the year of our Lord one thousand eight hundred and seven.
In the presence of   Signed John Dickey   Seal
N. Patteson
Abram Maury
Saml. Frierson

Page
(33)

Which foregoing last will and Testament of John Dickey was
duly proven in open court January Session 1808 by the oaths of
Abram Maury and Samuel Frierson (two of the subscribing witnesses thereto) to be the Act and Deed of John Dickey and the
same was ordered to be recorded whereupon David Frierson and
Benona Dickey qualified as Executors and rec.d letters Testa-
mantary.

JANE GARDNER'S Will - In the name of God amen, I Jane Gardner
of Williamson County and State of Tennessee considering the
undertainty of this mortal life and being of sound and perfect
mind and memory blessed be Almighty God for the same do make
and publish this my last will and Testament in manner and form
following that is to say, First I give and bequeath unto my
beloved son John Gardner one negro man named Harry upon his
paying one hundred and twenty dollars to be applied to the use
of Johnson Wood for the balance of the price of said negro,
and if he should refuse or neglect to pay the one hundred and
twenty dollars as aforesaid my will is that the said negro Harry should be sold to pay the said Wood and the balance of the
money arising from the sale should there be any to be paid to
my son John for his use and his heirs forever. I further give
to my son John aforesaid one cow and calf. Secondly, I give and
bequeath to my beloved son Richey Gardner one negro boy named
Simon during my said son Richey's natural life and at his death
my will is that the said negro boy Simon should decend to my
son William Gardner and should the said Negro Simon survive

Page
(34)

both my sons aforesaid to wit, Richey and William, then and
in that case my will is that the said negro boy Simon should be
free in case he behave well further it is my will that in consequence of my son Richey having the said negro boy Simon,
that he shall pay my son William aforesaid one hundred Dollars.
Thirdly: I give and bequeath to my beloved son Joseph Richey
twenty five dollars in merchandise whereas there is due from
John McKey forty pounds, should my son in law William Berry
collect said debt, I give and bequeath to my daughter Martha

one hundred dollars a part of said forty pounds to her and her
heirs forever. Item: I give and bequeath to my five other Daughters, to wit, Polly, Dawning, Molly Sumners, Nancy Sumners,
Rebekah Sumners and Anne Patterson to them and their heirs forever ten dollars each to be paid them by my sons Richey and William out of their own estate as soon as they can do it without
distressing themselves. Item: I give and bequeath to my daughter
Jane Gardner one colt which is now sucking and a new saddle also
one heifer and her increase that is now claimed by her to her
and her heirs forever. Item: I give and bequeath to my daughter
Hannah and my will is that she shall have the next colt that the
mare that I now have should bring, a new saddle, also one heifer
that she now claims to her and her heirs forever. Item: my will

Page
(35)

and desire is that my Executors hereafter named should pay all
my just debts out of the present growing crop. And lastly as to
all the rest, residue and remainder of my personal Estate, goods
and chattels of what kind and nature soever I give and bequeath
to my two sons Richey and William to be equally divided between
them to enable them to pay the several sums of money to the other
Legatees agreeable to this my will. Item: I do appoint my sons
John and Nicholas Scales whole and sole Executors of this my
last will and Testament hereby revoking all other wills by me
made. In Witness whereof I have hereunto set my hand and seal
this fifth day of September in the year of our Lord 1807.
Signed sealed and acknowledged
by the above named Jane Gardner   Signed
to be her last will and Testament   Jane Gardner
in the presence of us who have hereunto   x her mark
subscribed our names as witness in the
presence of this testatrix.
John Sumners, Joseph Sumners, James Patterson
Which foregoing recited will and Testament was duly proven in
Open Court January Session 1808 by the oaths of John Sumners and
James Patterson (two of the subscribing witnesses thereto) to
be the Act and Dec.d of Jane Gardner and the same was ordered
to be recorded: whereupon John Gardner came into court and
qualified as Executor thereto. An Inventory of the Estate of
Jane Gardner Dec.d: 2 negroes, 4 head of horses, 29 head of cat-
tle, 8 head of Sheep, 35 head of hogs, 6 Geese, 12 Ducks, chick-

Page
(36)

ens, 1 waggon and Gears, 3 plows, 4 hoes, 4 axes, 1 mattock,
1 cain hoe, 1 desk, 1 chest, 1 cupboard, 6 pewter plates, 3
delf ditto, 1 small bowl, 6 tin cups, 1 glass tumbler, 3 Glass
bottles, 4 pewter dishes, 2 pewter basons, 1 earthen crock, 4
pails, 1 large kettle, 3 potts, 2 ovens, 1 skillet, 1 pr. and
irons, 1 iron shovel, 3 pr. pot hooks, 1 pewter ladle, 1 iron
ladle, 1 flesh fork, 3 feather beds and furniture, 5 bedsteads,
10 chairs, 1 looking glass, 2 candlesticks, 1 pr. snuffers, 10
knives and 8 forks, 2 butcher knives, 2 screw augers, 2 chissels,
2 hammers, 1 rifle gun, shot bag and powder horn molds wipers and
screw driver, 1 fet addze, 2 brass cocks, 1 half pint measure
2 smoothing irons, 1 pr. pincers, 1 shoemakers hammer, 1 Bible,
2 Testaments, 1 Dialogue of Devils and several other books,

1 slate, 3 old saddles, 2 bridles, 1 new saddle, Sundry old
irons, 1 cotton wheel, 2 flax wheels, 3 pr. cards, 1 loom, 2
slays, 2 pr. harness, sundry accts. to the amount of $25.26½
sundry notes to the amt. of $10.10¾ doubtful, a flax hatchell,
2 padlocks, 1 cutting knife and box, 1 half Bu. measure, 2 wheat
riddles, 2 washing tubs, 1 churn, 1 spade, 1 tub, 3 salt barrels,
1 Razor and case, 1 shaving box, 3 meal bags, 4 cups and 5 saucers, 1 coffee mill. The above inventory is just of all the personal property that has come into my hands to the best of my
knowledge.

                         Signed,
                         John Gardner Extr.
                         12th April 1808
And at April Session 1808 the Court appointed John Baldridge
and William G. Boyd commissioners to value said Estate who made
the following report - April 30th 1808. We the undersigners have
appraised the Estate of Jane Gardner Dec.d agreeable to the
commission of this county court and say the Estate amounts to
$1685.75.

                         Signed
                         John Baldridge
                         William G. Boyd.

Page
(37)

WILLIAM APPLEBY'S Will - In the name of God amen the twenty
third day of November 1807 I William Appleby of the State of
Tennessee and Williamson County being in a low state of health,
but in perfect mind and memory thanks be given to God therefor
calling to mind the mortality of my body and knowing that it is
appointed for all men once to die, do make and ordain this my
last will and Testament, viz. principally and first of all I give
and recommend my soul to God that gave it and my body I recommend
to the earth, nothing doubting but at the General Resurrection
I shall receive the same again by the mighty power of God, and
as touching such worldly estate wherewith it hath pleased God
to bless me with in this life, I give, demise and dispose of
the same in the following manner and form. Item first: that all
my just and lawful debts be discharged with my funeral expences.
Item, Second: I give and bequeath to my well beloved and affec-
tionate Wife Agness my best bed and bed clothes and all her own
apparel, likewise all the cloathing that is bought for her and
not made up, one cow and calf, the young black mare and her
choice of the two women saddles. Item 3rd, I give and bequeath
to my son John Appleby one hundred acres of land out of a five
hundred acre survey which lies in Livingston County State of
Kentucky, to be equal to any in said survey: Item, 4th, I give
and bequeath to my son James Appleby fifty dollars in cash to be
paid within two years after the virtue of this will be in force.
Item 5th I give and bequeath to my son James Appleby fifty dollars in cash to be paid within two years after the virtue of
this will be in force. Item 5th, I give and bequeath to my son
William Appleby one hundred acres of land out of the aforesaid
survey in Kentucky: Item, 6th, I give and bequeath to my son
Daniel Appleby my bay mare and my own saddle and his apparel.
Item, 7th. I give and bequeath to my Daughter Elizabeth McCurdy
three dollars in cash: Item, 8th, I give and bequeath to my

Page
(38)

daughter Grissy McCurdy three dollars in cash. Item, 9th I
give and bequeath unto my daughter Jean Little three dollars
in cash Item, 10th. I give and bequeath to my sons David and
Samuel Appleby all the remainder of my part of the aforementioned
survey of land after taking two hundred acres before mentioned
out of it, to be divided equally betwixt them or the Executors
at their discretion to sell it and divide the price of it between them. Item, 11th-It is my will and desire that all the
remainder of the Estate after what has been mentioned be collected
both real and personal and to be disposed of to the best advantage for the support and education of those of the family that
are under age excepting my wearing apparel and the household
furniture which I allow to be at the disposal of my wife Agness
and my books I allow to be divided among my children and if
there is anything after schooling and raising the children to
divide it between my wife and her five children. I likewise

Page
(23)
constitute and ordain my trusty friends David McCurdy and John
Appleby to be my sole Executors of this my last will and Testament. In witness whereof I have hereunto set my hand and seal
the day and year above written.

Signed Sealed and delivered by   Signed
the said William Appleby as his   William Appleby
last will and Testament in presence   x   his mark
          of us - John Record
                John Calvert
Which foregoing recited Will and Testament was duly proven in
Open Court July Session 1808 by the oaths of John Record and
John Calvert (the subscribing witnesses thereto) to be the act
and deed of William Appleby and the same was ordered to be re-
corded - whereupon David McCurdy and John Appleby came into
Court and qualified as Executors and rec.d letters Testamentary.
An Inventory of the goods and chattels debts and credits of
William Appleby deceased viz, Debts to us known
In Georgia State for a waggon to Nat Hill ---------- $ 70
To William Appleby a balance of old acct.   20.56¼
     Credit due the Estate
By notes on Sundries left in the hands of James Appleby
in Georgia State to collect the amount   --------- 173
By the price of a horse in Georgia from
     Stephen Gray   -------------- 75
By a balance in the book by James Lamaster -------- 1.60
     A list of property   ) Not mentioned in the will.
One old waggon and hind geers   ) Three years of a lease of twen-
one old mare, one cow and calf) ty seven acres of land, one hand
two beds and clothing, two plows,) saw and chissel, one jack plane
and four hoes, two pair geers   ) one small pr. of steelyards,
one log chain two axes and foot) one broken waggon, in Georgia
adze, one Iron Wedge and draw-) State, one pair of stretchers,
ing knife   ) one spade, one pair saddle bags
                                  two old mill saws and a piece
                                  one hammer, one iron square.
Property in the will one bed and bed clothes bought for her,
all her apparel and all the cloathing, one cow and calf, one

young black mare, one saddle, on bay mare and saddle, one rifle
gun, two saddles, with household furniture and a number of books.
12th Oct. 1808   David McCurdy) Exors
   Returned to Oct. Session 1808   John Appleby)

Page
(40)   WILLIAM GREEN'S Will - In the name of God amen, the 23rd day of
Feby. 1809 - I William Green being sick in body but of perfect
memory thanks be to Almighty God and calling to Remembrance the
uncertain Estate transitory life and that all flesh must yield
unto Death when it shall please God to call, do make, constitute,
ordain and declare this my last will and Testament in manner and
form following, revoking and annulling by these presents all and
every Will and Wills heretofore by me made and other, and first,
being penitent for my Sins past, most humbly desire forgiveness
for the same, I give and commit my Soul unto Almighty God that
gave it me, and my body to be buried where it shall please my
Executors hereafter named to appoint, and now for the settling
of my Temperal Estate, as hath pleased God to bless me with, I
do order give and dispose the same in manner and form following
that is to say, first I will that my son Thomas Green, should
have one mare and colt, one cow and calf, one feather bed and
furniture, and I lend to my well beloved wife Mary Green my negro
man named Daniel as long as she remains my widow, and after she
marrieth or Deceses, I will that my son Thomas Green shall have
the said negro man Daniel, and the rest of my Estate I give to
my well beloved wife Mary Green to do as she thinks proper, to
do with in such manner as shall be to her mind to do and dispose
of all and everything, and I do leave my loving wife Mary Green
my Exetrix. and my son Thomas Green Executor with his mother
Mary Green. As Witness my hand and seal the date above written.
Attested by   Signed
J. W. White and John Andrews   William Green   (Seal)
Which will as above recited was duly proven in open Court April
Session 1809 by the oath of James White one of the subscribing
witnesses thereto, to be the Act and Deed of William Green.

Page
(41)   JOHN LAWRANCE'S Will - In the name of God amen the seventh day
of June in the year of our Lord one thousand eight hundred and
eight I John Lawrance of the State of Tennessee and County of
Williamson being in a low state of health but in sound mind and
memory thanks be given to God therefor calling to mind the mortality of my body and knowing that it is appointed all men once
to die do make and ordain this my last will and Testament, viz,
principally and first of all I give and recommend my soul to God
that gave it and my body I recommend to the earth, nothing doubting but at the General resurrection I shall receive the same
again by the mighty power of God and as touching such worldly
Estate wherewith it hath pleased God to bless me with in this
life, I give demise and dispose of the same in the following manner and form, first that all my just and lawful debts be discharged
with my funeral expenses, Second, I give and bequeath to my well
beloved wife Elizabeth to be at her disposal and my Executors,
all my stock of horses and cattle and hogs and waggon and cart
and all my household furniture and farming utensils, her side
saddle and all my books and my wearing apparel and all kitchen

furniture. I also will and bequeath to my son Abraham Lawrance two hundred and fifteen dollars by a note on James Malroy in the state of Georgia, to be disposed of at the discretion of the Executors as they think best for his advantage. I
also have two hundred dollars that is coming from my son Samuel Lawrance in Georgia a part of the price of a negro man I
left with him which I allow to be his property when that is
paid, I say I allow that two hundred Dollars to be disposed
of by my wife and Executors as they may think best for the
advantage of the family. I also will and bequeath to my Daughter Polly Lawrance one sorrel horse and saddle that she has now
in her possession, also one feather bed and furniture which now
goes by the name of hers, I also will and bequeath to my son
John Lawrance one mans saddle which goes by the name of his, I
also will and bequeath to my son Abraham Lawrance my saddle and
shot gun. I also will and bequeath to my daughter Margaret Harris

Page
(42)
twenty dollars out of estate in good property. I also will and
bequeath to my daughter Sarah Harris twenty dollars out of my
Estate to be paid in good property. I also will that in case
my special claims be obtained that whatever remains of them
clear of expences be disposed of as the Exectuoas may find best
for the use of my two sons John and Abraham Lawrance, I also will
and bequeath to my daughter Nancy Thomas two dollars. I also will
that the remainder of my money in Georgia that is not before
mentioned be laid out for land for the support of my wife and
children as long as she continues my widow. After that to be
equally divided between my two sons John and Abraham Lawrance.
likewise constitute make and ordain my wife Elizabeth Lawrance
and my trusty friends Jacob Lawrance and Allen Leeper to be my
sole Executors of this my last will and Testament. In witness
whereof I have hereunto set my hand and seal the day and year
above written.   Signed
                                John Lawrance   Seal

Signed sealed and delivered
by the said John Lawrance as
his last will and Testament
in presence of us - David McCurdy-James Coffey.
Which last Will and Testament as above recited was duly proven
in open Court October Session 1808 by the oaths of David McCurdy
and James Coffey, the subscribing witnesses thereto, to be the
act and deed of John Lawrance and at the same time all the Exec-

Page
(43)
utors therein named was qualified.

WILLIAM BULLOCK'S WILL - In the name of God amen I William Bullock of Williamson County being sick and weak but of sound and
perfect mind and memory do make and ordain this to be my last
will and Testament in manner and form as followeth first and
principally I give my soul to God who gave it me in humble hopes
of a joyful resurrection and my body to the ground to be entered
in Christian burial and touching worldly goods which it hath
pleased Almighty God to bless me. I dispose as followeth -
First I desire that my debts and funeral expenses be well and
truly paid. Item, I leave all my whole Estate after paying my
debts to my loving wife Frances during her life and then my desire

is that my daughter Elizabeth shall have one mare and one feather bed and covering and one cow and calf and my desire is that
she shall have all the goods and chattels that she hath worked
for since she came to the State of Tennessee and my desire is
that my son Nathan shall have one cow and calf and fifty dollars more than the rest of the children at mine or my wife's
death and still my desire is that my son Nathan shall have half
of all my stock that he may raise at my death, and still my desire is that my son Nathan shall have one bed and covering, and
at my wife's death what I leave not give away. My desire is that
the rest of my estate shall be sold and the money arising from
the sale my desire is that it shall be eq ually divided between
my son Nathan and Amos Elizabeth. Lastly I appoint my friend
John Williamson and my wife Executors of this my last will and
Testament ratifying confirming this and no other to be my said
last will and Testament. In witness whereof I have hereunto set
my hand and affixed my seal this thirteen day of January one
Thousand eight hundred and seven. Signed sealed published and
declared to be the last will and Testament of the Testator.
In the presence of us   Signed
John Williamson, Henry   William Bullock
Bailey, Jones Glover.   x his mark

Which foregoing recited will and Testament was duly proven in
open Court October Session 1808 by the oaths of John Williamson
and Henry Bailey two of the subscribing witnesses thereto, to be
the act and deed of William Bullock for the use and purposes
therein expressed and at the same time the executors therein appointed qualified as such.
Inventory of the estate of William Bullock, Dec.d.
One negro Jane, one note on Nathaniel Wych sixty four dollars
and ten cents a credit on said note of twenty dollars, 4 feather
beds and furniture, 3 mares, 6 head of cattle, 2 pots and han-
gers, 1 Dutch oven, 1 frying pan, 1 skillet, 1 grid iron, one
cane hoe, one broad ax, one handsaw, one hammer, one whetstone,
part of a sett of turning tools, one chissel, one weading hoe,
7 setting chairs, one drawing knife, one chest, 2 trunks, smoothing
iron, one lamp, 2 pails, 1 tub, 5 plates, 2 pewter basons, 1
Dish, 6 spoons, 2 tumblers, 1 wine glass, 1 mug, 1 pitcher, 1 case
of knives and forks, 5 cups, 6 saucers, 1 looking glass, 1 razor,
1 sugar box, 1 table, 1 loom and Gears that is to say 2 slays,
1 harness, 1 warping bars and spooling frame, 1 Bible, 1 Dialogue, 1 Testament, 1 Psalm book, 15 head of hogs, 3 cow hides,
1 bread tray, 1 sieve, 1 spice mortar, 1 side saddle, 1 box
with some old iron, 2 bottles, 2 jugs, 1 of leather, 1 hat, 2
shirts, 2 coats and sundry other wearing clothes, 1 spinning
wheel, 2 pair of cards, one bridle, 1 barrel, 1 ax, 1 pair of
cart wheels, 1 coffee pot, 1 grindstone, 1 pepper box, 2 augers,
1 pair scissors, 1 pair of Haimes, 1 Iron Wedge, 1 gun.
                         Signed   John Williamson) Exors.
                                  Frances Bullock)
                                        x her mark

Page
(45)

EPHRAIM ANDREW'S Will - In the name of God amen I Ephraim
Andrews of Williamson County do appoint and ordain this to be
my last will and Testament. Item. I lend to my beloved wife
Ann Andrews the whole of my estate both real and personal during her life or widowhood. Item, and all the rest of my estate
both real and personal after my wife's Decease or widowhood, I
desire should be equally divided amongst my six children, to
be equally divided amongst my six children, (to wit) George,
Knacy, Ephraim, Stacy, Elizabeth, and Nancy with the following
exceptions to wit, Item, I give and bequeath to my beloved wife
the sum of six hundred and eighty two dollars to be disposed of
as she may think proper. Item, I give and bequeath to my son
Knacy Andrews a tract of land containing one hundred acres
joining Benjamin Buggs line, running on his own line for complement. Item. I give to son Ephraim Andrews the one half of
the tract of land I now live on. Item. I lend to my Daughter
Elizabeth Young the other half of my land that I now live on
joining Borens and Biggers lines. Item. My will and desire is
that Pate, Vine and Nelson with their increase and whatsoever
part of my estate or the produce of it as may fall to the share
of my daughter Elizabeth than to remain in the hands of my
Executors hereafter named as long as her present husband shall
live and at his death her part of my estate is to be delivered
by them to her or in case of her dying before him my Executors
are hereby required and empowered to divide her part of my Estate
equally among such children as she may leave except Rebekah
Kyle, to which my desire is that she may have but one dollar.
Item. I give and bequeath to my grandson Howard Young the sum
of ten pounds cash to be laid out for him at the discretion of
my Executors after my wife's decease. Item my will and desire is
that the price with the hire of one negro fellow named Tom
that is now in the possission of George Andrews and William
Drumright, should be taken out of their part of the estate,
and the two hundred dollars that George Andrews paid the said
Drumright for Tom is to be reducted out of the P. Drumright's
part of said negro.

Page
(46)

Lastly I appoint my beloved wife Ann my son Knacy and
Benjamin Bugg to execute this my last will and Testament. In
witness whereof I have hereunto set my hand and seal this
Eighteenth day of July one Thousand Eight Hundred and Seven.
Signed sealed and pronounced by the testator as his last will
and Testament in presence of each other have subscribed our
names.   Signed
Test.   Ephraim Andrews   Seal
Miles Malone   x his mark
William Boring

Which foregoing recited Will and Testament was duly proven
in open Court January Session 1809 by the oaths of Miles Malone
and William Boring, the subscribing witnesses thereto, to be the
act and deed of Ephraim Andrews for the use and purposes therein
expressed - At which session Benjamin Bugg qualified as Executor and at April Session 1809 Ann Andrews and Knacy Andrews
came into Court and qualified likewise and received letters
Testamentory.

An Inventory of the Estate of Ephraim Andrews, Dec.d taken
April 6th 1809.
    1st the Household furniture.
    5 feather beds, 5 bolsters and 3 pillows for do., 6 pr.
sheets, 5 checked counterpains, two of compass work, Do. 4 bed
quilts, one do. of Em's and O.s, 2 Rose Blankets, 1 do. Dutch,
1 do. home made, 3 bedsteads and cards for Do., 2 walnut chests,
1 table of do., 6 chairs and 4 frames of Do., 1 large trunk,
1 do. small, 10 pewter basons, 14 plates, 5 dishes, 22 spoons,
1 case and 2 bottles, 4 do. common sort, 3 butter pots, 6 delf
plates, 11 saucers, 10 tea cups, 1 tea pot, 1 sugar dish, 1 cream
pot, 3 delf muggs, 1 do. an earthen one, 8 bowls, 1 pepper box,
1 salt seller, 1 funnel, pr. candlemoulds, 1 candle box, a ten
bale, 1 coffee mill, 1 coffee pot, 1 pr. fire dogs, pr. tongs and
shovels, 2 candlesticks, pr. snuffers, 1 looking glass, 1 stone
jug, 1 do. of Earth, 1 rifle gun, 1 do. smooth bore, 2 chamber
pots, 1 Razor and pr. lanuts, 2 pint tin cups, three books
Bailey's Dictionary, a Bible and Testament.
    2 nd of the kitchen furniture.
    1 spice mortar, 2 smoothing irons, 1 iron ladle, 2 Big Ket-
tles, 3 pots, 2 Dutch ovens, 2 skillets, 1 frying pan, pr. steelyards, 3 copper weights of 1 to ½ to and 2 ozs. 4 pr. pot hooks,
one bread tray, pr. of Bason moulds, plate and spoon, do. 1
tinkers ladle, 1 barrel of whiskey, 2 branding irons, 5 meal bags,
3 meal tubs, 1 flour tub, 4 water pails, 4 washing tubs, 4 salt
barrels, 1 small key with 4 or 5 Gallons of Brandy, 1 churn, 5
sides of leather, 4 sheepskins, 4 green hides, 2 half Bushels,
1 curry comb, 8 Baskets, a large bag of wheat, a parcel of Bacon,
a parcel of corn, a parcel of cotton, a parcel of flax, a parcel of old iron, 7 bells, a small bar of iron, 2 Ear bells, 1
cloth brush, 2 old saddles and bridles, 1 iron pot rack, 1 loom,
3 cotton wheels, 1 do. of lint, 4 Reeds and Gear for do., 6 pr.
cards, 1 pewter pint pot, 1 copper tea kettle, 4 sickles, 1
flax Hackle, 1 coopers adze.
    3rd - the plantation utensils.
    1 foot adze, 2 whipsaws, 2 do. of Brambles, 1 shoe hammer,
1 do. for nailing, 1 Handsaw, 4 screw augers, 1 Broad axe, 1
hand ax, 2 scythe blades, 1 chissel, 5 narrow axes, 4 pr. sheep
shears, 2 log chains, 1 halter do. 1 Jointer plane/iron, 4 pr.
drawing chains, 2 pr. Haims, 1 Horse Collar, 2 barshear plows,
1 Waggon and hind gear, 1 frae, pr. Iron Wedges, 1 yoke of oxen,
1 cart for do., pr. of old wheels of do., 1 grindstone, 3 small
gimblets, 1 do. spike, 10 weeking hoes, 3 do. sprouting, 1 pr.
Iron compasses.
    4th Bonds and Cash.

One bond on Kimbro Ogilvie for	---	$30
" Do. on Miles Malone		34
" Do. on Julis Neal		10
" Do. on William Nully		532.75
" Do. on N. P. Hardeman		110.
One cash lent Ephraim Andrews	-----	100
" to amount of a bond supposed to be $100 collected by S.E.Andrews of W. Williams in Virginia		100
" 2 five pound bonds left in Virginia for collection		33.33 1/3
" Cash in the hands of the Widow		66.25
Total amount		1016.33 1/3

****

5th - A List of the negros and stock
One negro man named Will, do. 1 Jeffery, do. Dick, Do. one
Abram, Do. Warrick, do. a boy Jacob, do.Starling, Jack, Bob,
Bill, the females, one woman Jenny, Darcas, Doll, Suck, Aim,
Size, the Girls, Lucy, Young Doll, Rachel Dilse - one do. a
negro man named Tom in the state of Virginia in the possession
of George Andrews and Wm. Drumright, with the hire of sd.
negro from the 10th of April 1798 till a distribution of the
said Estate, 6 head of horses, 26 head of cattle, 20 head of
sheep, 40 head of Hogs, 20 Ducks.
                     Signed Benjamin Bugg, Knacy Andrews,
Page   Ann Andrews.
(48)

JAMES GRAY'S Will
    In the name of God amen, I James Gray, do make this my last
Will and Testament in manner and form following to wit, first I
resign my Soul to the hands of the Almighty God who gave it me,
hoping in a remission of my sins through Jesus Christ and my
body I commit to the earth to be buried at the discretion of my
Executors hereafter named. As to my worldly estate I give and
bequeath as follows "First I give to my loving wife Suckey Gray
the use of and life estate to the Tract of Land whereon I now
live, and if the same should not be conveyed to me or my Representatives by Jas. Robertson whose Bond I now hoald for the conveyance of said land my Will is that she have her life Estate
in any lands that is or may be conveyed by virtue of said
Bond which I now hoald, the two Hundred Acre Tract called for in
said Bond excepted, which I have soald, I also give to my wife
during her life, the whole of the chattel Estate that I am at
this time possessed of consisting of negroes and Stock of
every description subjecting any part of it to the payment of
my Debts that my Executors hereafter named may think proper,
the balance to her during her life. Item, I give and bequeath to
my daughter Lucy Kearny the negroes which I have put in her
possession to wit, Joe, Joan, Jack, Charles, Nelly, Judity, Hardy, Anderson and Minty, to her and her heirs forever. Item, I
give and bequeath to my son Young A. Gray all the negroes which
I have put in his possession to wit, Starling, Bill, Sarah,
Franky and Patsey, to him and his heirs forever. Item, I give
and bequeath to my Daughter Suckey Booker the negroes which I
have put in her possession to wit, Jenny, Ephraim, Kissy, De-
Page   liah and James to have to her and her heirs forever. Item, I
(49)   give to my son James M. Gray, after the Death of my wife the
one half of the land on which I now life, to divide the same
quantity and quality with his brother Henry K. Gray being the
same which I have Robertsons bond for, two hundred acres in
said Bond (excepted) which is another tract and which I have
soald. I also give to him after the Death of my wife the one
third part of the negroes and chattel Estate that I leave her
in possession of, after the payment of my debts, and in case he
shall shall dye before he arrives at the age of twenty one I
will that my son Harry K. Gray shall have the whole of the land
that I now have or am in possession of under or through Robertson's Bond, being the Land where I now live, after the Death
of my wife, and if he dies under age I will that his third or

part of the negroes and chattels be divided between my two
youngest childrenor the Survivor of them. Item, I give to my
son Henry K. Gray after the death of my wife the one half of
the tract of land whereon I now live to divide quality and
quantity with his Brother James Gray and in case he dies before
he arrives to the age of twenty one, my will is that his
brother James have the whole of said Tract, as is to be conveyed to me by Robertsons Bond, I also give to my son Henry K.
Gray the one third of the chattel and negro estate that I willed
to my wife during her life, and in case he dies before he arrived at the age of twenty-one, my will is, that the said part
or third which he would be entitled to of the negroes and chattels be equally divided between my son James Gray and my Daughter Sarah S. R. Gray or the survivor of them. Item, I give and
bequeath to my Daughter Sally S. R. Gray after the death of my
wife the one third of the negroes and chattels Estate which I
have given to my wife during her life, and in case she should
die before she arrives to the age of twenty one, my will is that
her part or third shall be equally divided between my two youngest sons or the survivor of them. Item, I give and bequeath to

Page
((50))
my two youngest boys James M. Gray and Henry K. Gray all the
right of surplus warrants called for in Robertson's Bond to me
and the whole interest that I have in and to said Bond or in
case the one dies before he arrives to the age of twenty one,
then the whole interest of said bond to go to the survivor, that
is as before mentioned reserving a life Estate to my wife in
said land - my Will is that my Executors sell for the payment
of my just debts, one lot which I have in the Town of Franklin,
if they deem it expedient, if not my Will is that it go to my
three youngest children and the survivor of them. Item, I give
and bequeath to my daughter Sukey Booker and Sally S. R. Gray
all my right in and to an undivided moiety of land on Deers or
Spring Creek, being a tract of land of Three Thousand eight hundred and forty acres granted to Joseph and James Gray, on the
north side of Cumberland River in the County of Stewart, and
their heirs forever. Item, I give and bequeath to my son Young A
Gray one half of the claim which I have for lands in the State
of Georgia, in case he will recover the other half. I bequeath
to my three youngest children and the Survivor of them the remaining half, and in case young will not take on him the recovery
of my Georgia claim, I will that any one of my Legatees shall
have the half on their procuring the other half, for my three
youngest children. My will is that my friend William Dickson
have the guardianship of my son James till he arrives to the age
of twenty one with all the previledges that he as guardian can
have over him and his property. I also will that my son Young
A. Gray have the guardianship of my son Henry K. Gray till he
arrives to the age of twenty one with all the priviledges over
him and his Estate that a guardian could have. Lastly I consti-
Page
((51))
tute and appoint my loving wife Sucky Gray, my friend William
Dickson, my son Young A. Gray, and my friend Peter R. Booker
my Executrix and Executors to this my last will and Testament
containing eight pages hereby revoking any other Will or Wills.
In Testimony whereof I have hereunto set my hand and affixed my

seal this 20th day of January in the year of our Lord 1807.
Test.   J. Gray   Seal
John Hicks
Harrison Hicks
     Which foregoing recited will and Testament was duly proven
in open Court July Session 1809 by the Oaths of John Hicks and
Harrison Hicks the two subscribing witnesses thereto, to be the
Act and deed of James Gray, and the same was ordered to be re-
corded - whereupon Suckey Gray widow and relict of the said
James Gray, Dec.d and Young A. Gray two of the Executors therein
named, came into Court and qualified as Executors thereto and
received Letters Testamentary.

JOHN HIGGINS' Will - In the name of God amen I John Higgins of
the County of Williamson and State of Tennessee being very weak
in body but sound in mind and understanding, calling to mind the
mortallity of my body and that it is appointed for all men once
to die, I make and ordain this my last will and Testament that
is to principally and first of all I recommend my Soul into the
hands of God that gave it, and my body I recommend to the Earth
to be buried in a decent manner. And as to my Worldly Estate
which God has been ppleased to bless me with, I give and dispose
of in the following manner, after the Discharge of all Lawful
Demands against me. I will and ordain and bequeath to Martha my
beloved wife, my land and black mare and sorrel mare and all
my household furniture and all my working tools, my stock of
Cattle and Hogs, I will and bequeath to my two sons John and
Albert the two colts they now claim, and balance of my Estate
for to be sold, and equally divided amongst my children of
this will I ordain that my wife Martha and John Holbert to
be the Executors, I hereby ratify and confirm this to be my
last Will and Testament, and no other. In witness whereof I
have hereunto set my hand and Seal this 8th day of June in
the year of our Lord one thousand eight hundred and nine.
                                   John Higgins   Seal

Jeremiah Burns
John Pigg
Meriman Sandrum
     Which foregoing Recited Will and Testament was duly proven in
Open Court July Session 1809 by the oaths of Jeremiah Burns and
Meriman Sandrum two of the subscribing witnesses thereto, to be
the act and deed of John Higgins, deceased, and Martha Higgins,
widow, and relect of said Decedent and John Holbert the Executrix
and Executor therein named came into court and qualified as
Executors thereto and received letters Testamentary.

LUKE SMITH'S Will - In the name of God amen, I Luke Smith of the
County of Williamson and State of Tennessee being very po in
body, but in perfect mind and memory thanks be given unto God
calling unto mind the mortality of my body and knowing that it
is appointed for all men once to die, do make and ordain this
my last will and Testement, that is to say, principally and first
of all, I giv and recummend my Soul unto the hand of Almity God
that gave it, and my body I recummend to the Earth to be buried
in decent Cristian burial, at the discretion of my Executers,

Page
(53)

nothing doubting but at the general resurrection, I shall receive the same again by the mighty power of God, and as touching such world by astate it has pleas God to bles me with in
this life, I give devise and dispose of the same in the following manner and form. First of all I give and bequath to
Sione my dearly beloved wife the Articles as follows, the sorrel mare, and two cows and calvs and all the hogs, also one
Bed and furnetture and two Bedsteds and one table and one Wheele,
and what cheers thare is, and half of the Dresser afairs pur-
potionly divided, also one half of the pot mettel Also I give
to my well beloved Daughter Molinde Smith, whom I likewise
constitute make and ordain the sole Executrix of this my last
will and Testament, all and Singular the Gray fille and one cow
and calf, one bed and furniture, also half the Dresser afairs
and half the pot mettle, one Trunk and one side saddle, also
I give to my well beloved Sun Senneah Smith, whome I likewise
constitute make and ordain the sole Executrix of this my last
will and Testament all and Singular the sorrel horse coult, also
one yerling hefer and two year old steer, and one Bead and furnetture alsow all the tooels of avery cind also two books the
Dictionary and the Condordene, and my saddel and saddle bags
also I givs to my well beloved Sun William Smith whome I like
wise constitute make and ordaine the sole executrix of this
my last will and Testement all and Singular the following Arti-
cels, one yearling coult, also when the ballence the p roperty
is made sole of William to git so as to make up him aqual with
the rest of the children. Also it my dezier for my Sister
Elizebeth White for to take my Daughter Malinde and take care
of her.
    Signed Seeled published prononnced and declared by the said
Luke Smith as his last will and Testament in the presence of
us, who in the preence of each other have hearunto Subscribed
our names this twenty eight day of May Eighteen hundred and
nine.

                              Luke Smith   Seal
John Harden   Jaams Doyels   Delilah Harden
                   x his mark   x her mark.

Page
(54)

N.B. It is also my desier for my Brother William Smith and
William to be my axecuters.
    Which will and Testament as before recited was duly proven
in open Court July Session 1809 by the oaths of James Doyel
and John Harder two of the subscribing witnesses thereto, to be
the act and Deed of Luke Smith and the same was ordered to be
recorded.
    Edmund Cook. Division of his Estate.
    In Obedience to an order of the worshipful Court of William-
son County, caring date January Session 1809. I have proceeded
(with the Assistance of Col. John Witherspoon and Captain Nicholas Perkins) to divide the Estate of Edmund Cook Dec'd. between the several Legatees in manner and form following (to wit)
Mary Boyd late Mary Cook Drew Lot no. 1 which contained:
    One negro man named Charles aged 24 years and was
appraised to ---$575
    One girl named Winney aged 18 months appraised to----- 125
    In goods bought of said estate---------------------- 200.51
                                                          900.51

Henry Cook drew lot no. 2 which contained one
Negro woman named Nancy 26 years of age appraised to----$400.00
One Negro boy called Isham aged 5 years apprsd. to ----- 250.00
In Bonds for the Balance   250.51

                                                          900.51

Mary Cook drew lot no. 3 which contained one negro
woman named Jerno 25 years old, and appraised to $400.00
One boy named James 2 years old appraised to   100.00
In Bonds for the Balance   200.51

                                                         $900.51

John Cook drew lot no 4 which contained one negro
boy named Bob aged 7 years appraised to   300.00
One negro girl named Levenia 8 years old appraised ----   275.00
Bonds for the Balance   325.51

                                                         $900.51

Page
(55)

George E. Cook drew lot No. 5 which contained one
negro man named Sam aged 21 years apprs.d to ----------   500.00
One negro girl named Milly aged 5 years and apprs.d----   225.00
Bonds for the balance   175.51

                                                         $900.51

Given under my hand this 2nd day of May 1809.
                          Signed Armistead Boyd, Legal rep-
resentative of Mary Cook, Administratrix.
     I did assist with Nicholas Perkins in making the foregoing
Division and appropriation of the Estate of Edmund Cook Dec'd.
In Testimony whereof I have hereunto set my hand.
                          Signed John Witherspoon.
     Which Division as above recited was returned at July Ses-
sion 1809 and ordered to be Recorded.
     William Rutledge Acct. Current.
     We Samuel Perkins and Nicholas Scales, Commissioners ap-
pointed by the worshipful court of Williamson County to settle
with Alexander Rutledge Admr. on the Estate of Wm. Rutledge
Dec'd. have done the same as follows to wit: --------
     We find the said Admr. charged with amount of sales as
Per clerks certificate with   ------------------- 133.93½
     Also accts. returned of Inventory   11.95½
                          Cr.   Total $145.95
     The sd. Admr. has produced satisfactory vouchers for money
by him paid to the amt.   -------------------
     Given under our honor this 3rd day of July 1809.
                              Samuel Perkins
                              Nicholas Scales
     Which report as above recited was returned July Session
1809 by Sam'l Perkins and Nicholas Scales the Comr's. and
ordered to be recorded.

Page
(56)

     WILLIAM M.LOVES Will. - In the name of God amen I William
M. Love of Williamson County and State of Tennessee being weak
in body but in perfect mind and memory, do make and ordain
Joseph Love of Williamson County and William Ewing of Davidson
County my soul Executors of my Estate, and my body I recommend
to be buried in a decent Christian manner. First I wish all my
just debts to be paid. Second my accounts of notes and other
Book Debts, that are due me to be paid my Executors and to be

put to the use of paying Debts. Third, it is my wish that my
plantation on five mile creek in Williamson County I allow to
be sold at twelve months credit by my Executors, if there be a
balance of my debts not settled to be paid out of the money
arising from the sail of my land, the Balance to be equally
divided among my brothers and sisters except my sister Polly's
part, the one half of her part I allow her son Bennora Love,
to be collected by my Executors, to be put out upon interest
by them until he arrives at the age of twenty one, Forwith it
is my wish that my horse and saddle and my cattle and hogs to
be sold at twelve months credit by my Executors, and to be
equally divided between Joseph Love Junr. and John G. Love
my two brothers of Williamson County, my plough and grubbing
hoe, I allow my brother John G. Love, my trunk ax Iron Wedge and
ax drawing chains and sheep I allow my brother Joseph Love to
have my crop of corn and oats with my old corn to be equally
divided between my two Brothers Joseph Love and John G. Love
of Williamson County. I do hereby constitute and ordain this
my last Will and Testament, and do disannul all Wills, Legacies made by me. Wills confirmed ratified or ordained, that
this my last by me made. In witness whereof I have set my
hand this Sixteenth day of August one thousand eight hundred
and nine.

Page
(55)

Signed pronounced and declared in)
the presence of us, who in his pre-)   Signed
sents have set our hands the date)   William M. Love
above written.   )   Seal

Thomas Shannon, John Boyd, Edley Ewing
Which foregoing recited Will and Testament was duly proved
in open court October Session 1809., by the Oaths of John
Boyd and Edley Ewing, two of the subscribing witnesses thereto,
to be the Act and Deed of William M. Love and Joseph Love one
of the Exectuors therein named qualified thereto, and received
Letters and Testamentary.

Testr.   N. P. Hardeman, C.L.K.

William Love's Inventory -
Two hundred Acres of Land, 1 horse and saddle, 7 head of
cattle, 79 hogs and pigs, suncry accounts and notes to the amount
of $53.75 cents two shillings.

Jas. Love Ex.

returned to Oct. 1809

William Hunnell's Will State of Tennessee, Williamson County
In the name of God, amen, this being my last Will and Testament, after paying all my just debts I leave and bequeath
to my beloved wife and children one hundred acres of land on
Turnbull for their use, and if she should marry, said land is
to be sold and the money divided equally with my wife and children, and I leave five horses to be sold at twelve months credit, and all my stock of hogs except meet for the famyly - I
leave to my wife and children two mares and all the cattle for
their use, not to be sold and one hundred and fifty bushles of
corn on Turnbull for the use of the famyly and all the property
that is to be sold is to be sold at twelve months credit and
to be equally divided between my wife and children and the money
after after securing a warrant and bringing the above land

Page
(56)

****

threw the office is to be let out at Interest until my children comes of age - the crop where they now live is to be likewise sold and disposed in the same manner as above, except what the will make use of until the move to their home on Turnbull. In witness whereof I have hereunto set my hand and Seal this 9 day of October 1809. Hugh Allison and Peter Hunnel Executors to said Will.

Signed William Hunnel (Seal)
x - his mark

John Davy)
Robt. Love)

The Execution of which Will and Testament as before recited was duly proven in Open Court Oct. Session 1809 by the Oaths of John Davy and Robert Love the subscribing witnesses thereto, to be the Act and deed of William Hunnell and the same was ordered to be recorded.

Teste. N. P. Hardeman, C.W.C.

Page (59) Inventory of Merchandise Taken in John Wright's Store

101½	Yards	Calico	7 ps.	5	Remnants
62½	Do.	Do.		5	Remnants
45¼	Do.	Do.		5	" 12 yards red
	Calico 1. 1,2	Dark	Do. 1		
42¾	Do.	Striped	Calico	3	Remnants
2	Do.	Do.	Do.	1	"
8¾	Do.	Do.	Do.	1	"
6½	Do.	Do.	Do	2	"
2¼	Do.	Do.	Do.	1	"
2½	Do.	Do.	Do.	2	"
11¼	Do.	Do.	Do.	2	"
7¼	Do.	Do.	Do.	1	"
33¾	Do	Carolien	Muslin	2	Remnants
21½	Do.	Lead Col'd.	Do.	2	"
28	Do.	Do.	Do.	5	"
16	Do.	Do.	Do.	2	"
22	Do.	Blue	Do.	1	"
8½	Do.	Do.	Do.	1	"
6½	Gad 4/4	Do.	Do.	1	
3	Do.	Cotton	Shambrey	1	"
4	pieces	India Muslin	18 yards		
2½	"	Do.	Do.	16	"
1½	"	Do.	Do.	16	"
3	Do.	Do.	Do.	14	"
3	"	Do	Do.	12½	"
3	"	Do.	Do.	12½	"
1½	"	Do.	Do.	18	
2	"	Do.	Do.	14	"
29	"	Book Muslin Hdkfs.			

6 White Pocket Hdkfs.
13 Common Leno Shawls 6 Leno Jackets Worked
1 Common Leno Shawl 2½ yards of 4/4 Leno
3 Leno Shalwsl 3 do. Do. 4 yds. Leno 6/4
8 Yards Spotted Muslin
2 Do. Do
28 Do. Printed Do.
3¼ Do. Do. Do.
1 6/12 Dozen Printed Cotton Shawls 18½ Yds. Printed jeans.

	10	Yards	Printed Jeans
	$28\frac{3}{4}$	Do.	Jeans Olive
	$6\frac{1}{2}$	Do.	Durants
	20	"	Black Calimance
	20 1/6	"	Bumbosit
Page	6	"	Black Do.
(60)	26	Yards	Black Bumbosit
	24	"	Striped and Col'd. Nankeens
	33	"	Pillow Fustian
	20	"	Do. Do.
	20	"	Do. Do.
	$14\frac{3}{4}$	"	Black Velvet
	15	"	Thicksetts
	$19\frac{1}{4}$	"	Do.
	13	"	Olive Velvet
	$3\frac{3}{4}$	"	Black Do.
	$24\frac{1}{4}$	"	Card
	$22\frac{1}{2}$	"	Do.
	$13\frac{1}{2}$	"	Do.
	25	"	Do.
	$\frac{3}{4}$	"	Toclentte
	$1/\frac{3}{4}$	"	Swans Fawn
	$2\frac{1}{4}$	"	Do. Do.
	$\frac{3}{4}$	"	Do. Do.
	$\frac{1}{2}$	"	Do. Do.
	$1\frac{1}{4}$	"	Do. Do. 2 remnants
	$4\frac{1}{2}$	"	Do. Do. 2 "
	$4\frac{1}{2}$	"	Do. Do. 2 "
	3 1/8	"	Do. Do. 1 "
	7	"	Do. Do. "
	2	"	Do. Do. "
	$3\frac{3}{4}$	"	Do. Do. "
	4	"	Do. Do. "
	7	"	Bennets Card
	$8\frac{1}{2}$	"	Do. Do.
	$\frac{3}{4}$	"	Do. Vesting
	$11\frac{3}{4}$	"	Mix't. Cassamore
	$11\frac{1}{2}$	"	Do. Do.
	$9\frac{1}{2}$	"	Blue Do.
	17	"	Light Do.
	$2\frac{1}{4}$	"	Flesh col'd. Do.
	7	"	pine blue cloth
	$2\frac{3}{4}$	"	Mix'd. Do.
Page	4 1/8	"	Light dral Do. 2d. qty.
(61)	$6\frac{3}{4}$	"	Botts green 2d qty.
	$\frac{1}{2}$	"	Coating 1 yd. Damaged places
	$6\frac{3}{4}$	Yards	Drat Cloth
	$3\frac{1}{4}$	"	Brown Do.
	$9\frac{1}{2}$	"	Blue Do.
	2 3/8	"	Double mild drat
	$12\frac{1}{2}$	"	Cloth
	6	"	Mix't. Do.
	$2\frac{1}{4}$	"	Do. Do.
	$9\frac{3}{4}$	"	Do. Do.
	13 3/8	"	Coating
	4 3/8	"	Double milled drat common

$1\frac{3}{4}$ Yards Blue forest cloth
$18\frac{1}{2}$ " Plain
$5\frac{1}{2}$ " Do Do.
10 " Do. Do.
$18\frac{3}{4}$ " Do. Do.
12 " Brown Plains
$9\frac{3}{4}$ " Drat Do.
$10\frac{1}{2}$ " Mix't. Do.
13 " Kerney
15 " Plains
$23\frac{3}{4}$ " Drab Do.
1 Prs. Kerney
16 5/8 Yards Do.
1 Prs. White Kerney
8 $\frac{3}{4}$ Yards Coating
11 " Do.
$18\frac{3}{4}$ Backing Baire
$11\frac{1}{4}$ Yards Bear Skin
$3\frac{3}{4}$ " Do. Do.
$1\frac{3}{4}$ " Coating
$5\frac{1}{2}$ " Grey Do.
$23\frac{1}{2}$ " Brown flannell
8 5/8 " Grey Coating
15 " Damages Do.
27 " " "
45 " White Flannel 2 Prs.
$22\frac{1}{2}$ " Red " 1 "
20 " White " 1 "
22 " Yellow " 1 "
$10\frac{1}{2}$ " Red "
$12\frac{1}{2}$ " White "
$2\frac{1}{2}$ " Yellow "
Page (62) $22\frac{1}{2}$ " White "
21 " White "
$15\frac{3}{4}$ " Kenoal Cotton
3 Bonnets
17 Do.
8 Pair White Cotton hose
5 Do Do.
4 " " "
8 " " "
7 " " "
8 " " Woman's Do.
6 " " Mans Ribbed
6 " Do Do.
4 " Random Do.
6 " Cauke Do.
3 " White mens silk Do.
2 " Black
3 " White ribbed hose
3 " Lead col'd. Silk Gloves
11 " Mens Leather Do.
6 Womens Cotton Do.
4 "worsted hose
$9\frac{1}{2}$ Rheams writing paper

2 Gibson's Surveying
15 School Bibles
3-Goldsmith's England
1-Adelaide de Sansin
2-Tale of the Times
2-Directors
2-Volume of Civil War in England
1-Stephen de Bourbon
2-Franklin's Work
1-Immortal Waster
1-Huic
3-Dwight's Geography
9-Testaments
5-Scots Sessions
5-Clarissa Harlowe
4-grammars
$1\frac{1}{2}$ Doz. Mansons Spelling Book
41-Vicar Wakefield
8-Schoolmaster Assistants
4 Enticks Dictionary
4-Married Companions
6-Hymn Books, 2 Psalm Books
4-Roman Catholic Prayer Books
1-French revolution, 5 Church of England Prayer Books
4 7/12 Doz. Chap. Books
10/12 " Blank Books
9/12 " Do. Do.
1 5/12 " Do. Do.
10/12 " Do. Do.
1- " Small childrens Books reading made easy
2 Beauties of Poetry
11 Dozen of Primmers
1-Civil War Vendee
$1\frac{1}{2}$ Dozen black Morocco Pocket Books
11- " Red "
1 " Do. Do.
2 Blank Books
1-Large Ledger
1-Journal
$232\frac{3}{4}$-Yards Homespun 25 pieces
27- " Baleing 2 pieces
1 Ps. Webbing, 1ps. do. 1 ps. Do.
$\frac{3}{4}$ ps. Do.
2- " Straining Webb.
1- Do. Do.
8- Doz. Knives and Forks
2- " " "
2- " "
2 setts black Bone Carver
6-pitchers Do.
6 razors & Cases, 4 Razor straps
19 pr. shares large

51 pr. amall scissars
1 doz   "   Do.
2   "   Pen Knives
1 7/12   Doz. Do.
10/12   Do. Do.
2   Do. Do
5   Brass Ink Stands
1   Gross Head and Throat Buckles
5 Doz. Lursingle R. Buckles
6 Rasin

Page (64)

6 Do.
4 Doz. tea spoons
2   "   Do. Do.
3 Pair Steeve Sinks
6½ Gross Buttons
5 5/12 "   "
1   "   Do
2 4/12 "   Do.
1 10/12 "   Do.
4 8/12 "   Do.
5/12   "   Do.
6/12   "   Do.
1 1/3   "   Do.
2   "   Do.
7   "   Do.
1 Watch Case,5 large Bottles Snuff,
1 Small Do.
19 Bottles Mustard,9 papers ink,
   powder, 10 lb. White Spap.
57 Lb. Brown Soap,2 lb. Brown thread
2 5/16 lb, of twist
2¾ Gross quality binding
1¼   Do. Narrow
1½ prs. Silk Binding
2   "   Cotton ferritting
1 gross gartering
1 ps. figured Do.
1 ps. Black Ribbon
2 prs. Do. Do.
1 "   Do. Do.
1½ Doz. Apron Tape
6 prs. Tape
1½ Doz. roping
1 striped blanket
20 Do.   Do.
7-2½ paint Do.
1 3 "   Do.
2 pa. Rose Do.
1 Do. Do. Do.
2 Do. Do. Do.
1 Do. Do. Do.
4 Saddles and fixings
2   Do.   Do.

Page (65)

1   Do and plated stirrups
4 pair saddle bags
1 Silk umbrella

3½ pieces of velvet ribbon
6¾ Yards German Dowlas
118 lb. pepper
5 Barrels coffee
29 lbs chocolate
138 lbs Home Made Sugar
154 Lbs Imported   Do.
406 Lbs. Salt Peter
206 Lbs. rosin
48 Lbs. pepper
72 lb. raw ginger
20 Hundred segars
   Lot pipes
19 Lbs. spice
50 Lbs Brimstone
26½ lb. madder
36 Lb. Bohea Tea
10 Lb. Young Hyson Tea
13 Lb. Scouchong   Do.
10 Lb. Hyson Skin Do.
16 Lb. Cinamon
2¾ Lb. red wood
8 Lbs. ground ginger
8¼ lb. powder
7 Barrels Whiskey
1¾ lb of Indigo
5 HHdds. Whiskey 372 gallons
31½ Gallons Cogniac Brandy

31 Gallons New England Rum
20   "   "   "
6   "   Malaga Wine
12   "   Jamacia Sperits
12   "   Sherry
25   "   Lisbon   Do.
8   "   port wine
9   "   Jamacia Sperits
1   "   Acid
2/3 Barrel Herring
123 lb. James River Tobacco
26 Lb. Roll   Do.
1 pr. Boots
16 Pr. Shoes "
6   "   Fine
2 Cork Soal Slippers
3 Small Misses Do.
11 Pr. Course Do.
4 Tin Kettles
3 Do. Do.
1 Do. Do.
1 Bucket
2 Lanthrones
1 Tin Coffee Pot
3 Ditto. Do.

8 trumpets, 1 Sauce pan, 1 tea Kettle
4 Tin cannisters 1 tea pot 2 patty pans
1 Do.   Do.
1 large tin cannister,6 japaned cannisters
3 Sauce pans,2 bread trays,2 water plates
   2 side dished
5 pitchers, 1 Butter Boat, 1 Sauce Turean,
1 Soap dish
1 Mug, 10½ Doz.Black Bottles,3 Gal. Bottles
6 Half gallon Ditto
2 5/12 Doz. of Black Do.
1 Doz. Claret Do.
3 Small glass pitchers,1 8 lb. pewter,16½
   Gross small mould.
190 Quarters of Augers, 7 Axes, 13 Hoes,
   2 powder horns.
 3 Tobacco Boxes, 1do. do. 2 Horse fleams
 5 Cork screws
124 Bunches of garments, 76 strans black beads
   1 lot Backle Brushes, 93 lb lead, 1 pr.
   amsll scales, 1 pr. large Do.
 1 Sett Weights, 37 lb. Shingling nails, 18 8 Penny Do.
 9 Strans mock amber Do. 22 watch brass chains, 11 do. do.
 2 Steel ditto 24 Brass Scales, 13 glass Do. 1 Stork Buckle
 3 Pr. knee Buckles, 2 large garden fans 1 do. do. 1 do. do.
9 pr Shoes Boes, 3 Bugle necklaces, 1 pr. Ear Bobs.
1 Pr. Damaged ear bobs, 1 Breast pin and chain, 8 pr. common
   shoe boes, 1 ladies pocket book,5 Sticks Sealing Wax,1 Wreath,
   Lot lace and ribbon, 2 Gilt Lockets, 1 writing desk, 1show Box,
   10 Barrels Salt 2316, 2 lb. col'd. thread.
10 Oz. small wire, 5 5/12 Doz Gimblets, 1 2/12 doz. awl handles
 7 6/12 Doz Gun flints, 25 fishing lines, 2 bung borers.
 1 gross shoe tacks, 1 brass cock, 1 damaged chaffing dish.
 1 Bell 1 pr.Steelguards,5 girths, 1 Sardsingle, 1 lot damaged
   snuffers, 1 pr. steel do, 5 Bear skins, 3 Wolf Do., 1 Box
   Window Glass, 1 Scythe, 1/3 box chalk pipes.
 1 reel, 1 Barrel vinegar,74 hundred slays, 23 sifters, lot damaged work baskets, 1 Hat.

Page
(67)

 1 Large Kettle   ------- 114
 1 Kettle and pot---------- 160
 2 Potts ------------------ 90
   Sundry Castings   64
213 gallon Potts 17 lb. ea. 357
  10- 2   Do. 11   110
   5- 1   Do.   9   45
   4- 3   do. 17   68
   2 -Tea Kettles 15   30
   2 -Spiders and leds 20 Lb. 40
   1 -small oven and led   32
   3 -Large ovens   45 135
   1 -Do. Damaged   32
   1 -Do. Do.   32
   1 -Damaged Stew pot   14
   2 -Flat Botton Skillets 11½
   1 -Deep   "   "   11
   2- Do.   Do. 8½   17

```
1 pr. smallldogs      ----  26¾
1 small kettle        ----  16⅓
                            ─────
                            1404 ¼
```

3 Leading lines, 5 trunks, 1 table oak, 96 Gallon Tar.
333 lb. of tallow, 6 Doz. K. and forks, 8 doz. Do. Do. 1 Doz. Do.
6 Doz. Fr. Bone, 6 white Do. 6 Do. Do. 2 Doz Ebony, Do. 4 Doz.
Do. Do. 5 Doz. Do. Do. 3 Doz. Do. Do. White Bone, 2 Do. Do. 2
Doz., Do. Do. Common ½ Doz. Green Bone, Do. 4 Doz. Do. Do. Common, ½ Doz Green Bone Do. 4 Doz. Black Wood Do. 1 Doz. Sham
Buck Do. 1 Doz. Do. Do. 2 Doz. Do. Do. 1 Doz. Black Wood, Do.
Sham Buck Do. 3 8/12 Doz. Butcher knives 1½ Doz. Do. Do. 7
Jainers bits, 2/3 plane Do.
2 Doz. Tataned spoons, 7 Spool Bits, 4 Guage, 5 pr. Chissels,
5 Turners Chissels, 8 fireners, Do. 5 rasor straps, 5 Do. Do.
½ Doz. Bits. (sharp) ¼ Doz. Do. (Bent) 1 Doz. Do. Bent, 9 Doz.
Snaffle Do. bent, 5 Horselocks.
11 Snaffle Do. 6 9/12 Gimbles Common, 1 Coffee Mill.
1 Doz. Taylors Thimbles, ½ Doz. Brass Do. 1 gross awl blades
and 2 tacks, 10 4/12 Doz patent gimblets, 7/12 Shewing Boxes,
1 Iron Square.

Page
(68)

```
3 9/12 Dozen Double Bladed pen knives
5 3/12  "     Single Ditto
1 2/12  "     Ditto     Do.
2       Primers
3       Ditto     Do.
6       Pocket    Do.
3       Rasers    Do.
6       Do.       Do.
7       Do.       Do.
211  pair Butt Hinges, 11 pr. Ditto.  Ditto.
3       Ditto     Ditto
16 T Do.          Do.


3       Bung Borers
1½      doz Blacking Ball
10      M. Tacks
3       doz. Iron Tea Spoons
6 1/3 "    Pewter
7       Toy watches
3½      Doz. Iron Tea Spoons
3       Doz. Spectacles
3       Do.      Do/
3       Do.      Scissors
1 2/12 "         Do.
10/12  " -       Do.
5/12   "         Do.
2/12   "         Do.
5/12   "         Horse Fleams
6    Papers Ink Powder
4    Ps. Needles
2 fish hoops
20 Brace Bitts
11 Saw Sets
3 Inkstands
8 1/3 Prospect Hinges
```

Page
(69)

7 1/12 Doz. Common Lancets

```
 14  Oz. Brass pins
  1 Doz. Saddle Bag Fasting.
  3 M. Spriggs
 3½ Doz. Drawn Screws
1¼ Doz.   Do.   Do.
 3    "    Escutchers
 4    Do.
11    "    Prospect Locke
 2 gross Buttons
 3  Do.  Do.
 1  Do.  Do.
 1  Do.  Do.
 6  Pocket Books
1½ Gross Buttons
8/12   "    Do.
7/12   "    Do.
8/12   "    Do.
 1   Gross  Do.
10/12 Do. Do.
8/12   Doz. Do.
3½     Doz. Do.
 1 1/6  Twist
 1 Gross Heads and Threads
 2 Doz. Steel Do.
1¼  "  Thread Escutchers
 3 Sets plated heads and threads
 8 Sets rollen Do.
 2 pair martingale hooks
 4 Handles
 7 Doz. Pearl sleve links
 5 Brass  Do.     Do.
 6 Hat Buckles
 6 Screens
3½ Do.
 7  Sets plated Boxes
 1  Dozen Wood screens
 2  Watch Keys
 ¼  Gross Backing Awls
7½ Doz. Buttons
8½ Doz.     "
 1  Gross   "
 1  Doz.    "
 8  Doz.    "
 3  Packets 4½ G. Pins
 1  Grass Ferriting
1/3 prs of ribbon 7/6, 18/, 7/6,6/
   12/6, 12/7,8/3 and 15/
1/3  Dozen Hat Bands
 3 Chest Locks
¾ Nun's thread no. 30 ¼ No. 36
1/3  Do.  Do. No. 25
 2 10/12 Doz. Bobing
1½     "      Do.
 8  pair Silk Suspenders
5/12 Gross Heads and Threads
1½     "     Knitting Pins
 2  Bottoles Snuff
```

3½ Doz. Tooth Brushes
8 Oz. Nutmeg
7 Whetstones
2 Segar Boxes
2 Inkstands
19 Strand Beads
1 Card Shirt Wirs
2 pair Wool Cards No. 5
14 Do. Do.   No. 4
3 DO. Do.   No. 3
½ Gross Quarterly binding
   "   Shoe   Do.
1 Lb. Turkey Red
2 pieces Worsted Webbing
2 pieces Do. Do.
2 pieces Do. Do.
3 Reams writing paper

Page (71)
3½ Do. Dp.
6 Pocket Books
1 Doz. N. Snuff Boxes
1 piece Leopars Chintz 15½ yds
1 "   Green   Do. 18½
11 "   Trafalgar Do. 153¼
4 "   Do. Do. 24½
1 "   Do. Do. 21
1 "   Do Do. 29
8 "   Fancy Calico 96¼ Yds
1 "   Do. Do. 15¼
1 "   Do. Do. 9¼
1 "   Do. Do. 25¼
8 "   Do. Do. 141¼
7 "   Do. Do. 119¼
7 "   Do. Do. 34¼
2 pieces Printed Cambrick 5½ yds.
1 "   Dimity 11½ yds
1 "   Do. Do. 16¼ yds.
1 "   Do. Do. 5¼ yds.
1 "   Do. Do. 5¼
1 "   Do. Do 17½
1 "   Cambrick Do. 1
7¼ "   Black cord
14 "   Olive Do.
13½ "   Do. Do.
7 3/11 pieces olive cord
1 "   Do. Do.
3½ "   Do. Do.
6½ "   Do. Do.
7 1/11 "   White Do.
24 3/11 "   Velvet
33 "   Jeans
24 "   Fustian
24 "   Mixed Nankeen
23 Do. Do,
10¾ "   Do. Do.
14¼ "   White Jeans
9¼ "   India Dimity
Page (72)

2¼ Yds Tabby Cord Vesting
¼ "   Marsailes
10½ "   Printed Jeans
1½ "   Bennett's patent cord
7 "   Swansdown
2½ "   Do.
4 "   Do.
9 Vials Ladumun
3 " Castor Oil
(The Articles of medicine were
   left by Dr. D. B. Potter either
   to be sold or returned)
4 Vials Seveet Oil
8 "   British Oil
6 "   Spirits netre
11 "   Julip
2 "   Emitic Tartar
4 "   Balsam Copevis
29 "   Calomel
5 "   Essence Burgamot
3 "   Lemon
3 "   Dabby Elexer
28 "   Batemans Drops
12 " Godfrey Cordeal
3 "   Essence Mustard
11 / Scot's Pills
10 Dalby's Carminative
10 Medicamenton
24 Turlington's Balsom
3 Yatess Elexer
12 Vials Essence Pepper Mint
6 "   Balsom
1 Bottle Spirits Turpentine
1¾ Lb. Assifoedita
9 Oz. Camphire
3 Oz. Jalap
2 Bottles Cephalie Snuff
6 Lb. Winder Soap   (Page 73)
3 Lb. Rosin
2½ lb. Castel soap
2 Doz. Breast pins
7 Yards Plush
17 "   green Durante
17¾ "   red Do.
3½ "   Blue Do.
6 "   Purple Do.
9 White and Col'd. and Broad
   fringed shawls
12 Leno Shawls
7 Cross Barred Do.
4 Do. Do. Do.
9 Tact Handkerchiefs
16 Do. Do
12 Pocket Do. Col'd. Borders
3 Do. Do.

6   Pocket Handkerchiefs col'd. Borders
12 Book Muslin   Do.
19 Do.   Do   Do.
44 Small pocked faney Handkerchiefs
12 Red   "   Do
3   Printed Chintz Shawls
5   Do.   Purple Do.
1 4/14 Dozen Cotton Remants
  6/12   "   Do.   Do.
4   Tambord Large Shawls
9   Polecat Handkerchiefs
11 Pocket Handkerchiefs
6   Dozen Fancy Pocket Do.
$15\frac{3}{4}$ Lappet and Tambord Muslin
4 red pocket handkerchiefs
$1\frac{3}{4}$ Yards Lena Muslin
4 1/8 "   Do.   Do.
6 1/8 "   Do.   Do.
3 1/8 ")   Do.   Do.
5 1/8 "   Do.   Do.
10   Yds. Flowered Muslin
10   Do.   Do.   Do.
$3\frac{3}{4}$ "   Cambric   Do 6/4
$1\frac{1}{4}$ "   Muslin   Do. 6/4
$3\frac{1}{2}$ "   Glazed   Do. 6/4

Page
(74)

4   Yds. Glazed cambric
7   "   Do.   Do.
$4\frac{3}{4}$ "   Do.   Do.
3   "   Do.   Do.
$3\frac{1}{4}$ "   Do.   Do. Shirting
     "   Do.   Figured Do.
     "   Do.   Do.
$3\frac{3}{4}$ "   Do.   Do.
$1\frac{3}{4}$ "   Do.   Do.
20   "   Pink Cambric
$10\frac{1}{2}$ " Lead col'd. Muslin
30   "   Amotto   Do.
12   "   Shambry   Do.
17   "   Purple cotton Shawls
7   Pocket Hhdkf.
36 Do.   Do.
7 changeable and black silk hhdkfs.
$\frac{1}{2}$ yard cambrick
$1\frac{1}{2}$ "   Tabby velvet
4 ps. Irish Linnen $57\frac{1}{4}$ yds.
$6\frac{1}{4}$ Yds. Do.
$2\frac{1}{2}$ "   Do.
3   Porcupine Bonnetts
3   Straw   Do.
2   Do.   Do. Trimmed
5   Do.   Do.
1   Do.   Do.
3   Silk   Do.
40 Yds. Muslin 5 Remnants
7   "   Do. 3   Do.

```
                22½   Yards Chick
                14     "      Do.
                 8   Pr. Worsted Hose
                 2   pr. Men's ribbed hose.
                14   pr. Do.  Plain  Do.
                 3   pr. Woman's      Do.
                 3   pr. Do..  Lace   Do.
Page           10   pr. Womans       Do.
(75)            5   pr. Cotton gloves
                21 pr. Silk     "
                 2  Pr. Buck    Do.
                 1  Silk Umbrella
                 3   "      Do.
                 1 Cotton  Do.
                 4 ps. paper
                10 Yds. Bottle green cassimell
                10   "     Blue       Do.
                 8   "     Bennets Cord
                 8 yds. Double Milled R. Drab
                 4   "      Do/      Do.
                 6   "      Fine      "
                 4   "    Bottle green  Do.
                 8   "    Brown cloth
                 4   "    Fine mixed     Do.
                 2   "    Black cloth
                 2   "    Blue  Do.
                1½  "    Fine mixt.
                 7   "    Blue          Do.
                10   "    Grey mixed
                 2   "    forest cloth
                14   "    Drab coating
                12¾  "    Brown    Do.
                10¼  "    Grey Bath Coating
                14   "    Grey    "    Do.
                16¾  "    Brown         Do.
                12½  "    Drab Baire
                10¾  "    Blue Bear Skin
                14   "    Brown         Do.
                4½  "    Mix't. Cloth
                4½  "    Plains
                9½  "    Blue          Do.
                 ¾  "    Drab         Do.
                 1   /   Piece White Kersey
                25   Yds. Brown Do.
                17½  "      Green Do.
                21½  "      Mixed Do.
                22½  "      Brown Flannel
Page           22    "      Yellos   Do.
(76)           11½  "      White Flannel
               10½  "        Do.  Do.
               25½  "        Do.  Do.
               15    "      Yellow  Do.
                8½  "      red    Do.
                 ¾  "      Peeling
                 4  Pr. 9/4 Blankets
                 1  Pr. 8/4  Do.
                31  2½ paint Do.
                 ½  Pr. Rose Blankets
```

20 Striped Blankets
46 Yds. Dowlas
6 English Grammars
1 Vicar Wakefield
10 Testaments
1 Tell Tale of Times
4 Hymn Books
3 School Master's Assistants
4 Bibles
2 Volumns of History of England
1 Stephen D. Bourbon
1 Lord Rivers
1 Gandentia De Lucca
1 Beauties Poetry
1 Small Hymn Book
1 Vision Columbus
1 Vendu War   Page
2 Gibson's Surveying   (78)
3 Johnstone Dictionary
1 Large Bible
1 Washington Monuments
18 Maury Primmers
21 Blank Books
10 Reading Made Easy
45 New England Primmers
35 Chap. Books
34 Spelling Books
6 Volumns of Charlotte
11 Dwight's Geography

Page
(77)
6 Doz. 12 Pint Tumblers
11 "   "   "   Do.
13 Enameled Bowls
2 Flowers do.
1 Doz. White Do.
3 "   do. do.
5 Large Tin Camp Kettles
2   "   "   Buckets
7   "   "   do.
2 Camp Kettles
2 Large tin tea kettles
3   Do.   Do.
3 Calenders
1 Strainer
1 Large Pan
2 Wash Basins
6 Do. do.
1 Deep tin pan
1 Half gallon
2 Candle Moulds
1 Large Copper pot
8 "   do. do.
8 "   DO. do.
4 "   Tea Canisters
1 Japanned candle stand
   and snuffers

30 Tin pepper Boxes
89 Hundred Slays
2 Patty Pans
7 do. do.
3 Japanned Bread Trays
2 Jacks
1 Cream jug
3 Snuff Trays
15 Pasteboards
48 Wool Hats
1 Furr do.
1 Umbrella
2 Coat pads
1 9/12 Doz. Cow Hide Whips
3 Whips
2 Tin trumpets
1 Lantern
5 Girths
3 Corsingles
1 Whip saw
½ Doz. Bits
2 Curb Bits
1 Bear Skin
77 Box Cords
39 Leading Lines
2 Tin canisters
72½ lb. of pewter
8 Sifters
15¾ lb. of candles
29½ lb of soap
½ Box Spanish Segars
3 Pr. Ladies Kid
2 "   Morocco do.
2 "   Men's Leather Do.
7 "   do.   do.
29 Course do. do.
29 do do. do.
2 Women's do. do.
1 pr. Boots
200 Yds. Homespun Cloth
10 "   Check   do.
7½ "   Mix't.   do.
6 Chamber pots
8 Muggs
2 Tureans
2 Butter Boats
2 Tea Pots
7 Mustards
1 Milk Pan
14 Mustards
10 Peppers
1 Doz. Butter Plates
11 Vinegar Crewets
4 Quart Decanters
16 "   Bottles

5 5 large jars
2 2'd. size do.
1 gallon bottle
2½ "   do.

Page (79)

2 Gross pitchers
7¾ Yds. Homespun
3¼ "   White "
2 "   Dresses
13 "   Edging
2½ "   "
6¼ "   Lace
14 Oz. Barks
5 Yds. Velvet ribbon
5 " do. do.
½ Lot sewing silk
44 Buckle Brushes
6¾ Yds. spangled ribbon
2 "   Mix't. cord
3¾ "   Nankeen
24 Hat linings
3 Doz. Combs
17 Bunches Beads
2 Waiters
30 Lb. Madder
9 lb. Brimstone
25 lb. ground ginger
269 Qr. Screw Augers
9 Lb. glue
21 lb. madder
1 Drawing knife
3/¾ Powder
1 Keg Raisons
15 Axes
51½ lb pepper
15 gallons whiskey
29 lb. Coperas
¼ Barrel Fish
9 Awl shanks
179 lbs. copera rosin
17 lb. spice
3½ Spanish Indigo
1½ Lb. cloves
5¼ lb. salts
9¾   raisons
1¼ lb. flour sulphur

Page (80)

4 Pr. Steelyards
2¾ Lb. red Launders
1 Large Dish
25½ Lb. Chocolate
7 " Hyson Tea
4½ Boxes Window glase
89 Lb. 8'd nails
112 lb. Flooring Brads
10 Cane Hoes
120 Lb. James River Tobacco
59½ Small Roll Do.

3 Saddles
3 do
2 do
1 Woman's Saddle
1 Saddle
157 lb. of coffee
16½ lb. rare ginger
259 lb. salt petre
23 "   Alum
326 "   Sugar
300¼ "   Lead
36½ "   Blistered Steel
2871 "   Salt
29½ "   iron
134½ "   Andirons
224 Gallons Tar
3 Large kettles 5 9 lb.   177
2 8 gallon do.   60
5 6 Do. do.   29   145
4 4 do. do.   23   192
8 3 do. do.   18   144
8 2 do. do.   12   96
4 1 do. do.   8½   34
7 Spiders do. 13   91
1 Small Sugar Kettle   15
1 Stew pot ea. 15 lb. 21 lb. 36
2 Small spiders 13 lb.   26
4 large ovens   45   180
1 Second size   do.
15½ Waggon Boxes
   Cash on hand $450
1 pr. pistols
1 Title

Page (81)

1 Cupboard
12 chairs
1 looking glass
3 Window curtains
1 pr. Iron Fire Dogs
1 Dining Table
1 Breakfast do.
2 Stand
3 Beds and Furniture, bedstead
1 Horse
1 Cow
3 Negro men, Charles, Moses, Jack
1 "   Woman and 5 children
1 Mattryes
1 Waiter 1 writing desk
1 Bureau
   Dishes, plates, K. and fork.
   Table spoons and tea spoons,&
   china and Tea Board.
5½ Doz. Port Wine
1 Lot Bees Wax 17 ps.
½ Barrel sugar
2 Trunks

```
      1 dressing glass
        Kitchen furniture
      8¾ yds. course cloth negroes
      7 Remnants striped homespun 15 yds
      6 Do.    Plain    do.    12 do.
                Signed  E. Wright, Admr.
        Which Inventory of the estate of John Wright of John
      Wright Dec'd. as before recited was returned in open Court
      October Session 1809 by Elizabeth Wright the administratrix
      and ordered to be Recorded.
                    Teste, N. P. Hardeman, C.W.C.
```

Page (82)   JOHN HIGGINS' Inventory October 6th 1809 - A true Bill of the
Goods and Chattels of John Higgins, desseased.
```
        Article 1. Seventy Acres of Land
              2. Seven head of horns
              3. Thirteen Head of Cattle
              4. Sixteen Head of Hogs
              5. One still Tubbs and Casks
              6. One Waggon and four pair of gears
              7. Two ploughs
              8. four axes
              9. Six hoes
             10. One mattick
             11. Three augers
             12. One hand saw
             13. one chissel
             14. one Addz.
             15. one drawing knife
             16. one gimblet
             17. one Howel and Hammer
             18. One pair of nippers
             19 Two plains
             20. One cow
             21. One cutting knife and Steel
             22. One log chain
             23 2 Clippers
             24. One pair of Stretchers
             25. four saddles
             26. Seven Bridles
             27. One pair of saddle bags
             28. One spade
             29. One iron wedge
             30 Two guns
             31. One reap hook
             32. One round sham
             33. one pair of Compasses
             34. One riddle
Page (83)    35 Six Beds and furniture
             36. one pair of Bedsteads
             37. Three chests
             38. Two pots,one oven,one pan, and Tea Kettle
             39. Two Flat irons
             40. Two potracks
             41. Three pair of Pot Hooks
             42. Three pails three piggins and one wheelwright
             43. Two churns
             44. Three wheels
```

45- One Chuk Wreel
46- Drepers and furniture
47- One pair of shares
48- five bells
49- One looking glass
50- Two pair of scissors
51- Two sifters
52- Five chairs
53- Three Hides of Leather
54- One Hackle
55- Seven Slays
56- One pair Harness
57- Five books
58- four pair of cards
     two H. of steel
~   One case of Razors
     Two padlocks
     One set of working spools
     One brass ink stand
     Which Inventory of the Estate of John Higgins, Dec'd., as
before recited was returned in Open Court October Session
1809, by Martha Higgins and John Holbert the Executrix and
Executors - and ordered to be Recorded. Teste. N. P. Hardeman,
                                            C. W. C.

Page
(84)

     An Inventory of the Estate of James Gray, Dec'd. 26th of
September 1809, Viz.
     Twenty two negroes, seven head of horses, seven head of sheep,
a stock of hogs (say fifty) twelve head of horned cattle, nine
beds and furniture, eight bedsteads, three tables, eight chairs,
five trunks, one chest, one press, one small corner cupboard,
two looking Glass, two Tea Chests, one pair of fire Dogs, two
pair of Tongs, one shovel, one poker, two kettles, two pots,
three Dutch ovens, two Iron potracks, one pair of Smoothing
Irons, one meal Sifter, five water piggins, one churn, three
Bread Trays, a parcel of Barrels, one Sett of Smiths Tools,
one Safe, two pair of Brass Candlesticks, one pair of Steelgards, three chissels, four augers, one pair of sheep shears, one
rasp, two hand saws, one whip saw, one x cut, a small parcel
of Books, one old waggon, one cart, one spice mortar, one coffee
Mill, two kettles, one pair of waffle Irons, three Basons, a
parcel of old pewter, six cotton wheels, one loom, Slays, one
Harness, a Broken set of China, four Bowls, two hash Dishes,
thirteen custard cups, two Salt Sellers, two Tea Potts, a parcel of Wine Glasses, a parcel of Bottles, one Tea Board, Six
Waiters, a parcel of Baking pans, eleven plated, four Dishes
one coffee pot, three jugs, one knife box, one Dozen Knives and
forks, two whip saw files, four x cut saw files, one spike
Gimblet, two tin canisters, two brass chafin dishes, one iron
lamp, three pair of candle snuffers, five butter boats, two
Sugar Tabs, one mug, a small parcel of corn, three Saddles, one
Gunn, a parcel of Bacon, one carriage and Harness, one set of
Harness exclusive, two wooden Boxes, one Iron Square, one pair
of Compasses, one adze, a parcel of Geese, Turkeys, Ducks
Page
(85)
and chickens, a parcel of old Irons, two pair of Iron Traces,
six weeding hoes, four grubbing hoes, seven plough hoes, Seven
axes, one hatchett, one cotter, one Gouge, on Drawing knive,

a parcel of Wheat, say 40 Bushels, crop now on hand consisting
of corn and one barrell and a half of salt, one hogshead of
Tobacco, two pair of Pot Hooks, one bread Basket, one cullinder,
six Sickles, one griddle, one Grid Iron, three Sugar Boxes,
two Grind Stones, one pair of Iron Wedges, a parcel of loose
tobacco, perhaps two hundred weight, an open account against
Henry G. Kearny for L 167.10-1.

    Which Inventory of the Estate of James Gray Dec'd. as before
recited was returned in open Court October Session 1809 and
ordered to be recorded.

              Teste. N. P. Hardeman, C.W.C.

    ARTHUR FREEMAN'S Will - In the name of God amen I Arthur
Freeman of Williamson County and State of Tennessee considering
the uncertainty of this mortal life and being of a sound, perfect mind and memory, do make and publish this my last will
and Testament in manner and form following (that is to say)
during her natural life or widow hood the Tract of land whereon
I now live containing sixty three acres, one negro man named
Ben, my waggon cart and Geers, belonging to them, all of my
Stock of Horses, cattle and hogs, household and kitchen furniture and farming utensils, together with all the rest residence
and remainder of my estate of what nature or kind soever with
the Liberty of selling or disposing of any of the said property that can be spared to pay all of my just debts and to
support the family - and at my said wife's death or marriage,
all the property that then remains in my will and desire is,
Should be equally divided between all my children, by sale or
otherwise, as my Executors hereafter to be named may think
proper, with the exception, twenty-five dollars to be deducted

Page
(86)
out of my son James Freeman's part and added to my Son Miles
Freeman's part, the names of children are, James Freeman, Miles
Freeman, Betsy Freeman, Lucy Freeman, Nancy Freeman, Patsy
Freeman, and Rebecca Freeman. I hereby appoint my beloved wife
Polly Freeman and my friend Nicholas Scales Executors of this
my last will and Testament hereby revoking all other wills
by me made. In witness whereof I have hereunto set my hand
and Seal this 20th day of April in the year of our Lord one
Thousand eight Hundred and nine.

              Signed Arthur Freeman (Seal)
                    x   - his mark

Signed, sealed, published and
Declared by the above named Arthur Freeman to be his last Will
and Testament in the presence of us who have hereunto Subscribed
our names as Witnesses in the presence of the Testator, John
D. Hill, Burton Jordan, John Capell. Which Will and Testament
as before recited was duly proven in open Court October Session
1809 by the oaths of John D. Hill and Burton Jordan, John Capell

    Which Will and Testament as before recited was duly proven
in open Court October Session 1809 by the oaths of John D. Hill
and John Capell two of the Subscribing witnesses thereto, to
be the Act and deed of Arthur Freeman and the same was ordered
to be recorded, and Polly Freeman the Executor therein named qualified thereto and received Letters Testamentary.

              Teste N. P. Hardeman C. W. C.

Page
(87)

An Inventory of the Estate of Hardy Murfree Deacesed returned
to October Court in 1809:
One hundred thirty eight Dollars and 56 cents - Two Eagles
A note on Howell Adams, Dickson County, payable 1 Jan'y.
    1810 for two hundred and forty-five dollars. Supposed good.
A note on ditto, for two hundred and fortyfive dollars payable
1st of Jan. 1809/ Supposed good.
A note on Daniel Ross for five hundred and fifty dollars pay-
    able 1st March 1809. Supposed doubtful.
John Fly and Jere Fly note Ditto for two hundred and forty
    dollars, payable 6th of October 1809. Supposed good.
John Fly and Jere Fly note for Two Hundred and forty Dollars,
payable 6th October 1811. Supposed good.
Elizah Hunter signed Acct. for eleven shillings.
A note on William Neely for Two Hundred and eighteen dollars
    and eighty cents with two credits on it, one of forty dollars
    paid the deceased H. Murfree in corn, one of eighty dollars
    pd, W. H. Murfree in a note of James Finney the 20th July 1809
A balance due on Leon Record's note on the 7th September 1809,
Thirty-three dollars. Supposed good.
Henry Moore's note for Two Hundred Dollars, payable 27th March
    1809. Supposed good.
Molten Carter's note, Summer County, for forty-one dollars and
    25 cents.
Billington Taylor Signed Acc't. - fifteen 4½
Green Williamson's Signed Account for Two Pounds two Shillings
    and 5 d.
Samuel Brooks' Signed note for ten shillings and three pence.
John Carter's note for Eleven Dollars and 25 cts. Supposed
    good for nothing, payable 7th July 1805.
Martin Hall and Washington Thompson's note for fifty-one dol-
    lars and eighty-three cents payable 1st day December 1805
    with a credit on said note for three dollars and seventy four
    cents on the 15th Dec. 1804 the balance supposed to be a
    bad debt.
James Jordan's note indorsed to Hardy Murfree by Daniel Ross
    for three hundred dollars, payable the 1st day May 1808.
Eli Hope's Signed Account for twenty shillings.
John Fly and Jere Fly note for two hundred and forty dollars,
    payable 6th Oct. 1807 with a credit on it of Sixty-two
    dollars and fifty eight cents on the 15th March 1808. Also
Page   nine Dollars paid Mr. Hill for Bees, no date to sd. rec't.
(88) Edward Givens and John Hudson's note for one Hundred and Twenty
    six dollars, in cattle to be delivered in cattle. Supposed
    to be a doubtful debt.
James Matherrin's note for nineteen hundred and twenty dollars
    payable the 1st Jany. 1809 with interest from the Date
    supposed good, has a credit on said note for fifty dollars.
A parcel of Book Acc'ts. the amount not yet known as pr. his
    his books, some supposed good and some bad.
A draft on John Wright, Merch't. of Franklin, for seventy dol-
    lars supposed good drawn in favor of H. Murfree by H. Moore
An acknowledgement of fifty dollars, due by John Wright Dec'd.
Merchant in Franklin on a second order drawn by said Moore, or
as before the 1st day Jan'y. 1810. Supposed good.

Edward Givens note for two hundred and seventy-four dollars
    payable 1st Jany. 1811. Supposed good.
Howell Adams note payable 1st May 1808. Balance due thereon
    this 3rd October 1809. Thirty eight dollars and 32 cents.
John Hallum jr. Note for one hundred dollars payable in mer-
chantable gined cotton on or before the 1st Jany 1809. Supposed
good.
Charles Stevens and William Gray's note for twelve dollars.
5 beds, 3 bedsteads, 2 blue checked counterpins, two willow counterpains, 7 sheats, 1 Sell of calico curtin, 2 patched bed
quilts, 4 rose blankets, 1 blue homespun counterpin
1 pot, 1 kettle - 1 mare, 1 colt, 2 mules, 2 cows, 1 heifer, 2
    yearlings, 1 calf, 38 head of hogs
7 Indifferent Hoes, 7 indifferent axes, 3 grubbing hoes, 5
    plow irons, 3 pairs of chains, 2 augers, 1 chissel, 1 draw-
    ing knife, 1 handsaw
Negroes names at Stone's River as follows: 1 negro man named Jack.
    Supposed doubtful payable 2d day Sept. 1806
500 lb. of Ginned cotton now in Copi Sytles gin.
Henry Moore's note for thirty-eight Barrels of corn
Thomas Ryan Butler's note Balance due thereon for thirty-five
    dollars and 33 cts. Doubtful doubt.
Thomas Ryan Butler note for eight pounds seventeen shillings 16
    payable 31st day of October 1787 a doubtful debt.
Sam'l. Butler's for Sixteen Dollars payable 7th day of April
    1794 with a credit on the lack of three pounds
1 Ditto Woman Treacy, 1 boy Charles, 1 do. Jack, 1 do. Willie,
    1 do. fellow Dred, 1 do. Jack, 1 do. Sam, 1 do. Jeff, 1 do. girl
Nolley, 1 do. wench Jenny, 1 negro fellow Buster, 1 do. Cloey,
1 do. Old Frances, 1 girl Hanner, 1 woman Mill. Say negroes in
all at the different plantations, say where he lived Stone's River
on Martin's Tract on West Harper are fifty five as named above.
    61 head of cattle big and little, 32 head of sheep, 63 head of
hogs, and nine pence worth Carolina currency, a bad debt.
    1 boy child Natt, 1 ditto Warrick, 1 fellow Ben.
    Negroes names on the plantation whereon H. Murfree lived and on
West Harpeth on a Tract of Land called Martins Tract are as follows: One negro man George yellow, 1 do. Frank, 1 do. Tom, 1 do.
Daniel, 1 do. Will, 1 do. Davy, 1do. Fortune, 1 do, Ned, 1 do.
Bob, 1 do. Woman Sally her children as follows: one small girl
Bett, do. Kitty, Hetty, Charlotte.
    37 piggs, 3 mares and colts, 3 yearling colts, 2 bay mares, 1
Bay horse, 1 pided filly,1 black horse, 6 mules, 1 Jack Ass, 1
still and fifteen tubs, 1 old rifle, 1 old waggon and sett of
gear, 1 Bellows and vise, 2 indifferent hammers, 2 pair of old
tongs, 1 pair of fire dogs, 1 pair of Iron Tongs, 10axes, 1 Black
Grammar Box, 1 case and broken sett of bottles
    2 iron candle sticks, 2 brass do. , 1 pair silver speers,
½ dozen silver table spoons
    1 negro woman Selvy - her children as follows, 1 boy named Isham
1 girl Venus, 1 girl Sarah, one negro woman Cherry, her children
as follows 1 boy named Dred, 1 girl Nancy, 1 negro woman Abley-
her children as follows, 1 boy named Moses, a girl Edy, 1 boy Jacob, 1 boy named Ben, 1 negro boy Harry, 1 negro boy Tom, 1 do.
Frank.
    1 mugg, 4 salt sellers, 1 horn and tin tumbler, 1 decanter, 1

Page
(88)

Page
(90)

Wine glass, 1/3 doz do. Tea glasses, 15 Earthern plates,
1 pr. sugar tongs, 2 water plates, 2 Earthen Dishes, 1 turean, 3 Sauce Dishes, 1 Lettuce Plate, 1 Silver caster, 1
sword, 1 cloth Brush, 1 Indifferent umbrella, 12 silver-plated
handle forks, 11 do., do. knives, 6 Horn handle knives, 1 do.
fork, 2 ship carpenters ax, 1 drest fawn skin, 1 Washington's
picture, 4 cotton wheels, 1 linnen do., 3 pair of wool cards,
4 pr. of cotton cards, 5 reap hooks, 1 pair of smoothing irons,
1 sugar Dish, 1 Tea Pott, 1 Silver Tankard, 1 Butter Boat, 1 cake
dish, 1 milk pott, 1 pepper Box, 1 Tea Cannister, 1 Cream Pott,
1½ gallon Pott Tin, 8 small Bells for deer, 1 Lanthern, 1 pair
of steelyards, 1 canr., 1 wooden mortar and pessel, 1 shaving
kettle, 10 sides of Leather, 12 pieces of corkwood, 1 Bridle
Belt, and Bridoon, 1 old saddle, 2 pair of Hames, a parcel of
Geer, 1 small piece of Bukram, 1 piece of Live Wire, 41 hanks
of twine, 1 pair of bias scales, 1 loom, 4 Tubbs, 1 pail, 4
piggins, 1 churn, 5 milk keelers, 2 Wooden Bowls, 3 Potts and
one Dutch oven, 1 Iron Tea Kettle, 2 large do., 1 frying pan, 1
Spider, 2 pair of Pot Hooks, 1 Bread Tray, 1 Cantean, 3 sett of
loom harness, 3 barrells, 2 keggs, 1 Hatchett, 1 small earthern
Dish, 1 Flatt kegg, 1 small kegg Iron Hoped, 1 plow hoe mould,
2 cane hoes, 8 grown deer, 1 fawn, 1 small Bible, 2 saws, 1
saw sett, 3 hoops for Wheelnaves, 4 old cart saddles, 2 pair
of old Wells, 1 glass globe, 1 walnut Table, 1 meal chest, 2

Page
((91))

large hair trunks 1 do. Leather do., 1 small hair do., 1 5 hundred Slay, 3 geese, 1 Butter Pott, 1 mattress, 2 colts, 7
stocks of bees,

2½ yards of fringe, ¾ yds. of ditto, 2 yds. Blue Cloth,
2/4 Yds. of swansdown, 1½ yds. of striped waste cote, 8½ yds.
of calico, 2 yds. of flannel, 2 pieces of linnen, 2 yds. of
superfine blue cloth, 2 bales of twine.

15 piggs, 5 half grown hogs, 2 axes, 1 plow and gear, 2
W'd. hoes, 1 Wedge, 2 cows, 2 yearlings, 1 bare mare, a harricon
85 Bushels of Wheat, 25 Bushels of rye.

                       Signed David Dickinson, Adm.
                       of Hardy Murfree, Dec'd.

Which Inventory of the Estate of Hardy Murfree Deceased as before recited was returned in Open Court October Session 1809,
by David Dickinson one of the Administrators of said Deceased,
and ordered to be recorded.

                    Teste. N. P. Hardeman, C.W.C.

An Inventory of the Goods and Chattel rights and credits of
BENJAMIN COVINGTON, Deceased - By order of Court we, Presley
Hardin Gardner McConnico, and James Neely do appraise the goods
and chattels of Benjamin Covington, Dec'd., Viz.

4 steers	$34.50	1 bay horse	$60.00
6 steers yr. old	$27.00	1 steed colt	80.00
2 Heifers yr. old	9.00	6 hogs	15.00
3 Heifers 2 Yr. old	20.50	2 ditto	4.50
2 Bulls	20.00	18 shoats	6.00
1 Steer	10.50	1 Wagon and hind	
3 cows and calves	27.00	geers	100.00
1 cow and calf	9.00	1 plow and clev-	
4 cows and calves	39.00	ises	6.00
1 cow	7.00		

Page
(92)

19 herd of sheep	38.00	
1 mare and colt	85.00	
1 yellow mare	70.00	
1 do.	60.00	
1 Smoothing iron 3 axes, 1 handsaw, 1 slay	9.00	
1 chunk of lead, 1 bar of steel, 1 plow	6.07	
1 mattock, 2 weeding hoes, 1 pan	4.00	
6 saws and 10 pigs	14.00	
2 mens saddles	13.00	
1 flax wheel and 4 chairs,	4.50	
3 dishes,9 plates, 1 basin,22 spoons	18.00	
Part set of cups and saucers, 1 sugar dish, 5 bottles	2.00	
Knives and Forks, 2 Bibles and two other books	6.00	
2 beds & furniture	50.00	
1 chest,1 bucket & water vessel	8.00	
1 pot, 1 sifter & sundry articles	3.75	
1 musket gun,1 loom & hangings	13.00	
1 two-year old filly	50.00	
1 two-year old horse	30.00	
1 Dun mare and colt	20.00	
1 sorrel mare & colt	45.00	
1 bay mare 3 yr.old	85.00	
2 sides of leather 3 raw hides	9.00	
1 rifle gun, 1 looking glass	15.50	
1 pickling stand	0.50	
Cash	31.78	
Cash	80.00	
Cash	3.37	

An accepted order given by
John Greenlee to the mistake of David Hundspeth for
six pounds seven shillings six pence
Kentucky money   21.25

2 grind-stones	6.00	
2 pair of chains and hames	12.500
1 log chain	6.00	
1 scythe and pitch fork	3.00	
2 augers and drawing knife	1.50	
3 pr. Horse shoes and sundry pieces old iron	9.00	
2 Iron wedges	2.00	

An additional Inventory of the estate
of Benjamin Covington, Dec'd. as
returned July Session 1806 by the
Admrs. 201 share prize - 18.00
   $40. received of Benjamin Cotton.
   A memorandum of the Sale of property of Benjamin Covington,Dec'd.
Sept. 30,1801 as returned in Court
May Session 1803.

Presley Hardin Dr. 202 sheep		5.25
Richard Puckett	20 do.	5.30
Josh Braden	20 do.	4.30
Wm. McMullin	Do.	4.80
Wm. Fluallen one bay horse		86.25
Isaac Bateman 2 sheep		6.00
Sam'l. Merrit 1 mare		94.00
Wm. Davis one horse		50.00
Wm. Megah 1 mare		21.00
Jas. Williams do.		126.50
John Spence 1 cow & calf		17.00
Sam'l Curry do.		17.00
Henry Walker 1 steer		17.50
Rich'd. Orton 1 steer		12.25
Eli Stacy 1 do.		10.30
John Harness Grind-stone		1.60
Rich'd. Orton Grind-stone		1.60
Richard Orton Bed Blanket		5.30
Wm. Davis man's saddle		10.25
Wm. McGah 1 blanket		5.00
Gustis Holland 1 hogshead		1.00

   I certify this is a true Bill of
the sale.   Signed
     Teste   Richard Pucket, Ck.
                    x   his mark
Catherine Covington
        x   her mark

The above is a just inventory of the goods and chat-   her
tels rights and credits of Benjamin Covington. Signed Catherine   x
Covington, Administrator. Which Inventory of the Estate of   mark
Benjamin Covington Dec'd. was returned August Session 1801, by
the Admr. and ordered to be Recorded. Teste, N.P. Hardeman,C.W.C.

Page
(93)

Account of Sales of the Estate of Benjamin Covington Dec'd.
Sold on the 7th day of June 1803 as returned to August Session 1809.   by the Admr.

Isaac Laybot.	Dol. Ct.		Dol. Ct.
5 head of horses	185	Flax Wheel	1.76
1 sorrel filly	70	Hackle Teeth	.50
1 cow	15	1 Bible	2
1 do. and calf	10.50	1 poem Book	.33
3 cows and calves	40.50	1 Book	.33
1 Heifer	5.12½	1 Sive	.33
1 cow and calf	20.60	2 Blind Bridles	2
1 Heifer	6.87½	1 pitch fork	.75
12 Sheep	25.50	1 rifle gun	10.76
1 cow and calf	20.40	1 smooth Do.	1.
1 mare and colt	101.	Henry Kernay	
15 hogs	26.50	1 cow & calf	20.
1 Horse shoe	.25	1 Cow and calf	10.
1 Barshear plough	10.50	1 cow	10.
1 log chain	8	1 Do. and calf	12.75
3 pole axes	6.90	Rich'd. Orton	
2 Hoes	7.00	1 red steer	9.25
Gears	11.00	B. Bull	4.12½
Do.	5.70	1 steer	8.50
Iron Wedges	3	1 do.	9.
2 Clivises	1.50	1. do.	8.
3 Bells	2.15	1. do.	16.25
Drawing knife and		1 do.	8.
Sickle	1.33	1 do.	11
1 Blanket	2.60	1 do.	30.50
do.	2.60	2 do.	5.12½
1 Bed	18.00	1 do.	4.62
do.	15.51	1 do.	9.25
1 dish and Bason	5	1 do.	5.50
2 dishes	6.1	1 Bull	9.25
6 plates	5.35		
Old Pewter	1.31	Burrell McLemore	
A quart pot	1.31	1 Bay mare & colt	140.00
Crockery Ware	1.07	5 Sows & pigs	22.50
Knives and Forks	1.01	William Glover	
2 Bottles	.86	12 Hed Hoggs	19.5
Pott and Oven	5.59	1 chest	9.50
Flat Iron & Pot rack	2.01	Michael Kinnard	
Churn & pigin	.26	2 horse colts	47
1 churn	.78	Joseph Braden	
4 Chairs	2.1	1 grey stud	140
1 Bucket	2.1	James Neelly	
1 Loom and Gear	2	2 sets horse shoes	1.12½
Old water vessels	.12	Do.	1.52½
David Huston		Do.	1.75
Tea Kettle & old Pew-		1 Blanket	1.12½
ter	1.1	1 do.	1.25
1 Steer	8.12½	1 do.	1.20
Moses Chambers		1 plate & Tea Pot	3.32½
2 augers	90		
Benjamin Davis			
Hammer, Pincher &Nippers	1.95		

Page
(94)

```
John McKnight              Dol. Cts.
1 piece Steel (paid)          .25
  Dann Hill
2 Chairs                     1.
  George Davidson
1 Blanket                    4.50
1 do.                        4
  William McMullin
1 Bed Blanket                6.05
  Jesse Weathers
2 chissels                    .50
        Signed
      Isaac Lay, Admr.
      Catherine Covington
```

An account of a Sale made of a part of the property of Benjamin Covington Dec's., Aug. 1803.

Isaac Lay
2 Colts and sundry hogs 110.

        Signed
        Isaac Lay Admr. in right of his wife

An account of Bonds found amongst the papers of Benja. Covington Dec'd. by Isaac Lay Admr. and Catherine his wife.

```
John Greenlee and R.
  Hays                        51.75
Garner McConnico and
  Richard Puckett             73.
                             ─────────
                             124.75
                             $234.75
```

Signed Isaac Lay, Admr. in right of wife.
Returned to November Session 1803.
                        N. P. Hardeman, Clk.

Page
(9ʒ)

We James Boyd and Nicholas Scales being appointed by the worshipful Court of Williamson County to settle with Isaac Lay Administrator in right of his wife, on the Estate of Benjamin Covington, Dec'd. have done the same in the following manner. We find from a copy from Clerk's office of the amount of Scales and that he is charged with Cash, Bonds, and Amt. of Sales to the amount of ───────────── 2215.5

Administrator's vouchers to wit:
```
  Clerk's receipt for                              2.25
Thomas Stuart's rec't. for two fees               10.00
Richard Puckett (as guardian) rec't. for         594.18.5
Garner McConnica    do.       do.                 87.88
John Parks' Receipt                                2.00
Richard Puckett's rec't. for notes rec'd.
  for collection for                             769.96.5
An acc't. allowed for 7 gallons Whiskey
  for benefit of sales                             6.75
Crying the sales                                   2.00
2¼ bushels salt for the stock                      6.81
Administrators trouble                            20.00
```
A note inventoried for $51.66.7. There was credits at the time for $31 that was not deducted which leave 20.66.7
                Deducted from whole amt.
```
                             1522.50.7
                             ─────────
                              692.49.8
```
              Leaves due

Signed Nicholas Scales, James Boyd, Commissioners
12th January 1807
Returned to January Session 1807.

Page
(9⁵)
                    N. P. Hardeman,   C. W. C.
     State Tennessee, Williamson County. A just and true Statement
of the amt. of perishable property of John Hightower, Dec'd.
Sold Thursday 25th March 1802. Agreeable to an order of said
County Court that is 177 dollars and eighty cents.
                    Signed Polly Hightower, Admr.
Returned to April Session 1807.
                    N. P. Hardeman, C. W. C.
     Agreeable to an order of the County Court of Williamson at
April Session. We have proceeded to settle with Polly Hightower
alias Polly Sanders, Administrix of the Estate of John High-
tower, Dec'd:

Amount of property sold belonging to said Estate	$177.80
Hire of Negroes for the year 1802	149.65
Hire of negro Luke	88.00
Hire of negroes for the year 1803	200.40
Hire of negroes for the year 1804	294.00
Hire of Luke and Reuben 1806	100.00
Hire of negroes to Wm. Saunders 1805	300.00
Hire of negroes for the year 1806	200.00
Hire of negroes for the year 1807	322.62½
Contra Cr.	1832.47½
By pd. Lambert Clayton, John Hightowers note	82.60
pd. Richard Orton	11.87½
John Hurley for bringing family here	7.50
pd. Roger B. Sappington	5.00
pd Roger B. Sappington	20.00
Jesse Wharton	12.50
Lambert Clayton 1805 pd.	350.00
Costs on the above	20.29 1/3
pd. Alexander Davidson	31.90
pd. Stephen Childress for a judgmint obtained by	
John Rogers and Wm. Smith in Hamilton District	24.16
pd. John Dickinson	25.00
pd. Richard Hightower	88.00
pd. for keeping and boarding and clothing the	
children 4 years and schooling	160.00
	838.82¾

Page
(9⁷)
     Bal. due from Polley Sanders, Administratrix of
the Estate of John Hightower, Dec'd.. We find to be nine
hundred and ninety three dollars and sixty four cents.
Three hundred and twenty two dollars and Sixty two and ½
cents is not due until the 26th of March 1808 the Balance of
the $993.64¾ is now due. Given under our hands and this 16th
April 1807.
                    Signed C. Boyles
                         G. Hulme
Returned to April Session 1807.
                    N. P. Hardeman, C. W. C.

An inventory of the Goods and chattels rights and credits of
ELISHA CASH Deceased - as returned by Wm. Williams the Administrator -

Cash ninety-nine dollars 37½ cents $99.37½
Presley Hardin's Acct. eight dollars 25 cts.   8.25
Eli Stacy's acc't. one dollar   1.00
Howard Cash as Executor of Joseph Cash
Dr. to
Thirty-six pounds, North Carolina money - this is Disputed
and an uncertain debt.
One negro fellow named Harry, three head of cattle, one saddle
and bridle, one rifle gun, three quarters of a pound of pewter, two hundred Bushells of corn, one plow, one hoe, one ax,
one clivis, one freson, one pair of rope traces, one collar,
a pair of lines, two hats, one big coat, three close bodied
coats, one shirt, four pair of breeches, one pair of Stockings,
one pair of shoes, one pair of spurs, two handkerchiefs, one
razor, one pen knife, one cow hide, whip, hire of negro Harry
for one month six dollars.
                    Signed Wm. Williams, Administrator
Returned to February Session 1802.
                        N. P. Hardeman C.W.C.

Page
(98)

        An account of Sales of the Estate of Elisha Cash. Sold all
the property of Elisha Cash Dec'd. March 3d 1802. Joseph Rol-
ston bought one negro named Harry $505.
John Williams bought one horse   85.
Wm. Williams bought one horse   46.
    Do. Do.   one colt   51.
Henry Cook bought three head cattle   20.50
Samuel Curry one ax   3.12½
Wm. Williams one plough, clivis and freson   6
Samuel Curry one hoe   1.62½
    Do. do. pair of traces   50
Presley Hardin saddle and bridle   8.50
Elijah Williams Whip and Spurs   .50
Wm. Williams one rifle gun   15.
Chapman White one hat   4.25
John Hardin one hat   1.25
John Goff one big coat   4
Robert Read one coat, waist coat, Breeches and
    stockings   10.
Joseph Rolston, coat, waistcoat & breeches   6.
Chapman White, one coat and waistcoat & two pair
    of breeches and one shirt   6.
Joseph Rolston two handkerchiefs   1.25
    "   "   one pair of shoes   .50
William M. Mullins rasor and pen knife   1.
John Williams three quarters of pound of powder .50
Peter Edwards 120 bushels of corn   66.
John Rankin 40 Bushels of corn   22.40
Samuel Curry 40 Bushels of corn   24.40
                                             890.30
                        Signed
                        Wm. Williams, Administrator
Returned to May Session 1802
                        N. P. Hardeman

Page
(99)

Inventory of the property of DANIEL COX, dec'd., to wit:
two mares, one horse and one colt, one year old, four cows
and calves, one steer, two year old, on rifle gun, powder
horn and shot bag, two feather beds and furniture, six pewter plates, on bason, nine spoons, six knives and forks, five
tin cups, three earthen cups, two earthen plates and one jug,
one man's saddle and one woman's saddle, one little spinning
wheel, one pott, and pott hooks and one skillet, one sett of
shoemakers tools, one chopping ax, three hoes and one Drawing knife, one auger, one rasp and one file, one Hair Sifter,
one Skin Sifter, one set of Warping Spools, two water pails,
two keelers and one churn, one cann, one tray, one side leather,
and one whole skin of leather, one Bell, one pair cotton cards,—
one Bridle, one rasor, and one hone, one pair tug Traces and
Harness, one cow, one set plow Irons, two clivises, one sow
and nine pigs, seven raw Deer Skins.
    Given in by me - Signed Newton Cannon
               Feby. 4th, 1802
    Returned to February Session 1802.
          N. P. Hardeman, C.W.C.
    Chattel Estate of Daniel Cox, Deceased, sold at public
vendue March 8th 1802

	Dol.	Cts
One rifle gun, powder horn and shot bag, 6 pewter plates	10	
1 razar, 6 knives & forks & six spoons	1	50
1 hone, 1 rasor & 3 spoons	1	12½
1 Hair Sifter	1	12½
5 tin cups, 3 earthen cups, 2 eathen plates, 1 jug		50
2 water pails, 2 keelers, 1 cann & 1 Skin sifter	2	
1 feather Bed & furniture	15	
1 feather Bed & furniture	10	
1 Woman's Saddle	3	
1 set shoemakers Tools & 1 Rasp	2	
1 set plough Irons & 2 clivises	7	62 ½
3 Weeding Hoes	3	
1 man's Saddle	3	
1 flax wheel & 1 pr. cotton cards	2	
1 cow & Calf & 1 Bell	11	12½
1 cow & calf	11	12½
1 cow & calf	13	
1 Bay Mare	87.	50
1 Brown Mare	71	50
1 Yearling Colt	26	50
1 sorrel horse	71	50
1 chopping ax	2	50
1 Pott and Pott Hooks	2	50
1 Drawing Knife		75
1 pr. traces & Hames & 1 Auger		75
1 Steer two years old	5	75
1 Skillet	1	58½
1 side of cow leather, 1 tanned bear-skin	2	50
1 sow and nine piggs	3	
1 set Warping spools		50
1 churn		75

Page
((100))

	Dol.	Cts.
1 Cow and Calf	11	
1 Tray, 1 Bridle & one file		6½
1 cow	10	
7 Raw deer skins	3	
	403	2½

Signed Newton Cannon, Admr.
Returned to May Session 1802. N. P. Hardeman, C.W.C,
February the 3d, 1803. The Estate of Daniel Cox, Deceased.

Dr. to Newton Cannon	Dol.	Cts.
For Administration letter	0	.80
For Stampt paper for Inventory	0	.25
For stampt paper for notes		.87½
one day attending Court to Administer	1	
1 Day taking Inventory and taking to Court	1	
Two days hunting horses & putting up	2	
Keeping 4 head horses & feeding them 29 days	9	.50
Two days hunting and putting up cattle	2	
2 days going to Hardymans and back	2	
one day attending to the Lake	1	
1 day attending court to get the Estate settled	1	
	22	.42½

The above account of ~~Twentytwo~~ Dollars
and forty two ½ cents. Sworn before me this 28th Day of
October 1803.

                              Signed   Newton Cannon
                                       W. Wilson

Page
(101)

         We the under named Subscribers being appointed by the
County Court of Williamson to settle the Estate of Daniel
Cox deceased with Newton Cannon Administrator of sd. Estate
as find the above account of 22. 42½ to be just and the Balance of said Estate to amount to Three Hundred and eighty
dollars sixty cents. Given under our hands and seals this
28th day of October 1803.
                    Signed G. J. Wilson, J.P.   Seal
                           Samuel Bachman   Seal
Returned to November Session 1803.
                    N. P. Hardeman

         Inventory of the Estate of Andrew McMullin Deceased: 2
mares with their young colts, one yearling ditto, one cow and
calf, one steer, two years old, one do., three years old, 11
head of hogs, one rifle gun, with her accuberment, one man's
saddle, one woman's do., one set of plough Irons, one ax,
2 bells, one pot and Dutch Oven, 6 pewter plates, 2 basons,
one Dish, one feather bed, and its cloathing, one black
Walnut Chest, one Grubbing Hoe.
                    Signed Mary McMullin
Returned to August Session 1802.
                    N.P. Hardeman, C.W.C.
An account of the Estate of Andrew McMullin Dec'd. made Octo.
5th 1802.

	$	Cts.
Mary McMullin one ax --------------	1	.12½
One kettle	3	
One pot	1	.14½
One oven and lid	2	
Pewter	4	.75
Bed and Furniture	10	.75
W. Saddle	8	
One chest	1	.53
One Small Bull	1	.33 1/3
One colt	34	
One ditto	22	
Cow and calf	12	.50
10 Hoggs	10	.50
James McMullin 1 mans Saddle	5	.50
One rifle	10	.50
John Spencer one mare	40	
1 Bell		.87
Richard Orton one steer	9	.25
One mattock	1	.37½
John Goff, Plough Irons	10	
John Grimes one Mare	48	
Eli Stacy one Colt	18	
	262	0 1/3

Page (102)

                    Signed Rich'd. Puckett Ck.
            Returned to November Session 1802.
                        N. P. Hardeman, C.W.C.

An Inventory of the Goods and Chattels of JARED McCONNICO,
dec'd.: 8 pewter plates, 1 ditto Dish, 1 ditto, 6 Basons different sizes, 12 C. Dish, 1 smaller ditto,½ Doz. blue edged
plates, 1/3 Doz. green ditto, 2 White pint Bowls, 3 coffee
cups & 3 cups and Saucers, 3½ pint tumblers, 1 tin coffee pot,
1 ditto without a Handle, 2 tin cannisters, 1 large butter pot
cracked, 1 3-pint ditto, 1 2-Qt. Crack, 1 vinegar crewet, 1
pepper box, 1 pewter salt seller 1 3-qt. jugg, 2 black quart
bottles, 1 white bottle, 1 Earthen Dish (cracked), 1 pair fire
tongs, 1 State, 1 Grind Iron, 2 feather Beds, 1 small bed,
3 checked counterpains, 1 Bed quilt, 2 pair sheets, 1 pair old
Sheets, 1 Bed blanket, 2 Dutch Blankets, 1 Hair trunk, 2 chairs,
2 cotton wheels, one flax wheel, 1 meal Search, 1 Sifter,
2 slays or reeds, 2 pair cotton cards (old), 1 lamp, 1 pewter
candle mold, ½ Doz. knives and forks, 1 pair sadirons, 2 table
cloths, ½ Doz pewter spoons, 1 pair nippers, 1 pair horse
fleams, 1 Brass Inkstand, 1 Table, 1 Bible, 1 old Bible, 1
Young Man's Companion, 2 prayer books, 1 Watts' Hymns, 3 old
Books or parts of them, 2 pair pott hooks, 2 Iron Kettles,
2 Iron Potts, 1 Bell metal kettle, 1 washing tub, 1 water pail,
1 milk piggin, 1 tin Bucket, 1 frying pan, 1 tin cup and 1
qt. cann, 2 Bread trays, 1 pair shears, 1 Dutch oven, 1 pickling
Hogshead, 1 meal tub, 1 churn, 2 meal Baggs, 1 man's saddle, 1
Bridle, 2 Bits, 1 pair Saddle Bags, 2 Baskets, 1 Shot Gun, 1
Handsaw, 1 Lash Saw, one x cut saw, 2 Screw Augers, 1 Barrel
auger, 2 pott axes, one Broad ax, 1 cooper's Hatchett, 1 Dutch
plough, 1 Garden Hoe, 1 Drawing knife, 1 Key Hole file, 1 Claw
Hammer, 1 Shoe Hammer, 2 Chisels, 1 Saw rest, 3 Gimblets, 2

Page (103)

pair Iron Traces, 1 Lock Chain, 1 foot adze, 1 Grind Stone, 1 iron wedge, 1 horse coller, 1 pair Hames, 3 cows and calves, 1 cow, 2 Steers, 2 years old, one steer and one Heifer 1 year old, 1 Bull, 1 mare and yearling colt (Blaze), 1 mare and yearling colt (Bonny), 1 grey filley 3 years old, 27 shoats, 4 open sows, 5 strayed ditto, 22 hens and cocks, 11 Ducks, 1 flax Hackle, 250 Bushels Corn, 600 lb. Bacon, 40 lbs. Hog Lard.

Signed Jered McConnico, Admr.

Returned to May Session 1803.

N. P. Hardeman, C. W. C.

An Account of Sales of the Estate of Jared McConnico, Deceased, made agreeable to an order of Williamson County Court by Jared McConnico, Administrator 26th May 1803:

	$	Cts.
Thomas Walker 1 gray filley 3 years old	64	.50
John Williams, 1 yearling colt	19	
Samuel Curry, 1 mare (Blaze)	10	.25
Cash 1 pair Horse fleams and nippers		.52
1 pair Iron Traces	2	.53
1 saw sett		.12½
Eli Stacy, 1 sow and 6 shoats	7	
5 spaid sows	9	.75
1 steer	5	
William Glover, 1 Heifer	3	
William Mc Min 2 2-C. Bowls		.22
1 Slate		.26
1 pair Saddle Bags	3	
Joseph C. Cornwell, 1 Bed and furniture	40	
Ann McConnico, 1 small bed	13	
1 yearling colt	16	
David McMin 2 Screw Augers	1	.27
20 lb. Leaf Tobacco	1	.25
Jared McConnico, 1 steer $3, 1 Bull $10.12½	13	.12½
1 man's Saddle $8.50, one Ink Stand 18 cents	8	.68
1 x cut saw $4 one Barrel Auger 7½ cents	4	.7½
Heziah McConnico, 2 Sows and 21 Shoats	15	.75
1 Steer and 3 cows and calves	37	.25
1 cow	10	
8 Pewter plates and 6 Basons	7	.75
2 Dishes and 2 earthen ditto	5	.44
11 plates and 1 dish and cups	2	.32½
3 Tumblers and 1 Bottle	1	.20
1 Earthen Dish		.26
1 candle stick and snuffers		.40
1 pair tongs and 1 Gridinon	3	.41
Sundry Books	3	
1 Bed and furniture	40	
2 Dutch and one Bed Blanket	5	.56
1 counterpain and 1 trunk	8	.70
2 cotton wheels and 2 chairs	4	.90
1 flax wheel	3	.75
1 Hair and Lawn Sive	1	.27
2 reeds and 2 pair cards	2	.75
1 Lamp and 1 candle mold	1	.41
8 knives and forks	1	
1 pair Sad Irons	2	.37½
2 iron kettles and 2 pr. Pott Hooks	8	.70

Page
(104)

	Dol.	Cts.
2 Potts and 1 Dutch oven	4	.95½
1 Bell metal kettle	2	.51
1 Tubb, 1 pail and 1 piggin	1	.52
1 Tin Bucket	1	.55
1 frying pan	2	.12½
1 tin cup and qt. cann		.40
1 table and 2 Basketts	2	.87½
2 Trays and 1 pair shares		.37
1 pickling and 1 meal tubb	1	.25
1 churn and 2 meal baggs	1	.77
2 Table cloths and P. spoons	2	.50
1 Hand Saw and 1 Poll ax	4	.76
2 Hand Axes and 1 Shovel plough	4	1
1 Drawing knife and 1 G. Hoe		.88½
1 Hammer and 2 chisels and Saw	1	.10
1 Gimblet and 1 foot adze	1	.32½
1 pr. Traces and 1 lock chain	3	.63½
1 Shott gun and 2 Gimblets	3	.80
22 Fowls and 11 Ducks	2	1
1 Coller and Hames		.50
Heziah McConnico	2	.50
1 Grindstone and 1 iron wedge	2	.50
1 flax hackle	40	
1 bay mare	50	
1 two year old colt	9	
100 lb. Bacon	42	.50
500 lb ditto	3	.20
40 lb. Hogs lard	4	.11
40 lb. Twisted Tobacco	1	.91½
2 coffee potts	1	4½
2 cannisters and 1 Butter Pott		.86
1 Butter pott and 2 cracks		.61
1 Salt seller and 1 jug	1	.6
1 jug and 2 qt. Bottles	50	
150 Bushels corn		

Page
(105)

                    Total Amt. $642   .96
     The balance of the corn that was Inventoried was made use
of for the benefit of the Estate.   Session 180--
Returned to   N.P. Hardeman, C. W. C.

     Jan'y. 10th 1803. An Inventory of all the property of
James Glover, Senr. Dec'd. Viz.
     Cash 132.38 cents, 1 lb. Coffee, 1 lb. Loaf Sugar, 1
hone, 4 lbs glue, 4 oz. pepper, 1 rasor, 2 files, 1 Bed, and
furniture, 3 dishes, 5 plates 4 gimblets, 1 Bason, 1 Tin pan,
3 tin cups, 5 Spoons, 48 nails, 4 needles, 2 pr. cards, 1
gun, 2 saws, 1 axe, 1 foot adze, 1 frow, 1 wedge, 1 Drawing
knive, 1 Hammer, 1 Dutch Oven, 1 pr. pot hooks, 1 rundlet,
1 Bed card, 2 augers, 6 Horse Shoes, 3 Bells, 2 ear Bells,
3 chisels, 1 pair of Leather traces, 1 pair cart wheels, 1
knive, 1 waggon and geers, for 4 horses, 5 head of horses,
1 bread tray, 1 pepper Box, 3 pieces of Iron, Sundry wareing
clothes, 1 pair spectacles, 1 Seive, 1 pair hinges, 1 Bible,
1 plane Talk and Bet, 1 Bridle, 1 pot, 1 pair Stirrup irons,
1 hat, 1 Bond on Thos. Mason for 400 Dollars, 1 pair of Iron
Tugs, 1 negro wench named Alugail, one do. Molley, T empathy,

Arthur, Jemima, Mengo, Burrell, Hannah, Thomas, Tillman,
1 lock chain 62½ lbs. Salt, 1 meal Sack.
                              Signed
                         John Williamson
                         Jones Glover
                                   x   his mark

Page   Returned to Feby. Session 1803.
(106)   N. P. Hardeman, C. W. C.

An account of the Sale of the personal Estate of Jones Glover,
Dec'd 28th Feby.,1803.   Dol..   Cts.

	Dol..	Cts.
John M. Kinney 1 gray mare	46	
John Williamson 1 sorrel horse	60	
James Neely Esq. 1 Bay mare	50	
Lancaster Gloves 1 foot addz	1	8
1 drawing knife		85
Burrell McLemore 1 handsaw	1	25
1 axe	2	25
William Glover 1 hand Saw		75
1 frow	1	9
1 Iron wedge	1	8
1 pair Hames		61
Richard Williamson 1 sorrel horse	30	
John Spencer 1 bay mare	52	25
George Stramter 1 Bell	1	50
1 ditto	2	6
William Glover 1 Bell	1	30
Jones Glover Pewter	7	38
1 pair cards		62
1 pair trac es	1	50
Reuben Dotson, 1 ear bell		91
1 ditto		95
1 Bed Card		36
William Glover, one Bible		75
Richard Puckett 1 pair pot hooks	3	89
James B. Thompson 1 gun	1	13
Jones Glover Sundries		30
John Williamson Loaf sugar		90
Lancaster Glover R. & Hone		.50
William Bullock, Sundries	16	50
Edmond Withers, 1 pair cart wheels	2	28
William Glover 2 Blankets		17 1/3
Amos Bullock 1 knife	31	
1 Bed		30
Jones Glover 1 Bag	70	
Thomas Trice one waggon	3	
John Huston 2 leather collers	10	
Balaam Newsom H. and traces		60
John Huston 2 Bridles		
John Spencer 1 waggon wheel	2	
David Huston, 1 Lock chain	3	
Jones Glover, 1 negro woman (Melley)	112	
1 negro boy Mingo	210	
William Glover 1 negro man Arthur	620	
Burrell McLemore 1 negro woman (Aby)	206	

Page
(107)

	Dol.	Cts.
Richard Williamson (1 negro boy (Tom)		
Lancaster Glover 1 negro woman and children named		
Tempy and Tilman	580	
Burrell McLemore 1 negro girl Minney	490	
Benjamin Adams 1 negro girl Hannah	311	.25
Edmond Weathers, 1 runtlett		.50
Burrell McLemore, 1 negro boy Burrell	340	
Jesse Weathers, 1 Dutch oven	2	.8
Jones Glover 1 pott		.36
Benjamin Adams 1 hammer		.25
George Neelly old iron	1	.18
Lazarus Dotson 10 cups		.56
Henry Petty old iron tools		.70
Presley Hardin 1 plaine Stock and Bett		.61
Jones Glover 62 lb. Salt	4	.1
1 pair cards	1	.55

$2259 .6 1/3

Signed John Williamson) Admrs.
             Jones Glover   )

Page
(108)
    Inventory of the Estate of Noble Stockett, deceased; one
negro man named Jim, about 20 years of age, one sorrel mare
and colt, one Bay mare, one bay gelding and 2 year old colts,
four cows and calves, five yearlings, nine head of hogs,
three feather beds and furniture, two Bedsteads, three setting chairs, one table, seven pewter plates, two pewter
Basons, four table spoons, one cotton wheel, one flax wheel,
two trunks, four case knives, and six forks, one iron tea
kettle, one earthen bowl, seven tea cups and eight saucers,
one tea pot, 10 white metal tea spoons, five bottles one
Drinking glass, 1 cream cup, one pepper box, two tea cannisters, one Glass Salt Seller, three tin cups, three earthen
crocks, one tin pan, one candle stick, one pair of candle
snuffers, two pair scissors, one pair of Taylors/Shears, 1
ditto Goose, one Bible, one prayer Book, one Hymn Book, four
Books, one religious subjects, one rasor, one silver watch,
one cloth Brush, one water pail, one ditto Bucket, one washing
tub, one churn, one flat tub, two barrels, one womans Saddle, four bridles, one pair of Saddle Bags, one pair of Cotton cards, one ditto wool, one Sugar Box, a pair of flat
irons, one Iron pot, one Dutch oven, two large kettles, three
pair of pott hooks, one iron pot rack, one Bearshear plough
and cotter, one clivis, one pair of Iron Traces, two pair
of Hames, one Leather Horse coller, one Double Swingle Tree,
1 fine comb, one coarse,do., two axes, three hoes, one wedge,
one branding iron, one drawing knife, one small Bell, one
meal sifter.
                        Signed Robert Hulme, Admr.
                        Susanna Hulme, Admx.

Page
(109)
    Returned to May Session 1803
                N. P. Hardeman, C. W. C.

	$	Cts.
A memorandum of the Sale of the Estate of Noble Stockett, deceased:		
Robert Hulme - a negro man named Jim	, 400	
G. Hulme one black cow and calf	10	37½
James Borland one cow and calf	10	25
Robert Clayton one cow and calf	10	87½
Thomas Cormally one cow and calf	13	
Robert Hulme one sorrel mare and colt	118	50
James Campbell one bay mare	77	
John Porter one bay yearling colt	40	50
John Porter one sorrel yearling colt	42	50
John Porter one bay gelding	40	
Robert Hulme one Heifer	2	62½
Robert Hulme one heifer	3	50
G. Hulme one steer yearling	2	75
G. Hulme one steer yearling	2	
Robert Hulme one cotton wheel	3	12½
Robert Hulme one table	2	
Robert Hulme one feather bed furniture and quilt	27	
Jonathan Hopkins one feather bed	15	25
Henry Martin one feather bed, furniture, and bedstead	30	
Robert Hulme one trunk	5	50
George Martin one linnen wheel	4	
Robert Hulme sundries	3	75
James McCutchen one silver watch	18	62½
Robert Hulme three chairs	1	50
Robert Hulme Pewter	6	50
Thomas Speaks 4 knives and six forks	1	50
Sam'l McCutchen one book entitled Watch Nelson	1	
James Gault one Book		
John Porter one Bible		
James Borland three books		
James Gault one Book		31½
Thomas Garrot one small trunk	1	50
Robert Hulme 1 churn	1	50
Robert Hulme one pair of flat irons	2	53
Henry Martin one pair tailor shears	2	
John McCutchen two pair small shears		20
Thomas Garrott one Tailors Goose	1	8¼
James Borland one pair of cotton cards		25
John Porter one pair of cards		25
Wm. Thomason one iron kettle		
Robert Hulme one iron kettle		
Wm Thomason one small Dutch oven	7	6
Henry Martin one iron pott	8	
Robert Hulme one ladle and flesh fork	1	6
Robert Hulme one tea kettle	3	
Robert Hulme one pair iron chains	1	6
Ephraim Brown one pair of Hames	2	
Robert Hulme one meal sifter		62½
David Campbell one Blind Bridle	1	
Wm. Thomason one pair of Pott Hooks		50
James Campbell one bridle		62½
Robert Hulme one bridle		31
Robert Hulme two pair pott hooks		62½
Wm. Thomason one pair saddle Bags		12½

Page (110)

	$	Cts.
Robert Hulme one grubbing hoe		.50
Sam'l McCutchen one drawing knife		.32½
Sam'l McCutchen one leather horse coller	1	
Wm. Thomason one hoe		.62½
Robert Hulme one swingle tree		.82½
James Gault one axe	1	.12½
Robert Hulme one axe		.50
William Stockett one pr. double swingle trees		.50
Robert Hulme one crock		.27½
Robert Hulme one plough	6	
Robert Hulme one Washing Tub and Buckett		.76
Robert Hulme one water pail		.32½
James Patton four head of Hoggs	8	.25
Robert Hulme one Bell	1	
Robert Hulme one candle stick		.75
Robert Hulme five hoggs	10	

Returned to August Session 1803 by Robert Hulme and Susanna
Hulme the administrators.
                    N. P. Hardeman, C. W. C.

age
(111)   An Inventory of the Estate of WILLIAM MURREY, Dec'd., taken
1st August 1803: Surveyors Compasses, chaise scales and Di-
viders, Iveners Tools, one Jointer, Jack and Smoothing planes,
one handsaw, and two tenant Saws, eleven moulding planes,
three chisels, one moving guage, one reele, one pair of compasses, eight Bench plane bits, three files, one gouge, one
oil stone, two gimblets, one Brace and one bit, one large
screw auger, one sword, one loom, two pair Bedsteads, one table,
on cotton wheel, and one pair of cotton cards, one bed and
furniture, one woman's saddle, one narrow axe, one weeding hoe,
one grind stone, two smoothing irons, one caster stand, one
Bottle, one coffee pott, one tea kettle, one pewter dish, five
pewter plates, one set knives and forks, one tin ladle, two
Dutch ovens, one pair of hooks, one churn, two poles, one Sifter,
one washing tub, one brass candle stick, one large Butcher
knife, three books, viz., Pains writings, spelling Dictionary,
and the Constitution of the United States, and so forth. Given
under my hand this Day and Date above written.
                    Signed Thomas O. Due, administrator
                              x his mark
Returned to August Session 1803 by Thomas Due, Administrator
                    N. P. Hardeman, C. W. C.

Tennessee State   )   In obedience to an order of the Worshipful
Williamson County)   Court of the County aforesaid bearing sale
                    August Court 1803 the Subscribed has pro-
ceeded to make a true and perfect Inventory of the Chattel
Estate of Matcalf DeGraffenreid, Dec'd. of the county aforesaid in the manner and form following, viz:
    Terry, Negro man aged 49 years
    Ned   ditto   40
    James   30
    Solomon   28
    Matt   24
    Ben   14
    Ross   12

WILLIAMSON CO., TN - Wills - Inventories - Administrations   65

****

age
(112)

Jack, negro man aged 9
Godphrey   "   12
Dover negro   aged 9 years
Sawyer ditto   5
Mahomet ditto   6
Thomas, ditto   3
Silon, negro woman, aged 42 years, Jenny, do. aged 35, Abba,
ditto, aged 31, Charity do., aged 16, Naney, do. aged 14,
Winney do. 14, Meriah, do., girl aged 5.
2 work horses, Bay and Sorrel, 3 feather beds and furniture,
13 head Gision cows, 6 heifers, 2 year old and upward, 2 young
steers, 6 yearlings and 2 calves, 33 head hogs, 18 months old
and upward, 28 head hogs 1 year old and under, 2 Tables walnut
and poplar, 2 chests, 2 trunks and 1 cradle, 1 looking glass,
1 Safe, 1 British Muskett and nine chairs, 2 Earthen Dishes,
21 plates, 1 case and bottles, 4 quart bottles and 1 glass
sugar dish, 2 earthen tea potts and 3 bowls, ½ Doz. cups and
saucers, 1 milk and 1 cream pot, 1 tin Sugar Box and 10 knives
and forks, 1 large iron kettle and 2 iron potts, 2 Dutch ovens
9 stacks fodder, crop corn, supposed to be three hundred barrels, parcel of broke hemp, supposed to be one thousand weight,
3 Bearshear ploughs and 3 narrow axes, 6 weed hoes and 1 cans
hoe, 1 inch and 1/5 quarter auger, 1 frow, 1 hand saw and 1
iron wedge, 1 drawing knife, 3 pair chain traces, 3 pair Hames,
fixed with irons, 2 stacks, 1 tea kettle, 2 large spinning
wheels, 1 small wheel, 1 pair cart wheels.
                      Signed Henry Cook, Admr.
                      Nov. 7th 1803

Page
(113)

Returned to November Session 1803.   N. P. Hardeman, C. W. C.
State of Tennessee)
Williamson County) In Obedience to an order of the Worshipful
               Court of the County aforesaid bearing Date
November Session 1803. I, the Subscriber, have sold all the
chattel Estate of Metcalf DeGraffenreid Dec'd., that are
returned in the Inventory except the negroes which the following is a True Inventory of the said Sale -

                                        Dol. Cts.
Mary Ann DeGraffenreid bought -
1 Brown Cow $3 1 red cow $6   9
1 cow and calf $5.00 2 steers $4.50   9   .60
1 Safe and a parcel of Table furniture   4
1 Feather Bed and furniture   18
1 Ditto   15
1 ditto   15
1 Table, 1 chest and 1 trunk   4   .50
9 chairs $1.50 1 chest $1.50   3
1 table,1 trunk, 1 sugar Box,1 Looking glass3
1 chest, 1 pr. Sadirons $1.67 2 stacks
  fodder $6   7   .67
1 poll axe, 2 weed hoes $4.39,2 sows and
  11 pigs $10.10   14   .49
1 Bearshear plough and 2 sets geer   5   .50
1 large kettle $3.12½ 2 potts $3.12½   6   .25

	Dol.	Cts.
2 Dutch ovens $2.12½ 9 fat hogs $28.75	30	87½
14 young hogs $17.12½. 7 lots corn ten bar'ls.ea.$71½	88	13
1 bay horse $41 - 1 sorrel ditto $75.50	116	50
2 spinning wheels and 1 tea kettle	1	50
Chapman White bought -	$352	1½
1 stack fodder, $6.75 1 tub and parcel of oats $1	7	75
4 raw hides $3.50 6 fat hogs $20.75	24	25
Henry Cook bought	$ 32	
2 heifers $10 1 red cow $6.50	16	50
1 black cow and calf $7.75 1 yearling $2.25	10	
1 case and bottle $10.50 1 old musket $2.25	12	75
1 Bearshear plow $7.50 1 stack of blades $4	11	50
1 stack oats $8 1 parcel do. $1.10 Barrels corn $10	19	
1 cutting box $3.12 small shoats $8.50	11	50
2 fat hogs $7.25 4 pieces of tanned leather $5	12	25
2 pair cart wheels	2	
Philip Maury bought	95	50
3 lots corn ten Barl. ea.	30	25
1 frow $1.50 1 pair Hames and traces $3.25	4	75
2 stacks blades $5.37½.1 weed hoe $1	6	37½
2 stacks hay	4	12½
Nathan Farmer bought	$45	50
2 heifers and 1 steer	8	75
1 black heifer $8 1 red cow $7.60	15	60
A parcel fodder and shucks	1	75
Jordan Solomon bought	26	10
2 lots corn ten barrels ea.	22	25
1 stack blades	6	
Edmund Cook bought	28	25
18 young hogs	29	25
1 cradle $1.1 stack straw .12½	1	12½
Abram Whiteside bought	30	37½
10 barrels corn	10	
Frances Gunter bought	21	25
2 lots corn, 10 barrels ea.		
Henry Walker bought		
1 cow and calf	7	
15 barrels corn	15	
	$22	
Robert Guthrie bt. 3 lots corn 10 Bar'ls.	30	
William White bought		
1 Brindle heifer	4	50
1 cow and calf $6. 1 pied cow $6	12	
William Bright bought	16	50
1 cow and calf	8	
2 weeding hoes	1	50
	9	50
William M. Key bt. 1 red cow	7	
Abram M. DeGraffenreid bought 1 brindle cow	6	
Henry Holliday bought 1 Beershear plow	5	
Abraham Maury Senr. bt. 1 poll ax, 2 weed hoes	2	75
John White bought 1 stack blades,10 barrels corn	13.	50
Robert Davis bought		
1 top stack of fodder and shucks	2	
Joseph C. Cornwell bought		
2 lots corn, ten barrels ea.	20	75

Page (114)

Page (115)

                                                              Dol.   Cts.
Thomas Masterson bought
  1162lb. Hemp 4½ lb. ps. lb.   52   29
The crop of corn fell short sixty five barrels of the
Supposition returned in the Inventory made before the crop was
all gathered, the Balance of the Estate sold amounts to
eight hundred and twenty eight and thirty four cents. Given
under my hand this ninth Day of January eighteen hundred and
four.
              Signed Henry Cook, one of the Admrs.
Returned to January Session 1804.
                        N. P. Hardeman, C. W. C.

  In obedience to an Order form the Worshipful Court of Williamson County bearing date October Session 1804, I have proceeded to sell such part of the Slaves belonging to the Estate
of Metcalf Degraffenreid, Deceased, as is of value sufficient
to discharge all the debts due from said Estate, as far as I
know, or believe to be due. $ cts
One negro man named Solomon Sold C. White   460
one   "   boy   "   Ben   "   Wm. Williams   301   50
one   "   Do.   Jack   "   R, Puckett   290   25
                                                   1051   75
  Amounting in all to ten hundred and fifty one dollars
seventy five cents. Given under my hand at Franklin January
1st 1805.
              Signed Henry Cook, Admr.
Returned to January Session 1805.
                        N. P. Hardeman, C. W. C.

Page
(116)

  An inventory of the Estate of Jesse Blackshare Deceased,
taken the 26th day of July 1803 by Hannah Blackshare and Stephen
German administrators.
  1 woman saddle, a bond given by Joseph Wairs for dated the
25th of June 1803 for one hundred and twenty six acres of land
lying one the waters of big Harpeth, one year remaining of a
lease of fifty acres, 3 beds, 3 bedsteads and furniture, 1
wolling wheel and 1 linnen wheel, 1 dish and nine plates - 1
gun and powder horn, one shot bag, 2 ploughs and gear, 3 hoes
and 1 ax, 1 cart, a small parcel of leather, 16 head of geese,
43 head of hogs, 18 head of cattle, 43 head of hogs, 18 head of
cattle, 4 head of horses, 1 broad axe, 2 plains, 2 augers, 1
hand saw and some other tools, a set of Bricklars tools, Show-
makers tools, 1 chest and 1 box and a case and 10 Bottles, 6
chairs, 1 cradle, 1 looking glass, 3 basons, and 2 crocks, 1
set of tea ware, 4 bottles, 1 case of knives and forks, 1 blow-
ing trumpet and 2 tins, 3 Bibles, 2 Testaments and 2 Hymn Books,
2 spelling books and one pocket Book, 1 candle stick, pepper
box and inkstand, 2 pots and hooks and a kettle, 1 oven, one
skillet, 1 pan, salt supposed to be 2 bushels, a set of lancets, 1 rasar, 2 tables, 1 mans saddle, 3 bridles, 3 piggins,
and a churn, 1 piggin and washing tubb, 11 stand tubbs, 1 pair
of Iron wedges, 3 large gums, 1 slay and geers, 1 tame deer, 4
vials , 1 cag and bread tray, 1 pair of cards, 1 pair of smoothing irons, a quantity of corn, 7 dollars and 4 shillings due

5 dollars cash.

Returned to November Session 1803.

N.P. Hardeman, C.W.C.

	$	Ct
An account of the Sales of the Estate of Jesse Blackshare, deceased:		
Hannah Blackshare 3 feather beds and furniture	21	
ditto one woman's saddle	3	
ditto 1 cotton and flax wheel 1 p r. cards	2	.50
ditto 2 iron pots,2 do. kettles and oven and frying pan and skillet	5	
ditto 7 stand inke,1 sifter, 1 Bread tray	3	
ditto 15 head of hoggs	25	
ditto Corn in little crib	2	
John Porter smoothe bore gun,powder horn and shot-bag	10	
John Campbell 1 large Bareshare plow and swingle-tree	12	.62½
Thomas Blackshare 1 small do. 2 sets of geer and 2 clevises	1	
ditto 2 hilling hoes, 1 cane, do. one axe	2	
ditto a parcel of Shoe Leather	1	
Jacob Garrett 1 bore plain and one jack do	1	.40
Francis Hodge, 1 Broad ax 1 Howel,lauger,1 gouge	5	.25
Hannah Blackshare, 1 handsaw,1 drawing knife, 2 gimblets, 1 auger		.50
ditto Shoemakers tools		.25
John Porter set of Bricklayers tools	1	.25
Hannah Blackshare 1 chest and Box		.50
ditto 1 case and 10 bottles	1	
ditto 4 black bottles		.50
ditto ½ doz. chairs	1	
ditto 1 cradle		.16½
ditto 1 looking glass		.33
ditto 1 pewter dish, 7 plates 3 basons ½ dozen table spoons	1	
ditto. 2 crocks and 1 set of tin ware		.33
ditto 2 flat irons		.50
ditto ½ doz. knives and forks		.50
ditto Blowing trumpet		.8½
ditto 2 tin cups		.6
ditto 1 Bible,2 Testaments,2 Spelling books, and 1 Hymn Book		.50
Jacob Garrett 1 new Bible	1	
John Little 1 do do		.93¾
Aaron Overall 1 Hymn Book		.37½
Hannah Blackshare 1 coffee pot, 4 vials,1 pepper box, 1 candle stand		.50
Darsing Perry 1 pocket book		.75
John Porter 1 rasor and sett lancets	18.25	
ditto 1 cart	83.25	
Wm. Hulme 1 sorrel 2 year old colt	83.25	
Robt. Hulme 1 bay horse colt 1 year old past	71.25	
	$280.12	
Reuben Higgins 2 geese and 1 gander	3.25	
Robert Hulme 2 ditto and 1 ditto	3.32½	
Philip Walf 2 ditto and 1 ditto	3.66½	

		Dol.	Cts.
George Martin 3 geese		3	.54
Hannah Blackshare 2 geese and 1 gander		1	
John McAffee 1 gander			.83¾
Hannah Blackshare 2 geese and 1 gander			
Hannah Blackshare 1 bay horse		5	
ditto	1 bay filly	1	
ditto	3 small bells		.33
ditto	3 sows and piggs	3	
George Y. Peyton 1 sow and six shoats		11	.25
Robert Hulme 9 head of hogs		15	.37½
Hannah Blackshare 9 head of cattle		10	
John Porter 1 red cow and yearling		8	
Reuben Higgins 1 black heifer		8	.25
John McAffee 1 red bull		6	
James Wilson one black heifer		5	.12½
Martin Stanley 1 pied heifer		6	.25
Micajah West 1 red steer		6	
John McAfee 1 Black steer		7	.50
Abrm. Little red heifer with a white face		4	.26
ditto Brindle heifer		3	.51
John Porter plantation		40	
Hannah Blackshare 100 Bushels corn		10	
Miles McAffee 25 Bushels ditto		5	.75
Ditto 25 ditto		5	.75
John Hulme 25 ditto		5	.75
Martin Stanley 25 ditto		6	
Hannah Blackshare 1 saddle and 3 bridles		1	
ditto 2 bushels of salt		1	
ditto 2 iron wedges			.50
ditto 3 piggins, churn, washing tub			.50
James McCutchen 1 Bell and coller			.18¾
John McCutchen el bell and coller			.16½
Hannah Blackshare 1 slay geer and cog			.50
Sam'l. McCutchen 3 gums			.50
		194	.16¼
Hannah Blackshare, corn, skin and curry comb		4	.62½
Stephen German 2 skins		1	.25
		199	.94½

By virtue of Letters of Administration and Order of the
Court of Williamson County by us obtained we have proceeded
to sell the Estate of Jesse Blackshare deceased of which the
within and above is a true list, sold for us.
Signed Stephen Jarman, Admr.
Hannah Blackshare, Admx.
Returned to January Session 1804
N. P. Hardeman, C. W. C.

State of Tennessee - Agreeable to an order of the Worshipful
Court the County Court of Williamson to us directed we have
proceeded to settle with the Administrators of Jesse Blackshare Dec'd. which is as follows to wit: The Amt. of the sale
of the Estate of the aforesaid Jesse Blackshare,dec'd--$481.00¼
Debt due from James M. Neely --------- 2.33
483.33
279.00
Balance 204.33

Entered on $204.33 from 2'd Day of September 1803 until
the present day.   Dol. Cts.
                                                             22   .97
                                             Balance 227   .30
due from Hannah Blackshare, Admr. and Stephen German, Admr.
Errors excepted is $227.30
                    Signed G. Hulme
                         John Spencer
          pd. Contra   Cr.   Dol. Cts.
Paid Joseph Wairs   227   .3 0
  Doctor Hays   9
James McCormac for making a coffin   3
Jno Dickinson in Suits - Robt. and Geo. Hulme 2   .50
Silvanus Castleman Season of one Steed Horse 3   .50
Deaderick and Tatum proved   4   .92
Stephen German admr. for selling,collecting   3
Taxes on Land as pr. rect.   .31¼
N. P. Hardeman clerk for his services   3   .10
     Returned to July Session 1806   279

     The following is an Inventory of the Estate of JOHN JORDAN,
dec'd., to wit -
     4 negroes, 3 head horses, 9 head of cattle, 30 head hogs,
2 beds, bedsteads and furniture, 1 chest, 1 trunk, 4 chairs,
1 pot, 1 oven, 1 skillet, 1 cotton wheel, 1 pewter dish, 1
earthen dish, 6 pewter plates, 6 cups and saucers, 1 milk pot,
1 coffee pot, 5 tea spoons, 1 table, 6 table spoons, 1 pail,
2 piggins, 1 keeler, 1 looking glass, 5 knives and forks, 1
Bareshare plough, 1 falling axe, 1 hoe, 1 man's saddle, 1
Woman's Saddle, 1 Bridle, 2 pewter Basons, 1 pepper caster, 1
Salt seller, 1 pair pot hooks, 1 Sifter, 1 churn, 2 empty barrels
                    Signed Sally Jordan Admr.
               4th April 1804
Returned to April Session 1804
                    N. P. Hardeman, C. W. C.

     The following is the Sales of the Chattel Estate of John
Jordan, Dec'd., sold by the Administratrix on the 4th Day of
May 1805 at six months credit to wit: Dol. Cts.
Sally Jordan one negro girl named Teller   350
  Do.   do.   do   Jane   107
  Do.   do.   boy named Ace   310
  Do.   do.   do.   Ben.   100
  Do.   1 gray mare and filly   115
  Do.   1 brown horse   40
  Do. 2 beds, beadsteads and furniture   20
  Do. 1 chest,$1 do, 1 table 33½ cents   1   .33½
  do. 1 trunk 50 cents, 1 looking glass 25 cts.   .75
Burton Jordan 1 pewter dish and 6 pewter plates 4
Sally Jordan 2 ditto Basons and 5 Spoons   1
    Ditto 1 Earthen Dish 25 cents   .25
Ditto ½ Doz. Cups and Saucers, 1 cream pt, 5
    Tea Spoons   1
Ditto 1 Salt Seller   .25
Ditto 4 Knives and 5 forks   .25
James Downing 1 mans Saddle   7
Sally Jordan   1 womans ditto   1   .12½

		Dol.	Cts.
Sally Jordan	1 spinning wheel	2	.50
do.	1 Skillet and Led	1	
do.	1 coffee pot, .50,loven, and lid 1.50	2	
do.	1 pot and pot-hooks	1	.50
do.	1 pail and 1 piggin		.75
do.	1 churn and 1 keller	1	.25
do.	1 piggin .12½ cents, 1 weeding hoe 1.00	1	.12½
do.	1 falling axe	1	
do.	1 Bareshare plow, 2 clivises,1 swingle-tree	4	
Fred Brander	1 cow and calf $8.75	8	.75
Sally Jordan	1 cow and calf $8, heifers $10	18	
do.	2 yearlings $3.15½, 1 do. $1	4	.15½
do.	30 head of hogs	18	
do.	1 old sifter and Barrel 12½, 1 bridle $1.	1	.12½
do.	4 chairs	1	.25

                                    Total $1105   .74
                Signed Sarah Jordan, Admx.
Returned to July Session 1805.
                N. P. Hardeman, C. W. C.

        An Inventory of the Estate of JAMES MOORE, Deceased -
5 negroes, 6 head of horses, 548 dollars and 67 cents, 32 Head
of hogs, 11 head of cattle, 2 waggons, 8 pair of Harness, 8
horse collers,8 waggon bridles, 5 feather beds, 3 pair of Bedsteads, 6 pair and ½ of double blankets, 9 sheets, 4 coverlets,
1 rug, 1 Bed quilt, 3 Bolsters, 3 pillars, 2 rifle guns, 3
mens saddles, 2 women saddles, 1 hand screw, 1 waggon cover, 1
chest, 1 trunk, 1 cotton wheel, 1 flax wheel, 1 check reel, 4
set of plough irons, 4 chopping axes, 4 pots, 1 Hackle, 2 slates,
1 coffee mill, 2 pair of cards, 5 bags, 2 chairs, 1 pair of
Saddle bags, 4 riding bridles, 4 dishes, 6 pewter plates, 3
pewter basons, 10 table spoons, 6 tea spoons, 1 coffee pot,
6 earthen plates, 7 cups and Saucers, 1 earthen bason, 1 earthen
cup, 1 sugar bowl, 1 cream pot, 2 pitchers, 1 crock, 1 pickling
pot, 1 led canister, 2 jugs, 2 bottles, 5 knives and forks,
25 spools, 1 oven, 1 frying pan, 4 piggins, 2 smoothing irons,
2 pair of pot hooks, 1 pot rack, 1 pair of tongs, 1 shovel, 1
Broad axe, 3 planes, 7 augers, 1 handsaw, 1 square, 2 iron
wedges, 1 timber chain, 1 frow, 1 grind stone, 1 candle stick,
5 chissels, 1 drawing knife, 1 barrel, 1 keg, 1 curry comb, and
brush, 1 half Bushel, 1 cutting knife, 1 scythe, 4 Bells, 8
tin cups, 1 strainer, 3 hoes, 2 mattocks, 1 sifter, James Piggs'
and Peter Fitch note 50 dollars and 50 cents, Desperate Debt,
Sam'l. Southerland, Alexander Chisnhall note 37 dollars and 30
cents, Desperate Debt, Wm. Baldridge and James McCullock note
16 dollars and 23 cents. Desperate Debt Ashby Dunnagan and John
Ray note 8 dollars and 60 cents, Desperate Debt, Ashby and Wm.
Dunnagan Accounts 5 dollars and 62 cents, Desperate Debt.
                Signed
                David Robinson Admr.
                John Moore, Admr.
        Returned to April Session 1805.
                N. P. Hardeman, C. W. C.
An account of the Sale of the Estate of James Moore, dec'd:

Page (122)

Name	Item	Dol.	Cts.	Cts.
Catherine Moore	1 cow and calf	10		
Catherine Moore	1 cow and calf	10		
Catherine Moore	1 cow and calf	10		
ditto	1 cow	10		
ditto	2 heifers	8		
ditto	1 bull and heifer	6		
ditto	2 flat irons	1		
ditto	1 trunk	5		
ditto	1 chest	1	.50	
ditto	1 reel		.25	
ditto	1 flax wheel	2	.16½	
ditto	1 cotton wheel	2		
ditto	1 feather bed and furniture	41		
ditto	ditto	40		
John Moore	ditto	40		
Catherine Moore	1 feather bed and furniture	30		
ditto	ditto	10		
ditto	1 flax hackle	2		
ditto	1 coffee mill	1	.50	
ditto	25 working spools	1	.50	
ditto	2 slates		.66 2/3	
ditto	1 pair of cotton cards	1	.50	
ditto	ditto		.33 1/3	
James Neelly	3 plains	7		
Catherine Moore	1 Side Saddle and Bridle	12		
James Waldrip	1 mans Saddle and Bridle	12	.50	
Catherine Moore	ditto	11		
ditto	ditto	12		
Jediah Peck	1 Barsheal plow	7		
John Moore	ditto	3		
Catherine Moore	ditto	7		
John Moore	1 log chain	4		
ditto	1 pair of Double Traces	2	.25	
David Robinson	1 coopers Adze	1	.16 2/3	
John Neelly	1 Grind Stone	5		
Thomas Dixon	1 cutting knife and Steel	2		
John Moore	1 Scythe and Hangings	1		
David Robinson	2 pitch forks		.30	
ditto	1 Dung fork	1		
John Moore	1 bar of steel	2	.50	
Joel Hobbs	1 Broad axe	4		
John Moore	1 Pitching axe	2		
Catherine Moore	ditto	2	.50	
ditto	ditto	1	.50	
John Moore	1 lot of old Irons and Tools	1	.25	
ditto	1 frow		.83 1/3	
ditto	1 iron wedge		.91 2/3	
ditto	ditto		.66 2/3	
ditto	1 axe	1		
ditto	1 mattock	1		
Catherine Moore	ditto	1	.75	
David Robinson	1 Rifle gun	13		
John Moore	ditto	12		
Catherine Moore	1 big pot and hooks	4		
ditto	ditto	2		
ditto	ditto	1	.33 1/3	
ditto	1 Dutch oven	2		

Page (124)

		Dol.	Cts.
Catherine Moore	1 small kettle	1	.50
ditto	tongs and shovel	1	.50
ditto	1 double tree	1	.50
John Moore 2	2 screw augers	1	.12½
John Neelly	2 barrel augers	1	
John Moore	3 screw augers		.50
ditto	1 drawing knife and Square	1	.25
ditto	1 handsaw	2	.12½
ditto	1 small mare	1	.50
ditto	1 bay filly 2 yrs. old		.50
Catherine Moore	1 bay filly 2 yrs. old	1	.12½
ditto	1 frying pan		.50
ditto	2 weeding hoes	1	.12½
John Moore	1 bay filly 1 year old	89	
William Neelly	1 brown horse	49	
David Dobbins	1 bay horse	80	
Catherine Moore	1 Bay horse	42	
ditto	1 Sow	2	.50
ditto	2 head hogs	8	
Jesse White	2 sows	5	.75
Seth Barnes	1 sow and five pigs	2	
Catherine Moore	1 sow and four pigs	2	
John Moore	1 sow and seven pigs	3	.62½
Catherine Moore	1 barshear plow	3	
John Moore	1 pr. of chains and hames	6	.6¼
John Alsap	ditto	6	.9¼
Catherine Moore	2 leather collers	3	.12½
ditto	1 pair of chains and hames	5	.25
ditto	ditto	5	
James Hobbs	2 collers	3	
Catherine Moore	2 blind bridles	2	.25
John Alsap	1 blind bridle		.75
David Cummings	ditto	1	
John Moore	1 pair of leather lines		.55
Fredrick Pinkly	1 waggon and hind geers	96	
William Neelly	ditto	45	
Fredrick Pinkley	1 jack screw	8	
Catherine Moore	1 negro woman and chile	450	
ditto	1 negro girl	293	.25
Betsy Moore	ditto	202	
Catherine Moore	ditto	150	
ditto	1 pot rack	2	.25
James Fares	1 waggon cloth	7	
Abraham Walker	1 Bell		8
John Moore	ditto		.75
Catherine Moore	2 chairs		.50
ditto	2 bags	1	.75
ditto	1 bag	1	.51
John Moore	2 bags	4	
ditto	1 Barrel		.25
Catherine Moore	2 Slays	1	
John Moore	1 pair of saddle bags		.75

Catherine Moore, the dresser furniture, to wit: 3 dishes
6 plates, 3 pewter basons, 1o spoons, 6 tea spoons, 1 coffee
pott, 6 earthen basons, 1 earthen cup, 1 sugar Bowl, 1 cream

pot, 2 pitchers, 1 crock, 1 pickling pot, 1 tea cannister, 2
jugs, 2 bottles, 5 knives and forks, 4 pails, 8 tin cups. $18
    The foregoing is an account of the Sales of the Estate
of James Moore sold on the Sixth Day of June 1805 at twelve
months credit by order of Williamson County Court.
                        Signed
                        David Robinson and John Moore, Admrs.

page
(126)   Returned to July Session 1805.
                        N. P. Hardeman, C. W. C.

An Inventory of the Estate of DAVID DAVIS, Dec'd. in the County
of Williamson 16th of October 1805:
1 Bay horse, 2 barren cows, 5 head of young cattle, 14 head of
gentle hogs, 15 head of wild hogs, the getting uncertain, 1
feather bed and furniture, 1 silver tankard, 5 pewter plates,
5 pewter basons, 2 dishes, 1 coffee mill, 1 looking Glass, 1
trunk, 1 smooth core gun, 1 cross cut saw, 2 hand saws, 1 key
saw, 2 axes, 1 foot addze, 1 coopers addze, 1 drawing knife,
3 small chissels, 1 gouge, 1 crow, 1 round shave, 1 howell,
1 iron wedge, 2 weeding hoes, 1 iron pott, 1 Dutch oven, 1
skillet, 1 tub, 2 pails, 2 barrels, 3 keggs, 2 wheels, about 6
acres of corn, 1 quarter of cotton, 3 bowls, crokery ware, 1
tea pott, 5 cups and saucers, 5 knives, 5 forks, 1 pair fire
tongs, 1 frying pan, 1 chair, 1 hone, 1 small trunk.
                        Signed, Sarah Davis, Admx.
      Returned to October Session 1805.
                        N. P. Hardeman, C. W. C.
      A list of the articles sold at Public Vendue of the Estate
Page   of David Davis, Dec'd. November 23'd 1805
(127)   Sarah Davis 1 Bed and furniture   1 .50
        d itto   1 silver Tankard,5 pewter plates, 5 pewter Dol. Cts
                     basons,2 dishes, 5 knives and 6 forks   1 .50
        ditto   1 cotton wheel   1 .50
        ditto   1 skillet and firetongs   .40½
        ditto   14 head of hogs   2 .75
        ditto   6 acres of corn,2 stacks of fodder and
                     about 1 forth acre of cotton   7
        ditto   15 wild hogs   1 .37½
        ditto   1 cross-cut saw   4 .25
        ditto   2 axes   2
        ditto   2 cows and 5 head of young cattle   4
        ditto   1 pot and oven   1 .50
        ditto   2 trunks and 2 pair chains   1 .50
        ditto   1 coffee mill and looking glass   .75
        ditto   1 bail,2 hand saws, 1 Lock Saw, 3 chisels,
                     1 gouge,1 Iron Wedge and 2 hoes and Cooper's tools 3 .50
        Sam'l Wilson 2 small kegs   1 .25
        Sarah Davis 2 waggon wheels and 2 skins   1.50
        ditto   1 Tea pot,5 cups and Saucers and 3 Bowls .50
        ditto   2 pails, 1 Bar'l and Washing Tub   .25
        ditto   1 flax wheel and a small keg   .50
        ditto   1 chair   .12½
        ditto   1 frying pan   .25
        Abram Rodgers 1 Smooth Bore gun   7.12½
        Thomas Wilson 1 foot addze   1.50
        Arthur Pierce 1 Hone   1.25

	Dol.	Cts.
Edward Stepleton 1 pocket compass		.51
Sarah Davis 1 pair small Scales and Weights		.12½
Thomas Hotton 1 square and rounding knife		.12½
Sarah Davis 1 horse saddle and bridle	53	
ditto 1 negro woman named Dol	1	
Hames Davis 2 Geographys		.50

Returned to January Session 1806 by Sarah Davis, the Administratrix.
                    N. P. Hardeman, C. W. C.

Page
(128)
State of Tennessee)
Williamson County) In Obedience to an order of the worshipful Court of the County aforesaid bearing Date October Session
1805 the Subscriber has this day made a true and perfect Inventory of the Estate of Edmund Cook, Dec'd., in manner and form
as followith - Charles a negro man aged 21 years, Sam aged 18
years, Nancy a negro woman aged 24 years, Juner., a negro woman
aged 22 years, Bob a negro boy aged 4 years, Isham, a negro
Boy aged 2 years, Milley a negro girl aged 2 years, 3 feather
beds and furniture, 1 set of Bed curtains, 1 cradle and 1 corner cupboard, 2 sows and 11 pigs, 1 barrow 1 year old, 1390
lbs. pork, 5 cows with calf, 4 two year old Steers, 1 two year
old heifer, 2 one year old heifers, 1 Bay Mare 7 years old (with
foal), 1 bay filley 2 years old, 1 gray horse colt, one year
old, 1 four year old Steer, 1 Bond in the hands of H. Cook for
pt. of stud horse due 1st Jany. 1806 $225. One ditto in the
hands of ditto due 1st Jany 1807, $225. One Bond on H. Cook for
$76 due Jan'y. 1st 1806, for a young mare.
     The above Inventory made this thirteenth day of January
eighteen hundred and six. Given under my hand.
                         Signed
                    Mary Cook, Adminisx.

Page
(129)
Returned to January Session 1806.
                    N. P. Hardeman, C. W. C.
     In Obedience to an order of the Worshipful Court of William-
son County bearing date January Session 1806. I have proceeded
to sell the perishable property of belonging to the Estate of
Edmund Cook Dec'd. which is as followith -
     Mary Cook purchased 1 bay mare $120., 1 cow and calf $12,
1 heifer $5, 1 curtain and Bedstead and bed and furniture $50,
1 water canister, knife box and 1 iron pot $3.66 2/3 cents, 1
Scrubbing Brush 75 cents, 1 small bed and furniture $5. 1 Bull
$5., 1 Wheel and Cradle $1.50 - total $202.91 2/3 cents
     Henry Cook purchased 3 cows $26, 1 ditto $8, 2 calves $4,
4 steers $16.50, 1 heifer $5.,1 sow, 5 pigs and barrow $4, 1
steer $9, 1 sow and five pigs $3, 1 cupboard $3, 1 bed and fur-
niture $20, 1 young grey horse $60. Total $158.50
                    Signed Mary Boyd, Administratrix

Page
(130)
Returned to April Session 1809.
                    N. P. Hardeman, C. W. C
State of Tennessee)
Williamson County) In Obedience to an Order of said County Court
January Sessions, we have proceeded to settle with the Administra-
trixs of Edmund Cook deceased which is as follows to wit -
                                                       $ Cts.
Bond on Henry Cook due 15th day of March 1807   301   .00

                                                             Princpl
for ¼ of stud horse   355.59
 Bond on Henry Cook due lst day of Jany 1806
 for ¼ of a stud horse and a young mare   Int.   55.68½
Bond on Henry Cook for goods purchased at last
sale, due 25th of December next   P. 83.00
Goods bought at first sale by Mary Cook due lst   ) P/187.00
day of Jany 1807   ) Int.25.24½
Goods bought at last sale by A. Boyd due 25th
December next   15.71 2/3
    And find in the hands of the Administratrix the sums as
above stated. Given under our hands and seals this 8th day
of April 1809.
                        Signed G. Hulme
                            John Witherspoon.
            Returned to April Session 1809.

Page
(131)

        An Inventory of the Estate of Thomas Strickland, deceased,
taken 9th October 1804 by Tilpha Strickland, Admx. 1. 3 year
old horse, o one year colt, 1 Bridle and Saddle, 3 cows and
2 yearlings, 2 sows and pigs, 13 shoats, 1 Bed and furniture,
1 bedstead, 5 chairs, 1 pott, 1 Dutch oven, 1 pail, 1 piggin,
1 tub, 1 churn, 1 spinning wheel, 2 pair cards, one Bareshare
plow, 1 axe, 1 iron wedge, 2 baskets, Shoe Makers tools, 1
table, 1 Gum, 1 side leather, 1 raw cow hide, the crop of
corn and cotton, 7 cups and saucers, 1 tea pott, 2 pewter plates,
2 earthen plates, 1 decanter, 1 bottle, 1 pair pott hooks, 1
keeler, 1 bread tray, 1 gimblet, 1 bell, 1 old rifle and
shot bag.
                    Signed Tilpha Strickland
Returned to October Session 1804 - N. P. Hardeman, C. W. C.

An Account of the Sales of the Estate of Thomas Strickland,
deceased made by Tilpha Strickland Admr. of said deceased 1804
Tilpha Strickland 1 bed and furniture $23., ditto a parcel of
Tea Cups and Saucers .30 cents, ditto 5 chairs .75 cents, ditto
1 chair .25 cents, Joseph Slocumb 1 churn .66 2/3 cents, Tilpha
Strickland 1 Dutch oven $2.60, ditto 1 piggin .25 cents, ditto
1 lot of Coopers' Ware .76 cents, Riley Slocumb 1 axe and wedge
$3., Richard Orton 1 plow $4.75, Riley Slocumb 1 pr. of pincher's
hammers and awls $1.2½, Tilpha Strickland 1 woolen wheel and 2
pr. cards $2., Joseph Slocumb 1 horse bell .50 cents, Thomas
West one rifle gun $1.12½ cents, Ditto 1 sow $2.60, Joseph

Page
(132)

Slocumb six shoats $2.60, Tilpha Strickland 5 hogs $5.80, Abraham Whitesides one colt $44., Barnabas Beet one horse $62.50,
Isaac Crow 7 hoggs $15. Nathan Garner 1 saddle $6., Britain
Garner 2 Baskets .60 cents, John Blackman 1 cow $13., Enoch
Bateman 1 cow and yearling $12.25, John Patton 1 loom $7.,
Britain Garner 1 steer yearling $5., Tilpha Strickland 1 pot
hook and table $2.26, John Johnston 100 lb. of cotton $4,
3 hogs killed for the use of the family before the Sale, 1
side of leather made use of for the family and one cow dead.
                    Total amount $236.76 2 /3
    Errors excepted by me
                    Tilpha Strickland, this 4th Jany.1805
Returned to January Session 1805 - N. P. Hardeman, Clk.

An Inventory of the Perishable and other property of JOHN
HENDERSON deceased - 4 head of horse creatures, 1 rifle gun, shot
pouch , bullet moulds, 1 feather bed and its furniture, 1 pair
plow irons, 2 pair drawing chains, 2 pair of Hames and hangings,
1 pair Double trees, 2 clivises, 1 axe, 1 rasar, 22 head of
hogs, with about 10 acres Incian corn and his wearing clothes.
Eighty dollars on Robert Magness without either note or Book Account.   Signed John McCalpan, Admr.
     Returned to October Session 1804.
                                N. P. Hardeman, C. W. C.

(3) A memorandum of the estate of John Henderson, deceased, sold at
public vendue on the first day of November 1804.
John McCalpan Senr. a bed and furniture $30., George Mayfield 2
pr. of horse geers, stree and clivises $13.25, John McCalpan Senr.
a falling axe $3., Benjamin White a rifle gun and shot bag $41.,
John Gamble a crop of corn $50., John McCalpan a stock of hogs $30.
John McCalpan, Senr. a sorrel mare $50., Henry Rutherford a bay
horse $52. George Stewart a mare colt $26., William McCalpan a bay
mare $83, John McCalpan Senr. a lot of cloathing $5., John McCalpan, Jnr. a razor, George Steward a branding iron .55 cents, John
McCalpan cash $4.50.
                                    Total $396.67½
          Signed John McCalpan, Admr., Nov. 1st, 1804
     Returned to January Session 1805. N. P. Hardeman, C. W. C.

An Inventory of the Estate of MOSES McHUGH, deceased:
37 head of cattle, one waggon, Jackscrew and hind geers, fifteen
head of sheep, fourteen head of hogs, one rifle gun, shot bag,
and powder horn, one man's saddle, woman's saddle, one set of
plough irons, one set of double swingle trees, one pair of
stretchers, three clivises, three weeding hoes, two pair of
pot hooks, 1 cotton wheel, one linnen wheel, one pair of cotton cards, one pair of wool cards, one axe, one Iron Wedge,
seven pewter plates, three ditto dishes, five ditto basons, ten
ditto spoons, one pewter tankard, two earthen bowls, three piggins, two raw cow hides, 1 ditto, calf skin, some tanned Leather,
one smoothing iron, one hand saw, one chest, one loom, two pr.
of Weever's harness, three ditto slays, twenty spools, two
Bibles, two Testaments, two spelling books, three religious
books, one history, one shoe hammer, one pair of pinchers, one
razor, one hone, two iron pots, two Dutch ovens, four pair of
horse shoes, 1 grey gelding, two sorrel ditto, one Black ditto,
one black mare, one bay mare, one sorrel filley, one sorrel
mare and colt, 1 bay two year old colt, yearling ditto, two
feather beds and furniture, one note of hand on William Miller
of Kentucky for eighty pounds Virginia currency, due first day
of Septmr. next thirty of which is to be paid in property forty
four shillings like currency on Wm. Hall of the state aforesaid.
                     Signed Jane McHugh - her mark
Returned to April Session 1804.
                                N. P. Hardeman, C. W. C.

A Memorandum of the Sale of the Estate of Moses McHugh,dec'd.
Jane McHugh 2 feather beds and furniture $4, ditto 2 bedsteads $1,
ditto 1 cotton and 1 linnen wheel $2, ditto 1 chest .50, ditto
2 iron pots $1.50, ditto 1 iron kettle and 1 Dutch oven $1, ditto

3 pewter dishes $2, ditto 6 pewter basons, $2.50, ditto 7 pewter plates .50, ditto 7 pewter spoons .25, ditto 1 pewter tankard and 3 tins .50, ditto 2 earthen bowls .50, ditto 2 pair
of pot hooks .12½ cents, ditto 3 piggins .25, ditto 1 rifle
gun, shot bag, etc. $7.25, ditto 2 pair of Horse shoes .50 cents,
John Garrott 7 horse shoes .61 cents, Jane McHugh 1 hone and
razor .51 cents, ditto 9 books .50 cents, Jane M. Hugh 1 clivis .26 cents, ditto 1 pair of cotton and 1 pair of wool cards
.51, John Hinds 1 wheel spindle and Whirl .50, Jane M. Hugh 1
flax hackle $2.50, ditto 1 smoothing iron .66½ cents, ditto 1
Iron Wedge.34 1/3 cents, ditto 18 spools .25 cents, James M.
Neelly 1 Handsaw .60, Jane M. Hugh 2 weeding hoes $1.75, ditto
1 womans saddle .50 cents, ditto one man's saddle $10.50, ditto
4 tanned hides $1.75, Nancy M. Hugh 1 loom $2.25, Samuel Edmiston 1 Jack Screw $7.75, James M. Carmal 1 waggon $50., Samuel
White 1 pair of hind geers $3.12½, Jane McHugh 1 pair of ditto
$2.25, Samuel White 2 horse collers .50, Samuel McCutchan 1
Britchhand .27 cents, Jane McHugh 1 falling axe .50, ditto 1
pair of Streachers and Hangings $1.50, ditto 1 black horse $65.50,
John White 1 bay mare $40.50, Jane McHugh 1 black blaze-faced
mare $75.50, Nancy McHugh, 1 white horse $70., Samuel White 1
sorrel mare $50.25, Jane McHugh 1 sorrel horse $47., John White
some small swingle tree irons .75, Samuel White 1 sorrel colt
$16.62½, Jane McHugh 1 hoe .12½ cents, ditto 1 large plow $8.25,
James McHugh 1 sorrel filley $90, Ephraim Brown 1small bay filly
$26.50, Polly McHugh 1 Brown filley $52, Jane McHugh 1 red and
white Heifer $6., ditto 1 white face cow and calf $5, ditto one
broken-horn cow and calf $11.25, Jane McHugh 1 cow and calf $7.50,
Jacob Garrett 1 no-horned cow and calf $6., William Young 1
white face Steer $5., ditto 1 Black Steer with a white face
$9.40, ditto 1 Brindled short horned steer $4.51, ditto 1 pied
white back steer $4, ditto 1 white steer with a Black Head $5.1½,
John White 1 black stump tail ditto $2.55, Guilliam Clark, 1
Black and white steer $8, Polley McHugh 1 white Back heifer $6,
John Hartley 1 Black and white cow and calf $8.12½, Lancelot
Armstrong 1 Black and White steer $4.41, Jacob Garrot 1 cow
and yearling $6.50, Guilliam Clark 1 red and white heifer $9,
Jane McHugh 1 Black cow and yearling $6.30, James M. Neelly, 1
brindle cow $6, John Hartley 1 Stump tail Bull $3.25, John Hinds
1 brown cow $8, Jane McHugh 1 red heifer $6, James M. Neelly 1
red heifer with a white back $3.25, James Gault 1 dun coloured
steer $4.25, John White 1 red heifer $1.50, Robert Hulme 2 black
pided steers $6.25, Jane McHugh 3 sheep, $5.12½, Charles Brown
3 sheep $3.60, John White 3 sheep $3, Jane McHugh 13 head of
hogs $10, Charles Brown 3 sheep $5.

                    Signed Jane McHugh - her mark
        Returned to July Session 1804 - N. P. Hardeman, C. W. C.

    A memorandum of the sale of the balance of the estate of
Moses McHugh dec'd. 3rd November 1804 -
Nancy McHugh 1 white mare $81, Jane McHugh 3 head of small cat-
tle $3.25, Nancy McHugh 2 weaver's slays .25, Nath'l. Armstrong
1 shoemakers hammer .25.
                    Signed Jane McHugh, administratox
Returned to July Session 1807 - N. P. Hardeman, C. W. C.

    We the undersigned do hereby certify that agreeable to and

Order of the County Court of pleas and quarter sessions held
for Williamson County July Session 1807, to us directed, we
have settled with Jane McHugh, administratrix of Moses McHugh
deceased which is as follows to wit -
Jane McHugh Dr. to amount of first sale $881.18 2/3. Note on
William Miller of Kentucky for ₤ 85 due 20th October 1804 ½ due
in trade, the other ½ in cash on which a credit is entered by
the admx. for $178.33 1/3 $105. which she says she rec'd in
Trade, balance of principal property sold to be rec'd. for
the $105. sold for the amount of the second sale$81.75.
     Pd. contra cr. $1144.27.
     By travelling to Kentucky to collect the above Debt from
William Miller $20. By services rendered as Admistratrix $10.
By cash paid clerk for his services $4.10. By boarding and
clothing Jane McHugh infant daughter of Moses McHugh Dec'd.,
aged 7 years until the second Monday in October 1806 which is
3 years at $4. per year $12. Total $58.10
     Balance due for Adm. 1086.17, of which she is entitled to
her Dower as widow of the aforesaid Moses McHugh, deceased.
                    Signed G. Hulme and T. W. Stockett
     Returned to October Session 1807.
                         N. P. Hardeman, C. W. C.

Page
(138)   Inventory of the Goods and Chattels of WILLIAM ORTON, deceased
taken on the 8thday of October 1803 - One note on James Owen
payable 25th Decemr. 1803, 160 dollars, 1 note on Isaac Minor
payable 25th Decr. 1803 $60, 1 ditto on David Nolen payable
25th Decr. 1803 $25, 1 ditto on John Hill payable 25th Decr.
1803 $20, 1 ditto on William Wallis payable 10th Decr. 1803
$20, 1 ditto on Robert Chapman payable 25th decr. 1803 25 dol-
lars, 1 ditto on Ro. Chapman payable 25th June 1804 $20, 1
ditto on Sam'l Gentry, John Champ, endorsed by John Hill and
payable the 25th Decemr. 1803, $15. A verbal account against
Robt. Williams $13½, a verbal account against Wm. Wallis $5.
1 mare, 2 heifers, 2 steers, 1 steer at Pinkstons, 4 sows and
pigs and shoats, 7 wild hogs running about, John Hills, 1 sow
running at Reading Warmbells, a small crop of corn and cotton,
1 Stack of corn blades, 1 shovel, plow, double trees, some
clivises, 1 axe, 1 broad hoe, 1 cane hoe, 1 mans saddle, 1
womans ditto, 1 Dutch oven, 1 large pot, 1 pr. pot hooks,
2 sides of Leather in tan, 1 water pitcher, 7 plates, 4 Saucers and 3 cups, 1 decanter, 1 bottle, 1 tumbler, 1 pepper Box,
1 Salt celler, 5 table spoons, 4 knives and forks, 2 Brushes,
1 linnen wheel, 1 woolen wheel, 1 pair shears, 2 pails, 2 piggins, 2 baskets, 5 chairs, 2 barrels, 1 Bushel Grass Seed, 1
old Salt tub, an account of John Garner (Minor) 12 dollars,
1 yearling raw hide, 1 bell and coller, 1 file some salt.
                    signed Reading Wormbwell, Admr.
Returned to November Session 1803.
                         N. P. Hardeman, C. W. C.

Page
(139)   Inventory of the Estate of JOHN GARRETT, dec'd, which has not
been divided among the legatees -
Six head of horses, on yoke of oxen, one waggon, two log
chains, two pair of chain traces, three plows, one loom, thirty

head of hogs, twenty-three head of sheep, fifteen head of cattle, eight raw hides, one flax wheel, one counting reel, three
cotton wheels, three bedsteads, two tables, eleven chairs,
two pair of Saddle bags, one chest, one trunk, one handsaw,
one inch auger, one cross cut saw, one frew, one pair of iron
wedges, two pots, two kettles, one Dutch oven, one skillet,
one Tea Kettle, two pair of pot hooks, one flax hackle, two
washing tubs, two pails, one piggin, two slays and harness,
some tubs, and barrels, eight weeking hoes, two pewter dishes,
four plates, one butter pot, one tin pan, one pair of flat
irons, one churn, one spice mortar, one mans saddle, one womans saddle, some corn, the quantity unknown, one tea canister, three earthen dishes, thirteen plates, six tea cups,
twelve saucers, one large china Bowl, two ditto small one case
of knives and forks, one sugar dish, one tumbler, one cream
pot, two salt cerllers, one pepper box, two bottles, two
Decanters, six spoons, one coffee pot, one looking glass,
one large Bible, one four gallon keg and cock, six sides of
Tanned leather, four axes, seventeen pounds of iron, some
steel, one Bridle, one pair of Steelgards, about twenty pounds
tallow, number geese, four bells, two iron clivises, one grind
stone, one iron hammer, a quantity of hog lard, two scythes
and cradles, one grass scythe.

　　　　　　　　　　Signed Thomas Garrett, Jacob Garrett
Returned to　　　Session 1806.
　　　　　　　　　N. P. Hardeman, C. W. C.

Page
(140)
　　　Agreeable to an order of the Worshipful the County Court to
us directed we have proceeded to sell the estate of John Garrett deceased which is as follows to wit:
Thomas Speaks 2 weeding hoes $1, Janney Garrett 2 flat irons
$1.53, Barthalomew Stovall 2 iron wedges $2.2, Bartholomew
Stovall 1 axe $2.75, Thos. Speaks 1 hoe $1, Jenny Garrett tea
kettle .60, James Jackson, 1 axe, hoe, gimblet, chisel and ladel
.80, George Stramlar 1 Scythe and some old irons .56¼ cents,
Jacob Garrett swingle tree, padlock and cotter $1.25, John
D. Garrett 2 hoes $1.25, Jacob Garrett 1 flax hackle .40 cents,
James Hartgrave 1 grindstone $1.4, Thomas Speaks 1 cross-cut
saw $4, Jacob Garrett 1 handsaw, Jacob Garrett, 1 frow, .95,
Dempsey Nash 1 large kettle and candlestick .35, John D. Garrett
1 iron pot and hooks $3, Jacob Garrett 1 Iron pot $4, John D.
Garrett 1 washing tub .52, Jenny D. Garrett 1 Bucket .12½,
Barthew. Stovall 1 side undressed leather $2.12½, George
Hulme 1 side undressed leather $2. 1 cent, William Ivy 1
side undressed leather .50 cents, James Jackson do. do. do.
$1.80, Robert Johnston 1 do. do. do. .60 cents, John Crowder
do. do. do. $1.40, John Boyer 1 Iron Kettle and old iron $5.7
John Blair 1 cotton wheel $2., Henry Martin 1 bareshear plow
Page
(141)
$4, John D. Garrett 1 shovel plow .75 cents, Thomas Garrett
1 weeding hoe .12½, Izrael Mayfield 1 cow and calf $14.25,
Robert Johnston 1 cow and yearling $9, Dempsey Nash 1 young
white cow and calf $9.25, William Cowen 1 cow and calf $9.25,
William Cowen 1 cow and calf $13.30, William Cowen 1 cow and
calf $16, Sam'l. Meddleton 1 white heifer $12.26, Isaac
Wright 1 heifer $4.85, Isaac Wright 1 heifer $3.30, Dempsey
Nash 1 Bull $3, Jacob Garrett 1 Bull $1.12½, Jenny Garrett
1 yearling colt $19.50, John Harding 2 sows $5.25, John D.

****

Garrett 1 yearling $1.26, Henry Martin 1 shovel plow .61, John
D. Garrett 1 sow and pigs $4.30, Isaac Wright 1 sow and pigs
$3.3, William Hanell 4 hogs $10.25, John D. Garrett 4 hogs
$9, Dempsey Nash 4 hogs $7.25, Jacob Garrett 4 hogs $5, Jacob
Garrett 4 hogs $3.75, Patrick Deviling 2 wheels $1.26, Patrick
Develing 1 loom $7.25, John Alsup 1 skillet .37½, Patrick
Develing 2 pair harness and 1 slay $1.25, Izrael Mayfield 1
piece steel $1.60, James Hargrove 1 barrel .40, Wm. Honell 4
hogs $6.25, John Crowder 1 sow and pigs $3.13¼, David Wren 1
sow and pigs $3.25, John D. Garrett 1 sow and pigs $2.25,

Page
(142)

Daniel Cowen 1 yoke oxen $66.50, Daniel Cowen 1 log chain $8.
Henry Martin 5 sheep $12., Daniel Durham 5 sheep $12.25, Wil-
liam Ivy 5 sheep $9.20, Leven Edney 5 sheep $10.55, Thomas
Speaks 6 sheep $8.75, William Ivey 1 bell .50, George Stramler
1 scythe and old iron .37, John D. Garrett 1 ax $3.12½, John
Compton 1 horse colt $60.25, Samuel White 1 gray horse $48.50,
Dempsey Nash 1 sorrel filley $71.80, Jenny Garrett 1 grey mare
$30. Dan'l. A. Durham 1 waggon $11.12½, John D. Garrett 8
barrels corn $11.12½, John Blair 8 barrels corn $10.81¼,
John Jones 8 barrels corn $10.26, John Alsup 8 barrels corn
$10.26, John D. Garrett 8 barrels corn $10.20¼, Dempsey Nash
8 barrels corn $10.51, Hardy Murphy 1 raw hide $2, do. do.,
do. do. $1.50, do. do. do. do. .75 cents, do., do. do. do. $1.65,
do. do. do. do. $2.90, do. do. do. do. $4.5, do. do. do. do. .45
cents, Henry Martin 1 log chain $1.50, do. do. 1 pr Steelyards
$5., Thomas Garrett 1 spice mortar .50, John D. Garrett 1 pr.

Page
(143)

chains $2.31¼, James David 2 chair frames .50, John D. Gar-
rett 1 walnut table $2.62½, Dempsey Nash 1 Bedstead $2, David
Wren 1 Bedstead $1.75, John D. Garrett 1 trunk $3, Thomas
Garrett 1 looking glass $1, Jacob Garrett 1 large Bible $7.20,
John McCollum 1 bay horse $80, Jenny Garrett 1 bedstead .25,
Jacob Garrett 1 chest $1.25, Dempsey Nash 1 water pail .75,
Jenny Garrett 1 cake tallow $2.2, John Jones, 1 coke tallow
.38, Jacob Garrett hogs lard $1, Benja. Dunn 1 churn .82, Jen-
ny Garrett 1 cooler .12½, do. do. 1 Barrel .12½ cents, John
Hulme 1 barrel .19¾, Thomas Garrett 1 barrel .20, Henry Mar-
tin 11 geese $8.75, Robert Hulme 11 geese $8.13½, Joseph
Dawson 1 man's saddle $2.60, James David 2 chairs .75 cents,
John D. Garrett 2 chairs $1, James David 2 chairs .82½, John
D. Garrett 2 chairs $1.12½, Henry Martin 1 table $1.50, John
McCollum 4 pewter plates $1.50, John Jones 1 pewter dish $1,
Henry Martin 1 do. $2, John D. Garrett 1 tin pan and coffee
pot $1, do. do. ½ dozen knives and forks $3., Sam'l. Meddle-
ton ½ Doz white plates 1 salt celler and pepper box $1.6½,

Page
(144)

George Stramlar 1 white dish .56, do. do. do. .12½, do. 1 earthern dish and plate .30, Jenney Garrett 5 earthern plates
.60 cents, Joseph Dawson 4 cups and 5 Saucers .67, do. do.
2 cups and 5 saucers .17, Dan'l. Durham ½ ping Decanter and
tumbler $1, John Porter 2 bowls and cream pot .26, John Camp-
bell ½ pint decanter and tea pot .58, Dempsey Nash 1 China
Bowl $1.7¼, do. do. 2 bottles .50, George Stramlar 1 quart
bottle .30, John D. Garrett 1 bottle .50, Thomas Garrett, 1
counting reel .50, do. do. 1 wheel $1, James David 1 pair of
gears $3, Benja. Dunn 3 sheep $10.12½. Returned to July Session 1806. N. P. Hardeman, C. W. C.

Memorandum of the Sale of the Balance of the Estate of John
Garrett deceased - William Mattocks 4 barrels corn $5.50, Henry
Hunter 4 barrels corn $5.50, Henry Hunter 4 barrels corn $5.60,
William Mattocks 4 barrels corn $5.75, Henry Hunter 4 barrels
corn $5.65, John Jones 4 barrels corn $5.75, John Jones 12 bush-
els $3.50, Dan'l. Durham 3 hogs $4.12½, Isaac Wright 4 hogs $4,
Isaac Wright 6 pigs $2.25, James Hardgrove 1 ax and pr. saddle
bags, John D. Garrett 1 pr. saddle bags $2.75, Jacob Garrett

Page
(145)

1 bell .28, James Hardgrove 1 barrel .30, John D. Garret, 1
Butter pot $1.75, Jonathan Betts tobacco .61, James Hardgrove
tobacco .61 cents, Thomas Alsup old Gun Barrel .34, John D.
Garrett 4 hogs, Bridle and Auger $3.62½, Thomas Garret 1 bell
.50 cents.
                    Signed Jacob Garrett - Thomas Garrett
     Returned to January Session 1807.
                         N. P. Hardeman C.W.C.

A n Inventory of the Estate of JAMES GAY, deceased; one sorrel horse, four pai of overalls, one pack saddle, one pair
of shoes half worn, one pair yarn socks, 2 waistcoats, one
pair saddle bags, five worn shirts, one meal bag, one bell
one great coat and hat, shoe leather, 1 bed tick, razor and
case.
                    Signed J. Goyne, Admr. - 15th July 1806
     Returned to July Session 1806. N. P. Hardeman, C. W. C.
     Supplementary Inventory of the Estate of James Gay, de-
ceased - 1 Black Horse old and of little value.
                    Signed John Goyne, Admr.
Returned to October Session 1806. N. P. Hardeman, C. W. C.

Page
(146)

     An account of the Sales of the Estate of James Gay, deceased,
made 9th of August 1806 - John Baldridge one sorrel horse, one
bell $20.75 John Goyne 1 black saddle .12½, ditto 1 pair of
old saddle bags .25, John Baldridge 1 razor and case .25, ditto
1 pr. of shoes .25, John Goyne 1 lot of leather .50, ditto 1
bag, ditto 1 big coat .37½, Jesse Tarkington 1 lot of cloaths
.50, John Baldridge 1 pair of locks .75, John Goyne 1 lot of
cloaths $4.62½, ditto 1 bed tick $1.
                    Signed John Goyne
Returned to October Session 1806. N.P. Hardeman, C.W.C.
     A Supplemental amount of sales of the Estate of James Gay,
deceased, made 8th October 1806. One black Horse sold to Elijah
Richardson $20.
     Signed John Goyne, Admr. Returned to January Session 1807.
                         N. P. Hardeman, C. W. C.

Page
(147)

     Agreeable to an order made by the County Court of Pleas and
quarter-sessions held for the County of Williamson in the State
of Tennessee at the Courthouse in the town of Franklin on the
second Monday in April, we have proceeded to settle with John
Goyne, Administrator of James Gay, deceased, which is as follows to wit - To mending and washing $2.50, to expences when
said Gay was sick $10, to burial expenses $10, to collecting
property together $5., to attending Court $5., to Jesse Wharton

for services $5, to cash pd. Doctor Sappington $1.87½, to keeping horse $6, to cash lent $2, to cash paid N. P. Hardeman,
Clk. $3.10 - total $59.22½. Amount of the sale of said Estate
$49.87½. Balance due Administrator $9.35. Given under our
hands this 14th April 1808.
    Signed G. Hulme, Sion Hunt. Returned to July Session 1808.
            N. P. Hardeman, C. W. C.

Page
(148)   WILLIAM McKNIGHT'S Nuncupative Will - State of Tennessee, Williamson County - Memorandum that on the third day of Novemr. in the
year of our Lord, one Thousand eight Hundred and five, in the
County and State aforesaid, by an accident of horses running
way with a waggon, William McKnight received a bodily bruise,
which caused his death, he being in sound mind and memory did
make and declare his last will and Testament, Nuncupative, in
these or the like words following, that is to say, I wish there
to be no Sale of my property but that my family keep it together and improve it to the best advantage, and when the family
grow up to divide it equally among them. These or the like
words to that amount the said William McKnight decalred in the
presence of the Subscribers, with intention that the same should
be his last Will and Testament, wherefore he desired them or
some of them to bear witness. Given under our hands and Seals
this 15th day of April 1806.
    Signed David Shannon -(Seal) John McKnight -(Seal) and
Samuel McKnight (Seal)
    Which foregoing receited Nuncupative Will was duly proven in
Open Court April Session 1806 by the oaths of David Shannon,
John McKnight and Samuel McKnight, to be the Nuncupative Will
of William McKnight deceased, and the same was ordered to be
recorded.
           N. P. Hardeman, C. W. C.

Page
(149)   An Inventory of the Estate of William McKnight deceased - one
negro woman and two children, a note on Mathew M. Gough for
twenty-seven dollars, due the first day of October 1806. Balance
of a note on Isaac Williams for six dollars and fifty cents,
due the first of March 1806, five head of horses, three grown
ones and two colts, 18 head of cattle, six grown ones, and
eight young ones, ten head of sheep, about sixty head of hogs,
consisting of sows, shoats and pigs, two plows and three hoes,
four axes, and one Log Chain, one pair of Double Trees and
Clivises, four plains and six chisels, hand saw and drawing
knife, four gimblets and four augers, one rasp, one file, pair
compasses, two gauges, one wheel wright screw, one hammer, three
wheels, two cotton and one flax, four bedsteads, three beds
and furniture, a cupboard, chest and table, seven chairs, one
loom, one kettle, one pot, two ovens, one looking glass, one
large Bowl, three small ones, six cups and saucers, four Glass
Tumblers, a pint decanter and a pint flask, six Delf plates,
one pewter dish, two Basons, one mug and earthen crock, two
smoothing irons, one gun, one pair of pinchers, six awls and
tacks, three saddles, two mens saddles, one womans saddle, all
about halfworn, one barrel or tub, three little pails, one large
one, one churn, and keeler, two pair of cotton cards, one Iron
Wedge, a note on John Perryman for $4.85 cents Judgment against
Heatwell Miles for $14.45½, a bond upon Julius Sanders and

William Logan for two hundred and twenty-eight acres of land
considered a doubtful debt.
    Signed David Shannon, John McKnight, Admrs.
    Returned to July Session 1806 - N. P. Hardeman, C. W. C.

Page
(150)

    An Inventory of the property of JAMES PATTON, deceased.
13 negroes, 14 horses, 46 head of cattle, 240 head of hogs,
20 head of sheep, 1200 bushels of corn, 75 bushels of rye, 16
Bushels of wheat, 8000 wt. of seed cotton, 1 waggon and geers,
3 plows and 5 clivises, 9 hoes, 6 axes, 1 cross-cut saw, 1
Hand Saw, 1 foot addze, 3 augers, 3 chissels, 1 lock chain,
1 Drawing Knife, 1 Iron Wedge, 1 frow, 1 gun, 2 grubbing hoes,
8 Bells, 5 stocks of fodder, 1 loom, 8 slays and 2 sets of
Harness, to cash and notes $182, 6 beds and furniture, 1 look-
ing glass, 2 flat irons, 1 tea canister, 1 set of cups and
saucers, 1 tea pot, 26 plates, 9 dishes, 5 Basons, 2 coffee
pots, ½ doz. knives and forks, 9 spoons, 11 tins, 1 pitcher
and tumbler, 1 decanter, 2 candlesticks, 2 slates, 1 kettle,
2 pots, 2 ovens, 4 pails, 1 tub, 3 keelers, 1 churn, 2 sifters,
14 chairs, 1 table, 8 barrels, 3 bushels of salt, 4 saddles,
4 reap hooks, 19 books, 2 cotton wheels, 3 pair of cards, 1
lock, 1 set of spools, 3 bee gums, 1 pot rack, 2 pair of pot
hooks, 2 keys, 15 geese. The above is a true Inventory of the
property of James Patton, Dec'd.
    Signed Margaret Patton, Admx., James Patton, Admr.
    Returned to January Session 1807. N. P. Hardeman, C.W.C.
    An account of the sales of the Estate of James Patton, Dec'd.
Margaret Patton 1 mare $5.75, Charity Upshaw 1 mare and colt
$200., Margaret Patton 1 mare and colt $120, James Patton 1
mare $75, Robert Patton 1 mare, horse and colt $200, John
Dawson 1 horse $65, Margaret Patton 1 mare $80, James Patton 1

Page
(151)

horse $100, Margaret Patton 1 colt $35, ditto 1 horse $55, do.,
1 colt $13, Charity Upshaw 1 negro girl $250, James Patton 1
negro boy $350, John Dawson 1 negro girl $300, Robert Patton
1 negro girl $250, Margaret Patton 1 negro boy $300, ditto 1
negro boy $150, ditto 1 negro boy $150, ditto one negro boy
$100, ditto 1 negro man $400, ditto one negro man $400, ditto
1 negro girl $100, ditto 2 negro women $700, ditto 35 head of
cattle $248., ditto 200 head of hogs, $200, ditto 27 head of
sheep $47, ditto 15 geese $4, ditto 1200 bushels of corn $98,
ditto 75 bushels of rye $15, ditto 16 bushels of wheat $6,
ditto 5 stacks of fodder $3, ditto 1 waggon and geers $18,
ditto 3 plows $3.50, ditto 9 hoes and 6 axes $6, ditto 1 cross-
cut saw, handsaw, foot addze, 2 augers and 3 chissels $6.25,
ditto 1 lockchain and drawing knife $1, ditto 1 iron wedge and
frow .25, James Patton 1 rifle gun $6, Margaret Patton 4 beds
$35, Charity Upshaw 2 beds $4, Margaret Patton 1 looking glass
$1, ditto 1 set of cups and saucers and tea pot $1.50, ditto
26 plates and 9 dishes $12, ditto 5 basons and 2 coffee pots
$4, ditto ½ dozen knives and forks and 9 spoons $1.25, ditto

Page
(152)

11 tin cups, 1 pitcher and glass $1550, Margaret Patton 1 de-
canter and 2 candlesticks $1, ditto 2 slates, 2 Sifters, 14
Chairs and table $2.50, ditto 1 kettle, 2 pots, and 2 ovens
$4, ditto 1 loom, 8 slays, 2 sets harness $10, ditto 4 pails,
1 tub, 3 keelers and 1 churn $1.25, ditto 8 barrels, 7 saddles,
and 19 books $6., ditto 3 bushels, salt, 4 reap hooks, 2
grubbing hoes $1.50, ditto 2 cotton wheels and 3 pair of cards
$3., ditto 8 bells, 1 padlock and sheep shears $1.50, ditto

****

1 set of spools, 3 bee gums, and 5 clivises $3.75, ditto 1
pot rack, 2 pair of pot hooks and 2 cags $1, ditto 8000 lbs.
seed cotton $260

The above contains a true account of the chattel estate
of James Patton deceased, as sold by the Administrator and
Administratrix on the 16th day of March 1807 at 12 months cre-
dit, this the 14th day of April 1807.
Signed James Patton Admr. Margaret Patton Admx.
Returned to April Session 1807.
N. P. Hardeman, C. W. C.

Page
(153)
An account of the Sales of the Estate of John Ingram, deceased:
Susanna Ingram 1 negro man Tibe $351, Frances Ingram 1 negro
man and wife $450. Susanna Ingram 1 woman and child $250,
Thomas Ingram 1 negro boy $405,, John M. Christian 1 negro girl
$340, Sam'l. Ingram 1 negro boy $270, Thomas Ingram for Betsy
1 negro boy $150, Susanna Ingram Junr. 1 negro girl $161. Susanna Ingram 1 Brown horse $31, Sam'l Ingram 1 gray mare $31,
Thomas Ingram 1 sorrel horse $63, Susanna Ingram 1 bay horse
$31, Nick Seales 1 grey colt $10, Susanna Ingram 1 Cow and
calf $8, John M. Cuiston 1 cow and calf $8.50, Susanna Ingram
1 cow and calf $8, Wilson Davis, 1 cow and calf $7, Susanna
Ingram 1 cow and calf $7, John M. Cuiston 1 yearling $2.1,
ditto ditto $3.26, Samuel Perkins 1 yearling $2, Elijah Downing 1 cow and calf $8.75, Susanna Ingram 12 head hogs $20,
Thomas Ingram 1 watch $19, Susanna Ingram 2 cotton wheels $2.1
Frances Ingram 1 bed and furniture $26.26, Samuel Ingram 1 bed
and furniture $20.25, John M. Cuiston 1 bed $20, Thomas Ingram
1 bed $21.50, Susanna Ingram Junr. 1 bed $18, Thomas Ingram 1
bed $14, James Neal sundries $4.25, Susanna Ingram sundries
irons $2.50, Minos Cannon frow and hammer $2., Alexander Rout-
Page
(154)
stone 1 axe $1, Benjamin Arthur $2.50, Susanna Ingram 1 bare-
shear plow $5., John M. Cuiston kettle and skillet $2.1, Susanna Ingram Senr. 1 falling axe $1.25, Susanna Ingram sundry
pewter $5.25, Susanna Ingram 1 looking glass $1.26, James Neal
1 keg $1.50, Johnson Wood 1 slate .53, Susanna Ingram 1 jug
$1.51, Susanna Ingram sundry pot metal, etc. $3., Minos Cannon
1 pr. G. Shares .38, Susanna Ingram 4 chairs $1.1. Total $2643.
Returned to July Session 1807. N. P. Hardeman, C. W. C.

We William Wilson and Nicholas Scales being appointed Com-
missioners at October Session 1807 to settle with Thomas Ingram, Administrator on the estate of John Ingram, deceased,
have done the same in the following manner - $ Ct
We find that the Admr. is charged with amt. of sales-2904   56
We also find him charged with a note given by Wittshire
G. Poal to Susanna Ingram for as a Doubtful Debt, for
which has been rec'd. in full for said note   51 6¼
Total Amt.   2955 .61.6
Admr. produced satisfactory vouchers for money paid
to amount   178. 6
$ 2777.61.6

We believe the Admr. is entitled to an allowance for the
Clerks fees and when the amt. can be ascertained, we are wil-
ling to allow it in this Settlement.
Signed Nicholas Scales, W. Wilson, Comrs.
Returned to January Session 1808. N. P. Hardeman, C.W.C.

'age
155)

The following is a just and true Inventory of the Chattel Estate of WILLIAM BRIDGES as came to my hands this 15th of
October 1806.
    1 sorrel mare and colt, 1 bay ditto, ditto 1 pole axe, 1
Bell, 1 cow and calf, 1 ditto. ditto 1 yearling, 44 head of
hogs, 2 head of sheep, 1 bed and bed cloaths, ½ dozen pewter
plates, 1 pewter dish, 1 Dutch oven, ½ dozen knives and forks,
½ dozen ditto table spoons, ½ dozen tin cups, 1 Bearshare
plow, 1 shovel plough, 1 clivis, 150 Bushels of corn. Supposed
small parcel of unbroke flax. Inventory taken by me this 15th
day of October 1806. Signed Terry Bridges, Admr. of Wilson
Bridges, deceased. Returned to October Session 1806.
                        N. P. Hardeman, C. W. C.

Memorandum of the Sale of the Estate of Wm. Bridges, deceased
Nancy Bridges 1 feather bed, furniture and bedstead $2,
ditto one pewter dish and tin pan .50, ditto 1 Dutch oven and
2 water pails $4.50, Charles Campbell 1 Bell and coller.$0
Nancy Bridges 1 flax wheel and cotton cards $4, Patrick Hulme
5 pewter plates and 2 spoons $2, John Campbell 5 tin cups .53
Robert Prewitt 1 lamp .13½, ditto 4 knives and 2 forks .31,
John McCollum 1 Basket .26, Sam'l Edmiston 2 clivises $1.30,
Robert Prewitt 1 shovel plow $2.3, John Prewett 1 poll axe $2
Charles Campbell 1 Barshare plow %5.50, Thomas Hulme 1 saddle $2.6¼, John Prewitt 1 Bridle $1.51, Terry Bridges 3 barrows $15.75, John McCollum 2 sows and 15 shoats $17, John
Page   McCollum 2 sows and 15 shoats $17.13½, Nancy Bridges 4 bar-
(156)   rels corn $2, Ephraim Brown 5 barrels corn $5.65, John Prewitt 5 barrels corn, ditto 5 barrels corn $6, Wm. Young 4
barrels ¾ bushels of corn $4.98, James Brown 1 bay colt $20.
Nancy Bridges 1 cow and calf $4, ditto 1 heifer yearling $1,
Patrick Campbell 1 bay mare $50, James McHugh 1 blazing star
colt $31.53, Thomas Hulme 1 sorrel mare $107., Nancy Bridges
1 ewe $1, Terry Bridges a parcel of Pumpkins $1.25, James
Miller 1 cow and yearling $8.62½, Patrick Deviling some un-
broke flax .50, John Pruitt 1 Lease of Land $19, C. Funk-
houser 1 note of $7, Terry Bridges 1 cow $9.
                 Total - $281.83½
Signed Terry Bridges, Admr. Returned to January Session 1807.
                        N. P. Hardeman, C. W. C.

The Inventory of the Estate of CATHERINE MOORE, deceased
5 negroes, 4 horses, 54 hogs, 14 head of cattle, 1 flax hackle, 1 coffee mill, 25 warping spools, 2 slates, 3 mens saddles, 1 side saddle, 2 flat irons, 1 trunk, 1 chest, 1 reel,
1 flax wheel, 1 cotton wheel, 2 plows, 2 axes, 1 mattock, 3
pots, 1 Dutch oven, 1 kettle, 2 pair of hooks, 1 pair of
tongs, and shovel, 1 double tree, 1 frying pan, 3 hoes, 2
pair of chains and hames, a crop of corn, 2 pair of cards,
2 collers, 2 blind bridles, 1 pot rack, 4 chairs, 3 bags, 3
slays, 1 sifter, 2 tubs, 1 churn, 3 pails, 1 tea kettle, 1
coffee pot, 4 pewter dishes, 6 pewter plates, 6 earthen plates,
6 tea cups and saucers, 3 pewter basons, 1 bottle, 1 jug,
Page   1 tea canister, 15 spoons, 2 crocks, 1 pitcher, 6 sheets, 2
(157)   coverletts, 1 quilt, 1 rug, 3 pair of blankets 3 beds 2
pair of bedsteads.

Signed
David Robinson, John Moore
Returned to October Session 1806.   N. P. Hardeman, C. W. C.

A list of the property of Catherine Moore, deceased. Sold November 27th 1806 by giving twelve months credit:

John Moore 1 plow and irons $6, Jesse Sparkman 1 plow $3.12½, John Moore hames and chains $6.75, Jesse Sparkman 1 axe $2.87½, Jediah Peck Bridle chains and hames $5.25, John Moore ditto $2.25, David Dobbins 1 mattock $2.50, John Moore 2 weeding hoes $1.90, Moses Sprinkler 1 weeding hoe $1, James Huey 1 oven $2.50, Thomas Latta one pot $3.80, Betsy Moore one oven $1, John Moore 1 beig pot $7.62½ Jesse White 1 little pot $2, Thomas Latta 1 frying pan $2.20, Jesse Sparkman 1 tub $1.1, Betsy Moore 1 earthen crock .40 cents, Betsy Moore 1 coffee pot $1, Betsey Moore ½ dozen earthen plates .66, Betsy Moore set of cups and saucers $1.3, Betsy Moore 1 tea cannister .25, Henry Moore 1 tumbler and bowl .30, Betsy Moore ½ dozen pewter plates $3., Jesse White 1 pewter dish $1.30, Charles Robinson one pewter dish

$1550, John Moore one pewter dish $2.75, William Sparkman 1 pewter bason $2, Charles Robinson 1 big spoon .60, John Neelly 3 spoons .25, John Moore ½ dozen spoons .80, ditto ditto .80, David Dobbins 1 pewter bason and salt seller $1.12½, Thomas Latta 1 pitcher .75, Betsy Moore 1 strainer .51, John Armstrong 1 tea kettle $3.25, Jesse Sparkman 1 water pail .88, John Moore 1 water pail .50, William Neelly 1 small pail .25, Frederick Mobary 1 churn $1.75, John Moore 1 pair smoothing irons $2, Betsy Moore 1 pr. cotton cards .50, Caleb Manley 1 flax hackle $3.80, Robert Wilkins 2 pair shears .75, Claud McCollum 1 pair cards .25, Robert Wilkins 1 coffee mill $2.25, William Sparkman 4 knives and forks .50, Betsy Moore 1 trunk $4, Robert Wilkins 1 cut reel $1.25, John Moore 1 little wheel $4, Robert Wilkins 25 spools $2.10, Betsy Moore 1 slay .80, John Moore 1 slay and harness $1.75, ditto 1 slay $1.40, Jacob McCollum 1 beig chest $3.37½, John Moore 1 bed and furniture $42.25, Gray Sims ditto ditto $40.75, Elisha Hunter Senr. 1 bed and furniture $40, Samuel Andrews 1 mans Saddle and Bridle $15.25, Jesse White 1 saddle $11.75, Moses Sprinkle 1 saddle $5.12½, Alexander Moore

1 slate .40, Sion Record 1 negro woman named Diana $361, John Robinson 1 negro girl $304, William Simpson 1 negro boy $281., John Moore 1 negro girl $254, Isaac McCollum 8 barrels of corn $12.56, Alexander Moore 1 negro boy $200, Isaac McCollum 8 barrels of corn $12.50, Jesse White 8 barrels of corn $12.25, John Farrar 8 barrels of corn $12.25, Thomas Taylor 4 head of hogs $27.25, Elijah Hunter 4 head of hogs $20.10, ditto ditto $17.5, Thrasher McCollum 1 boar hog $2.65, Claud McCollum 1 sow $3, Carter Bethell 6 head of hogs $15.12½, Swanson Johnston 2 sows and pigs $12.76, Claud McCollum 1 sow $5.7, Thrasher McCollum 1 sow and pig $3.31, Isaac McCollum 2 hogs $6.26, ditto 3 hogs $4.30, John Moore 7 head of hogs $7, Carter Bethell 1 cow and calf $15, George Glascock 1 cow and calf $14.12½, John Moore 1 cow and calf $13.50, ditto one cow $13.50, Ezekiel Harbilson 1 bull $7.12½, Isaac McCollum 1 steer $6.50, Thrasher McCollum 1 steer $4.61, Claud McCollum 1 heifer $6.25, John Moore 1 heifer $10.15, Luke Patterson 4 yearlings $16.50, Joab Patterson 1 bay mare $50., Robert Page 1 pot rack $3.62½,

Betsy Moore 1 tub .50, David Robinson 1 vessel .50, Charles Robinson 1 crock $1.83, Gilbert Patterson 1 jug $2.87, Thomas

Latta earthen pot .12½, John Moore 1 pr. tongs and shovel $3.75,
ditto 2 chairs $1, Robert Wilkins 2 chairs .41, Moses Sprinkle
1 curry comb .33, Thomas Latta shoe brush .35, ditto double
tree irons .88, John Moore 1 candle stick and Snuffers .29,
Gilbert Patterson 1 cag .19, Alexander Moore 1 bell $1.52, Wil-
liam Lea 1 bell $1.75, Robert Wilkins 1 bell $1.51, John Armstrong 1 meal bag $2.27, William Harrilson 1 meal bag $2.27,
John Armstrong 1 meal bag .76, Samuel Andrews 1 sifter .15, David Robinson 1 sugar cup .27, Alexander Moore 1 bay mare $100.,
John Moore 1 colt $15.25, Robert Wilking 1 sorrel mare $50.
                    Signed David Robinson) Administrators
                            John Moore   )
Returned to January Session 1807. N. P. Hardeman, C. W. C.

age
161)

An Inventory of the Estate of WILLIAM RUTLEDGE, deceased, taken
this 5th Day of January 1807 by Alexander Rutledge, Administrator,
Agreeable to an Order of the County Court of Williamson (viz.)
  1 black mare, 1 cow and calf, 1 yearling, 15 head of hogs, 1
rifle gun, 1 shot pouch, 1 mans saddle and blanket, 1 pot, 2
spinning wheels (cotton), 1 washing tub, 2 Water pails, 1 loom,
1 cow hide and half of steer hide, ½ dozen chairs and ½ dozen
tin cups, ½ in. whip saw, 1 hoe, 1 horse coller, 1 axe, 1 mattock, 1 clivis, a set of double tree irons, 1 churn, 1 bell, 1
pr. double triggers, a list of debts due as appear from a memorandum found amongst this a/c's - Jesse Foster 25 cents, John
Folks 50 cents, Alex Rutledge 37½ cents, Jesse Foster 25 cents,
Robt. Ore 25 cents, John Folks 25 cents, Edward Elam 12½ cents,
John Hail 12½ cents, Wm. Alexander 12½ cents, Presley Hampton
12½ cents, Humphrey Baker 12½ cents, Robt. Ore 45½ cents, old
Mr. Fielder $2.50 cents, money rec'd. of Edmison $1.50, William
Irvine $5.
                    Signed Alex'r. Rutledge, Admr.
            Returned to January Session 1807. N. P. Hardeman, C. W. C.

An account of the Sales of the Estate of WILLIAM RUTLEDGE, deceased, sold the 26th day of January 1807 at 6 months credit:
Alexander Rutledge 1 cotton wheel $1.25, Margaret Rutledge 1
cotton wheel $1.76, Robert Winsett 1 falling axe $1.6¼, Robert
Pailey 1 Bell $1, James Patterson 1 mattock $2, Alexander Rutledge 1 clivis .54, ditto one horse coller .14, Margaret Rutledge 1 churn .56, ditto 1 piggin ½ doz. tin cups .81, ditto one
small pail .51, Margaret Rutledge 1 washing tub .31, William

age
162)

Rutledge Jun+r. 1 rifle gun and shot pouch $30, James Gault
1 raw hide $2.40, Johnson Wood half steer hide $1.78, Alexander
Rutledge ½ dozen chairs $3.73, Thomas Sutherland ½ price of a
whip-saw $6.6¼, Margaret Rutledge 1 cow and calf .12½, John
Barnhart 1 mare $33, Margaret Rutledge 1 pot $3, Alexander
Routston 1 yearling $3.50, Wilson Davis 1 mans saddle $1.51,
James Wilburn 1 loom $6.25, James Patterson 1 hoe .25, Robert
Paisley 1 choice of 4 hogs out of 12 $9.75, Thompson Wood 2
choices of 4 hogs $7.12½, Elijah Rutledge 3 hogs missing $2.,
Alexander Rutledge 1 blanket $1.50, ditto 1 set swingle tree
irons .12.
                    Signed Alexander Rutledge Admr.
            Returned to April Session 1807. N. P. Hardeman, C. W. C.

An Inventory of the Property of John P. Perkins, deceased -
2 negroes, Abraham and Pammey in possession of William M. Key,
hired until 25th of December next, one negro woman named Annekey
hired to Philip Maury until 25th day of December next, one negro woman named Milkey hired to Jonathan Phillips, one negro
boy named William about eight years old and one ditto child
5 or 6 months old in possession of the said Phillips, one negro boy about sixteen years old named Peter, 2 black horses
about 6 years old, 1 ball ditto 16 years old, 1 ditto called
Sabbeen 10 or 12 years old, 1 brown mare and colt, the mare
14 or 15 years old, 1 black colt 3 years old, 1 bay colt 2
years old, 1 brown ditto 1 year old, 1 red cow and calf, 2
pided steers about 3 years old, 1 brown ditto 1 year old, 1 red
cow and calf, 2 pided steers about 3 years old, 20 head of
hogs, 5 old sheep and 4 lambs, 3 bedsteads and furniture, 1
folding table, 1 dressing ditto, 2 card ditto, 4 large trunks,
4 small ditto, 6 chairs, 1 small ditto, 1 cotton wheel, one
flax ditto, 1 pr. cotton cards, 1 broch jack, 1 check reel,
3 smoothing irons, 3 pewter dishes, 1 earthen ditto,(cracked)
6 ditto plates, 2 ditto basons, 6 ditto spoons, $\frac{1}{2}$ dozen knives
and forks, 1 pewter soak spoon, 1 earthen bowl, 1 china ditto,
1 mug cracked, 2 glass tumblers, 3 do. stock glass, 2 tea cups,
7 saucers, 6 silver tea spoons, 2 combs course and fine, 1
quart decanter, 1 vinegar cruet, pepper box and castor, 2 qt.
bottles, 2 pint ditto, 1 sugar dish, 1 small butter pot, pr. old
hand irons, 1 odd ditto, shovel and tongs, 2 pair pot hooks, 2
iron pot racks, 2 iron kettles, 1 small pot, 1 Dutch oven, 1 skillet, 1 frying pan, 1 iron dish, 1 large pot, with a leg out,
1 tea kettle, 2 copper coffee pots, 1 tin ditto, 1 tin cup, 1
tea pot, 2 washing tubbs, 2 pails, 2 piggins, 3 keelers, 1 churn,
1 flat tub, 2 small ditto, 4 bread trays, 3 old barrels, a half
bushel, 1 hand Saw, 1 Inch chissel, 1 Inch Auger, 1 pr. nippers, 1 shoe hammer, 6 awls, 1 axe, 1 Barshare plough, 1 small
ditto, 1 wing for ditto, 2 old weeding hoes, 2 cane ditto, 3 pr.
drawing chains, 2 pair hames, 1 riding carriage and geers out
of repair, an old stage waggon out of repair, some old iron, 1
large waiter, 3 small ditto, 14 bake pans, 1 cow, 2 heifers,
2 year old, 2 yearlings, 1 sheep, 1 old shot gun, 1 sword, 1
pr. holsters, some plank for flooring and walnut ditto, 2 looking glasses, both broke, an obligation on Nathaniel Harris of
Petersburg, Virginia, payable the first day of January 1807
for the sum of three hundred dollars, a doubtful debt - 1 note
on Philip Maury (payable) doubtful debt, for the sum of forty
dollars, 1 note on William Mackay for one Hundred and Thirty
Dollars, payable in cotton, payable the 25th of December 1807.
One note on Peter Perkins and Leah Perkins pd, the first day of
November 1802. An obligation on William and Michael Robertson
for four hundred and forty acres of land lying in Davidson
County on the East side of Harpeth one mile above the narrows.
This list contains all the property that has yet come into my
possession this 11th day of May 1807.
                    Signed Dan'l. Perkins.
        Returned to July Session 1807.   N. P. Hardeman, C. W. C.

Page
(164)

An Inventory of the Estate of WELCOME HODGES, deceased - 160
acres of land, 5 head of horse creatures, 8 head of cattle, 17

head of hogs, 1 dish, 3 beds, Bedsteads and furniture, 1 loom,
1 riding chair, and harness, 2 trunks, 2 pots, 1 oven, 1
skillet, 2 pair of hooks, 1 oven lid, 1 pr. of Dog Irons, 1
potrack, shovel and tongs, 2 flat irons, 1 frying pan, 3
axes, 2 hoes, 1 plow, 2 waggon wheels and axle tree, 1 coffee
mill, 1 shot gun and pouch, 9 pewter plates, 2 dishes, 3 basons, 4 spoons, 1 table, 1 big wheel and powdering tub, 7
chairs, 1 womans saddle, 1 mans saddle, 2 bridles, 1 pr. steelyards, 1 umbrella, a little earthen ware, 1 handsaw, 1 augers,
some tin ware, some wooden vessels, 1 sifter, 1 pr. Drawing
chairs and coller.
                    Signed Edmond Hodges, Admr.
Returned to July Session 1807.
                         N. P. Hardeman, C. W. C.

Page   An account of the Sales of the Estate of Welcome Hodges,
(165)   dec'd. Sold the 13th Day of August 1807.
         Edmond Hodges 1 roan horse colt $19, Reuben George 1 bay
mare and colt $45, William Bowers 1 bay horse $72.50, Edmond
Hodges 1 black horse $42.50, Alexander Rolston 1 riding chair
and harness $18.50, Edmond Hodges 1 cow and calf and 1 old
cow $18, ditto 1 white heifer $8, ditto 1 do. cow and calf $15,
James Billingsly 1 brown motly cow $10.12½, William Towler 1
red cow and calf $11, Nathaniel Kimbro 7 head of hogs $14.51,
Robert McClellen 1 shot gun, pouch,etc. $12.32½, James Bil-
lingsly 1 loom and old clivis $7.21, Edmond Hodges 1 table $2.1,
John Depriest 1 desk $15.75 and one umbrella $1.25, Barnett Elliott 1 bed, bedstead and cord $20.1, Moses Friel 1 pewter ba-
son $3.25, ditto 1 do. dish and 3 plates $2., Edmond Hodges 1
small smoothing iron .75, ditto 1 large ditto $1.6, ditto a
quantity of earthen ware $2.1, ditto 1 pair of steelgards $2.26,
William Beavers 1 trunk $4.25, Edmond Hodges 1 pair of Barshare
irons $3.58, John Depriest 1 frying pan $2.26, Edmond Hodges a
quantity of pot metal $5.25, ditto 2 beds and furniture, 2 bed-
steads, etc $20, Reuben George 1 old Handsaw $1.25, Edmond Hodges
1 coffee mill $1.6, James Downing 3 chairs and 2 frames $2.50,
Sterling Brown 1 falling axe $2.28½, Benjamin Arthurs 1 mans
Page   saddle $6, Sterling Brown 1 Grind-stone $1, Robert Orr 2 four-
(166)   wheels of a waggon $4.50, Edmond Hodges 1 pr. chains and 1
leather coller $3.2, ditto 2 bells .15. Total amt. $402.97½
                    Signed Edmund Hodges
                         x his mark
Returned to April Session 1808. N. P. Hardeman, C. W. C.

     An Inventory of the Estate came into our hands of Samuel
Clark, deceased, late of Williamson County.
     Cash - 1 negro man named Watt, 35 years old, 1 negro woman
named Judah 18 years and 2 small children by the names of
Allen and Lewis, 2 negro girls over twelve named Orrey and Mol-
ley, 1 under twelve named Mary, a Negro boy under twelve named
Frank, a note on Josiah Ellet $59.50 cents, an account on Col.
Christman $7.40¼, on Alexancer Ray $4.50¾ on John Warine $1.87,
James House Senr. $5, John Hall $10, William House $1.56¼, James
House Jr. $38¼, George Busse 75 cents, Jacob Rager 58½ cents
James Downing 62 cents, Arthur Fuller 50 cents, Israel M. Carrel
$2.25, Riley Murrey 25 cents, Isaac Rogers 50 cents, Ephraim

Givens 50 cents, Thomas Miles 62½ cents, 3 years lease of 25
acres cleared land, now in corn and cotton, 3 feather beds and
furniture, 1 small childrens bed, 1 large walnut chest, 1 large
trunk, 1 small ditto, 1 walnut table, 1 loom and weaving ne-
cessaries, 1 mans saddle, 1 womans do, 1 shot gun and shot pouch
1 old rifle, 1 Bible, 1 Shridon's Dictionary, 1 History, 3
jugs, 1 funnel, 2 coffee pots, 1 tea pot, 1 tea kettle, 1 tin
canister, 2 pepper boxes, 1 spice mortar, 2 candle sticks, ½

Page
(167)

pint Decanter, ½ Dozen earthen plates, 2 earthen dishes, 1
pewter dish, and bason, Bottle camphire, 1 large pewter spoon,
4 small ditto, half dozen knives and forks, case of rasars, 1
hand saw, 1 Drawing knife, 1 pair of compasses, 2 Screw Augers,
1 large gimblet, 1 lamp, 3 chissels, 3 axes, 1 grind-stone, 5
hoes, 1 plow hoe, 1 plow, 1 coulter plow, 1 hogshead, 3 barrels, 1 washing tub, 1 well bucket, 1 cotton wheel, pair cotton
cards, pair wool ditto, 2 pails, 3 kettles, 2 pots, 2 ovens,
3 pair pot hooks, 1 pair flat irons, 1 skillet, an old waggon
and some gger, 2 bridles, 1 grey horse, 1 black filley, 6 cows,
5 calves, 4 yearlings, 3 grown hogs, parcel of old irons, 12
shoats, 1 pair saddle bags, pair iron wedges, 4 bells, 1 sifter,
1 butter pot, 1 churn, 9 small hogs killed and used after the
death of the deceased for the use of the family - corn to the
amount of Seventy five bushels used by the family for provisions.
                    Signed William Martin, Admr.
                      Virginia Clark, Admx.
Returned to July Session 1807. N. P. Hardeman, C. W. C.
    An additional Inventory of the Estate of Samuel Clark, de-
ceased - 3 coats, 3 pair breeches, 2 shirts, 5 waists coats,
2 pair stockings, 1 pair shoes, cotton receipt for $48.45 at
$15 pr. hundred, hire of a negro fellow $40 for six months,
hire of a negro girl $8.25 cents, 3 hogs, 24 $ cash.
                    Signed William Martin, Admr.
                      Virginia Clark Admx.
Returned to October Session 1807. N. P. Hardeman, C. W. C.

Page
(168)

An account of the Sale of the perishable Estate of Samuel Clark
   deceased disposed of the 15th of August 1807 -
Virginia Clark the crop growing $15, 1 feather bed and furniture
$25, one ditto $15, one ditto $15, 1 small bed (children's)
$4, William Martin case razors $1.50, William Nolen money
scales $1, Inkstand .16½ cents, Bartholomew Stovall ditto .16¼
cents, William House shot moulds .25, ditto knee buckles and
hat do. .12 cents, Joseph Howell ½ dozen awls .6¼ cents, Isaac
Mason Junr. lancets .31¼, Virginia Clark tea kettle $1.50, ditto
.80, ditto .60, ditto 12½, Benjamin Gambrel pepper box .25, Virginia Clark coffee pot ditto $1, William Nolen candlestick .75,
William Martin crass-cock .25, Virginia Clark .30, ditto .75,
ditto .75, ditto $1.50, ditto .25, Bartholomew Stovall 1 jug
.50, Virginia Clark 1 ditto .90, 1 table $2.26, one trunk $4,
one chest $7, Richard Orton pair steelgards $4.12½, ditto one
trunk $2.5, Virginia Clark side saddle $7, ditto clothes of
the dec'd. .12½, James Downing steel $1, old Irons $1.13, Horse
shoes .51, Virginia Clark 1 lamp .29, Bartholomew Stovall 1 small
gouge .6¼, Izrael M. Carrel 1 plain .58¾, ditto 1 hand-saw .58,

Page
(169)

George Bussee 1 drawing knife and gimblet .75, B. Stovall 3
old books and dictionary $2, ditto flat irons $1, William House
saddle bags $3.50, Abram Mason plough mould and bell $1, Vir-

ginia   Clark 2 hoes .50 cents, 2 axes $2.70, 1 plough hoe.51
cents, 1 cotter .28 cents, 1 plow hoe .31, 1 grubbing hoe .62½
 cents, 2 Hilling Hoes.50 cents, Benjamin Gambrell 1 mans saddle
$21.25, Virginia Clark 2 ovens $4.57, Abram Walker oven led .37,
Virginia Clark 1 pot $3.77, one ditto $1, Fire shovel and pot
hooks .35, 1 skillet and log chain $5.65, 1 sifter $2.25, Jacob
Waggoner 1 barrel .62, Virginia Clark 1 ditto .26, 1 Bell $1.,
1 pail .15, 1 small water vessel .25, 1 churn.30 cents, 1 barrel
15 cents 1 tub .25 cents, 1 meal bag.25 cents, 1 hogshead.50
cents, 1 keeler.12½ cents pot-hooks, candlestick and flesh forks
.25 cents, 2 clevises $1.2, one bucket $1.1 cent, John Depriest
old waggon and gear $40.50, Virginia Clark 1 double tree.25 cents,
3 old chairs 56 cents, 1 wheel and 2 pair cards $2.75, 1 loom .25
cents, 2 old Bridles .36 cents, 1 old horse $32, one filley $40,
16 hogs $18.56, two cows and calves $26.27, Lawson Hobson 1 ditto $12., Virginia Clark 2 ditto $27.25, Benjamin Gambrel 1 ditto
$11, two bells $1.76, 1 young steer $6.25, two yearlings $6.6,
1 yearling $5.1 one bee hive $1.50, Benjamin Gambrill 3 clivises and pr. snuffers .75, ½ pint decanter 12½ cents, 1 pr.
pinchers .30 cents, John Mathews grind stone $2., Virginia
Clark 1 filley $40.

Page
(170)

              Signed William Martin Admr.
              Virginia Clark Admx.
     Returned to October Session 1807. N. P. Hardeman, C. W. C.

An Inventory of the Estate of John Noland, deceased, taken the
10th day of July 1807 -
3 head of Horse Creatures, 1 cow and calf, 9 head of hogs, 1
kittle, 2 Dutch ovens, 1 pot, 1 smoothing iron, 1 hoe, set of
plow irons, 1 sede saddle, 2 beds and furniture with other household furniture, 1 iron wedge, 2 screw augers, 1 drawing knive, an
account upon William Hooker for a cow worth 10 dollars.
     Signed Thomas Hooker - Easter Noland, Admrs.
     Returned to July Session 1807. N. P. Hardeman, C. W. C.
     An account of the Sales of the perishable property of the
Estate of John Noland, Dec'd., sold the 10th day of August 1807:
John Noland 1 bay horse $6, Esther Noland 1 bay horse $6, Esther Noland 1 brown horse $12, Esther Noland 1 cow and calf $6,
Esther Noland 1 cow $3, Esther Noland all the household furni-
ture $12., John Noland 1 watch, 3 augers, 1 drawing knife, 1
plow, one hoe, one axe, 1 iron wedge $7.6. Total $52.6
              Signed Esther Noland, Admr.
     Returned to January Session 1808. N. P. Hardeman, C. W. C.

Page
(171)

An Inventory of the Estate of JASON WADSWORTH, deceased -
50 acres of land, 1 horse, 5 head of cattle, 10 head of hogs, 1
horse, 5 head of cattle, 10 head of hogs, 1 rifle gun, 1 cart,
1 plow hoe, 2 weeding hoes, 1 mattock, 1 axe, 1 iron wedge, 1
auger, 2 chissels, 1 handsaw, 2 feather beds, 1 wheel, 2 pair
of cotton cards, 2 chairs, two pewter dishes, 3 ditto basons,
2 plates, dozen spoons, 4 pint tins, 3 pots, 1 looking glass,
1 tea caniater, 2 water pails, 1 churn, 1 hair sive, 1 flat
iron, 1 jug, 2 iron clivises, 1 lock chain, 1 mans saddle, 1
hunting saddle.
              Signed Obediance Wadsworth, Admx.
     Returned to October Session 1807. N. P. Hardeman, C. W. C.

An account of the Sales of the Estate of Jason Wadsworth,
deceased, sold at public auction the 2d. day of April 1808 -
5 head of cattle $29, one plow shear $3.50, 2 feather beds
and furniture #30, one mattock $2.75, 1 whip $1.72, two hoes
.75 cents, one pot $2, 1 oven $1.6¼, one axe $1.6¼, one tea-
kettle $1.25, 2 chairs 78 cents, 2 clivises .72¼ cents $1.50¼,
shoe hammers and pinchers .75 cents, pewter $1.25, 2 jugs $2,
one canister .57½ cents, 1 glass 32¼ cents, 1 can .31, 2 clivises
$1.3, one chain .32 cents, 1 horse coller .26 cents, knives
and forks .35 cents, 1 crock 13½ cents, shot pouch and powder horn .51 cents, 1 sifter 13½ cents, one pail 7 cents, 8
spoons .32¼, shoe files .34¼ cents, 6 buckles 9¼ cents, 3 Bridles bits .61 cents, 1 horse $61, one saddle $11.1, one Bridle
12½ cents one chest .33 cents. Total amount $149.32½
Signed Obediance Wadsworth.
Returned to July Session 1808. N. P. Hardeman, C.W.C.

Page
(172)
An Inventory of the Estate of Edith HAY, deceased - 1 negro woman, 1 two year old colt in the range, 1 cow, 1 feather bed and
furniture, 1 womans saddle and bridle, 1 large pot, 1 oven,½
dozen earthen plates, 1 pitcher, 2 punch bowls, 1 pewter dish,
two pewter plates, 1 bason, 1 coffee pot, ½ dozen knives and
forks, 3 iron spoons, 4 tea spoons, 1 axe and hoe, 1 drawing knife, 2 flat irons, 1 tub and 2 piggins, 2 jugs, 2 slays,
and one harness, 1 candle stick and snuffers, 4 fowls.
Returned to April Session 1807. N.P. Hardeman, C.W.C.
This is an additional Inventory of the chattel Estate of
Edith Hay deceased, which has come to my knowledge since I re-
turned the former inventory which is one note on Nathaniel
Wych for forty six dillars sixty six and two thirds cents.
Apl. 11th, 1808.
Signed Rich'd. Hay - Returned to April Session 1808
N. P. Hardeman, C. W. C.

An account of the sale of the personal property of the Estate of Edith Hay, deceased, on the 9th day of May 1807:
Richard Hay one axe $2.87½, Amos Bullock 1 pot and hangers
$3.25, Balaam Hay 1 Dutch oven $2, William Glover 1 dish $1.25
Pewter $1, William Williams 1 candle stand and snuffers .40,
James Gibson 1 case and knives and forks .85, sundrys .50,
Francis McCall 1 coffee pot .40, Richard Bently 1 set flat
irons $2.37½, Balaam Hay 1 drawing knife .75, William Glover
1 jug $1.57, John B. Gibson 1 jug $2.35, Richard Hay 1 slay
Page
(173)
and harness $1.10, James Gibson 1 Slay and Harness .40, John
Geary 1 washing tub .40 cents, 2 pails .51 cents, James Gibson 1 hoe .74, Richard Hay tea spoons and salt-stand .50,
James Gibson ½ doz. plates $1, ditto ditto bowls .75 cents,
1 pitcher .86, Edith Hay 1 side saddle $8, John Geary spun
cotton $2.35, Joel Stephens 1 bed $41., John Black fowls $1.
31¼, John Geary 1 cow $8, Balaam Hay 1 horse $18, Richard
Hay 42½ lbs. cotton at six cents pr. pound $2.55, John B.
Gibson 1 negro woman named Cheary $402.6, Cash $11.62½, Note
on Nath'l. Wych $46.66 2/3. Returned to July Session 1807.
N. P. Hardeman, C. W. C.

State of Tennessee, Williamson County Settlement made this
9th day of July 1808 between David Squier and James Hicks,

Commissioners, appointed by order of said County Court to settle
on behalf of the heirs of Edith Hay dec'd. with Richard Hay, Administrator of the said Edith Hay deceased -
    The said Rich'd. Hay, Admr. makes the following return of
assets in his hands to wit: 1 note on John B. Gibson for $404.41,
1 do. on Nathaniel Wych $46.66 2/3, 1 do. Joel Stevens $41, 1
do. Balaam Hay $20.75, Cash in hand $11.62½, 1 note on Richard
Hay $7.2½, 1 do. John Geary $11.26, 1 do. John Black $1.31¼,
1 do. Edith Hay $8, 1 do. James Gibson $5.10, 1 note on William Glover $4.40, 1 do. Richard Bently $2.37½, 1 do. William
Williams .40, 1 do. Amos Bullock $3.25. Total $567.57¼.
    The said Rich'd. Hay as Admr. sets forth his claim against the
Estate of aforesaid and preys the following credits (to wit)
For 4 days waggoning at 12/ per day $8.00, for do. riding to
hire a negro for the dec'd. $2., for 2 do. for bringing a negro
woman to the sale $1.00, Doctor's fees .50, for services as Ad-
ministrator $20, for services pd. Patrick Gibson for selling the
Estate $1.,for Clark fees vs. the Estate of said Defendant $2.
for cash pd. John Atkinson one of the Legatees $48.40 2/3, for
do. John Lindsey for said Dec'd. $9.22, for note owed Dec'd. for
$45.41 2/3 due 1st October 1804 $45.41 2/3. Total $147.47.
Interest on the same $9.93. Balance due the Estate $420.10¼.
4 Legatees each $105.2½. Returned to July Session 1808.
              N. P. Hardeman, C.W.C.

An Inventory of the Estate of MICHAEL WARREN, Dec'd. -
2 plows, 1 clivis, 2 pair stretchers, 2 corn hoes, 2 grubbing
ditto, 3 axes, 1 drawing knife, 1 log chain, 4 plates, 3 pair
hooks, 1 skillet, 5 pails, 2 buckets, 1 churn 1 keg, 2 pewter
dishes, 1 saucer, 8 pewter plates, 22 table spoons, 1 flax-
haakle, 1 pr. shears, 3 coffee pots, 1 candlestick, 1 tea canister, 1 tin kettle, 11 tin cups, 3 jugs, 2 tea kettles, 2 crocks,
2 smoothing irons, 8 knives and forks, 1 pound wool, quantity
clean flax, 2 trunks, 2 chests, 1 case razors, 1 pair fire-tongs,
1 pr. nippers, 1 iron wedge, 1 bar steel, 1 bar lead, 2 pair
Bridle bits, 1 meat axe, 1 curry comb, 1whetstone, 1 frying pan,
1 chair, 1 shot gun and powder horn, 1 keg nails and sundry
pieces of Iron, 1 womans saddle, 1 mans ditto, 1 waggon and harness, 4 riding bridles, 11 head horses, 1 flax wheel, 1 pair
cotton cards, 2 bags, 1 bed cord, 17 head cattle, sundry books,
4 beds and furniture, 1 looking glass, 1 dozen delf plates, 2
dishes delf, 6 glasses, 1 set tea ware, 1 pair scales, 1 pair
candle molds, 1 pr. wool shares, 40 yards muslin, 2 reap hooks,
1 halter chain, 1 saddle blanket.
          Signed David Craig, Alex. Miller.
Returned to October Session 1807. N. P. Hardeman, C.W.C.
    An account of the Sales of the Estate of Michael Warren,dec'd.:
Ezekiel Lampkins .62½ cents, John Elliott $1.31½, Alex. Miller $3,
John Elliott .81¼, Thomas Adams .87½, Thomas Adams .75, John Mil-
ler .91, David Craig $4.25, John Elliott $2.56½, James Craig .41¼,
Robert Sellers $1, Thomas Adams $2.1, Alex Miller $5., William
Adams $1.12½, Alex Montgomery $2.25, John Gillespie .60, Isaac
Sellers .40, William McLean .50, Thomas Reardon $2.50, Thomas
Reardon $2.75, Robert McLain .60, John Collie .80, William Mc-
Lain $1, Thomas Adams $1.62½, John B. McMahon .75, John B. McMa-
hon .25, John B. McMahon .80, Olsimus Kindrick .95, John Collie

$1, William Blakely .62½, Alex Miller $2.25, James Craig .26¼, John Collie .50, John Gillaspie $1, Alexander Miller $1, Thomas Reardon .62½, Alex Miller $1.43, James Craig $5, David Orton .75, Robert McLain $4.53, Isaac Sellers $11.77, William Gurley $60.75, David B. Thomas $76.25, James Fitzgerald $50.

Page
(176)
James Fitzgerald $61.50, Thomas Adams $1.6, William McLain .60, David Craig $5, Alex Miller $3.80, Mark Edwards $8.60, John Gillespie $4.62½, Thomas Adams .32½, William Adams $3.12½, Thomas Reardon $11.10, Thomas Caldwell $14.25, Thomas Reardon $11, David Hines $11.30, John Elliott $14, William Blakely $8.25, Isaac Sellers $9.40, Matt Johnston $13.62½, David Hines $13.52½, David Hines $15.12½, John F. Cowsart $14.51, Isaac Sellers $12, George White $5, William McMahon $6, David Craig $18, William Adams .52, Alex Montgomery .40, James Craig $57.50, Isaac Brooks $12.50, John F. Cowsart $108., John Hood $73.12, David Craig $3, John Jamison $3.75, Alex Miller $5.25, John Lindsey $2.12½, James Fitzgerald $1.5, William McLain $3.37½, William Adams $2.22, Alex Gillespie $9.60, David Craig $27.25, James Copeland $20, David Craig $7, Henry David .6¼, Alex Miller $50.50, David Craig $53.50, William Adams $6.12½, John Collie .55, David craig $14, David Craig $4.50, David Craig $7, John Collie .35, George White $2, David Craig $10, John Ray $1.75, William Adams $1, James Copeland $3.12½, David Craig $19, David Craig $15, John White .75, Alex Miller $1.12½, Samuel Cox $4, James Fitzgerald .80, David Craig .50, David Craig $3.6¼, Alex Montgomery $101., David Craig $45, David Craig $7, Alex Miller $7, Alex Miller $1. Total amount $1235.22¼.

The above is a just and true acc't. of Sales of Michael Warren dec'd. Sold by us the 5th and 6th days of Novr. 1807 being $1235.22½ cents.

Signed David Craig and Alex Miller, Admrs. Returned to October Session 1808. N. P. Hardeman, C. W. C.

Page
(177)
An Inventory of the Chattel Estate of DEMPSEY KENNEDY, dec'd.: 1 stud horse, 2 geldings, 1 mans saddle, 1 womans ditto, 1 pr. saddle bags, wearing apparel.

Signed John Kennedy, Admr. 13th October 1807. Returned to October Session 1807. N. P. Hardeman, C.W.C.

An Inventory of the Estate of THOMAS ROGERS, dec'd: 1 colt, 2 mares, 9 head cattle, 11 head of hogs, 2 beds and furniture, 2 pots, 2 ovens, 1 skillet, 1 pr. flat irons, 1 pr. Dog Irons, 1 axe, 1 Iron Wedge, 1 Weeding Hoe, 1 lease of Land containing 7 or 8 acres cleared, Table furniture, plates, dishes, knives and forks.
Signed William Beard, Admr. Returned to October Session 1807.
N. P. Hardeman, C. W. C.

An account of the sales of the Estate of Thomas Rogers, dec'd. Sold 5th November 1807

Sophia Rogers 2 beds and furniture, 2 cotton wheels, pewter, chests, pots, oven, skillet, piggin, hourse and furniture $20. Moses Parks 1 pair fire dogs $4.87½, Stephen Brooks 1 oven $3.18¾, Robert Calvert 1 skillet $1.68¾, John Mitchell 1 cow $9.60¼, Lawn. Johnston 1 steer $3.6¼, William Willet 1 heifer $6, Joel Hobbs 1 steer $6.50, one heifer $6.75, Sophia Rogers 1 heifer $6.87½ ditto $8.12½, Greenberry Rogers 1 saddle $6.37½, John McCracken 1 draw-

Page
(178)

ing knife .37½, John McDaniel 1 colt $40.50, James Swanson 1 mare $102.50, George Glascock 3 barrows $5.37½, William Willet 2 sows $6.12½, William Beard 1 iron wedge .75, Sophia Rogers 1 axe $1.75, ditto 1 hoe .68¾, ditto 5 barrows $23.1. Total amount $265.71¼.

Signed William Beard, Administrator on the estate of Thomas Rogers, dec'd. Returned to January Session 1808.
N. P. Hardeman, C. W. C.

Charles Campbell admr. returns the following list of the property of JOHN CAMPBELL, deceased in his hands -
James Campbell due the Estate $1.50, John Brady ditto ditto $9.00, John Campbell ditto ditto $12.00, John Pruitt ditto ditto $4.00, Patrick Campbell 1 book, Charles Campbell for Schooling $6.00.

Signed Charles Campbell.
Returned to April Session 1808. N. P. Hardeman, C. W. C.

An Inventory of the Estate of John Shumale Dec'd.: 1 horse $10, three beds and furniture $37.50, one Bible 75 cents, knives and forks $1.25, spoons cups and bottle .75 cents

Page
(179)

An Inventory of the Estate of WILLIAM DAVIS, dec'd: 3 head of horses, 6 head of hogs, 1 bed and furniture, 1 pot and small kettle, 1 cotton wheel, 1 table, 5 chairs, 1 falling axe, 1 drawing knife, 1 handsaw, 1 mans saddle and bridle, a small portion of shelf furniture, some corn supposed to be about 90 bushels, 5 weavers slays, 1 razor and shaving box, 1 pair shoe brushes, 1 washing tub, 1 churn, 1 pail, 1 note on Richard Venable for 4 dollars, 1 note on William Tolly and William Churchwell for $15 payable in beef.

Returned to January Session 1808 by Elizabeth Davis, administratrix. N. P. Hardeman, C.W.C.

An account of the Sales of the Estate of William Davis, deceased, as sold on the 5th day of Feby. 1808:
John McKnight 1 saddle, bridle and blanket $2.50, James M. Knight 1 coller, hames and clivis, Robert McKnight 1 pail and cooler .50, Thomas Shannon $1.12½, Andrew Keigler 2 chairs $1.60, 2 do. $1.40, James McKnight 1 chair 62½ wt. 1 wheel $2, Mathew Benthall 1 bedstead and cord $2.12½, Sam'l. B. McKnight sundries .50, James McKnight sundries $3, James McKnight 1 drawing knife $1.62½, Sam'l. B. McKnight sundries .50, James McKnight sundries $3, James McKnight 1 drawing knife $1.62½, and 1 axe $1.35, 1 table $3.76, 1 pot and hooks $3.68¼, Robert McKnight Senr. 1 pan $2.50, James McKnight 2 sows $3, Mathew Benthall 2 sows $5, Robert McKnight Junr. 2 sows $4.90, Mathew M. Gough 1 razor and box .94, Elizabeth Davis 1 horse $45. 1 bed $19, Mathew M. Gough 1 kettle $1.13¼, Sam'l. B. McKnight, tea ware $3, James Elliott knives and forks $2.50, John Boyd ½ dozen spoons $1.50, James

Page
(180)

McKnight 1 mug .28, 1 crock .68¾, Thomas Shannon 3 glasses .82½, James Shannon 1 bowl .38, Thomas Shannon sundries .66 2/3, Polly Shannon 1 dish $2.60, David Shannon 4 barrels corn $2.17½, John Boyd barrels corn $17.67, Elizabeth Davis slays $4, 1 mare and colt $26, Thomas Shannon 1 basket .26, Robert McKnight do. .29.

Signed Elizabeth Davis, Admx. Returned to July Session 1808. N. P. Hardeman, C. W. C.

Page
(181)

An account of the sales of the Estate of JOHN GAMBLING, deceased. Sold the 5th day of February 1808: Polley Gambling 1
feather bed and furniture $15, ditto ditto $15, Wm. Hutcheson
1 little wheel $2.50, Polley Gambling 1 lot of dishes and delf $4.
William Wilson 1 milk keller .33, James White 1 churn .31¼, Polley Gambling 1 Smoothing Iron .57¼, Ivey Burnim 1 pot and pot
hooks $3.50, Polley Gambling 1 mare and saddle $25, John White
1 mare $32. ditto 1 bay horse colt $30, Gersham Hunt 1 red steer
$5.50, Polley Gambling 1 red cow and yearling $7.26, ditto 1
red cow and pided calf $9, ditto 1 sow $1.50, Joshua Burnham
1 sow $2, Polley Gambling 1 pr of fire dogs $3, Gersham Hunt 1
stone tukler .37½, James White 1 frying pan $1, Joshua Burnham 1
axe $1.62½, James White 1 axe $2, William Robbins 1 weeding hoe
$1, Polley Gambling 1 little chair .41, ditto 4 chairs $1.50,
John White 1 chest $2.6¼, William Snell 1 ivory comb .50, Polley
Gambrel 1 kettle, 1 oven and pot rack 1 skillet $6.75, ditto 1
pr. cotton cards $1.52, ditto 1 pale .12½, ditto 1 piggin .28,
ditto 1 table $1.25, John White 1 bottle .31¼, David Tade 1 pack

Page
(182)

saddle, David T. Alexander 1 cow and calf $12, Lemuel White 1
cow and calf $14, Lemuel White 2 heifer yearlings $8.12½, Isaac
Acuff 1 cow $11, Polley Gambling 1 red cow $5, 1 stud colt 2
years old not found till since the sale.
      Returned to April Session 1808 by John White, Admr.
      N. P. Hardeman, C.W.C.
      The following contains a true account of all the chattel Es-
tate of Jonathan Davis deceased, as has come into my hands as
Administrator to wit -
      Six head of horses, 3 of which is running in the range on Duck
River and was at the death of the Deceased, 14 head of cattle,
8 of which is running in the range on Duck river, as above stated.
19 head of hogs 9 of which is running at large on Duck River as
above stated, 1 waggon, 4 pair of gears, 1 waggon cover, 1 log
chain, 1 Barshare plough, 1 shovel plow, 3 falling axes, 2 weeding
hoes, 2 carpenters chisels, 1 auger, 1 drawing knife, 1 fish gig,
1 coopers addze, 1 flax hackle, 1 jointer, 1 compass, 1 shoemakers hammer and pinchers, 1 rifle gun, 1 shot pouch, 1 sprouting hoe, 1 pot, 1 oven, 1 skillet, 2 pair pot hooks, 3 water pails
2 churns, 3 bridles, 1 washing tub, ½ dozen case knives and forks,
2 feather bedsand furniture, 6 pewter plates, 3 pewter basons, 6 tin
cups, 3 raw hides, 4 sides of tanned leather, 1 meal bag, 6 framed
chairs, 1 iron wedge, 1 flat iron, 2 gimbletts, 1 set of frizens,
1 clivis, 2 wheels, 1 flax and 1 cotton, 4 books, 2 mens saddles,
1 pair of cotton cards, 1 six hundred slay, 4 table spoons, 1
pepper box, 1 womans saddle, 1 earthen dish, 1 old chest, 1 old
trunk, 1 hog which was killed for the support of the family since
the death of the deceased, Simeon Hinds' assumpsit for $110,
Isaac Bells assumpsit for $2, Alener Vaughn assumpsit for .50
cents, 2 pr. of Bridle bits, corn growing on 7 acres of ground,

Page
(183)

but does not know what quantity, William Claytons assumpset for
$7.50, John Davis' $9.50, Wright Williams' assumpset for $1,
Zachariah Martin's assumpset for $1, Eight pounds of tallow
1 canoe on Duck River, 1 sifter, 2 Bridle Bits.
                        Signed
                        Amos Davis, Admr.

Returned to January Session 1808   N. P. Hardeman, Admr.

An additional Inventory of the Estate of JONATHAN DAVIS, dec'd.:
87½ cents in the hands of Jonathan Martin, 1 bell. The amount
of the corn that was inventoried by me as part of the Estate of
Jonathan Davis, deceased, measured 94 bushels, allowing 2 measures
of short corn or nubbins for one at 50 cents per bushel $47.
                    Signed Amos Davis.
Returned to October Session 1808. N. P. Hardeman, C. W. C.
    An account of the Sales of the Estate of Jonathan Davis, de-
ceased February and March 1808:
    Nancy Davis 1 bed and furniture $5.50, ditto ditto $4.16 2/3,
1 chest and small trunk $2, 1 flat iron .34 1/3, 1 dish and pep-
per box $1.2, 1 Dutch oven and hooks $1.76, 1 large pot and hooks
$2.50, 1 skillet .33 1/3, 6 pewter plates and 3 basons $2, 6
knives and forks and 4 spoons .51, 5 tin cups .66 1/3, 1 tub, pail
and piggin .82½, 1 cotton and 1 flax wheel $3.50, 1 slay and 1
sifter .76, 1 Bible .76, 2 churns .76, 1 pair cotton cards .61,
1 bag and tallow .76, 2 chairs .26, 1 colt $18.58, 1 axe $15, 1
side saddle .13½ cents, 1 Bridle .28 cents, 1 sow and 4 pigs $3.2.
Total $52.52½ cents.

Page
(184)

Oliver Williams 1 book jointer and Iron $1.25, John Pillow 1
drawing knife .83, Mathew Rosenblum 1 rifle and shot bag $7.37½,
2 barrows $11.77, 1 cow and calf $13.3, 1 cow and calf $9.28,
John Fowlkes 1 panel leather $1.84, ditto .51, John Davis 2 raw
cow hides $5.37½, 1 brown colt $40, Wright Williams 1 pocket
compass .81¼, 1 mans saddle $6.63, 1 black mare $50, Stephen
Clayton 1 cow and yearling $11.12½, Samuel Fitzpatrick 1 cow and
yearling $9, Hartwell Hyde 1 bull $5.50, 1 waggon and hind geer
$50, Amos Davis 1 sorrel horse $68, 9 hogs $27.50, 1 hoe .50½,
Hannah Fleming 1 black mare $52.50, William Clayton 1 small rund-
let .55, 2 bridles .51, 1 old sow .60, David Smith 2 chisels and
auger $1.29, 1 Bar share $5.75, Jesse Davis 1 shoe hammer and
pinchers .81¼, 1 iron wedge .81¼, 1 axe $1.25, 1 log chain $4.25, 1
grubbing hoe $1.37½, Dan'l. Davis 1 howell .51, 1 white-faced
heifer $11.50, Rich'd. W. Hyde 2 books $1.29, 1 cow and calf
$19.32½, 1 double tree $2.50, Samuel Venable 1 saddle $6.1, John
Clarke 2 sows and 2 pigs $5.23 1/3, John Eaton 2 sows $7.9,
Joseph Jackson 2 barrows $11.1, Mathew Benthall 1 cow and calf
$13.51, Edmund Ribers 1 cow and calf $20.6¼, John Depriest 2
yearlings $6.85, John McClellan 1 bay horse $60.25, Wiltshire
Jordan 1 pr. traces and hames $1.28, John Perryman 1 pr. traces
and hames $2, 1 axe $1.62½, William Edmondson 2 sets hip straps

Page
(185)

$2.75, James McKnight 2 hoes $1.52, Morgan Fitzpatrick 1 plow
hoe $3.   Total $609.1¼.
    The foregoing account of Sales of the Estate of Jonathan Davis
deceased as sold the 5th day of February and 3rd day of March
is true to the best of my knowledge.
                    Signed Amos Davis, Admr.
Amos Davis, Administrator of Jonathan Davis, deceased, makes a
further return of sales property - which has come into his hands
since his former return: 1 bay mare rec'd. in part payment of
a trade. Debt due the Estate from Simeon Hynes as formerly mentioned $74. 1 bell $1. Total $75.
Decr. 1808.
                    Signed Amos Davis, Admr. of Jonathan Davis, dec'd.
Returned to January Session 1809. N. P. Hardeman, C.W.C.

185

An Inventory of the Estate of JOHN PAGE, deceased, July 8,1808
15 negroes, 15 head of horses, 23 head of cattle, 23 head of
sheep, 7 feather beds and furniture, 1 trunk, 2 chests, 11 pewter plates, 3 dishes, 8 basons, 2 tables, 10 chairs, 3 cotton
wheels, 1 flax wheel, 3 pair of cards, 3 iron kettles, 3 pots,
2 ovens, 1 skillet, 1 griddle iron, 1 pair of steelgards, 3
pair of pot hooks, 1 shot gun, 1 rifle gun, 3 barshares, 1 shovel,
plough, 4 pair of Drawing chains, 4 weeding hoes, 2 broad axes,
4 falling axes, 2 sickles, 1 whip saw, 1 looking glass, 1 handsaw, 1 foot addze, 3 augers, 1 horse cart, some coopers ware, 1
coffee pot, 2 stone jugs, 2 crocker, 2 glass bottles, 2 black
Jacks, some cups and saucers, 5 milk bowls, 9 table spoons, 1
case of knives and forks, 1 weavers loom, 4 slays, 2 saddles,
2 iron wedges, 1 frow, 2 flat irons, 1 claw hammer, 1 pair of
sheep shears, 1 check reel, 1 hackle, 1 meal sifter, 2 bread
trays, 1 brass inkstand, 73 head of hogs, 1 grubbing hoe, 1
branding iron, 4 plain bits, 1 drawing knife, 2 bolts and clivises, 14 pieces of leather, 36 geese, great and small, 6 tin
cups, 1 candle mould. The within in an Inventory of the goods and
chattels of John Page, dec'd. to the best of my knowledge.
Signedm Lovey Page
x   her mark
Returned to July Session 1808. N. P. Hardeman, C. W. C.

Page
(186)

An Account of the Sale of the property of John Page, deceased:
Henry Ingram 1 cotton wheel $2, Lovey Page 1 ditto $1.12½,
Josiah Wooldridge 1 flax wheel $1.66½, Henry Ingram 1 clock reel
$1.18¾, Lovey Page 1 cotton wheel $1.12½, Andrew Craig 1 plow
share $3.25, Lazarus Crawford 1 cane hoe $1.55, Andrew Perkins
1 adze .76, Peter Pinkston 1 broad axe .81, Lovey Page 3 axes
$2.62½, 1 tub and 2 pails .50, Andrew Pickens 1 axe $1.25, Thomas Parsons 1 handsaw $1.26, Josiah Wooldridge 1 lot of old
tools .25, Richard Wood 2 augers .35, Henry Ingram 2 chissels
.56¼, William Locke 1 pare of compasses and Square .50, Joel
Stevens 1 frow $2, Amos Rounsavall 1 shovel plough and hoe $1.31¼,
Lovey Page 4 hoes $1, Turner Pinkston 1 whip saw $4.18¾, Henry
Ingram 1 pair hames and chains $3.56¼, Lovey Page 2 ploughs and
geers $5.50, Lovey Page 1 swingle tree and clivis $1.6¼, William
Alexander 1 ditto $4.12½, 2 pails, tub, and churn $1, ten chairs
$2, 2 bread trays and sifter .12½, 1 kettle, 2 pots, 1 oven, 2
pair of hooks, 1 table and sundry other articles $13.50, 3 pair
of cards $1.6¼, 1 gun and shot bag $4, Hugh McBride 1 pair of
wedges $1.75, Lovey Page 1 trunk $2.25, 1 chest $1, 1 feather
bed and furniture $25, 3 ditto $107.12½, Coleman Wheaton 1 feather bed and furniture $28.50, John Nichols ditto $30, Lovey
Page 1 chest $2.75, 1 feather bed and so forth $27, 1 bedstead
.50, 1 loom and appurtenances $7.50, Josiah Wooldridge 2 plains
.33, 2 chissels and gimbletts .33, Lovey Page 1 waggon hammer .30

Page
(187)

William Garley 1 Dutch oven $1.53, Joel Vaughn 1 Spider $1.75,
William Mansker 1 pot $3.56¼, George Mansker 2 kettles $3.75,
Jeremiah Wade 1 Bay Mare $38.2, George Mansker 1 sorrel mare $62,
Charles Stevens 1 sorrel horse $50.12½, Lovey Page 1 bay mare
$46.12½, 1 grey horse $16.50, Nathan Scruggs 1 grey horse $41,
William Bennett 1 bay mare $13, Lovey Page 1 black mare $10,
David Shannon Senr. 1 grey colt $16.37½, Henry Stevens 1 sorrel
filly $28, Levy Ferrell 1 sorrel colt $17.50, John McClelland
1 ditto $26.2, James Hungerford 1 grey colt $56.12½, Robert
McLennon 1 sorrel filley $36.12½, William Stevens Junr. 1 black
and 1 red steer $10.52, John Patterson 1 pided cow and yearling

$12, James McBride 1 red heifer $6, 1 red cow and yearling $17.12½
John West 1 pided cow $11.75, Lovey Page 1 black cow and yearling
$10.25, 1 ditto $10.56¼, William Stevens, Junr. 1 red heifer $10,
Lovey Page 1 white cow $10, Edward Stevens 1 pided yearling $3,
James McBride 1 red heifer $3.77, William Stevens Senr. 1 pided
steer $10.6¼, Lovey Page 1 pided cow and yearling $10., Wm. Bar-
ker 1 pided cow and yearling $12.52, William Stevens 1 black
cow and yearling $14, Lovey Page 1 pided heifer $10.50, William
Stevens, Junr. 1 spotted cow $3.50, 1 sandy do. $5., Joel Stevens
1 spotted sow $5.25, Lovey Page 1 white sow $3.6¼ 1 do and 4
pigs $2.50, Nathan Scruggs 3 sows and pigs $16.31, James Downing
1 pair of steelgards $4.50, Lovey Page 1 looking glass .83½,
Peter Pinkston 2 sickles .76, Lovey Page 1 candle stick and moulds
.25, David Shannon Senr. 1 flax hackle $2.38, Peter Pinkston 1
stone jug $2.2, Lovey Page 1 womans saddle $5, ditto 1 mans saddle
$2.64, George Mansker 1 small keg .52, Turner Pinkston 1 large
keg .75, Henry Jordan 1 rifle gun and shot bag $13.76, ditto 1
small jug .51, Turner Pinkston 1 barrel .25, Lovey Page 1 pickling tub .25, Turner Pinkston 1 table $1.6¼, John McKnight,1
parcel of stave timber $2, William Stevens Senr. 1 stand $1.32½,
ditto 1 open headed stand .80, Turner Pinkston 1 ditto .80,
John Watson 1 ditto .81¾, Turner Pinkston 1 ditto $1.26, William
Mansker 1 ditto $1.17, Lovey Page 2 ditto, $1.50, Beverley Ridley
1 ditto $1.55½, William Stevens, Junr. 1 cart $15.62½, John
Depriest 1 raw hide $2.25, 1 ditto do $2, Joseph Howell 5 sheep
$10.12½, John Depriest 3 sheep $6.51, 3 ditto $7.6¼, Lovey Page
2 ditto $4, John Crawford 6 ditto $13.25, John Patterson 1 side of
leather $2.25, John Depriest 1 ditto $4.25, Arthur Fulgum 1 ditto
$2.1, John Depriest 1 ditto $2.50, 1 ditto $2.82, William Lock 1
decanter .37, Robert McKnight 1 hammer and 2 gimblets .65,Peter
Pinkston 1 black Jack .40, Robert McKnight 1 black jack .63,
Lewis Stevens 20 geese $11.6¼, Lovey Page 12 ditto $6.25, the
Estate indebted to Peter Pinkston for crying the sale $4, Joel
Vaughn as clerk $1.75, David Shannon as ditto $1.
Returned to January Session 1809. N. P. Hardeman, C. W. C.

(Page 188)
(Page 189)

    An Inventory of the Estate of THOMAS SHARP, dec'd., taken this
9th February 1808 -
    1 sorrel horse, 1 old saddle and bridle, account against Charles
Patterson $36, ditto against B. Watkins $2.37½, some saddles,tools,
and needles, 1 cloth coat and 1 cotton ditto, 2 pair stockings,
1 blanket, great coat, 1 pair overalls of velvet, 1 pair ditto
of nankeen, 1 pr. ditto of tow and a woman's pr. of cloth, 6
handkerchiefs and 2 shirts, 1 pair of boots, 1 hat, 1 pair of
flannel slips, and shirt of ditto, 1 waist coat of Swansdown, 1
old of ditto, 2 other waist coats, 1 dozen sadlers awls and 100
tacks, 3 remnants of silk tashe, 1 pocket knife, 1 lancet, 1
thimble, 4 horse shoes, 1 inkstand, 1 wallet and Inkstand, 1 wallet and saddle blanket, 1 pair of scissors, 1 vial of stuff or
medicine, 1 pinch back ring, 1 Breast pin.
    Signed Jacob Harder. Returned to April Session 1808.
            N. P. Hardeman, C.W.C.

Page
(190)   An Account of the Sales of the Estate of THOMAS SHARP, deceased
    Sold the 10th day of May 1808: William Bright one spur .25, 1
pr. worsted stockings $1.26, 1 flannel shirt .37½, Jacob Harder

1 pr. shoe boots $1.50, 1 saddler's hammer .75, a lot of saddler's
tools .75, 1 pair of velvet pantaloons $4.50, 1 Breast pin $1,
1 pinch Back ring .31¼, 2½ dozen needles .37½, a lot of saddlers
awls .37½, 1 knife and 2 lots of B. $1.31¼, 1 Handkerchief .37½,
2 handkerchiefs .25, 1 lot of silk tathe .75, 1 lot of materials
.33, 2 accounts at .37½, 1 on Charles Patton 36, 1 on B. Watkins
$2.37½, 1 saddle blanket $1.41¼, 1 waist coat $1, 1 pair nankeen
pantaloons .50, 1 pr. suspenders .12½, 1 wallet and inkstand .50,
1 cloth coat $5, 1 sorrel horse $18, James Deal 4 horse shoes .25,
1 old bridle .50, 2 neck handkerchiefs $1, 1 hat, $1.12½, 1 shirt
$1.55, 1 ditto $1.82, Clayton Talbot 1 pr. of Tow pantaloons $1,
Peter Pinkston 1 pr. of cotton stockings $1, Martin Stanley 1 check
handkerchief .71, 1 Waistcoat $1.1, 1 old saddle $2.1, 2 pr. pantaloons one of steps .26, Ludwell Estes 1 Blanket Great Coat $1.42,
2 Waist coats .41, John Sappington 1 cotton coat $1.12½

(Page 191)

Signed Jacob Harder, Admr.
Returned to July Session 1808. N. P. Hardeman, C. W. C.

An Inventory of the Estate of BURWELL THORNTON, deceased, sold the
21st day of June 1806.
   Edward Swanson 1 mare, saddle, bridle and saddle bags .50 dol.
Saddle bags $12. ditto several articles of clothing $12,David
Samaster 1 shirt $2.25. Total $64.25
   Signed John Gatling, crier Edward Swanson, Admr.
   Returned to July Session 1806. N. P. Hardeman, C. W. C.

Page (192)

An Inventory of the property of WILLIAM S. MULLIN, deceased -
7 negroes, 5 head of horses, 21 head of cattle, 50 head of hogs,
corn and fodder, 2 feather beds and furniture, 1 small chaff
ditto, 2 tables, 3 chests, 1 candle stand, 2 cupboards, 1 dozen
chairs, 2 small ditto, 1 loom, 2 linnen wheels, 2 cotton ditto,
5 dishes, 5 basons, 2 tin pans, 32 plates, 4 bowls, 1 sugar bowl,
2 cream pots, 2 pepper boxes, 1 salt seller, 1 butter boat, 1 cruit,
3 tumblers, 1 dozen pewter tea spoons, 1 set of cups and saucers,
2 tin cups, 1 mug, 1 dozen knives and forks, 1 coffee pot, 9 books,
1 hone, 1 case of razors, 1 looking glass, 1 clothes brush, 1 pair
shovel and tongs, 1 pair sheep shears, 1 spice mortar, 1 candlestick
and snuffers, 2 kettles, 3 pots, 2 Dutch ovens, 1 frying pan, 2
iron racks, 1 spider, ½ dozen table spoons, 2 guns, powder and shot,
6 sides of leather, 2 flat irons, 1 waggon and gear, 4 plows, 7
hoes, 1 spade, 1 cotter plow, 1 pair of wedges, 4 chopping axes,
1 hewing ditto, 1 frow, 1 cross cut saw, and set, 1 handsaw, 1
foot adze, 1 grind stone, a parcel of water vessels, a parcel of
pickling tubs, 1 churn, 5 pair cotton cards, some weaving gear,
1 half bushel, 1 riddle, 3 sifters, 1 cot, a parcel of old irons,
3 augers, 3 chissels, 1 hackle, 1 curry comb, and 3 bells, 2 saddles, 1 pair pinchers, 1 hammer. The amount of the A/c and notes
against William Mullin $17.75 cents against Joshua Mullin $103.16
cents - against Jesse Mullin $23, against Henry Key $5.50, against
Charles Campbell $4, against Daniel Cowan $3.86½, against Sarah
Robertson .75, against John Gordon $119, against Elijah Renshaw
balance $8,
      Signed Mary Mullin x her mark J.T. Elliston.
Returned to April Session 1806. N. P. Hardeman, C. W. C.

An additional Inventory of the Estate of William S. Mullin,dec'd.
   A parcel of wild hogs, some corn and bacon, some more acts.
against Joshua Mullin $10.50, one axe.
                    Signed Mary Mullin Admx.
                         J. T. Elliston, Admr.
Bill of Sale of the above --
Hogs sold running in the woods $13., corn sold $9.68¾, bacon
ditto $6.75, Axe sold $1.25.
                    Signed Mary Mullin Admx.
                         J. T. Elliston Admr.
Returned to October Session 1806. N. P. Hardeman, C. W. C.
An additional Inventory of the Estate of William S. Mullin, dec'd.:
1 negro, 1 head of cattle, 1 hog, 4 saucers, 2 dishes, 1 poranger,
1 pr. pot hooks, 1 tea kettle, 1 washing tub, parcel of crocks,
1 pair of cards, 1 half bushel, 1 riddle, 1 chissell, 1 powder horn,
3 files, 2 eules, 1 pair steelgards, 6 vials, 4 gimblets, 1 log
chain, 1 drawing knife, 1 gouge, 1 howell, a parcel of baskets
and beans, 1 lock and hinges, 1 scythe, 3 bushels of potatoes, 1
sun dial, a parcel of Seed cotton, an account against Wm. Young
$28.12½ cents.
                    Signed Mary Mullin - J. T. Elliston.
An Additional Inventory of the Estate of Wm. S. Mullin, dec'd.
More acts. against William Mullin Junr. $12.50, acct. against
Hanks for rent corn $13, Some act. for the hire of negroes from
the death of the William S. Mullin to the time of sale act. against
W. L. Marr $13, against Capt. Demombro $18.25, against Josiah
Mullin $18, against Sneed $9.25, against Lintz $11.62½.
                    Signed J. T. Elliston, Admr.
                         Mary Mullin, Admx.
Returned to April Session 1807. N. P. Hardeman, C. W. C.

An Additional Inventory of the Estate of William S. Mullin,dec'd.:
An account against Joseph T. Elliston $12.82½.
                    Signed Mary Mullin, Admx.
                         J. T. Elliston, Admr.
Returned to October Session 1807. N. P. Hardeman, C. W. C.

An account of the sales of the Estate of William S. Mullin,dec'd.
8 negroes $2,577.27, 5 horses $198.43¼ cents, 22 head of cattle
$132.73¾, 51 head of hogs $30.31½, 278½ bushels of corn $44,
3 stacks of fodder $6.50½, 2 feather beds and furniture $50.,
1 chaff bed $3.25, 1 table, 1 candlestand, 1 set cups and saucers,
3 tumblers, 1 crewet, salt seller, 2 pr. boxes, 1 sugar bowl, 2
tin pans, 6 dishes, 5 basons, 6 spoons, 12 knives and forks, 20
plates, 1 mug, 2 cups, shovel and tongs, morter candlestick,
snuffers, looking glass, clothes brush, 4 saucers, 3 bowls, 1
cream jug, 6 tea spoons, 1 table $19.00, 3 chests $3.50, 2 cupboards $6.3, 12 chairs and 2 small ditto $7.59¾, 1 loom $5.25,
2 linnen wheels $4.28, 2 cotton wheels $5.68¾, 1 dish, 6 plates
1 bason, 2 spoons $6.1, 3 plates, 6 tea spoons, 1 butter pot, bowl,
1 cream jug and poranger .12½, 9 books $4.56, 1 hone $2, 1 case
razors .80, 1 pr. sheep shears, 1 kettle, 2 ovens, 2 flat irons
.40, 2 pot racks $2, 1 kettle $5, 1 pot and hooks $2.90, 1 dish
.50, 2 pots $1.62½, 1 frying pan .82½, 1 spider and tea kettle .50
2 guns $6, powder and shot $2.11½, Leather $5.10½, 1 waggon $20.12½
2 pair chains and britching $4, 1 ditto ditto coller $2.68,

Page
(195)

Coller and old irons $2, two plows and old iron $2, two plows
$4.76, 1 cotton ditto $2.75, 7 hoes, 1 axe $6.66½, 1 spade $1.70,
1 pr. wedges $2.18, 3 chopping axes .77, 1 cross-cut saw $4.25,
1 Handsaw $1.1, 1 foot adze $1.50, 1 grind stone $1.12½, water
vessels and tub $1, 1 pickling tub and crock $2.12½,
    1 churn .37½ cents, 6 pr. cards $1.82, weaving gear $2.76,
    2 half bushels .62½ cents, 2 riddles .37½, 3 sifters $1.18½,
1 cott $1.26, 3 augers .51,
    4 chissels $1, 1 haskle $2.13¼, 2 saddles $7.50, 1 pr. pin-
chers and hammer .62½ cents
    3 files and 2 rules, .30, 1 pr. steelgards .25,
    1 horn and 6 vials .33¼ cents, 4 gimblets .45 cents
    1 log chain $1.1 Drawing knife and gauge .25½ cents
    1 Howell .51 cents, baskets and beans .50 cents
    1 lock and hinges $1.9, 1 Scythe .50 cents, 3 bushels po-
tatoes $1, 1 sun dial .25 cents, a panel of seed cotton $24.
Total $3228.40.
                Signed Mary Mullin, Admx.
                    J. T. Elliston, Admr. of William S.
Mullin, Deceased.
        Returned to July Session 1806. N. P. Hardeman, C. W. C.

An Inventory of the Estate of SAMUEL HOUSTON, deceased:
Notes due $417, 1 waggon and geer, 1 negro girl, 3 horses, 5
head of cattle, 8 head of hogs, 2 plows, 5 axes, 1 cross cut
saw, 1 iron wedge, some carpenters tools, 3 feather beds and
furniture, 1 trunk, 1 kettle, 2 pots, 2 ovens, 1 jug, 1 crock,
2 spinning wheels, 2 pair of cotton cards, 1 log chain, some
pewter, knives and forks, 4 chairs, 2 smoothing irons, 2 bells,
1 cloth loom, and harness, 1 side saddle, 2 bed cards, 1 iron pot
rack, due by assumpsit $15, 1 churn, 1 pail, 1 canister, 1 slate,
some books, 1 looking glass, some vials and bottles, some iron
scraps, some remnants of leather, 4 dear skins, 2 pad-locks,
2 flour barrels, some pottry, 1 cotter, 1 weeding hoe, iron shovel,
1 curry comb, 1 case of razors and shaving box, 1 umbrella,
some shoe tools, some shot, fifty barrels of corn, 900 weight of
fodder, 32 dollars in cash, 1 curb, bridle, 1 sifter and bread
tray, some flax and cotton. The within is a just and true Inventory of the Estate of Samuel Houston, deceased, that came to
my hands, taken this 12th day of April, 1809.
                Signed Sidney Houston - x her mark
        Returned to April Session 1809. N. P. Hardeman, C. W. C.

An Inventory of the Estate of John Tapley, deceased:
1 negro man named Sam, ditto Napper, 1 ditto ditto Fanny, 1 horse,
1 mare, Stephen Chipley's agreement to pay $18 per month for the
hire of 2 negroes for 6 months, a desperate debt, 1 note on Robert
McLemore for $24, on ditto with credit to the amount of $253.33 1/3
1 note on Thomas Newman for $10, Newman is not known to us, 1
note on Charles Smith for $30. 1 note on John Dabney for $10, 1
note on Thomas H. Perkins for $100, cash in the hands of Thomas
Edmiston $44.32, 1 thimble, 1 shaving box, 1 small book (Smith's
 Geography), 1 umbrella, 1 rifle gun, 2 blankets, 1 saddle, 1
hone, 1 set surveying instruments, 1 small bottle, 1 tobacco box
2 pocket books, 1 pair boots, 3 coats, 1 pair saddle bags, 1 bell,
5 pair pantaloons, 7 waistcoats, 1 cravat, 1 bridle, 1 inkstand,
1 case of razors, 1 pair short breeches, 2 shirts, 6 pair locks,

Page
(196)

2 handkerchiefs, 2 pair stockings, 1 large bag, 2 small clothes bags, cash in the hands of Thomas H. Perkins $24 which he received of Edward Warren, an obligation on Robert Grinder in favor of John Tapley and Thomas H. Perkins, to make a deed to a tract of land lying on the waters of West Harpeth, granted to Robert Hays by virtue of John Grinders warrant for his services in the Continental war, an order drawn by Nelson on John Anderson for $70 in favor of Peter Perkins and by him assigned to John Tapley, cash $260.36½. Supposed to be part of the price of a negro John Tapley. Sold to Robert McLemore, which money we have paid to said McLemore, a quantity of corn, sundry papers in Peter R. Booker's hands.

Signed Thomas H. Perkins)

T. H. Edmiston   ) Admrs.

Returned to April Session 1809. N. P. Hardeman, C.W.C.

Memorandum of property sold and negroes hired, belonging to the Estate of John Tapley, deceased:

Page (198)
David Squire 1 umbrella .25, Thomas H. Perkins 1 rifle gun $16.51, Thomas Edmiston 1 blanket $2.50, Robert H. Perkins 1 saddle $10, Daniel McMahon 1 hone .52, Thomas H. Perkins compasses and chain $15.62½, Edmond Chitwood 1 tukler and tobacco box .51, John McCandless 2 pocket books $1.25, Edward Warren 1 pair boots $3.50, Caleb Manley 1 coat $9.75, David Squire 1 negro woman Agney $20.87½, Caleb Manley 1 negro woman Fanny $27.50, George Stramlar 1 negro man Napper $51, Peter Perkins 1 negro man Sam $51, Robert McLemore 1 negro man Lawson $55.25, James McCandless 1 pair saddle bags $3.6¼, John Witherspoon 1 bell $1, ditto 1 pr. pantaloons, 1 cravat and waistcoat $8, Thomas H. Perkins 1 bay mare $45, Nicholas T. Perkins 1 bridle $4, Robert McLemore 1 horse $35.12½, Josephas Harris 1 inkstand and case razors .81¼, Amos Bullock 1 coat $3, John M. McCandless 2 pr. pantaloons and waist coat $1, ditto 2 waistcoats, 1 pr. breeches $1.56¼, George Davidson 1 coat waist coat $3.68¼, Gregory Wilson 2 shirts $2.77, George Davidson 2 pr. pantaloons $2.76, Zachariah Drake 3 waistcoats $1, John McCandless 2 waist coats $1.56¼, Samuel E. Goodridge 2 pr. socks $1.56, 2 pr. ditto $1.56¼, John McCandless 1 pr. ditto, 2 handkerchiefs .63¼, ditto 2 pr. stockings 1 pr. socks $2.19¾, ditto one large bag 2 cloth bags .59, Hendley Stone 10 barrels corn $10, Robert McLemore 10 barrels ditto $10.4, Richard Huse takes balance of corn.

Signed Thomas H. Perkins)

Th. Edmiston   ) Administrators

Returned to April Session 1809

Page (199)
An Inventory of the Estate of ROBERT CARLILE, deceased: 4 head of horses, 7 head of cow beasts, 20 head of hogs, 2 beds and furniture, 1 spinning wheel, 1 chest, 1 plow and gear, 2 hoes, 2 mens saddles and bridles, 1 dish, 7 plates, ½ dozen knives and forks, 5 spoons, 1 coffee pot, part of a set of cups and saucers, ½ dozen tea spoons, 1 pitcher, 1 stone jug, 2 axes, 1 iron wedge, some shoemaker's tools, 1 smoothing iron, 6 chairs, 1 churn, 3 piggins, 1 bason, 1 Dutch oven, 1 kettle, some corn, some cotton, 2 decanters, 1 drawing knife, 2 chissels, 1 handsaw, 1 meal sifter, and one pair of geese.

Signed S. Childress.

Returned to April Session 1809 by Stephen Childress, the Administrator. N. P. Hardeman, C. W. C.

An Inventory of the Estate of JAMES JOHNSON, deceased: 1 lease
of land, 10 acres, 3 head of horses, 5 head of cattle, 10 head
of hogs, 1 barshare plow, 8 plates, 7 spoons, set of knives and
forks, 1 feather bed and furniture, 1 mans saddle, 150 bushels
of corn, 1 razor, and shaving box, 1 clivis, 1 tin bucket, and
pails, 1 pr. cotton cards, 1 small box, 3 tin cups, 1 delf bowl,
1 walnut table.
     Returned to January Session 1809 by James Gault and Grace
Johnson, the Admr. and Administratrix. N. P. Hardeman, C. W. C

An Inventory of the Estate of JAMES MAYFIELD, deceased: 1 horse,
between 9 and 10 acres of corn, 1 sow, 4 books, 2 blankets, 3
yards of grey coating, 1 bridle.
                    Signed John Mayfield
Returned to October Session 1808. N. P. Hardeman, C. W. C.
     A supplemental Inventory of the Estate of James Mayfield, de-
ceased: 2 razars, 1 padlock, 1 ball of tape, a debt of $16. due
from John McCalpan, together with sundry wearing apparel.
                    Signed John Mayfield, Admr.
     Returned to January Session 1809.
     An account of the Sales of the Estate of James Mayfield, dec'd.:
John Wooton 1 bridle $2, James Walker 1 book Currin's Speeches $4,
James Mayfield 1 do. Franklin's Works, .75, John Champ 1 do. The
Dream Dictionary .75, James Walker do. the Hive .50, Francis
Donaldson 2 blankets $6.60, J. L. Fielder 3 yards of grey coating
$6.81¼, John Mayfield a horse $40, John Champ crop of corn $20.12½,
John Mayfield a sow $5.12½.
                    Signed John Mayfield.
     Returned to January Session 1809. N. P. Hardeman, C. W. C.

An Inventory of the Estate of MICHAEL ROBINSON, dec'd., taken the
9th day of July 1808: 1 waggon with the gears and other furniture,
2 horses, 1 case of bottles, 1 large Jug, tongs and shovel, 1
skillet, 1 pot, 1 oven, lid, 2 pot racks, 2 flat irons, 1 frying
pans, 1 morter and pestle, 2 axes, 3 weeding hoes, 2 pewter dishes,
1 bason, 3 spoons, 1 earthen bowl, 1 pitcher, 1 auger, 1 drawing
knife, 2 bells, 1 handsaw, half dozen knives and forks, 3 dishes,
18 plates, 3 basons, ½ dozen tea cups and saucers, 1 jug, 1 chamber pot, 1 canister, 7½ yards linnen, 11 sheets, 2 blankets, 3
spoons, 1 chest, 2 hand towels $202.37½ cents, 2 cags, 1 pail,
several small articles too tedious to mention, 1 receipt from
James Robinson of five dollars lent to him.
     Signed David Robinson, attorney in fact for Wm. Cocke, Exor.
Returned to July Session 1808. N. P. Hardeman, C. W. C.

Inventory of the Estate of FRANCIS MCCALL, deceased: 2 head of
horses, 12 head of cattle, 5 head of hogs, 3 feather beds, bedsteads and furniture, 1 cupboard, 1 table, 3 pots, 1 kettle, 1
oven, 1 skillet, 1 pot rack, 3 pair pot hooks, 3 chairs, 1 looking glass, some books, some brittle ware, such as Queen's ware,
some pewter, knives and forks, spoons and other cupboard furniture, 1 plough, 1 hoe, 3 augers, 1 handsaw, 2 chissels, 3 pails
1 washing tub, 1 shoe hammer, pinchers and nippers, 2 smoothing
irons, 1 flax wheel, 1 big wheel, 1 loom and tackling, 1 woman's
saddle, 1 pickling tub, 1 canister, 1 tin pepper box and carver's
knife box, 1 axe, 1 iron wedge, 1 clivis and swingle tree, 1
bridle, 1 foot adze, 1 drawing knife, 7 geese, 1 pr. stirrup

Irons,, 1 debt on Jacob Whitehead for $26.75, $40. in work
on said Whitehead.
            Signed Catren McCall and Thomas McCrory, Admrs.
        Returned to October Session 1808. N. P. Hardeman, C.W.C.

        An Account of the Sale of the Estate of FRANCIS McCALL,
deceased, sold the 10th Day of Dec. 1808: 1 cupboard $7.25,
cupboard furniture $5.78, Table and 3 chairs $1.50, 3 beds,
bedsteads, and furniture $20, looking glass .75, pr. stirrups
irons .50, 1 auger .85, pot rack and smoothing irons $1.56,
bridle and buckles .12½, handsaw $1.55, foot addze $2.76, 2 augers
and 2 chissels $1, pot and skillet, oven and hooks $1.75, 1 eleven
gallon pot $2.25, 1 kettle and hooks $6.21½, loom and tackling
$6.50, womans saddle $3, big wheel, 3 pails and washing tub $2,
1 pickling tub .60, plow irons, clivis, axe and iron wedge $5.96,
six geese $6, two horses $42.50, 1 cow and calf $8, one cow $10,
one bull $8, 1 cow $11.25, 1 ditto $12.50, 1 steer $5.11, 2
heifers $10.10, 2 ditto $8.35, 1 steer $4.25, five head of hogs
$3, 1 hoe .8½, 3 books.11 ½, shoe tools $2.12½.
        Returned to January Session 1809. N. P. Hardeman, C.W.C.

Page
(203)

        An Inventory of the perishable Estate of JOHN PATTON,
deceased, Jan. 9th, 1809: 1 negro man named Jim, 1 negro woman
and child, 10 head of cattle, 4 sows and pigs, 1 waggon and hind
gears, 1 set of plough irons, 1 cutting box and knife, 1
carrying knife, 1 drawing knife and hand saw, 3 hoes and 2 axes,
1 spade, 1 set chain traces, 3 beds and furniture, 2 trunks, 1
sugar chest, 1 sugar canister, 1 tea board, 2 tables, 1 looking
glass, 1 tea kettle, 4 candle sticks, 1 coffee pot, 3 pewter
basons, 6 table spoons, cupboard furniture, 1 tin box, 6 chairs,
1 pair fire dogs, 1 loom, 1 spinning wheel, a number of books,
dough tray, 1 iron kettle, 1 large pot, 1 small pot, 2 ovens, 1
skillet, 1 grid iron, 3 bee hives, 1 cut reel, a parcel of
saddles, 1 pot rack, 1 pair pot hooks, 1 coffee mill, 2 pails,
60 barrels corn, 1 pr. steelgards, 1 iron wedge, 1 pr. sad irons,
1 hackle, 1 lanthern.
            Signed Lawrence Bass, Admr.
        Returned to January Session 1809. N. P. Hardeman, C. W. C.
        Additional Inventory of the Estate of John Patton, dec'd.:
Mrs. Robertson, balance $4.00 desperate, William Caldwell balance
desperate, Moses Akins, balance $70.87½ desperate, David Cum-
mings balance $13.66½ desperate, Arch'l. McReynolds $2.50 desperate, Patrick Lyons $6.37½ desperate, Joel Lewis $12.4 desperate, James Walker $2.50, desperate, John Childress, Junr.
$48.12½ desperate, Samuel Mitchel $2.00 desperate, Spear Roach
$2.25 desperate, John Dillehunty $9.25 desperate, John Gillaspie
$45.87½ desperate, John Boyd $7.37½ desperate, Daniel Joslin .37½

Page
(204)

desperate, David McGavock $3.62½ desperate, John C. Phillips .50
desperate, John May .50 desperate, John Brownlee $1.50, desperate,
General James Robertson $75.12½ desperate, Samuel Donelson acc't.
pro. $1.75 desperate. Total $324.74.
        In the above list of accounts, some of the persons therein
named have left the County and probably will not return, others
are insolvent and others have accounts against the Estate-
To which is to be added the following acc'ts.: Thomas Talbot's
account $9.75 desperate, Wm. T. Lewis $9. desperate, Hugh Black
.57 desperate.

Signed Lawrence Bass, Admr. Returned to April Session 1809.
N. P. Hardeman, C. W. C.
     Additional Inventory of the Estate of John Patton, dec'd:
Andrew Fitzpatrick balance $2., desperate, Andrew Wilson $100.
desperate, James Wilson, balance $25., Philip Fishburn Ł 72 North
Carolina currency $180 desperate, George Patton $200. desperate
William Love and transferred by William T. Lewis for Ł 9.7 equal
to $23.37½ desperate, Robert Franklin Ł 1.8.6 equal to $3.56¼
desperate, John Cramp Ł 75.17.7 equal to $189.70 desperate, George
S. Allen and due bill $6.25, Michael Salter and John Shackleford
$1075 desperate, Michael Salter and John Shackleford $1500.
John Cain Articles of Agreement for money lent $182.50 desperate
 William Parkers due Bill $4.50 desperate. Total $3491.88¼.
 Robert Hays obligation for 400 acres of land,desperate, William
Caldwell's note for 37 barrels of corn, Judgment against John
Maclin for $9, desperate.
     Signed Lawrence Bass, Admr. Returned to April Session 1809.
N. P. Hardeman, C. W. C.
     A Schedule of the Sale of the personal or chattel property
of John Patton, deceased,by Lawrence Bass, administrator (viz):
1 white steer and heifer $3, 1 white and red heifer $3, Brindled
ditto $2.75, 1 white and red ditto $".50, 1 brindled $4.75, 1
cow and calf $8.50, 1 ditto $7.6¼, 1 cow and calf $10.25, 1 ditto
$9.50, 1 sow $3.25, 7 shoats $3.50, 1 sow $3.00., 1 sow and pigs
$6. 1 sow and 7 pigs $7.75, 1 waggon and gear $21, 1 set plough
irons $3.56¼, 1 cutting knife steel $1.00, 1 pitch fork .56¼,
1 currying knife $3.66¼, saw and drawing knife $2.62½, 2 hoes,1.12½
2 acres $2.56¼, 1 spade .87½, 1 mattock 1.6¼, 1 garden hoe .31,
1 howel .25, 1 coopers adze .87½, 5 chissels .81¼, 2 pair harness ropes .62½, clivis frizens $1.76, Clivis links .56¼, old
irons $2.81¼, nippers pinchers, rasps $1., Buckle $2.00, Hammers,
knives and shares .82, Box and saddle trimmings $1.65, chains
1.13¼, 2 beds and furniture $50, 1 grids stone .81¼, 2 books .43¾,
1 iron wedge 81¼, 1 meal box .25, 1 kettle $6990, 1 large pot $6¼
.12½, 1 small pot $2.75, 1 broken oven .25, 1 skillet and oven .62½
1 grid iron .81¼, 1 pot rack hooks $2.18¾, 2 piggins .25, 1 churn
.87½, 1 coffee mill .65¼, 1 hackle $3.22½, 1 lanthorn .25, 3
bee hives $2.50, 30 barrels corn $16.50, lot of corn by the barrel
1.00. Total $30.
     L negro man Jim $350.50, 1 bedstead .6¼, 1 old saddle $1.06½,
1 counterpain $5.00, 1 trunk .50, 1 small box .50, 1 tin box
.25, 1 sugar box .62½, Table and cupboard furniture $11.25, look-
ing glass $1.50, 1 table .30, candle sticks and snuffers $2.43¼,
1 candle stick .25, 1 tea kettle $2.87½, 1 coffee pot .43¾, 6
chairs $2.13½, old chairs .56¼, cotton wheel $1.25m flax wheel
$3.50, 1 check reel $1., loam and Bars $8., fire dogs $3.25, 2 flat
irons $1.81¼, 1 pr. steelgards $3. 12 books $4.6. Total $642.98¾
     Total amount of the sale of the chattel Estate sold at
nine months credit on the 20th day of February 1809.
     The charge in the foregoing account of sales of 30 barrels
of corn sold for $16.50 is to be added to the above amount as
it is not extended, it is also a conjectural amot. of corn, as
it was the balance in the crib after selling the lot of 30 barrels. Total amot. $659.48¾.
     Signed Lawrence Bass. Returned to April Session 1809.
          N. P.Hardeman, C.W.C.

Page
(205)

Page
(206)

Page
(207)
An Account of the Sales of the Estate of Robert Carlile, deceased:
Sarah Carlile the widow 1 bed $20, ditto 1 bed $5,1 spinning
wheel .50, ditto one chest $1, 1 dish, 7 plates, knives, and
forks, 5 spoons, 1 coffee pot, saucers, tea spoons, pitcher jug,
and smoothing iron, 6 chairs $2, 1 churn and piggin $1, 1 bason
.25, 1 Dutch oven .50, parcel cotton $5, decanter crewet .50,
meal sifter kettle and geese $1.75, 1 bridle $1, corn $2, 2 cows
and calves $10, Stephen Childress 2 axes $2.25, 1 wedge and shoe
tools $1.12½, 1 heifer and cow and calf $10.50, 1 mare and colt
$40, 1 sorrel mare $81, Eli Spurlin, handsaw chisels and drawing knife $3, 20 head of hogs $36, George Marlin 1 plow and geer
$5.62, James Black 1 cane hoe $1, Hardin Perkins 1 saddle .37½
John Porter 1 bay mare $40, Thomas H. Perkins 1 mans saddle $2.51.
    The above sold by Stephen Childress, Admr. Returned to
January Session 1810. N. P. Hardeman, C. W. C.

    An additional Inventory of the Estate of John Higgins,dec'd.:
    Whiskey in Kentucky $22. Returned to January Session 1810.
N. P. Hardeman, C. W. C.

    Inventory of the Estate of ARTHUR FREEMAN, Deceased:
1 Negro man named Ben, 4 head of horses, 4 head of cattle, 23 head
of hogs, 1 waggon and hind geer, 1 pr. hames, traces and back
hand, 1 cart, 1 plow, 1 hoe, 2 axes, 1 saddle, 2 pots, 1 kettle,
1 slay and 2 harnesses, 9 pewter plates, 3 basons, 2 dishes, 7
knives and forks, 4 earthen plates, 4 cups and 6 saucers, 6 silver
tea spoons, 1 small looking glass, 4 tin cups, 1 bedstead, 8 chairs,
3 trunks, 1 shot gun, 1 log chain, 1 pair Taylor's shears, 2
jugs, 1 decanter, 1 small tumbler, 1 pr. plated spurs, 1 table, 1
coffee pot, 1 tea canister, 1 candlestick, 1 candle mould, 2 flat
irons, 7 pewter spoons, 3 old books, 1 pair candle snuffers, 5
beds and furniture, 3 hammers, 2 chissels, 1 drawing knife, 1 womans saddle, 3 bridles, 2 gimblets, 1 handsaw, 1 pr. leather
traces, 3 collers, 2 churns, 4 pails, 2 bags, 2 iron wedges, 4
table cloths, 2 tubs, 1 flat stand, 1 meal sifter, 2 bread trays,
45 lb. cotton, 3 baskets, 110 barrels corn, 4 stacks blades,
1 shuttle, 2½ bushels wheat, 1 pocket book, some potatoes, 1
pepper box, 2 bottles and 6 vials with medicine in some of them,
1 grind stone, 1 pr. shoe brushes,$12 cash, 2 bells, 1 curry
comb, 1 trumpet, 2 pr. pot hooks, 1 flesh fork, 2 cotton wheels,
2 pr. cards, 1 snuff bottle, 6 awl blades, 1 pegging awl, a
claim for money in Virginia but the amount not known, 4 pr. knit-
ting needles, 2 butcher knives, 1 pr. shoe buckles, 1 pr. silver
studs broke, 1 silk money purse, wearing clothes, consisting
of coats, jackets, breeches, shirts, stockings, etc., 1 raw cow
hide, a small quantity of powder and shot, 1 gold breast pin.
    Signed Polly Freeman, Executrix. Returned to January
Session 1810. N. P. Hardeman, C. W. C.

Page
(209)
    An Account of the Sales of the Estate of WILLIAM LOVE,
Deceased: David B. Love 1 sow $4.75, John G. Love 65 head of
hogs $65, ditto 200 acres of land $1800, ditto 5 head of hogs
$17, John Marr 1 heifer $6.6¼, John G. Love 1 heifer $7.87½,
ditto 1 heifer $2.92½, John House 1 steer $11, Thomas Mayfield
1 cow $10.62, William Hess 5 head of hogs $15, ditto 5 head

hogs $15.45, David B. Love 1 saddle $5, Henry Hughes 1 horse
$97, John House 1 steer $2, John G. Love 1 cow $9, William Hess
5 head of hogs $12.75. Total $2081.44¼.
     Signed Joseph Love, Executor. Returned to January Session 1810. N. P. Hardeman, C. W. C

     Inventory of the Estate of JAMES CRAFTON, deceased:
8 negroes, Ellick, Sindey, Eny, Moses, Mary, Sam, Meriah and
Charles, 1 waggon, 2 pair of geers, 1 horse, 2 cows, yearlings,
1 chest, 1 table, 3 beds and furniture, 1 small trunk, 1 woman's saddle, 2 spinning wheels, 2 pr. cotton cards, 1 pot, 1
pr. pot hooks, 1 washing tub, 1 pail, 2 piggins, 2 pewter dishes,
2 basons, seven pewter plates, 5 spoons, 4 knives and forks,
1 smoothing iron, tobacco, quantity unknown. Taken by us this
tenth day of January 1810.
     Signed John Crafton and Daniel Wilkes. Returned to January
Session 1810. N. P. Hardeman, C. W. C.

Page
(210)
We, David Shannon and Oliver Williams, two of the Justices of
the Peace for the County of Williamson being appointed as
Commissioners by the County Court of Williamson at their January Session 1810 to settle with Sarah Davis, widow and Administratrix of David Davis, deceased, have done the same in
the following manner, to wit: We find from the face of the
papers produced to us, on Settlement that she has sold the
Estate of the deceased for the sum of $101.72 and that she has
paid the sum of $102.56.To Peter R. Booker as rec't. filed
$2.50, to R. P. Currin as pr. rec't filed $15.70, to Arthur
Pierce as pr. rec't filed $51.14, to N. P. Hardeman Clk. $21.22.5
to Margaret Davis $3, to Daniel Perkins, Treasurer, $6., to
John Page $3. Total $102.56.5
     Signed O. Williams and D. Shannon. Returned to January
Session 1810. N. P. Hardeman, C. W. C.

     An Account of the Sales of the Estate of JOHN HIGGINS,
deceased: Martha Higgins 3 saddles and gun $20, James Higgins
1 rifle gun $10, Martha Higgins 1 waggon $25, Abraham Biller
1 still and tubs $132, William Higgins 1 mare $51, James Higgins 1 colt $7, Albert Higgins 1 mare $46, 65 gallon whiskey
sold for $22. Total $313.
     Signed John Holbert, Exor. Returned to January Session
1810. N. P. Hardeman, C. W. C.

Page
(211)
     Dr. William Parham in account with the orphans of William
C. Hill, deceased, January 1st, 1810.
     To the hire of the negroes for the year 1809 $177.76.
     To balance p. contra ------------   -   19.52
1810 January 1st   Cr.
By allowance made for keeping negro woman Cloe $4.95
By board of Martha, James C. and H. M. Hill for the year
1809 $105., by cash paid Nichol and McAlister pr. rec't No.
1 $17, by cash pd Neilson K. and Mitchell pr. rec't. No. 2 for
M. H. $3.12½, by cash pad Neilson K and Mitchell pr. rec't.No
2for James C. Hill $3.12½, do. do. do. pr. rec't. no. 2 for
H. W. Hill $3.37½, do. do. do. for 1 do. for H. W. H. pr.
rec't. No. 4 $2.50, do. for schooling J. C. H. and H. W. C.
for the year 1809 $16, do. paid for returning guardian acc't.

for .66 2/4. Balance due the Orphans for year 1809 only $19.52.
Total $177.76.
      Signed William Parham, Guardian.   Returned to January Session
1810. N. P. Hardeman, C. W. C.

      An Account of the Sales of the Estate of SAMUEL Houston, dec'd.
Sold 27th of May 1809.
Lydia Houston (Hewston?) 1 plow $3, oven and lid $2, small pot
.75, broken oven .25, 1 pot $2, cotton wheel $1, shelf and furniture $6, churn .50, flat irons $1.25, loom $1, bed cord .50,
1 pr. cotton cards $1.3, chairs $1. one axe $2.75, 1 bed $8, do.
$16.50, ditto $12.50, books $2, umbrella $1.37½, 2 axes and wedge
$2.37½, slate .76, hand axe $2.12½, curry comb .50, tray and
sifter .50, side saddle and circingle $2, 2 padlocks $1, 2 jugs
and 2 barrels $1.62½, cow, calf, and bell $16.25, leather and deer
skin $2.62½, 1 sorrel filley $58, looking glass vials and trunk .75,
1 heifer $6, 1 bull yearling $3, heifer yearling $2.50, 1 bay mare
$111, pr. hames and traces $5.1, cotton $1, kettle $3, crib corn
$2, 1 pot rack $2.2.

Lydia Houston 14 head hogs $19.25, two barrows $9, 1 pot rack
$2.2.   Total $259.69½
David Houston 1 cotton wheel $1.87½, 1 black filley $48, sorrel
filley $58. Total $107.87½
James Houston razors, case and box $1.25
John Marr 1 bell $1.31¼, 1 poll axe $1.50, shott and shovel
plow $2.18¾. Total $5.
Grosee Shapp 1 cow and calf $15.6¼, Charles Boyles 1 lot of
tools $5.50, lot of old irons $3, hames and traces, bridle $5,
back hander horse chain $2, holter chain and line $1.50, T. $17.
Henry Ingram lock chain $5, cow and calf $15,--T. $20.
2 dressed deer skins $2.3, hoe and shovel .53,--T. $2.96.
Samuel Williams 1 waggon and hind geer $78. Total $515.81¾
                    Signed Lidey Houston
                              x   her mark.
Returned to January Session 1810. N. P. Hardeman, C. W. C.

State of Tennessee) We, the Subscribers, Commissioners, appointed
Williamson County) by the Worshippful Court of said County at
                    January Court 1810 to settle with Sampson
Sawyers, Administrator in right of his wife on the Estate of
Samuel Clark, deceased, have done the same as follows, to wit:
and find from the face of the papers produced to us on Settlement,
that they have sold the estate of the deceased for the sum of
(together) with hire of negroes acc'ts $858.18¼, out of which
sum they have paid as here below expressed $779.76½. Balance
due the Estate $78.41¾.
      An Acc't. to John and Thomas Childress $106.75, Deaderick
and Sommerville Acc't. $6.76, William Polk Acc't. $2.50, Benja-
mine Gabrills note $40, John Sappington's Acc't. $6.50, Samuel
Clark Senr. Acc't. $3.41¼, William Nolen Acc't. $12.50, Richard
S. Henderson Acc't. $28, William Nolen order $9.83¼, Abraham
Whitesides Acc't. $8.87½, George Bussey acc't. $8.87½, Jason
Thompson's note $48.51, cash paid for taxes for $8.62½, Thomas
Lightfoot Acc't. $10.5. Total $303.76½.
      William Martin's Account for Cash paid Thomas Stewart for
advice $5. Total $308.75½.

Cash pd. for making coffin for sd. deceased $5.
                          Total $313.76½
For boarding and schooling four children infants of the deceased
6 months or up to this date 12th January 1810 -- $300
For keeping two negro children up to this
     present date -------------------- ----------   56.
William Martin expense to North Carolina to settle
     the benefit of sd. deceased ------------   10.
Allowance made to the Admr. and Admx. each $50   50.

                                              $779.76½

     In Pursuance to an Order to us directed from the Worshipful
Court of Williamson County, we have settled with Sampson Sawyer's
Admr. in right of his wife and William Martin Admr. of the Estate of Sam'l. Clark, deceased, and on settlement thereof we
find that the said Administrators stand indebted to the said Estate the sum of $78.41¾ cents, which settlement is in full of
all acc'ts. that was presented to us by the Admrs. previous to
this date, Given under our hands and Seals this 12th day of
January 1810.
                    Signed S. Green -- (Seal)
                           O. Williams -(Seal)
          N. P. Hardeman, C. W. C.

Page
(214)

          JOSEPH COLES' Will - In the name of God Amen - I Joseph
     Coles of Williamson County, State of Tennessee, being of sound
     disposition mind and memory and understanding do constitute,
     make and ordain this my last Will and Testament, first I give
     to my Brother Thomas Cole and my Sister Elizabeth Cole my Tract
     of Land lying on Little Harpeth - containing three hundred and
     twenty acres to be equal between them. I also give to Thomas
     Cole one grey mare known by the name of Jin, two feather beds
     and furniture and all my wearing apparel and three trunks, and all
     my farming utencils, I further give to Elizabeth Cole one negro
     boy named Jack and a sorrel horse, I give to my brother Samuel
     Cole one grey mare known by the name of Febey. I give to my brother
     John Cole, one mare colt of a reneish colour, I give to my sister
     Nancy Cole one hundred dollars in cash to be paid to her by my
     Executor herein after named. I give to my sister Mary Cockey
     twenty-five cents to be paid by my Executor to her. I give to my
     Brother Philip Cole twenty-five cents to be paid to him by my
     Executor. I give to my half Brother William Cole one dollar to
     be paid by my Executor. All the balance of my property that is
     not disposed of, I request that my Executor may sell and after
     paying himself for services done about the Execution of this my
     Will, the Balance to be paid unto my Sister Nancy Cole for her
     use after paying all my just debts and funeral charges I do here-
     by appoint my brother Thomas Cole sole Executor of this my last
     Will and Testament, revoking all others heretofore made by me.
Page
(215)   In witness hereof I have set my hand and affixed my Seal this 20th
     day of July eighteen hundred and nine.
                    Signed Joseph Cole (Seal)
     Signed, sealed in the presence of Dan'l. Perkins, Sam'l. McCutchen,
     Sam'l. Edmiston.
          The Execution of which Will and Testament as before recited

was duly proven in Open Court January Session 1810 by the oaths
of Daniel Perkins and Samuel Edmiston two of the subscribing
witnesses thereto to be the Act and Deed of Joseph Coles and the
same was ordered to be recorded and Thomas Cole the Executor therein named qualified as Executor thereto, and received Letters Testamentary.
Teste N. P. Hardeman, C. W. C.

EVAN MITCHELL'S Will - In the name of God Amen - I Evan Mitchell of the State of Tennessee and County of Williamson being
sick and infirm in body but of sound and perfect memory knowing
that it is apointed unto all men once to die, I do make and ordain this my last Will and Testament in maner as folows, first I
recomend my Soule ... who gave it me hoping that I shall receive
it again at the general resurrection, Second I recomend my bode
to be deceantly burried at the discration of my wife and friends
in Christian like maner and as fore my worldly goods whitch it hath
pleased God to blise me with, first I give and bequath unto my
loving wife Charity Mitchell after my lawful debts is all payed,
the use of a negro woman named Jeney with her increase, together
with all my stock and Household furniture during her widowhood and
if she should never marry during her natural life to be equally
devided between my daughter Elizabeth Benton and my sone Hamblen
Hares and my sone David Alen at my loving wife's death or marage,
by heiring out the afores'd. Janey with her increase, until my
youngest sone David Alen is twenty one years of age, L do apoint
my loving wife Charity Mitchel as Executrix of this my last Will
and Testament. In witness my hand and Seal this 16th day of August in the year of our Lord 1809.
Signed Evan Michell -- (Seal)
Teste:
James Allison, Wm. Ogilvie -
Which Will and Testament as before recited was duly proven in
open Court April Session 1810 by the oath of James Allison one of the
Subscribing witnesses thereto, to be the Act and Deed of Evan
Mitchell, and the same was ordered to be recorded and Charity
Mitchell the Executrix therein named qualified as Executrix there-
to and received Letters Testamentary.
Teste N. P. Hardeman, C. W. C.

JOHN T. PRIEST'S Will - In the name of God amen, I John T.
Priest of Williamson County and State of Tennessee being low and
weak in body but sound in mind and memory do make and constitute
this my last Will and Testament in manner and form following (viz),
first I resign my soul into the hands of Almighty God, who gave
it me, looking for redemption only through Jesus Christ the Savior
of the World.
Item I desire thal all my just debts be paid to effect which
I desire that my beloved wife Mary may sell my lott or lotts in
the town of Franklin and such other property as she may deem necessary in such manner as her judgment may direct. Item, I give and
bequaath to my beloved wife Mary all the residue of my Estate both
real and personal during her natural life or widowhood, either to
dispose of or keep together as she may deem expedient for the purpose of maintaining herself and my nine youngest children (viz.)
Jenney, James, John, Moses, Fanney, David, Elizabeth, Abram, and
Rhodey Love, and at the expiration of her life or widowhood, to be

equally divided between my above named children, the other two
Thomas and Mary Rivers being already provided for. I do hereby
constitute and appoint my beloved wife Mary Priest executrix of
this my last Will and Testament. In witness whereof I have hereunto set my hand and affixed my seal this first day of Novr.
1809.
              Signed John T. Priest   -- Seal
                    x his mark
Teste: Abram Maury
       Robert Davis
     The Execution of which Will and Testament as before recited
wad duly proven in open Court April Session 1810 by the Oaths of
Abram Maury and Robert Davis, the two Subcribing Witnessed thereto
to be the Act and Deed of John T. Priest and the same was ordered
to be recorded, and Mary Priest, the Executrix thereto, and received Letters Testamentary.
              Teste, N. P. Hardeman, C. W. C.

     JOSEPH COLE'S Inventory - State of Tennessee, Williamson
County. Inventory of the personal property of Joseph Cole, dec'd.
1810. Thomas Cole's legacies, 1 gray mare, 2 feather beds and
furniture, 3 trunks, 1 barshear plough, 1 shear and cotter, 1
pair of hames and 2 pair of traces, 2 axes, 1 Bell, 1 hammer, the
wearing apparel, legatee Elizabeth Cole, 1 negro boy Jack, 1 sorrel horse, legatee Samuel Cole, 1 gray mare by name Febey, legatee

Page (218)

John Cole, 1 mare colt, a parcel of corn, a small bulk of rye,
1 old saddle and bridle, 1 pair of pocket pistols, and moulds, ½
dozen silver tea spoons and tongs, 3 small glasses, 50 gallons
whisleu, 1 raser, 1 pair saddle bags, ½ dozen knives and forks,
cash came to hand $176.93¾, note of hand on John D. Garrett $20.85,
note of hand on Samuel Edmonston $6. Note of hand on Carr Allen
for $8. Balance of a note on Thomas Sappington for $50. Ephraim
Brown book account $5.81¼. Wm. Sneed book account $2.37½. Certificate for Jury allowance $2. Book account Samuel Edmonston $1.50.
     Signed Thomas Cole, Exs. Returned to April Session 1810.
N. P. Hardeman, C. W. C.
     1810 April 7th. A list of property sold by Thomas Cole, Exe-
cutrix of Joseph Cole, deceast -
     Thomas Cole 50 gallons whiskey at 40 cents $20., John McCute
chen 1 razor .40, Thomas Cole 1 pr. saddle bags .85, T. W. Stockett ½ dozen knives and forks $1.e, same 3 small glasses at 37½
cents $1., Thomas Cole ½ dozen silver tea spoons and tongs $3.75,
same 1 pr. pocket pistols and moulds $2.37½, Joseph Stockett 1
old bridle and saddle $2., Thomas Cole 1 Bulk of rye $8., Thomas
Cole 40 barrels corn at .62½ cents $20. Total $59.87½
     Returned to April Session 1810 by Thomas Cole, Exor.
N. P. Hardeman, C. W. C.

Page (219)

     The Estate of Joseph Cole Dr. to Thomas Cole, Exr. cr.
To allowance made Thomas Cole as Executor of the Estate of Jo-
seph Cole deceased ------------------- ----- $200
To Cash paid Bradford printer as pr. rect.   2.50
Cash paid Charles A. Burton as pr. rec't.   9.00
To funeral Expenses   3.00
To cash paid the clerk as pr. receipt   2.35

Total $216.85
Balance due the estate $117. Total $333.85.
     Contra Cr.
By cash $176.93¾, by the amount of Sales of sd. deceased $59.37½,
By one note on John D. Garrett $20.85, by Samuel Edmondson note
$6.00, by Carr Allen's note $8, by Balance of Thomas Sappington's
note $50., by an acc't. on John Duffield .50, by an acc't. on
Ephraim Brown $5.81¼, by an acc't. on William Sneed $2.37½, by
Clark's Sertificate on Juror allowance $2., by no account on
Samuel Edmondson $1.50. Total $333.85.
     The above notes not collected at this time. Also the above
accounts.
     The above Settlement was made by us agreeable to an order of
the County Court of Williamson to us directed from the April Session 1810. Given under our hand this 11th April 1810.
     Signed S. Green, John Crawford. Returned to April Session
1810. N. P. Hardeman, C. W. C.

age
220)   The remaining part of the contract between Jonathan Davis,
dec'd. and Simeon Hinds $35, 1 canoe $1.50 - Total $36.50.
     The above is a full Statement of all the effects of the
above named Jonathan Davis before this time unaccounted for.
          Signed Amos Davis. Returned to April Session
1810. N. P. Hardeman, C. W. C.

     Agreeable to an order of the Worshipful Court of Williamson
County to us directed, we met and took into consideration the sit-
uation and value as hereinafter expressed of the Estate of Samuel Clark, deceased, and report as followeth to wit - That being
informed by one of the Administrators of said Estate (William
Martin) that there are debts due by the Estate which are yet
unpaid, deem it therefore improper to proceed to a division at
this time agreeable to the instructions of said order to us directed, but are of opinion that the negroes belonging to said Estate
be hired out until said debts be fully discharged, the names,
ages, and the value we hereunto affix to wit: Matt about 35 yrs.
of age $425, Dick 25 yrs. of age $500, Frank 12 yrs. $325, Jude
20 Yrs. $325, Orra 18 yrs. $450, Milley 17 yrs. $400, Mary 13 Yrs.
$400, Allen 6 yrs. $200, Lewis 4 yrs. $160, Caroline 1 yr. $100.
     Given under our hands and Seals this thirteenth day of Feby.
1810.
     Signed William Christman,(Seal), John H. Crockett (Seal),
John Smith (Seal). Returned to April Session 1810. N.P.Hardeman,C.W.

age
221)   Agreeable to the opinion and instructions of the Commissioners
as above expressed, we the Administrators, proceeded to hire out
the negroes belonging to said Estate on the 24th Feby. until the
31st day of December next, for the following sums, to wit.:
     Walt for the sum of $40, Dick ditto $40, Frank ditto $20,
Orra ditto $40, Molly ditto $40, Mary ditto $31, Judd and her 3
children $10. Total $221. Given under our hands and Seals this
24th February 1810.
     Signed William Martin (Seal) and Sampson Sawyers (Seal)
Returned to April Session 1810. N. P. Hardeman, C. W. C.

     Account of Sales of the Estate of James CRAFTON, dec'd. made
on the 9th Day of Feby. 1810:

****

John Crafton 1 sorrel horse $15, ditto 1 waggon and hind gears
$50, ditto 1 Bedstead and furniture $16.66 2/3, ditto 1 bed and
furniture $15, one ditto ditto $8, ditto 1 chest $3.1 1 table
$2.50, one womans saddle $12, ditto 2 pewter basons and 3 plates
$3, ditto 2 dishes, 4 pewter plates, quantity knives and forks $4,
ditto 1 cotton wheel $2, 1 pr. cotton cards $1, ditto 1 pr. cotton cards .75, 1 Smoothing Iron .75, ditto 1 small trunk $1.50,
1 cotton wheel $2.50, ditto 1 pot $3, one tub and 3 pails $2, dit-
to 1 cow and calf $12, one ditto ditto $12, ditto 1 yearling $3.25
1 ditto ditto $3. Total $172.71 2/3.
     State of Tennessee, Williamson County, April Term 1810.
The within is a just and true amount of the Sale of the Estate of
James Crafton, deceased, sold by us on the 9th Day of Feby.1810,
amounting to $172.71 2/3 cents.
     Signed Daniel Wilkes, Admr. (Seal). Returned to April Session
1810. N. P. Hardeman, C. W. C.

     Inventory of the moveable Estate of William BERRY, deceased,
this the 23rd day of February 1810 by us which consists of the
following articles: 4 head of horses, 15 head of cattle, 1 negro
wench, 1 cutting knife and steel, 9 head of sheep, 1 Iron candle
stick, 12 head of hogs, 22 geese, 1 sett plow irons, 3 chain traces,
2 hoes, 1 log chain, clivises, double trees, 1 waggon, 2 axes,
12 chairs, 4 beds, 4 pots, 1 Table, 2 trunks, 2 wheels, 1 iron
crock, 1 pr. of tongs, 2 saddles, 6 wooden vessels, 2 pewter
dishes, 12 pewter plates, 2 pewter basons, 6 tin cups, 1 tin pan,
½ dozen spoons, ½ dozen knives and forks, 2 crocks, 1 pitcher,
sett tea cups and saucers, 1 looking glass, 1 clock reel, 1 loom
and gears, 1 smoothing iron, 1 Hackle.
     Signed James Miller and James Berry, Admrs.
     Returned to April Session 1810. N. P. Hardeman, C. W. C.

     MICHAEL KINNARD'S Inventory - 1 note of hand George Kinnard
$45, 1 note on Michael Kinnard $47.50, 1 note on John Kinnard
$46.50, 1 note on Lewis Stevens $15. 1 note on Nathaniel Kinnard
$45, 1 note on Anthony D. Kinnard $88, 1 note on James Thompson
$81.50, 1 ditto on James Jones $51, 1 ditto on William Mathews
$15.25, 1 ditto on George Laton $20.76, negro man and negro boy, 1
mare and colt, 1 cow and calf, and yearling, 8 shoats and pigs,
corn, quantity not known, mans saddle, clothes and trunk, handsaw
chissel and gouge.
     Returned to April Session 1810. N. P. Hardeman, C. W. C.

Page
(223)

     JOHN CHAMP'S Will - In the name of God amen I John Champ
being sick of body, but perfect in mind, do think proper to make
this my last Will and Testament, in such a manner as to do Justice
to myself and every just creditor I have - as to my body I consign
it to its Mother Earth, my Soul I commit to the benificent and
merciful God of Heaven and Earth in whom I trust - with regard to
mypproperty I would have it disposed of in the following manner
to wit, the Estate left me by my father to be sold and that together with what I already have oweing me I wish to have appropriated to the use of paying my just debts and should there be
any left, which I presume there will, I wish it to be added to the
mass of my estate after making the above appropriations, I would
have remain with my wife during her widowhood or until my youngest
child Artimitia shall arrive to full age in the event of her

Page
(224)

marriage I would have the whole of my Estate taken into the possession of the Exectuors of this my last Will and Testament to be by
them kept until the arrival to age of my aforesaid youngest child
Artimitia, except the household furniture, which I think is the produce of her own Industry and likewise the kitchen furniture provided she does not convert none of my present Estate into such
articles, but should she not marry, I would have the whole Estate
remain with her as aforesaid until the arrival to full age of our
youngest child, confidently hoping that she will have each child
tolerably well educated, and when the period of the aforesaid child's
age shall arrive, I wish an equal Distribution made of my Estate
among my wife and each child, so as that they shall severally have
an equaly proportion one with another, my Brothers Thomas and
Robert Champ, I wish to be the Executors of this my last will and
Testament and I do hereby nominate and appoint them for that purpose.
Teste: John Mayfield, John L. Fielder, Robert Olive.
                    Signed John Champ.
        Which foregoing recited Will and Testament was duly proven in
Open Court July Session 1810 by the Oaths of John Mayfield and John
L. Fielder, two of the Subscribing witnesses thereto to be the Act
and Deed of John Champ and the same was ordered to be Recorded.
                    N. P. Hardeman, C. W. C.
1810 Oct. Session Thomas Champ qualified as Executor to the above
Will.

Page
(225)

State of Tennessee, Williamson County - In pursuance of an order to
us directed from the Worshipful County Court of Williamson of April
Session 1810, we have proceeded to Diveide the Estate of Samuel
Clark, deceased, between his sd. widow and legatees agreeably to
law, and we do divide and distribute the same in the following
manner to wit - to the sd. widow Virginia (now the wife of Sampson
Sawyer) we allot a certain negro fellow named Dick, valued to five
hundred dollars and one other negro boy named Lewis valued to one
hundred and sixty dollars, making together three dollars more than
sd. widow's proportional part of sd. Estate which she is hereafter
to account for with those who are by law entitled to receive the same.
The before named two negroes, we have alloted to the sd. Widow
Virginia subject o an equitable and proportional part of such debts
as may hereafter come against the sd. Estate. The remainder of the
Estate we allot to those in equal proportion who are by law entitled
to the same. Given our hands this 9th day July 1810.
        Signed John H. Crockett, S. Green, Wm. Christmas, John Smith.
Returned to July Session 1810. N. P. Hardeman, C. C. W.

Page
(226)

        An Inventory of the property of JOSEPH ROBERTS, deceased -
July 7, 1810: 14 hoggs, 1 mare, 3 cows and calves, 2 yearlings,
2 feather beds and furniture, a full sett of cabinet makers tools, 1
pot, 1 Dutch oven and lid, 1 skillet and led, 3 bedsteads, ½ dozen
chairs, 1 table, 1 beauro, 1 cotton wheel, 1 flat iron, 1 cupboard,
9 plates, 1 sett of knives and forks, 2 large bowls, 2 pitchers,
1 large bottle and a quantity of plank not know how much, 1 grind-
stone, about 3 acres of ground of a Lean for one year after this,
1 axe, 5 stands of bees, 1 washing tub, water pail and looking glass.
        Returned to July Session 1810 by William Brown, Administrator.
                    N. P. Hardeman, C.W.C.

Memorandum of the Estate of Thomas G. Caldwell - 1 negro
boy about 17 years old named Peter, 1 receipt on Charles Polk
for two horses valued at L 80 to be paid in land on Elk River,
1 note on Lydal B. Estess for $60 eleven of sd. dollars is paid,
1 note on William German $62.20¼, which said German is insolvent,
2 beds and furniture, 1 trunk, 2 wheels, 1 real, 1 dozen plates,
Set cups and Saucers, 1 bason, 2 dishes, 2 glass tumblers, 1 glass
pitcher, 1 coffee pot, 1 tea pot and coffee mill, 10 knives and
forks, 2 barshare plows, 1 ax, 2 hoes, 1 iron wedge, saw, auger,
and drawing knife, 2 pots and hooks, 1 oven, 6 plates, 1 set of
spools, 2 smoothing irons, 2 pair drawing chains, and hames, 1
churn, 1 slate and some books, 2 bedsteads and cards, 5 chairs,
1 looking glass, 1 rasar, and strop, 1 mans saddle, 21 head of
cattle, 22 head hogs and some pigs.
    Signed Mary Caldwell. Returned to July Session 1810.
N. P. Hardeman, C. W. C.

Page
(227)

List of the vendue of WILLIAM BERRY'S Estate as Dec'd.:
    James McCutchan 1 log chain $4.25, David McCord 1 cutting
knife and reel $2.25, George Allen 1 large kettle $3.37½, Martha
Berry 1 pr. horse gears, 1 plow, 1 pr. of double trees and clivises and swingle tree $3.25, William Alexander 1 pr. hames,
1 chain, 1 back band $1.43¾, Martha Berry 1 falling axe $2.25,
Charles Adams 1 falling axe .62½, Martha Berry 2 hoes .25, William Johnson 2 house chairs .75, Martha Berry 4 house chairs $2.
Abram Summers 3 house chairs $2.25, James Miller 2 house chairs
$1.26, James Miller 1 house chair .65, Martha Berry 1 table $1.25,
Thomas Berry 1 Bedstead, bed and beding $11., William Beaty 1 bed
$7, 1 ditto $9, Martha Berry 1 trunk $1.25, James Berry 1 trunk
.75, Martha Berry 1 cotton wheel $1.56½, 1 flax do. $1.50, John
Eaton 1 reel .30, James Berry 1 iron crock $2.1¼, John Depriest
1 pr. fire tongs .50, James Berry 1 mans saddle $4.18¾, Martha
Berry 1 womans ditto $6., ditto 1 weaver's reel .50, Jesse Livesy
1 loom and geers $6., Alexander Johnson 1 iron candle stick .12½,
Amos Davis 1 smoothing iron $1, James Berry 1 flax hackle $3.4½
Valentine Allen ½ dozen pewter plates $2.76, John Clark 1 pewter
bason $1., James McCutchan 1 pewter dish $1.50, David Spain 1
pail .35, Adam Miller 1 small pail .27, Valentine Allen 1 small
pail .30, William Walls 1 pickling tub .75, William Hickman 1

Page
(228)

Jack Screw $2.75, John Brim 1 looking glass $1., Martha Berry
negro Fillis $175.6¼, William Banks 10½ wt. of feathers $4.,
James Andrew 10 head of sheep $14.62½, Henry Scales 2 bull year
old calves $3.25, John Bostick 1 black stear $2.55, Adam Miller
1 black heiffer $2.52½, John Clark 1 red and white heifer $4.,
John Bostick 1 white steer $3.50, ditto 1 brindle steer $3.50,
Valentine Allen 1 sorrel horse 4 yrs. old $45., ditto 1 bay mare
$73,, Edward McNeal 1 grey mare and colt $73.37½, Thomas Berry
1 waggon $33. April 30th 1810.
    Signed James Miller and James Berry, Admrs.
Returned to July Session 1810. N. P. Hardeman, C. W. C.

    List of the sale of William Alexander of the Estate of Wil-
liam Berry, deceased, viz: six head of cattle at $23.55½, March
30th 1810.
    Signed William Alexander. Returned to July Session
1810. N. P. Hardeman, C. W. C.

April 30th 1810, an Allowance for the Widow and children
for one year by William Wilson, Robert Donnalson , Abram Summers.
as follows 1250 wt. of bacon, at 12½ pr. pound $156.¼ - 127½ Bush-
els of corn at _____.

The above allowance paid in the following articles, viz.
of corn .33 1/3 per bushel, 40 bushels of wheat at .33 1/3 per
bushel, of bacon at .12 1/2 pr lb., 1 mare $40, 1 bed at $21, 2
cows at $18, 22 geese at $14, dresser furniture in part $6, three
pots at $8.12, hogs at $50 - Total $157.

We do certify that the above articles were valued to the widow for a years maintainance at the price annexed to them.
    Signed Robert Donaldson, Abraham Summers, W. Wilson.
    James Miller and James Berry, Admrs.
    Returned to July Session 1810. N. P. Hardeman, C. W. C.

An Inventory of the Estate of Evan Mitchell, dec'd. to wit:
1 negro girl named Jenny $400, 1 horse $56.66 2/3, 7 head of cattle $28, 2 beds and furniture $61.66 2/3, 1 chest and 2 trunks
$7.75, 1 pot and 1 oven $4.20, 4 basons, 2 dishes, 6 plates $4.66
1/3, 6 spoons and 6 knives and forks $1.55, 5 chairs wheel and cart
$5, 2 flat irons .75, 1 plow, 1 hoe, 2 axes $4.91 2/3, 1 handsaw
1 drawing knife $1, 1 hammer .40, 1 table and 2 bells $5.50, 1 pr.
iron traces $2.50, 2 sows and 10 shoats $6.68½. Total $586.44

We, the Subscribers, after being duly sworn have valued the
above Estate as above. Signed Richard Ogilvie, Kimbrough Ogilvie,
and Henry Bailey. Sworn to and subscribed before me this 7th day
of July 1810. James Allison, J. P. Returned to July Session 1810.
N. P. Hardeman, C. W. C.

Page
(230)

An Inventory of the Estate of JOHN PRIEST at his Decease of
which Mary Priest, the Executrix, has knowledge: 4 head of horses,
viz: 1 gelding and 3 mares, 9 head of cattle, viz.: 4 cows, 2
2-year olds and 3 yearlings, 44 head of hogs little and big,
2 beds, 4 blankets, 4 counterpanes, Sheets, 2 bedsteads, 1 table,
4 chairs, 1 flax wheel, 1 cotton wheel, 2 pails, 1 tub, 1 half
bushel, 1 churn, 4 barrels, 3 pots, 2 ovens, 1 frying pan, 1 sifter, 5 earthen plates, 4 pewter plates, 3 pewter dishes, 1 bason,
4 knives and forks, 2 bowls, 1 coffee pot, 1 tea pot, ½ dozen
cups and saucers, 2 bottles, 1 turner, 1 crewet, 1 wine glass,
1 table, ½ dozen tea spoons, 1 loom, 2 plows and geer, 3 hoes, 1
cart, 1 ladys saddle, 2 bridles, 2 axes, 2 bells, 1 pr. flat irons,
1 handsaw, 1 drawing knife, 1 smooth bored gun, 1 deed from Abram
Maury to John Priest dated ye 5th Novr. 1809 for two lotts in
Franklin No. 66 and No. 76 not recorded - one of thirty dollars
from Robert Bevill to John Priest due 7th Octo. 1809, Desperate
one of the above property that was sold one the 4th of May 1810
by Thomas Hulme to satisfy three Executions against John Priest
deceased, one at the instance of John Sample and Co., one at the
instance of Thomas Masterson the following - 2 beds, bedstead
and furniture, 1 table, 4 chairs, 3 pots, 2 ovens, 1 frying pan,
1 sifter, 5 earthen plates, 4 pewter plates, 3 pewter dishes, 1
bason, 4 knives and forks, 2 bowls, 1 coffee pot, 1 tea pot, ½ doz.
tea spoons, 2 ploughs, 1 geer, 3 hoes, 1 cart, 1 ladies saddle and
2 bridles, 1 red and white cow, red and white ditto with white face,
1 brindle cow with white face, 1 black cow with white shoulders
and face, 2 two-year olds and 3 yearlings, making the nine stated

ge
(31)

in the Inventory, also 1 grey mare and 1 sorrel horse, 5 sows, 2
barrows and 13 pigs, 4 chairs, 2 pails, 1 tub, 1 flax wheel, 1
cotton wheel, 1 half bushel, 1 churn, 8 barrels.
                    Signed Mary Priest
                         x her mark
Returned to July Session 1810. N. P. Hardeman, C. W. C.

        In pursuance of an Order of Williamson County Court April
Session 1810 to us directed we have measured the lines of the Land
deeded to John Patton, deceased, out of a grant Number 43 that was
formerly granted to William Collingsworth for 640 acres and find
that there was deeded to sd. John Patton three hundred and sixty
seven acres and thirty four poles. And that said John Patton had
deeded to James Wilson 48 acres and 150 poles of that land and the
balance according to the direction of sd. Court we have divided
among the heirs and distributees of sd. John Patton in the following manner to wit - Sally Patton one hundred and six acres, as

age
(232)

her dower, beginning at a small dogwood and dead mulberry near the
east end of the mill dam and a little north of sd. dam, thence west
twenty two poles crossing little Harpeth below the Mill House and
crossing a Spring Branch to a sugar tree in all 88 poles, thence
south 29 poles to a stone, between two spring branches thence west
68 poles to a stump and stake between the Franklin road and Beesley's
fence, thence south 3 degrees east 93 poles to a small hickory near
Crockett's field thence east 164 poles to two haw bushes on James
Wilson line thence north his line 35 poles to a sugar tree, Wilson's
corner, thence north 10 degrees west to the beginning - No. 1 Hannah Patton twenty one acres forty seven poles, begins at an ash
southwest corner of the original survey, thence north three degrees west 45 poles to a small hickory corner to the Dower thence
east 78 poles to a box elder thence south 42½ poles to a poppaw,
thence west to the beginning No. 2 John Patton twenty-two acres
twenty seven poles begins at a box elder corner to Hannah Patton's,
thence east 86 poles to two haw bushes on James Wilson's line,
thence south with sd. Wilsons line 40½ poles to a horn beam Wilson's corner, thence west 86 poles to a poppaw south east corner
to Hannah P atton, thence north 42 poles to the beginning - No.
3 John Cunningham and Polley his wife nineteen acres and one
hundred and fifty-two poles begins at a sugar tree Wilson's Corner,
thence north ten degrees west 66½ poles to a mulberry near the mill
pond thence East 52 poles to an Iron Wood near Wilson's fence,
thence south 66½poles to a white oak, thence west 44 poles to the
beginning no. 4, Drucilla Stainback formerly Drucilla Patton, twenty four acres fifty one poles, begins at a walnut near a large artificial mount, thence north 29 poles to a small horn beam one the
west bank of Little Harpeth thence east 103½ poles to a hickory
and a small sugar tree on Wilson's line, thence south with his line
47 poles to an iron wood Cunningham's Corner on Wilson's west boundary line, thence west 52 poles to a mulberry near the pond, thence
north 10 degrees West 18 poles to a dogwood and dead mulberry. Beginning corner to the Dower, thence west 43 poles to the beginning,
No. 5. Betsy Patton twenty acres and twenty poles. Begins at an
ash ten poles east of Little Harpeth, thence East 92 poles to a small
sugar tree and hickory on James Wilson's line being a stake, thence
west 92 poles to a road, thence south 35 poles to the Beginning. No.
6-Thomas Patton twenty acres and twenty poles begins at a red oak

on Crockett's line thence south 35 poles to a stake Betsy Patton's corner, thence west 92 poles to a small elm on the side
of the road, thence north 35 poles to a stake on Crockett's
line, thence east 92 poles to the beginning - No. 7 Nancy Bass
formerly Nancy Patton twenty-five acres fifty-six poles. Begins
at a walnut near a large artificial mount on the west side of
Little Harpeth thence north with Drucilla Stainback line 29 poles
to a small horn beam on the bank of Little Harpeth thence east ten
poles to an ash Betsy Patton's corner, thence north 70 poles to a
stake on Crockett's line, Thomas Patton's corner, thence west with
Crockett's line 44 poles to a sugar tree, thence south crossing
Little Harpeth in all 99 poles to a stake, thence east to the beginning - No. 8. James Patton nineteen acres, one hundred and twenty-two poles. Begins at a sugar tree, runs east 6 poles to a stone
Nancy Bass' corner, thence north 14 poles to a horn beam, thence
west 77 poles to an ash on the side of a path being George Patton's
corner on Crockett's line, thence south three degrees east 43 poles
to a stake and stump on the side of the road being the north west
corner of the Dower right, thence east 68 poles to a Stone between
two Spring branches, thence north to the Beginning. No. 9, George
Patton nineteen acres and one hundred poles begins at a small horn
beam being north east corner to James Patton runs west 77 poles to
an ash his other corner, thence north 40 poles to a Sugar tree,
William Patton's corner, thence east with his line 80 poles to a
White Oak on Nancy Bass' line, thence south 40 poles to the beginning. No. 10. William Patton twenty acres and eighty poles. Begins at a white oak on Nancy Bass' line, George Patton's corner,
thence west eighty poles to a Sugar tree on Cockrell's line, thence
north 3 degrees west 41 poles to a poplar, Beginning corner to the
original Survey on Crockett's line, thence east 80 poles to a Sugar
tree, thence south 40 poles to Beginning. Given from under our
hands and Seals this 10th Day of July 1810.
        Signed J. Bruff, (Seal)
            John Holt (Seal)
            James Bradley (Seal)
            Samuel Wilson (Seal)
            James Davis (Seal)   Com'rs. and Surveyors.
Returned to July Session 1810. N. P. Hardeman, C. W. C.

(Page 234)

(Page 235)

        An Inventory of the Goods and Chattels rights and Credits of
JOHN CHAMP, deceased, to wit - 4 negroes to wit, Ailse, Nance,
George, and London, 2 mares and one colt, 2 cows and calf, one
yearling, 39 head of hogs, 2 beds and furniture, 3 bedsteads, 1
single tree, 5 chairs, 1 soop spoon, 1 cotton wheel, 2 linnen
wheels and check real, 1 Dutch oven, 2 pots, 1 kettle, 3 poles, 2
churns, 1 cooler, 1 stone jug, 3 bottles, 1 pickling pot, 2 cow
bells, 2 pair stirrup irons, 1 pr. steelgards, 1 pr. Taylor's
shears, 4 books, 1 chest and table, 4 weaver's slays, 2 pr. geer,
1 washing tub, 2 pot racks, 2 pr. pot hooks, 1 plow collar, hames
and chains, 1 clivis and twisted link, 1 axe and hoe, 12 pewter
plates, 2 dishes, 1 bason, 4 tin cups, 12 spoons, case knives and
forks, tea pot, and salt sellers, 1 pr. cotton cards, 1 smoothing
irons, 2 bridles, and a side saddle, 1 loom, 1 pr. Samples and
3 shuttles, 8 Drakes, 2 Ducks, 2 ganders, 1 basket, 1 oil stone,
1 case rasors and shaving box, 2 gimblets, 1 screw auger, a quantity
of old iron, 3 notes on John Mayfield, one for $150 each payable

the first day of March 1812, one note on Tolliver Brady $15,
payable August 1809, one note on John L. Fielder for $20.
    Signed Thomas Champ.
    Returned to October Session 1810. N. P. Hardeman, C.W.C.

An account of the Sales of the Estate of WILLIAM HUNNELL, dec'd.
Sold on the 20th Novr., 1809 -
    Robert Caniday 1 side leather $1.25, Benjamin Brown 1 ditto
$1.12½, Peter Honoll 1 ditto $1.12, Robert Caniday 1 ditto $1.00,
Peter Honoll 1 ditto $1.50, Hugh Allison 1 ditto $1.21½, Andrew
McMahon $3.15, some brick bands $1., Richard Hart 1 set of cooper's tools $4.82½, Peter Honoll handsaw and compasses $4., Joseph
Dewey double traces and irons $3.40, Elisha Williams 40 pounds iron
$6.75, Samuel Williams 6 hogs $8.12½, Benjamin Brown 17 head of
hogs $22.50, James Prichett 9 head of hogs $12, Ambros Cobb 18
head of hogs $26.75, John Jones 9 head of hogs $9.10, Isiah
Davey 10 barrels of corn $7.35, Henry Inman 10 barrels of corn
$7.12½, Andrew Mahan 10 barrels corn $7.51½. Total $134.80½.
    An account of Sales of the Estate of William Hunnell, de-
ceased. Sold 30th Decr. 1809: Robert Canaday 3 hogs $6.12½, Robt.
Shannon 12 shotes $8.25, John Reeves 1 hog $3.25, William Cenney
1 hog $3.25, Andrew McMahon 1 hog $3.40, James Cenney 1 hog $3.15,
Robert Shannon 2 hogs $3., Jered Puckett 2 horses $36 and $40,
David Witherspoon 1 filley $47., Peter Honall 1 mare $32., Hugh
Allison 1 mare $23. Total $208.42.
    Given under our hands this 8th day of Octr. 1810.
    Signed Peter Honoll and Hugh Allison. Returned to October
Session 1810. N. P. Hardeman, C. W. C.

Page
(237)
An Inventory of the Estate of JAMES MCCUTCHAN, deceased -
2 head of horses, 8 head of cattle, 3 feather beds and furniture,
1 walnut chest, 1 table, 7 pewter plates, 1 pewter dish, 1 pewter bason, 1 tin pan, 4 tin cups, 3 earthen plates, 1 tea pot,
4 tea cups and 3 saucers, 4 bowls, 1 pitcher, 1 coffee pot, 2
bottles, 4 forks, 5 knives, one cotton wheel, 1 linnen wheel, 1
pr. of cotton and 1 pr. of wool cards, 7 chairs, 2 bedsteads, 1
iron kettle and lid, 1 Dutch oven and lid, 1 iron pot, 1 iron pot
rack, 1 iron chain to hang a pot on, 1 smoothing iron, 1 mans
saddle, 1 womans saddle, 1 reap hook, 1 claw hammer, 1 pr. pinchers, 2 shoe brushes, 1 looking glass, 2 barrels, 1 pr. of rope
traces, 2 shuck collars, 1 barshare plow, 1 small Bible, 1 Dictionary, with 7 other books on Different Subjects, 3 water pails,
1 coffee mill, 1 bar of iron, 1 small box, 1 axe, 2 weeding hoes,
1 mattock, 3 horse bells, 1 candle stick, 2 bridles, ½ dozen tea
spoons, 1 pr. double trees, 2 clivises, 34 head of hogs, 1 half
of the crop of corn and cotton growing on the plantation, 1 iron
wedge, 7 geese, 1 note on Jonathan Hopkins for $100, one note on
Robert Hulme for $10. One note on Robert Clayton for $7 returned
by me the Administratrix.
    Signed Hannah McCutchan. Returned to October Session 1810.
N. P. Hardeman, C. W. C.
    A Sypplemental Inventory of the Estate of Ephraim Andrews
deceased: 1 cupboard, 1 negro named Jerry, 1 negro named Milley,
6 delf bowls, 6 delf plates, 1 case bottles, 1 bond, on Benjamin
Bugg of $63 due, 1 note on Knacy Andrews of $100 due 26th July
1809, 1 note on Richard Locke $25, credit with $11. Returned to
January Session 1811. N. P. Hardeman, C. W. C.

ge
(38)   A List of the Sale of the Estate of James McCutchan: Cupboard and crockery ware $2.50, (to Hannah McCutchan), Thomas L. Robertson 1 feather bed $14.50, Hannah McCutchan 1 feather bed and furniture $12, Hannah McCutchan 1 small feather bed and furniture $5, William Sargent 1 walnut chest $4.50, John Porter 1 Dictionary $4.67, Hannah McCutchan 3 books $1.66, Thomas L. Robertson 1 book history of the United States $1.6¼, David Pinkerton 1 book Webster on Book-keeping,.50, John McCutchan 2 books $1.50, Hannah McCutchan 1 Bell .25,, Hannah McCutchan 1 hammer and pr. of pinchers .75, Elisha Reynolds 1 coffee mill $1.12½, John McAffee 1 pr. of shoe brushes .20, John McAffee 2 bells, 2 rings, chain and bridle bitt $1, John Porter 1 Sickle .50, John L. Fielder 1 iron wedge .93¾, John Porter 1 mattock $1.6¼, Elisha Reynolds 1 Bar of Iron $3, William McCutchan 1 mans saddle $8, Hannah McCutchan 1 ladies saddle $1, Hannah McCutchan 1 tubb and 2 piggins .25, Neal Hopkins 1 iron pot .25, Hannah McCutchan 2 iron kettles $1, Hannah McCutchan 1 small barrel .6¼, Elisha Reynolds 1 cotton wheel and pair cords $1.75, Hannah McCutchan 1 poll axe $1, Hannah McCutchan 1 linnen wheel and pr. of cards $2, ditto 3 sitting chairs and 2 small ditto $1, ditto 2 chairs .6¼, ditto 1 sorrel horse $10, Jason Hopkins 1 sorrel horse $42, Hannah McCutchan 1 red cow and calf and heifer $4, Winifred Hopkins white back heifer $4.50, Hannah McCutchan 34 head of hoggs $8.52, ditto ½ crop of corn $1, ditto ditto $2.56¼, William McCutchan 1 rasar and shaving box .37½, Hannah McCutchan 1 plow .50, Neal Hopkins 2 clivises 2 rigs, 1 shuck collar and rope traces .12½, John McAffee 1 pr. of Double trees and shuck collar .50, Neal Hopkins 1 looking glass .6¼, Hannah McCutchan 1 small box .6¼, Hannah McCutchan 2 weeding
age
239) hoes .50, ditto i ron pot rack .75, Robert Hulme 1 cow and calf $12, Jason Hopkins 1 heifer $4.12½, Hannah McCutchan 6 geese $1. Total $165.9¾.

      I do certify the above to be a true return of the Sale of the Estate of James McCutchan, deceased -

                Hannah McCutchan, administratrix of
James McCutchan, dec'd. Returned to January Session 1811.
        N. P. Hardeman, C. W. C.

      An Inventory of the Goods and Chattels-rights and Credits of Thomas HOPE, deceased, that have come to the hands of Thomas Berry, his Administrator - A note upon William Perry for $50, ditto William Hemphill and David P. Anderson for $16, ditto Edley Ewing for $50, ditto John Clark and Basil Berry for $50. ditto Edley Ewing for $50, ditto William Perry for $10, ditto William Berry for $52, ditto Daniel Perkins, balance due thereon for $26. 32 cents, ditto on David P. Anderson for $8.50, ditto William Sargent for $50, ditto Edley Ewing for $50, ditto John Prewitt and Edley Ewing balance due for $19, ditto on Basil Berry for $60, ditto on David P. Anderson balance due thereon for $7.50, ditto John Harvey for $5, 1 feather bed and furniture, 1 horse saddle and bridle, 1 cow and calf, 1 yearling, 1 Dutch oven, a few articles of wearing apparel, 80 bushels of corn, 33 yds of cloth, 2 pewter dishes, 3 pewter basons, 6 pewter plates, 10 dollars lent to widow Hope, $4 lent to Mary Ann Taylor, 1 small skillet.
      Signed Thomas Berry. Returned to January Session 1811.
        N. P. Hardeman, C. W. C.

ge
40)

          Agreeable to a Commission to us directed from the Worshipful
Court of Williamson County, Tennessee, to settle the accoumpt
current of the Estate of John Pryor, deceased, with Hendley Stone,
Administrator in right of his wife Elizabeth, Administratrix, of
the Estate of the said Deceased and as guardian for Peter Pryor and
Green Pryor, orphans of the said John, Dec'd., we have assembled
ourselves together this 29th day of December 1810 and report as
follows (viz.) L.S.D.
          The Estate of John Pryor, deceased, in accoumpt current with
Hendley Stone Dr. - 1799 Jany. 15th To balance due as pr. Record
from Pittsylvania Court, Virginia, settled January 15th 1799
£1.18.11$\frac{3}{4}$,
          1799 Jany. 29th To Cash paid John Brown pro. Acct.£3.11.4$\frac{1}{2}$
1807 May 12th. To cash paid Col. Peter Perkins as pr. award
of Artubrators debt. damages £150.
          To Expence and trouble of settling said Estate as Administra-
trix- Total £223.0.4$\frac{1}{2}$. Deduct 1/3 of which is 74.6.9. Balance
due Mr. Stone £148.13.5$\frac{1}{2}$
          Peter Pryor and Green Pryor orphans of John Pryor, dec'd.
Dr. To Hendley Stone, guardian, to said orphans. L.S.D.
          January 1804 To boarding cloathing, schooling, books, paper,
and other expenditures from the year 1804 up to the present date
as pr. vouchers rendered amounting to £326.13.6.
          Allowance made for Guardianship £86.16.9.
          Up to the present date   £413.10.3
Cr. By balance from Virginia as pr. Record £2.8.3
          By hire of sundry negroes and rent of lands Pittsylvania,
Virginia from December 1803 up to the present date as pr. vouchers
rendered amounting to £417.2.3 and £413.10.3. Balance due the orphans £3.12.0. Given from under our hands this the day and date
above written. Signed N. Perkins and S. Childress.
          Returned to   Dan'l. Perkins and Edw'd. Warren.
January Session 1811. N. P. Hardeman, Clk.

          A List of Property sold by THOMAS CHAMPS, Executor, of
John Champ, deceased, of Williamson County on the 30th of October 1810, to wit: Andrew Baldridge 1 loom $3.25, John Mayfield
1 bedstead .56$\frac{1}{4}$, Christian Hughes 2 ganders and 10 Ducks $1.75,
Andrew Baldridge 1 plow and gears 3.12\frac{1}{2}$, Robert Baldridge by his
wife 1 iron oven 3.78\frac{3}{4}$, Dr. John White 1 axe 2.6\frac{1}{4}$, James Moore
1 hoe .75, Frederick Owen 1 pot $1.50, ditto 1 tub and piggin .75,
James Walker 2 pails .90, Mary Champ 1 pot and hooks .25, Mary
Champ 2 bells .56$\frac{1}{4}$, Robert Henderson 1 churn .56$\frac{1}{4}$, James Walker
1 keeler and some iron .90, James Moore 2 slays, harness and shut-
tle $2, Christian Hughes 2 slays $1.25, Joel Riggs 12 hogs $25.75,
ditto 8 hogs in the woods $10.25, Mary Champ 1 sorrel mare and
sorrel colt in the range on Duck River $16, Nelson Fields 1 grey
mare $32, John Mayfield 1 old cow and yearling $7.50, Christian
Hughes 1 long wheel 1.62\frac{1}{2}$, Joel Riggs 1 pot rack 2.6\frac{1}{4}$, James
Moore 1 basket .6$\frac{1}{4}$, Peter Reaves 1 chain .25, John Campbell 1
jug, $1.25, Mary Champ 1 Bible .31$\frac{1}{4}$, G. Hunt 1 book .37$\frac{1}{2}$, James
Walker 1 case of razors $1.85, Richard Hightower 1 pair Shares
.75, John Hill 1 reel $1.25, Mary Champ 1 bottle .12$\frac{1}{2}$, Robert
Baldridge 1 bottle and jarr .44, Frederick Owen 1 bason and 5
plates $2, James Moore 1 pair steelgards $2.50, Frederick Owen
1 chest $2.50, Mary Champ some old pewter $3.50, Frederick Owan
1 bedstead $2, G. Hunt 2 reaping hooks .64, Frederick Owen 1 bed-

stead $2, G. Hunt 2 reaping hooks .64, Frederick Owen Senr. 1
 Bedstead .80, Peter Reaves 1 drawing chain and collar $2.75,
Nimrod Williams 1 inch auger .50, John McCalpan 4 chairs $1.56¼,
John L. Fielder 1 table .41¾, Frederick Owen 1 saddle womans
$7, Mary Champ 2 beds and furniture $23, James Walker 1 cow and
calf $8, Nath'l. Herbert 13 hogs $11, Peter Reaves 1 cradle and
tea pot $2.25. Total $198.9¾.

NB-4 hogs returned in the Inventory was made use of by the
family of John Champ, deceased, which were not sold.

I certify the within is a true copy of the list of the property of John Champ, deceased, sold by me.

Signed Thomas Champ, Exor. Returned to January Session 1811.
N. P. Hardeman, C. W. C.

The Administratrix of the Estate of JOHN PAGE, dec'd. Dr.
To the amount of Sales as per certificate of the clerk $1151.67¼

242

310.64

Balance due the Estate on a Settlement with
the Court $841.3¼

CR - By sundry receipts as follows to wit:
By receipt No. 1 $55.35½, by ditto 2 .75, by voucher 3 $50.21,
by ditto 4 $1.87½, by ditto 5 $2, by ditto 6 $7.36¼, by ditto 7
$2, by ditto 8 $34.48½, by ditto 9 $3.18¾, by ditto 10 $5.64,
by ditto 11 $5.98, by ditto 12 $40.11, by ditto 13 $12.20, by
ditto 14 $7.30, by ditto 15 $7.1¼, by ditto 16 $1, by ditto 17
$26.6¼, by ditto 18 $8.25, by ditto 19 .60, by ditto 20 $33.34,
by ditto 21 .50, by ditto 22 $5.40. Total $310.64.

The above Settlement was made in consequence of an order
to us directed from the worshipful Court of Williamson October
Session 1810. Given under our hands this 14th January 1811.
                     S. Green
                     Nicholas Scales

ge
43)

Balance due the Estate of JOHN PAGE, deceased, as will appear by the within Settlement -$841.3¼.

To an allowance made the Administratrix of John Page, dec'd.
for her services   ------   41.0¾

To an allowance made the same for the maintainance of four
small children for two years ---100

Balance due the Estate --- 700.

The above Settlement was made in consequence of an additional
commission to us directed from the January Session 1811. Given
under our hands this 19th January 1811.
                Signed S. Green
                  James Black.
Returned to January Session 1811. N. P. Hardeman, C. W. C.

Dr. William Parham, Guardian. In account with the Orphans
of William C. Hill, deceased - 1811 Jany 1st to John Warren for
the hire of a negro in a broom field pr. note for the year 1810
$40, To Talbott and Reed for the hire of a negro man Isham pr.
note 1810 $84, to Potts, etc, for the hire of negro man Toby
pr. note 1810 $60, to Jacob Harder note for the hire of negro man
Lewis pr. note 1810 $65, To Sion Record and John Wilkins for hire
of negro boy Jerry per note for 1810 $35, to the hire of Easter and
her children pr. self 1810 $30, to the hire of Phil a negro boy pr.
self $25. Total $339

CR

By Cash paid Edwd. Harrison for boarding and schooling James C.
and Henry W. Hill pr. rect. No. 1 $102.66 2/3, ditto paid D.
Caldwell for Martha, James C. and H. W. Hill per rect. $2.29 1/3
ditto Nichol and McAlester for J. C. and H. W. Hill pr. rec't.
No. 4 $13.12 1/3, ditto Henry Hill pr. rec't. No. 5 $11.12 1/3,
ditto James C. Hill pr. rec't. No. 5 $12.25, ditto Martha Hill
pr. rec't. No. 6 $13.75, ditto ditto pr. rec't. No. 7 $7.50, ditto
ditto No. 8 $3.6 1/3, ditto To boarding Martha Hill for the year
$35.

'age
244)

To cash paid John Branch for a chest for Martha Hill pr. rec't.
no. 9 $4.50, ditto paid Wilson King and Mitchell per rec't. no.
10 $3.75, ditto for making returns as per rect. no. 12 .62 1/3.
    Balance due the orphans of William C. Hill, deceased $127.84
Returned to January Session 1811. N. P. Hardeman, C. W. C.

    THOMAS SIMMONS' Will - In the name of God amen I Thomas
Simmons of Caswell County and State of North Carolina knowing the
certainty of Death and being very weak in body but having my
perfect sense and reason do make this my last will and Testament
as touching such worldly estate as it hath pleased God to bless me
with, I dispose of the same as follows: Item to my dear wife Priscilla my plantation with one hundred and fifty seven acres of land
the plantation tools, one third of the stock, one third part of
the household further also five negroes to wit Phillis, Fanney,
Tom, Rachel, and Isbell, her, my dear wife, to have and to hold
her lifetime and at her death the negroes to be praised and equally
divided among all my children that is to say Martha and Priscilla
to have their part paid them in money by the other Legatees who
has the negroes - Item, I leave old Lucy, Milley, Dilcey, Young
Lucy and Reuben at my death to be valued and equally divided among
Hannah Graves, Martha, Priscilla, Keziah, Sarah and Thomas, and
for Martha and Priscilla to have their parts paid them in money
by the other legatees. Item. I leave my son Alexancer one hundred and
seventy acres of land lying in the northeast corner of my Survey
including a spring and part of the cleared land, one negro boy
named Aaron, one feather bed and furniture, one mare named little
bay Pol, one cow and calf, and two chairs, saddle and bridle to
be kept in the possession of my wife during her life in case she
should not marry and at her death the boy hired and the land
rented for his support, and if he die without heir, the land to
return, to his brother Thomas and the rent of his Estate to be
equally amongst all his sisters and brothers. Item, I give to my
son Thomas one hundred and fifty seven acres of land with the
plantation and after the death of my wife in case he should want
I give him liberty to settle and clear not interrupting his mother
her lifetime, also one negroe boy named Sam, one feather bed and
furniture, one cow and calf, two chairs, to him and his heirs forever and I do hereby revoke disannul and make void all other wills,
heretofore made by me and pronounce this to be my last Will and
Testament, I appoint Thomas Graves and my son Thomas Simmons the
Executors of this my last Will and Testament. In witness whereof
I have hereunto set my hand and Seal this 5th day of October 1794.
                          Thomas Simmons (Seal)
Teste, Charles Taylor and Butler Murphey.
    October Court 1794. This Will was proved by Charles Taylor
and Butler Murphey and ordered to be recorded.

Page
(245)

A true copy. Teste Ad. Murphey C. C. Teste Alex Murphey, D. C.
Which copy as before recited was presented in open court April
Session 1811 by Thomas Simmons one of the Executors therein named
and ordered to be recorded.
          Teste N. P. Hardeman, C. W. C.

Page
(246)   An Inventory of the Estate of THOMAS SIMMONS, deceased, which
was by his Will loaned to his son Alexander during his life, then
by his Will to be divided between all the children of said Thomas,
dec'd., taken by me the Executor of said Thomas this 11th of April
1811: 1 negro man named Aaron, 1 woman named Philis, 1 boy named
Charles, 1 ditto named Reuben, 1 negro boy named Lee, 1 ditto named
Stephen, 1 feather bed, blanket, and pillar, 1 axe, 1 tin trumpet.
          Signed Thomas Simmons, Executor of the last Will and Testament
of Thomas Simmons deceased. Sworn to in open Court, April Session
1811. N.P. Hardeman, C. W. C.

          An Account of Sales of the Estate of EPHRAIM ANDREWS. dec'd.
Sold the 21st, 22nd, 24th and 25th day Jan'y. 1811. As returned by
Knacy Andrews and Benjamin Bugg, the Executors, at April Session
1811: Knacy Andrews a shovel and pr. tongs $2.75, pr. flat irons
$2.25, 1 froe .50, 1 jug .50, 1 cloth brush .25, funnel .25, 1
old negro fellow Will .25, 1 halter chain $2, 1 negro Dolly and two
children, Dolly and Jerry, mulato boy John $337, 1 kettle $3, pr.
steelgards $5.12½, 2 chamber pots .75, 1 scythe $3.50, 1 keg of
tobacco $3.25, 1 rundlet and vinegar $1, bag of snapshot 12½, 2
books $1.25, pr. cotton cards $2, goard of sugar $1.79, 1 stone
pot $2.25, 1 table cloth and 2 towels $1.50, 6½ yds. linen $3,
bag of spun cotton $4.80, case and bottles $3, bed and furniture
$62.25, Bedstead and undertick $3, 1 cow $10, parcel of weaving
geer and slay $1, Slay and geer $2.35, 1 do. $2, basket .26, Bar'l.
and meal .30, 1 pr. of turkeys, $1, lot 1 plank .12½, 1 hill of
potatoes .50, queensware $1.30, 3 pr. of cards $1.56, phial .7,
1 coffee pot 1 cent, 6½ yards mix't. cloth $3.62½, 1 negro girl
Lucy $259. Total $1386.9
          James Allison 2 pr. sheep shears .81¼, Loamie Stephens 2 pr.
sheep shears .85, 2 bridles $1, pr. fire dogs $2.31¼, 1 plow $5.76,
pr. of geers $2.50, 1 washing tub $1.1, 1 cow $8.50. Total $21.73¼
          Joel Stephens 1/5 chain $1.50, 1 do. $1.75, 2 bags do. $1.30.
          William Glover 1 tongue chain and 2 breast do $1.6¼, 1 old
sorrel horse $18.50, old mare $51.25, 1 bay horse $72.75. 10 bushel
wheat 1st choice $5.6¼, 1 potato hill $1.1, a quantity of cotton
$9.12½, to amount brought from John Baker's Acc't. $7.75. Total
$166.51.
          John Ogilvie 4 augers and 1 chizzel $1.75, 1 skillet $1.75,
David Pinkston 1 broad axe $3.25, old pewter $1.63, bowl and pitcher .56½, delf ware and tea spoons .50, 10 yds. of baging $2.80,
total $8.74¼.
          John Robinson 1 axe $1.75, 1 bramble saw $2.75, 1 bag of
Page   cotton .28, 1 pr. of turkeys $1.
(247)   Thomas Wilson 1 old axe .37½, tin bucket and old drawing
knife and 2 clivises and pins .50, Peter Pinkston 1 candle stick
.43¾, 1 flour tub $1.76, bag of fruit .50, peas and beans .18¾,
white sugar .37½, spun cotton $5.6¾, 1 bag, 41 pr. of bagging
$1.43¾, 2 yds. of do. $1.18¾, 11½ yds of wadling cloth $4.25,
spun cotton .83¾ - total $16.44½

Thomas Allison 1 poll axe $1.75, George H. Allen 1 jointer and
iron .25, 1 grindstone $2.87½, William Young 1 box of old lumber
$1.62½, brindle cow $8.2, 10 yds. shirting $4.18¾, Alexander
Bennet 6 plates $4.62½, 1 bottle .83, 1 bottle of camphire .50,
8 yards cloth $4.

John Ewin 1 negro girl Size $422, Thomas Bradley 1 negro
woman Amey and boy child Bob $572, Cornelius Mathews 1 negro
fellow Dick $531, William A. Price 1 kettle $7, the 5th lot of
corn 8 Bar'ls $9, Ephraim Andrews 1 bason and dish molds and 1
ladle $61, 1 negro fellow Abraham $575, 1 negro woman and 2 children Susan, Will, and Milly $715, 2 old negroes Jeffrey and Jenney
$10, 1 kettle $6, 1 piggin .37½, tub and rye $2, cart and stears
$60, 2 hogs 5th choice of fat $4, 2 hogs 6th choice $4.25, 2 do.
7 do. $4, 2 do. 8th do. $3.50, 1 young sorrel horse $60, one
filley $60, 1 cow and calf $10.62 1/3, one do. $8.1, S. Wheel
$3.37½, 1 gin .70, one basket and cotton $2, 1 do. of flax $1,
pr. wts. and scales $1.1, one Bull $14, one loom $8, 1st choice
of 10 hogs unfat $22, 2nd do. 10th do. $12, 3rd choice of hogs,
10th do. $6.50, 200 lb. cotton $5.50, 29 ducks $2, Whiskey Bar-
rel $1, 3 turkeys $1.50, 1 sive .25. Total $1682.58½.

Clement Walls 1 pot and hooks $3, Will Stevens 1 Dutch oven
$2.12½, 1 meal tub .50, 1 washing tub .54, 1 churn .80, 1 barrel
.12½, 1 tub .25, 2 chairs $1.50, 2 do. $2, 2 do. $1.50. Total $9.34

Page
(248)
Benjamin Bugg 1 handsaw $1.75, 1 howel .50, 1 log chain
$2.6¼, 4 sickles $2.6¼, 3 gimblets .43¾, 1 axe $1.6¼, spoon
molds $7.50, pr. old hoops $1.25, 1 crop $4.50, negro Jacob
$418, negro Worick $589, negro woman and 2 children Dorcas,
Rachel, and Dilcy $620, negro boy Starting $440, candle molds
.59 pot and hooks $1.75, 1 bramble saw and files $13.25, 2 hoes
$2.12½, 1 scythe $1, 2 first choice of fat hogs $14, peas and
beans .37½, old lumber .50, 2 chairs $1.1-cotton wheel $2.61,
1 pot rack $3.50, 1 bread tray .25, 1 tub and old iron .62½,
small trick .50, basket of cotton $1.37½, 1 do .27, 1 dish $3.1-
ald $2, 2 books $1, box of knives and forks $2, 1 do. $3.62½,
spice mortar $1.30 4 bowls $1.12¼, tea cups .75, mug .12½,
3 tumblers .76, crockery ware .20, goard of sugar $1.29, 3 table
cloths $1.60, 1 table cloth and 2 towels .50, 1 chest $4 1 trunk
$5.62½, 1 bag .50, 1 chest $7.52, 1 bed, bedstead and furniture
$1, bed and furniture $61, one bedstead $2.10, cupboard $30,
10 yards bagging $2.90, old sadale .31, tea kettle $3.37½,
bag and 14 bushels of wheat $7.37½, 1 topstack $1.30, 2 riddles
.25, 1 wire sive $1.50, set of lancets .25, 2 turkeys .54, 1
table .6¼, 1 piggin .12½, 1 rat trap .6½, 1 bottle .39, 8 barrels of corn $8.65, 1 bocket 6¼, 1 pitcher .65, 10 bushels of
wheat $4.37½, 1 tray .14, 3 pr. cards .79, 1 Double tree and
tray .18¾, pr. wipers .25, 10 yds. of shirting $4.12½. Total
$2291.54.

Michael Kinnard 1 branding iron .50, one bag $1.75.
1½ bushels measure .51, one waggon and hind gears $60, 1 wag-
gon cover and tar bucket $2.25, bought from Joel Stevens a/c
$4.65. Total $69.57.

James Joyce 1 pot and hooks and ladle $2, 2 bells $1.65,
1 bag of wool .18¾, 1 bag $1.76, 5 baskets .75, 6 plates $3.7¼,
1 crewet .26, Hugh Pinkston 1 axe .56¼, 1 hoe $1.12½, 2 heifers
and 1 stear $96¼, 2 stears $5.50, two do. $6.6¼, 1 bason $1.68¾.
Total $23.90.

Gideon Hansley 2 hammers .62½, 2 hoes $1.37½, 1 bag of

fruit .90, one bag $1.75, 1 bason $1.75. Total $6.40

William Alexander 4 sheep first choice $13.62½, Alexander
Johnstone 1 Dutch oven $2, Queensware $1.6¼, looking glass .50,
coffee mill .75, 1 top stack shucks and blades $1.31¼, 25 Doze.
of oats and parcel of fodder $3. Total $8.62¼.

John R. Tankersley 1 red heifer $4.50, 1 side of leather
$1.90, bag of coffee .53, 8 barrels corn $9.62½, 1 Almanac .14.
Total $16.2½, John Pillow 2nd lot of sheep 4 - $10.50, 4 sheep
third choice $8. Total $18.

Ephraim Bugg 3¾ yds. of cloth $2, Richard Ranolds 5 sheep
last choice, Robert McConnel 1 barshear plough $4.51, 1 plow hoe
.38½, 1 cow $9, Total $13.89½.

George Kinnard washing tub $1, one pail .30, one do. .26,
old half bushel .7¼, 1 tub .56, 2 chairs $1.50, waggon cover $2.
one tar bucket .25, pitcher .65, 6 plates $1.60, 8 bar'ls. corn
$8.30, 8 bar'ls. do. $9, the balance of corn $1.1, one churn and
tray .17. Total $21.22¼.

John Watts 1 rifle gun $10.13½, Nelson Chapman 1 bell .57½,
shirt mans $1, 200 lb. of seed cotton $5.6¼, Elijah Mayfield 1
whip saw and files, $16.65, George Welbone 1 smooth bore gun $6,
William Tucker Junr. a bag of picked cotton 57., 1 do. .30, one
spinning wheel $2.1, 1 do $1.51, Leather $1.50 pr. cartwheels
$1.55. Total $5.45.

Charles Dowd 2 hoes $1, 2 do. $1.15½, 2 do. $1.50, 2 hoes
$1.50, 1 small wheel $2.26, 1 pr. pewter $2.1, 1 bag .45, pr.
cards $1.38, pr. wool cards .81. Total $12.4½.

Josiah Wilson p. geers $2.81¼, churn and peas .12½, ½ dozen
spoons .64, Richard Ogilvie pr. old geer $1.25, Wark Smith 2 hogs
2nd choice unfat $5, 2nd choice $11.2 ,do. 3rd choice $7.5, 2
do. 4th choice $5, 3 phials .50. Total $28.25

George Maneo Sr. 1 sorrel mare $91, John Baker to sundries
as pr. account curt. $13.1, Joseph Glover 1 cow $7, 1 pewter dish
$2, Edward Scruggs 1 cow $8.37½, Val. Allen 1 cow $6.15, 1 do
$6, Greenberry Dean curry comb and Drag .32, 1 table $2.62½, 4
spoons .39½. Total $3.34

Kimbro Ogilvie 1 whip saw $3, 200 lbs of seed cotton $5.12½,
slay and geer .56¼. Total $8.68¾.

Josiah White 1 bag of fruit .50, 4 plates $1.90, Bar'l. and
salt $7.50, 200 lb. seed cotton $5.37½. Total $15.27½

Charles Stevens 1 bag $1.75, Box flax and bell .50, brought
from William Stevens Acc't. $5.25. Total $7.50.

Lewis Manco 1 bag $1.77, side soal leather $4.36, 1 bag
$1.75, John Dalton Bar'l. lime .7, candle box .32¼, 1 bag and wool
.50, 6 lots of wheat 10 bushels $5, 1 blade stack $3.1 4th choice
of hogs 10 head $5, cow and calf $10. Total $25.90¼.

Hugh McBride 1 side leather $2.90, bar steel .90, parcel of
thread $3.6¼. Total $6.86¼.

Tapley Andrews 7 spoons .57¼, p. pewter $2.31¼, 1 dish $1.31¼,
coffee pot and cups .75. Total $4.94¾.

Abram Cole 2 basons $3.1, Julian Neal 1 pewter dish $1.75, 1
knife .31¼, 8 bar'ls of corn $9.12½, 10 bushels of wheat $5,
7th lot of wheat 13 bushels $5.63½, 12¼ yds. of cloth $4.56¼.
Total $17.26.

Lancaster Glover pr. of wool cards .80, 2 bowls .45, Amt. of
Charles Locke's account $9.39. Total $10.64

Page
(251)

Benjamin Little 2 butcher knives .50, 200 lb. cotton $5, Richard
S. Locke 1 stone pot and cream pot $1, Blue thread .62½, phial
of lintseed oil .50, 1 hill of potatoes .37½, do. 42½, 6½
bushels wheat $2.84 1/3, 1 tub and basket, pr. cards .50, chest
wheat, bag and flax seed .25. Total $6.41¾.

John Oslin 11½ yds. of linnen $5.5, Robert Rogers bunch flax
$2, basket and blankets $2.50, pr. of turkeys $1, one foot adze
.62½, 6 earthen plates $1.50, cups and saucers .75. Total $9.37½.

Charles Hooks bag of fruit $2.30, bed and furniture $56.6¼, 1
do. $65, Patrick Gibson 2 ear bells .45, William Borin 2 turkeys
.54, Obediah Driskell 200 lb. of seed cotton $6, William Legate
8 barrels of corn $9, Nich Neal 1 bottle .37½. Total amount sold
$7874.85.

Signed Knacy Andrews, Benjamin Bugg, Exors.

State of Tennessee, Williamson County St. agreably to a n
order of the worshipful Court of Williamson County April Session
1811. We Oliver Williams and Sion Hunt two justices of the peace
for said County appointed to settle with Joseph T. Elison, Admr.
of WILLIAM MULLIN, dec'd., do the same in the following manner
to wit from the face of the papers produced to us we find the
Admr. sold the Estate of the Dec'd for $3259.8

Interest rec'd. on Chapman, etc. $104.80, an acc't. against
William Mullin, Junr. $184.25, do. Joshua Mullin $113.66, do.
John Gordon Debt $119 Interest $20, ditto William Young $28.12½,
do. on Jesse Mullin $26.37½, do. on Ben Shaw $8, do. on Hanks $13,
do. on J. T. Ellison $8, do. on Charles Campbell $4, do. on

Page
(252)

Henry Key $5.50, do. on Mat Robertson .75, a judgment on Chapman
and others $550., to the hire of negroes before the sale $70.12½
For cotton $24, an Account against Daniel Cowen $3.87½.
Whole amount $4542.53 - $773.97 sum of $3768.56.

Pr. Contra Cr.
As per voucher No. 1 $29, ditto no 2 $4.12½, ditto No. 3
$3.59¾, ditto No. 4 $10, ditto no. 5 $18.50, ditto no. 6 $1.87½,
ditto no. 7 $1.25, ditto no. 8 $11.45, ditto no. 9, $4, ditto
no. 10, $5.37½, ditto no. 11 $27.42, ditto no. 12 $12.62½, ditto
no. 13 $11.45, ditto no. 14 $3, ditto no. 15 $7.66 2/3, ditto
no. 16 $357.71, ditto no. 17 $74.20, ditto no. 18 $9.25, ditto
pd. R. White no. 19 $42.50, ditto N. Wilkinson No. 20 $21.25,
Not collected of Campbell, Henry Key and Cowan as charges against
Admr. $13.87½, as per voucher $21, An allowance made to the
Administrator Joseph T. Ellison for his services in collecting
of debts due the Estate $100. Total $773.97.

Balance due the Estate in the hands of the Admr. J.T.E.
$3768.56. The annexed settlement was made by us, Oliver Williams
and Sion Hunt, Justices appointed by the County Court to settle with the Admr. of William S. Mullin. Dec'd. this 11th day
of April 1811.

Signed O. Williams, J. C. and S. Hunt, J. 6.
Returned to April Session 1811. N. P. Hardeman, C.W.C.

Page
(253)

1807 - Feby. 10th. - Polley Pate Dr. to Lancaster Glover, her
guardian, 1 5/8 yards of ladies' coating $3.50 pr. yd., 2½ yds.
of white flannel at .75 pr. yd. $1.87½, 1 pair of shoes $1.12½,
paid Taylor for making riding dress $1, black velvet silk and ½
buttons for dress .60

1807 - April - Expences from Virginia $17, 1 spelling book .37½,
3 months schooling $1.50, 9 months schooling $5.25,
1809 - January - 1 quire paper .37½. Total $34.68½.
1807 - Feb. 10 - Elizabeth Pate Dr. to Lancaster Glover her Guardian 1¼ yds. white flannel .75, per yd. $1.50, 1 pr. shoes .75,
Taylor for making dress $1., Velvet silk and buttons for dress .60,
1807 - Apl. - Expences from Virginia $17, ½ quire of paper and
spelling book .62½, 6 months schooling $3.50,
1808 Jany. 3 months schooling $2, 1 yd. muslin and quart of tar
.75. Total $34.45½/
1807 Apl. 4th . Person G. Pate Dr. to Lancaster Glover his Guardian
1 ciphering and slate and book, 1 quire paper and spelling book .87½,
expense from Virginia $17, July 1807- 1 Arithmetic $1, September
12 ½ quire paper .25, Octo. 8th. 3 months schooling $2, 1808 Decr.
25, 6 months schooling, 83 days schooling, 1½ quire paper, 1 hat
and quart tar, 1 hat - $34.32½

(Page
254)

     Lancaster Glover ,Guardian Dr. to Polley Pate, Eliza, and
Nancy Pate and Person G. Pate, heirs of Hardy PATE, deceased, $559.93
Interest on 400 from the 25th Decr. 1804 to 8th April 1811 $150.
Interest on $159.93. 7 mills from 28th Feby. 1803 to 8th Apl.1811
$68.37.5.
          Signed Lancaster Glover. Returned to April Session
1811. N. P. Hardeman, C. W. C.

     State of Tennessee, Williamson County - This day agreeable to
an order of the County Court of Williamson, we, William Wilson and
Samuel Perkins have proceeded to settle with Benjamin M. Cuistan,
Administrator in right of his wife of JOHN JORDAN, deceased, and
find the sales of the Estate as appears by the Clerks certificate
amounting to one thousand one hundred and five dollars and seventy
four cents, since which they have paid as by the anex'd. Statement
and vouchers herewith appearing the sum of eighty seven dollars,
twenty-one and a fourth cents, which leaves a balance due the Estate of one Thousand and eighteen dollars and fifty one ¾ cents
as appearing below. Given under our hands this 9th day of March
1811.
          W. Wilson, J. P. Sam'l. Perkins, J. P.
John Jordan, Admr.
          In account with Estate of John Jordan.
     To amt. of sales of the Estate John Jordan, deceased, as p.
clerks' certificate $1105.74
               CR.
By Am't. pd John Anderson as p. acc't. and rec'd. $85.92¼
By amt. pd. Sherriff p. receipt. $1.30.
                              Total $87.22¼

Page
(255)
     JAMES BUFORD'S Will - In the name of God amen I, James Buford,
of the County of Williamson and State of Tennessee, weak of body
but of perfect sound mind and memory, blessed be God for it, and
calling to mind the mortality of my body and knowing that it is
appointed for all men once to die, I have therefore thought proper to make and ordain this my last Will and Testament and first
principally, I give and recommend my Soul to Almighty God, that
first gave it and my body I recomend to the Earth to be buried
in a decent and Christian manner, by the direction of my Executors
whom I shall hereafter appoint and as touching of my worldly Estate wherewith it hath pleased God to bless me in this life, I give

demise and dispose of in the following manner (viz.) - First I
give to my Daughter Sicila the property that she has already
had. Then I give to my son Hennery the property that he has already had. Then I give to my daughter Frankey the property that
she has already had. Then I give to my son Charles the property
that he has already had. Then I give to my Daughter Charlotte the
property that she has already had and a negro boy Harry. Then I
give to my son James the property that he has already had and a negro
boy Peter. Then I give to my son Edward the following named negroes,
one boy named Dick, and one named Stephen and the plantation whereon I now live after giving James Luster the one fifth part on the
value, provided that James Luster makes Hennery Buford a title to
the tract of Land whereon Hennery Buford lives in Virginia if
not Henry Buford is to have the part that is left to James Luster,
Edward is to have three good cowes and calves and a steer, three
sows and piggs, and one years provision of pork. Then I give to
my daughter Pricila the property that she has already had. Then I
give to my Daughter Katherine the property that she has already
had. Then I give to my grand son Duncan Cameron sixty pounds to be
paid in cash. The balance of my negroes that has not been named
to wit, Andrew, Suckey, Darby, Pat, Jude, Gloster, Fanny, and Sam
and their increase if any is to be equally divided among my three
daughters Charlotte, Pricilla and Catherine and James Luster provided that James will make Hennery Buford a wright to the Land
before mentioned, otherwise that part left to James Luster is to
go to Hennery Buford my will is that all Debts due to me by note or
book acp't, is to go to pay all my just debts, and if there should
not be a sufficiency to satisfy the debts it is to be made out of
that part of my estate that has not been already given, and the
balance of my stock of cattle, horses, and hodges with my household and kitching furniture and farming tools, and all my other
property that has not been named my will is that it shall be equally
divided among the whole of my children except my stock of sheep,
which is to be equally divided betwen James, Edward, Pricilla, and
Katherine and my Will and desire is that my son Spencer Buford,
my son Charles, my son James and my son Edward Buford to be sole
Executors to this my last Will and Testament. In witness whereof
I have hereunto set my hand and affixed my Seal this the tenth
day of April eighteen hundred and eleven.
                    James Buford
                  x his mark
Signed, sealed and acknowledged in the presence of Elisha Dodson,
Gabriel Buford, and Alexander Mebane - Which foregoing recited Will
and Testament of James Buford, deceased, was presented in Court
July Session 1811, and proved by the oaths of Elisha Dodson, Gabriel Buford, and Alexander Mebane, subscribing witnesses thereto,
to be the Act and deed of James Buford and the same was ordered to
be recorded and Spencer Buford, Charles Buford, James Buford and
Edward Buford came into court and qualified as Executors thereto and
received Letters Testamentary.
          N. P. Hardeman, Clerk of Williamson County Court

     Inventory of the Estate of Charles Taylor, Dec'd.: 1 bay Horse,
two years old, note on George Stramlar for $4.3½, 15½ yards home-
spun linen, one dollar cash.
               Signed Henry H. Atkinson, Admr. July 13th, 1811.
Returned to July Session 1811. N. P. Hardeman, C. W. C.

April 27th 1811. The amount of the Sail of the property of
THOMAS SIMMONS, deceased, which was loned to his son Alexander du
dureing his life, there to be sold and equally divided amongst all
his Sisters and Brother - Thomas Simmons to six negroes vizt.
Aaron, Phillis, Charles, Ruben, Lee and Stephen $16.05
1 trumpet .25, Daniel Adams 1 feather bed and furniture $16.25,
Jerdan Soloman 1 axe .87½. Total $1622.37½.
Returned to July Session 1811.
N. P. Hardeman, C. W. C.

Page
(258)

Inventory of the Amount of Sail together with all Debts due
and Accounts comeing to the Estate of MICHAEL KENNARD, dec'd. under
the Administration of LEWIS STEVENS and MICHAEL KENNARD, dec'd:
Notes on demand the 4th November 1810 - to one note on George
Kenard amount $45.50, to one do. do. on Lewis Stevens $15., to
one do. do. on Anthony Kennard $88, to one do. do. on John Kennard
$46.50, to one do. do. on James Thompson $88.50, to one do. do.
on James Thompson 47.50, to one do. do. on Nathaniel Kinnard $45.,
to one do. do. on William Matthews $15.25, to one do. do. on
George Seaton $20.76, Notes on demand the 12th of February 1811,
to one note on Nathaniel Kennard $8, to one do. do. on Anthony
Kennard $6.18¾, to do. do. on John Curry $2.37½, to do. do. on
Carey Morgan $4.38½, to do. do. on Robert Moore $4.30, to do. do.
on George Seaton $1.46, to do. do. on George Bennett $50.81½,
to do. do. on John Kennard $4.12½, to do. do. on William Caldwell
$3.37½, Notes on demand 11th February 1811 - to one note on Nel-
son Chapman $2.31¼, to a do. do. on Mark Michel $500, to do. do.
on James Thompson $2.6¼, to do. do. on Curtis Hooks $2.25, to do.
do. on Nathaniel Kennard $2.13½, to do. do. on Anthony Kennard
$4.23½, to do. do. on Michael Kennard $38.25, to do. do. on Lewis
Stevens $21.50, to do. do. on Betty Hooks $8, to note George
Kennard on demand 23rd Feby 1811 amount $288.91½, to note of Ben-
ton Harris rec'd. the money the 12th May 1810 $17.20, to note
one John Kennard on Demand the 17th Jany. 1811 $50.73, to one
dollar account against Loammie Stevens $1, to money received $1.61
Total $1384.41¼.
Signed Michael Kennard and Lewis Stevens
Returned to July Session 1811. Teste N. P. Hardeman, C. W. C.

Page
(259)

Account of Sales of the Estate of WILLIAM BULLOCK, Dec'd.
taken 10th December 1810 by John Williamson - Amos Bullock 1 pott
and hooks, do. do. 1 pott and hooks $1.37½, Nathan Bullock 1
Dutch oven $1.87½, Charles Boyles 1 lott augers and hammer .50,
Amos Bullock 1 iron wedge .82¼, ditto ditto 1 lott chissels .51,
ditto ditto 1 hand saw $1.56¼, ditto ditto 1 cart and wheels $8.12½,
Nathan Bullock 1 skillet, hoe, etc. $1, ditto ditto 1 bason, dish
and spoons $3.50, John Hay 1 coffee pot, cups and saucers $1.25,
Amos Bullock 1 bottle, knives, forks, etc., $1.25, ditto, ditto
1 table .26, Thomas Jones 1 grid iron .71, Nathan Bullock loom
and gears $3, William May cards and wheel $2, Amos Bullock trunk
and chair $1.50, James House 3 chairs .81¼, Elizabeth Bullock,
flat irons, books, and Sugr. Dish $1.62½, Amos Bullock feather
bed and furniture $18.37½, Sylvanus Sturdivant bed and furniture
$7.75, Elizabeth Bullock looking glass and towell $1, Amos Bullock

1 jugg .50, Sylvanus Sturdivant 1 axe .56¼, Amos Bullock 1 bedstead $1.50, Nathan Bullock 1 barrel .25, George Neelly 1 steer
$2.76, Nathan Bullock 1 sorrel mare $57.25, Amos Bullock 1 sorrel horse $18.75, do. do. leather and pail .89, George Sleeker
parcel piggs $6.12½, George Davidson 9 hoggs $13, James Terryl
1 negro girl Jane $400.25, Jacob Rowland 1 stone jugg .50, Nathan
Bullock 1 whet stone .33, Nathan Bullock 1 cane hoe .25, Amos
Bullock 1 churn and pail .25, do. do. 1 bell $1.1, Nathan Bullock
1 grind-stone $1.76, do. do. 1 broad axe .25, Eliza Bullock 1
chamber pott .25, Amos Bullock 1 note due from Nath'l. Wyche $15.25,
Total amount of Sales of the Estate of William Bullock, dec'd. ,
by John Williamson, Exor. Returned to July Session 1811.
N. P. Hardeman, Clk.

Page
(260)

JOHN NOWLIN'S Will - In the name of God amen I, John Nowlin, of the State of Tennessee and County of Williamson, being
of sound mind and memory and calling to mind the uncertainty of
life have thought proper to dispose of what it hath pleased God
to confer on me and for that purpose do make and ordain this in-
strument of writing to be my last Will and Testament, hereby revoking all former Wills by me heretofore made and shall now dispose of my estate in the following manner to wit - Item, I give
and bequeath to Bartholomew Stovall and his wife Aggey Stovall
one dollar. Item, I give and bequeath to my son Golsbey Nowlin
one dollar to him, his heirs and assigns forever. Item, I give
and bequeath unto my son-in-law John Duffy and his wife Salley
Duffey one silver dollar to them, their heirs, and assigns forever. Item, I give and bequeath unto my wife Anney Nowlin my corner cupboard with all its contents of crockery ware and also two
beads and bedstead and furniture, the saddle and bridle now called
hers, together with two horse-kind of her choice out of my stock
at my Deceasee, to her, her heirs and assigns forever. Item, it
is my Will and desire that they whole of my estate both real and
personal of every kind of discription, except fifty dollars, to
be equally divided between my two sons to wit, Littleberry Nowlin,
and David Nowlin to them, their heirs and assigns forever. And
the fifty dollars reserves in the above gift I give and bequeath
to my wife Anney Nowlin to her, her heirs and assigns forever.
And lastly I do hereby appoint my Brother William and his son
General Lee Nowlin Executors of this my last Will and Testament.
And as I before said hereby revoking all other Wills and confirming this and this only to be my last Will and Testament. In witness whereof I have hereunto set my hand and affixed my seal this
23rd day of September in the year of our Lord 1808. Interlined
before signed with the words wife and dollar.
Signed John Nowlin - (Seal) - Signed, sealed and
acknowledged in presents of William Christmas, J. Solomon, John
Jobe, General L. Nowlin, which Will and Testament as before recited was duly proven in open Court October Session 1811 by the
oaths of Jordan, Solomon and General L. Nowlin, two of the subscribing witnesses thereto, to be the act and deed of John Nowlin and the same was ordered to be Recorded and William Nowlin
and General Lee Nowlin, the Executors named therein, came into
Court and qualified as Executors thereto, and received Letters
Testamentary.
N. P. Hardeman, C. W. C. (In places this name is spelled
Nolin)

Page
(261)

Inventory of the Estate of JOHN NOWLIN, deceased - William Nowlin and General Lee Nowlin, Executors of the last Will and Testament of John Nowlin, deceased, report to the Court of please and quarter sessions for the County of Williamson October Turm 1811, the following Inventory of the goods and chattels of the said John Nowlin, deceased, which have come to their hands previous to the filing of this inventory, also the following List of Debts which from the books and papers of the said John Nowlin, deceased, appears to be due and owing to him. The're is 13 head of horses, 29 head of cattle, 12 head of sheep, 69 head of hogs, 8 chairs, 3 feather beds and bedsteads, 2 chests, 2 trunks, 1 table, 1 mans saddle, 4 pr. of gear, 5 axes, 2 wedges, 1 frow, 1 rifle gun, shot pouch and powder horn, 5 hoes, 3 plows, 1 cross cut saw, 1 hand saw, 2 augers, 1 drawing knife, 1 pair of sheep shears, 1 pair of dog irons, 1 Spouting hoe, 2 ovens and lids, 3 pots, 1 skillet, 1 kettle, 3 pair pot hooks, 2 pot racks, 1 loom, warping bars, and spools, spool frames, 1 pair of fire tongs and shovel, 2 washing tubs, 1 churn, 1 can, 8 piggins, 2 kelars, 1 candle stand, 2 cotton wheels, 1 flax wheel, 1 check reel, 4 empty salt barrels, $3\frac{1}{2}$ barrels of brandy, $\frac{1}{2}$ barrel of whiskey, 4 sickles, 1 pair of steelgards, 1 barrel with some vinegar in it, 3 empty barrels, 1 barrel with some salt in it, 3 empty whiskey barrels, 1 halter chain and coller, 1 pair of double trees, 2 steel traps, 1 flax hackle, 8 bee stands, 1 gallon, half quant, pint and funnel, 5 clivises, 1 waggon, 2 pair of hames and 1 pair chains, 2 pair of brick bands, 1 log chain, 1 rawhide, 1 side of upper leather, 2 tame dear, 1 still, 9 tubs, 1 singling stand and 1 doubling cags, 1 cowhide whip, 1 tub of tallow, 1 tub of fat, 1 side and a half of sole leather, 2 empty barrels, 1 sifter, 4 baskets, 1 Bible and some other books, a parcel of flax and cotton, 2 flat irons, 3 horse collers, a quantity of Sheaf oats, also a quantity of fodder, some rye, 4 stacks of hay, his wearing cloaths, two cribs with corn in them, also a quantity of corn standing in the field, 1 branding iron, 2 gimblets, 1 claw hammer, and whetstone and a handsaw file, a grind stone, 2 meal bags, 1 tomahawk, 17 head of geese, 12 head of Turkeys, 1 case of razors, 3 horse shoes, and piece, 1 negro man named Abel and Ned, 7 dressed deer skins, 3 old bridles, a web of cloth in he loom and filling for it which will be wove out and made up for the negroes $33.75 in cash, 1 pair of Buckskin breeches, 1 pair of Spectacles, Isaac Mason, Dr. by Book Act. .50, Mr. Venable Dr. .66 2/3, Israel M. Carrell Dr. $3.33, William Fielder Dr. 4.93\frac{3}{4}$, Augusty Holland Dr. $1.75, , John Chitwood 4.16\frac{1}{4}$, Edmund Chitwood, Dr. $2.50, old Mr. Venable, Dr.bad $1.85, Mr. Little Dr. $5.33, John Harkins Dr. $2.50, Mr. Asteen 3.12\frac{1}{2}$, Jesse Asteen Dr. $5.91, William Price Dr. by note $9.8, Alexr. McDonald Dr. by order 1.92\frac{1}{2}$, William M. Grider by order $3.00, Nathaniel Aldridge Dr. by note $5, James Downing by order $5, William Wilcockson dr. $1, William Rutledge Dr. $6.46, Armez McCray dr. $1.25, J. Taylor Dr. .75, Peter Gillum and Jesse Hurd by note 666.66\frac{1}{4}$, George Mansker, Senr. $5, two feather beds, bedsteads, and furniture and cupboard and its contents, 1 womans saddle, and bridle, Alexr. Simpson Dr. $12, A. Fargerson Dr. $3.50, Wm. Brooks Dr. .62$\frac{1}{2}$, H. Bell Dr. $12, bad debt, 1 other bed and furniture, Daniel Willis Dr. $8.75, fifty dollars to be paid to the old ladey when collected, also one other negro named Ned. Signed Gen'l. L. Nowlin, Exor. Returned to Octo. Session 1811. N.P. Hardeman, C.W.C.

Page
(262)

Account of Sales of the estate of John Nowlin, Deceased.
A return of the amount of the Sale of John Nowlin, Dec'd., property as given in by William and General L. Nowlin, Executors, of the said John Nowlin after delivering the legacies specified in the face of the Will, is as follows (to wit): William Nowlin, Senr. dr., ½ whiskey $5.00, Walter Kinnard 2 lbs brandy $63, 1 steel trap $1.31¼, 1 do. $5, 2 plows $6.32¼, 2 axes $2.75, 1 frow $1.25, 1 tomahack .81¼, 1 log chain $4.50, 1 set of swingle trees $2.50, 1 flax hackle $2.56¼, gimblet, whetstone, and hammer $1.13, 1 weeding hoe .40, 1 do. do. .75, 1 do. do. .25, 1 gallon and other measures $2.2, 1 pair of sheep shares .75, weeding hoe .90, 1 pair
(Page 263) of catton cards, 1 do. of wool cards .63, 1 cotton wheel $1., cutting knife and box $3.50, 1 cut real $1.75, 1 Dutch oven $2.50, 1 small pot $1.25, some leather $4., 1 waggon and geer $30., 1 skillet and lead $1.50, 1 pot $3.44¾, 1 kettle and hooks $4., 1 oven $2.50, 1 cotton wheel $1.10, 1 barrel and churn .56¼, 1 patern of skins $3.25, 1 do. $1.12.5, 1 dressed deerskin $1.29, 2 do. do. .76, 1 set of Dog Irons $3.62½, 1 bed and furniture $22.25, 1 do. do. $24.25, 1 do. do. $20.26, 1 do. do. $7.12½, 1 mare and colt $40., 1 horse $30.1, 1 colt $32.50, 1 mare $32.76, 1 mare $40.50, 1 colt $15., 1 roan horse colt $30, 1 black colt $20., 1 black filley $30.75, 1 bay filley $26.6¼, 1 negro fellow Ned $504., 5 head of hogs $12.50, 3 head do. $9., 10 head do. $32.6¼, 8 head do. $22.25, 9 head do. $35.37½, 10 head do. $35.25, 9 head do. $33., 7 head do. $22.62½, 7 head do. $19., 8 head do. $39.12½, 1 boar $4., 1 sow $7.62½, 11 head of sheep $27.92, 4 shoats $3.25, 1 rifle gun $16.76, 1 side of Leather $3., 1 drawing knife .75,
(Page 264) 2 iron wedges $1.46¼, 1 cow and calf $10., 1 do. do. $11.12½, 1 do. do. $8.6¼, 1 do. do. $8.25, 1 do. do. $13., 1 do. do. $8.32½, 1 do. do. $10.62½, 1 heifer and steer $12., 1 do. do. $7., 1 do. do. $9., 1 do. do. $9., 1 do. do. $7.1, 2 do. do. $9.1, 1 Bull and Heifer $11., 1 filley $11.85, 19 geese $11.25, 1st choice of hay stacks $5.56, 2nd choice of do. $3.50, 3rd choice of do. $3., 4th choice of do. $2.26, 1 stable of soft oats $6., 1 do. do. $4.6¼, oats, rye and fodder $.1, Oats in 1 side of the C. C. $4.51, do. do. do. $10.25, do. do. do. $4.64¼, 1 weeding hoe .92, 3 horse collars .75, 1 cross cut saw $6., 4 barrels $3.50, 1 ax $2.43¾, 1 axe $2.37½, 1 barrel $1.25, 1 do. .87½, 1 barrel of soap $9., some soap .50, 1 mans saddle $17.37½, 4 sickles $2.50, 1 tub of hogs lard $4.35, 1 barrel of tallow $9., a barrel with some salt $2., 1 pot full of salt $3.6¼, 1 scythe $1.50, hames and chains $1., 1 flax wheel $2., some leather $1.87½, 1 poll axe $1.75, some tobacco .26, 1 trunk $1.50, 2 piggins .43¾, 1 pail .16½, 1 can .25, some coopers ware .88¾, 1 piggin .25, 1 washing tub .75, 1 do. do. .45, 2 augers $1.45, 2 meal bags $2.72½, 1 sifter and tray .87½, 1 handsaw $2.25, 2 pot racks $2.61½, 1 haulter chain $1.16, 1 frying pan .32¼, 1 churn .56¼, 4 baskets $1.47¼, 1 pair of flat irons $2., 1 ladle and tray .18¾, 1 candle stand .25, 1 pr. of steelgards $3.75, 2 chests $11.50, 1 table $1., 1 couch .20, some books .50, some cotton $10.25, some flax $5.31½, 1 rope haulter .25, 1 raw hide $4.5, 1 still and other fixing $61.50, 28 barrels of corn $28.69¼, 20 barrels do. $20.4, 1st lot of corn 8 barrels $9.25, 2nd lot of corn 8 barrels $9.50, 3rd do. do. $10. 4th do. do. $10.6¼, 5th do. do. $10.6¼, 6th do. do. $10.6¼, 7th do. do. $10, 8th do. do. $9.82½, 9th do. do. $10., 10th do. do. $9.50, 11th do. do. $9., 12th do. do. $9., 13th do. do. $9., 2

tame deer $2.12½, 1 black steer $11., 1 pided steer $10., 1
grind-stone $3.25, the flock of turkeys $4., 8 beed stands $13.5½,
9 chairs $3.5, 1 pair of leather breeches $4., 1 big chest $5.,
1 bell and coller $2., 1 shovel and tongs .25, 1 negro man Abe
$525., 1 cag of vinegar $4.1, 1 rope .50, 9 still tubs $3., 1
sow and pigs $1.2, 1 blind bridle .30, lincey cloth $6.57¼, 1
loom $6., 8 head of cattle on D. River $45.69, - Total $2600.69
        Amount in the whole errors excepted of the Sale of John
Nowlin, Deceased, property.
        Signed Gen'l. L. Nowlin, Exr. Returned to January Session
1812. N. P. Hardeman, C. W. C.

        WILLIAM CHRISTMAS' Will - In the name of God amen, I, William
Christman, of the County of Williamson in the State of Tennessee,
being now in a lowe state of health but of perfect sound mind
and memory do ordain and establish this my last Will and Testament
first it is my Will and desire that all my lawful debts be paid
out of my estate by my Executors hereafter named out of my bonds,
notes, and accounts if they should be found sufficient to discharge my debts, and if not I do hereby fully authorise and empower my executors or any one of them to sell and dispose of any
Tract or Tracts of land that I have by Deed, Grant or entry, given
my said executors or either of them full power to make and Execute Deed or Deeds of Consequences or to make Transfers of entrys
platts, or certificate to all or such tracts of land they or either of them may dispose of at a good and fair price except the

Page
(265)

Tract of land I now live on the east side of Mill Creek being the
Tract which I purchased of Bennet Philips and the adjoining lands
thereto which I purchased of Henry Butler and one of John Buchanan
which is not to be sold or disposed of by my Executors, but the
same will hereafter be disposed of by this Will. Item, I give and
bequeath to my grand-son William Christmas Marr the land and plantation I now live on, being the two tracts I purchased of Bennet
Philips, one of Henry Butler, and one from John Buchanan to him,
his heirs and assigns forever and I do also give to my grand-son
William Christmas Marrs two negroes to wit, one negro boy named
Adam and negro girl named Mary now in the possession of his father
Josiah Marrs, also one bed and all the furniture belonging to
the same that his mother had also one horse or mare, saddle and
bridle of the value of one hundred dollars to him and his heirs
forever, and it is also my wish and desire that he should be
maintained out of the estate hereafter lent to my wife and should
he die before he comes of age or marry and hacving no living
issue, in that case it is my will and desire that the whole of
the estate given him be equally divided between my two daughters
Patsey Green and Sally Jones Dyer, share and share alike, to
them and their heirs forever. Item, I lend to my wife Abegail
during her natural life the Tract of Land and Plantation whereon
I now live with the dwelling house and all other outhouses and
also six sows and pigs and pork for the first year after my decease. Also five cows and calves, two horses, one named Jack
and the other named Dick which I had from Kidd and Henry Conway
and I also lend her during her natural life all my household and
kitchen furniture except the clokk and its case which I give to
my daughter Sally Jones Dyer to be taken immediately after my death

and the deske and book case and case of bottles, I give to my
Daughter Patsey Green to be taken away at the same time the clock
is, and after the death of my wife, it is my will and desire that
all my household and kitchen furniture lent to my wife be equally
divided between my two daughters Patsey Green and Sally Jones Dyer
share and share alike to them and their heirs forever. Item, it

Page
(266)
is my Will and desire that the right of one thousand acres of
land on the clear fork of Cumberland River which I gave to my
daughter Polley Graves Connelly be confirmed to her and her heirs
and I also wish her to get out of the Sales of my land one hundred
dollars in cash and I do now confirm all the property heretofore
given her to remain as her property to her and her heirs. Item
I give and bequeath to my daughter Patsey Green, her heirs, all
the property I heretofore gave her on that she had out of my estate, her heirs, and I do also give and bequeath to my said Daughters Patsey Green and Sally Jones Dyer their heirs the whole of
my estate not heretofore given including my land and stock to be
divided equally between them, and whenever the Death of my wife
and if my grand son William C. Marrs dies without lawfull issue
or marries then and in that case the whole of my estate as well
real as personal to be equally divided between my said Daughters
Patsey and Sally aforesaid to them their heirs forever, share and
share alike to include entrys, bond for land titles, grants, deeds,
etc. It is my Will and desire that my Executors or either of them
sell and dispose of all my land in the State of Tennessee, giving
at least eighteen months credits together with all the Stock not
heretofore given or lent to my wife and the proceeds of such Sale
or Sales when collected to be equally divided between my two daughters Patsey Green and Sally Jones Dyer to them and their heirs
forever, Share and Share alike, and should any bonds,notes, or accounts that I have pay the debts that I owe and if any Surplus should
remain my Will and desire is that the same be divided between my
said two daughters aforesaid and it is further my Will and desire
that my two daughters,to wit Patsey Green and Sally Jones Dyer
have all my negroes except one negro fellow named Bobb.

I wish sold by my Executors after my death to remain to them
and their heirs, the negroes to be equally divided between them,
my will and desire is that my Executors hereafter named shall have
full power and authority in selling and disposing of my land to
Page
(267)
make and Execute Deed or Deeds. Deeds of conveyance either by General or Special Warrantee, as they may make the contract and all
monies arising from such sale or sales after my debts are paid to
be equally divided between my said two daughters Patsey and Salley, my daughter Polley having received her portion of what I
could give her heretofore. And lastly I do appoint Sherwood Green
and Joel Dyer my sons in law my Executors to this my las Will and
Testament with the full powers above given them, hereby revoking
and disannulling all and every will by me heretofore made. In testimony whereof the said William Christmas hath set his hand and
Seal this 31st of October 1811 (arrased and interlined before
signed.)
Signed William Christmas - Seal
Signed, sealed, published and declared to be the last Will
and Testament of William Christmas before us - B. Searcy and James

Vaulx, which Will and Testament as before recited was duly proven in Open Court January Session 1812 by the oaths of Bennett
Searcy and James Vaulx the Subscribing witnesses thereto, to be
the Act and Deed of William Christmas and the same was ordered
to be Recorded - and Sherwood Green and Joel Dyer the Executors
therein named came into Court and qualified as Executors therto
and received Letters Testamentary.

    N. P. Hardeman, C. W. C.

    An Inventory of the estate of William Christmas, deceased:
4 feather beds, 4 boulsters, 1 white sett of bed curtins, 1 striped
ditto, two common setting chairs, 6 windsor ditto, 1 candle-stand,
2 walnut tables, 1 clock, 1 looking glass, 2 brass candle sticks,
1 meal sifter, 2 spinning wheels, 1 tea kettle, 5 bedsteads,
and four cards, 2 iron potts, 1 large kettle, 2 washing tubbs,
2 water pails, 1 coffee mill, 1 sett flat irons, 1 desk and
book case, 1 bottle case, 2 trunks hair, 1 chest, 1 china press,
2 tea potts, 20 cups and saucers, 2 bowls, 1 cream pot, 3
tumblers glass, 4 salt cellars, 2 pepper boxes, 1 cream pot, 2
Tea canisters, 10 plates earthern, 1 loaf sugar, 15lb brown
sugar, 2 large maps, 10 bushels barley, red clover seed, 1 side-
saddle, 1 old hand-saw, 1 churn for milk, 8 empty barrels and
large quantity of Soap, about 150 lb salt, 1 saw-hammer, 1 garden hose, 1 kettle, 2 old Dutch ovens, 1200 lbs pork, Salts or
thereabouts, 500 lbs. old bacon or thereabouts, 1 pair of pot-
hooks, 2 plows, 2 adzes, 2 grind-stones, 118 head of cattle,
7 head or horses, waggon wheel bar, 1 pair of old cart wheels,
30 barrels of corn, 2 weeding hoes, 5 geese, 7 turkeys, 1 small
rundle washing bowl, the silver cup and fork worn by Colonel
Christmas on his arm, 1 razor, 1 shaving box, 3 white counterpins
11 striped counterpins, 8 bed quilts, 1 3-pint blanket, 11
sheets white cotton, 6 pillows and cases, 6 knives and forks,
1 pair of old bed curtins, 4 pair window curtins, 1 shot-gun
powder and flask, 1 mans saddle, 2 hucaback table cloths, 4
plain ditto, 2 new bed ticks, 3 pieces hoop iron, 52 lb. bar
iron, 1 negro man named Julets, 1 ditto named Bobb, 1 ditto
boy, ditto Adam, one negro woman named Dinah.

Page
(268)

Names Notes	Date	Amt. Cts.	When Due
John Davis	Oct. 30,'11-	$17.83	--5th Dec. 1809
John Allen	June 5,1809	5.0	
Lewis Evins	1 Dec. 1809	1.0	
Elm Holmes	1 March 1811	.75	
Sherwood Green	2nd.Oct.1811	$285.	
do.	Mem.	$120	
Theo. Shute	14th Nov. 1811	$ 25.22½	--15th Nov. 1811
Edwd. Gregory	29th Oct. 1811	50.	--- 29th April 1812
Edw. Wilson	30th Jan'y.1811	1.20	
Gideon Pillow	9th April 1811	150.	---9th July 1811
William Tutor	8th April 1810	158.	---8th Oct. 1811
Richard Howard	30th Aug. 1810	8.	
Dawson Howard	25th Nov. 1811	47.	-- 26th Nov. 1811
William McGimsey	9th April 1810-	$150.	-9th April 1812
John Jones	27th Oct., 1810--	$100	- 1st April 1811
Arthur Harris	28th Oct. 1811--	$76.66	- 7th Nov. 1811
William B. Pope	30th Oct. 1811	$51.25	- 3rd July 1811
John Haywood		$5.62½	

Names Notes	Date	Amt.	When due
John H. Campbell	26th Oct. 1811	$9.75	5th Nov. 1811
Benj. Marcel	30th Oct. 1811	56.52	10th Nov. 1811
John Crawford	30th Oct. 1811	52.15	9th Nov. 1811
Stephen Debow,	29th Oct. 1811	40.	25th Dec. 1811
John Murrey	30th Oct. 1811	17.60	9th Nov. 1811
P. Meachem	29th Oct. 1811	23.	30th Oct. 1811
Samuel Weakley	12th Nov. 1811	62.63	13th Nov. 1811
William P. Anderson		33.33 1/3	
Calvin Wheaton	4th Aug. 1807	14.25	
B. G. Stewart	29th Oct. 1811	6	7th Nov. 1811
R. L. D. Shores	17th Dec. 1810	6.25	
William McClure	19th Oct. 1811	3.62½	
William G. Maginson	5th July 1811	.62½	
Elisha Prossett	9th Aug. 1808	6.26	
John Currey	1st Oct. 1811	.75	
A. Stubblefield	8th Feby. 1811	3.50	
W. Brackin	3rd Dec. 1811	15.30	4th Dec. 1811

Page
(269)   Joseph Coleman   320 acres of land and warrant
Sampson Sawyers' Note for------ $3.   horse worth $50.
Henry Lyon's notes $10.
Simpson Harris' note $11.
Patrick Lyons ditto $15
Moses Fish accepted aid by Dr. William Dickinson for $33.33,
1 note on James Tygard $130, with a credit on it for $100, Bal-
ance due $30, Cash on hand at the time of taking this Inventory
$55.12¾, John Andrews $13., William P. Anderson $32.58½, John
Bowen $15.39, Hugh F. Bell $12.56¼, John Coleman $73.25, Henry
Conway $27.90, Enoch P. Connall $10.66, Robert H. dyer $9.50,
Ephraim B. Davidson $6.50, Augustin Davis $2.50, John Griffin .50,
Garrot Goslold heirs $22.61, John Green .25, William Green $2.14,
Thomas Harney $18.72½, John Haywood $5.39, Thomas Johnson $10.39,
Turner Lane $11.35, William Montgomery $12.73, Col William Moore
$6.25, McLemore, Watkins and Mitchell $17.6¼, G. L. Nolin $37.93,
William Nelson $18.93, William Mitchell $73.67, Edward Mitchell
$5.70, Stephen Montgomery $62.60, John Overton $63.22, William
Outlaw $9., Robert Prince $150, Henry Pughe $13.62½, Stines Pil-
low .50, Reuben Searcy $22.60, Robert Searcy $4.50, Francis Taylor $12.25, James Taylor $22.25, Robert Weakley $5.25, Joseph
Woolfolk $2.32½, James Ralston $7.60, William Merrill $9.85,
William Good $11.43, Edward Simmons $1.75, Benjamin Blackman
$1.87½, Edward Given $3.80, McLemore and Given $11.50, Phillips
and Campbell $4.20, William Dickson $27., John Primm .75.
      State of Tennessee, Williamson County - The above is an in-
ventory of the goods and chattels, notes and open Acc'ts. (so
far as has come to our knowledge, or so far as we at present
can ascertain of the estate of William Christmas, deceased, returned to April Session 1812 by us.
                  Signed S. Green and Joel Dyer, Executors
      Returned to April Session 1812. N. P. Hardeman, C. W. C.

age
271)   An account of the sales of the Estate of William Christmas
deceased: Benjamin Gamble 1 mans saddle $15., Ansalom Nolen chains,
clevis and single tree, ditto, ditto, 1 plow, Benjamin Gambill, 1
axe .16¼, Joel Dyer 1 axe $2., James Haley 1 plow $1.75.

Joel Dyer 1 sythe and cradle $3.6¼, Sherwood Green 3 bars sheet
iron $3.25, Isaac Nicholson 2 raw hides $3, James Scott 1 spade
$1.55, ditto ditto 52 lb. bar iron $6.50, William L. Watson 1
grind-stone .78, Joseph Hall 1 ditto ditto $1, Joel Dyer 1 shot
gun $22, James Bradley a parcel of Barley $2.83, Sherwood Green
1 bay mare $28, Nelson Fields 1 sorrel colt $14, Isaac Mason 1
mare and colt $15, Thomas Griggs 17 hoggs $13.25, Willie I.
Davis 43 hogs $28.6¼, Isaac Battle 13 ditto $7, Henry McClure
22 ditto $9.55, Caleb Willis 1 stear $3.30, Allen Nolen 2 stears
$12.25, William Nolen 1 ditto $4, Caleb Williams 1 brindle steer
$3, William Nolen 1 white and red steer $1.12½, Joel Dyer 1 stack
oats $8.75, ditto ditto 1 crib corn $30, ditto ditto 7 turkeys
$2.50, ditto ditto 5 geese $2.52, Izrael M. Carrel a parcel of
oats $1.6¼, Sherwood Green 2 large maps $2,
        State of Tennessee, Williamson County - The above is an
account of sales of the Estate of William Christmas, deceased,
returned to April Session 1812 (the balance of the articles that
is in the inventory and not sold is detained by the widow, and of
course accountable for by
            Signed S. Green and Joel Dyer, Executors.
        Returned to April Session 1812. N. P. Hardeman C. W. C.

age
272)   JOEL PARRISH'S Nuncupative Will - In the name of God amen I, Joel
          Parrish, of the County of Williamson, State of Tennessee, being
          weak of body but of sound and perfect mind and memory blessed be
          Almighty God for the same, do make and publish this my last Will
          and Testament in manner and form following that is to say, after
          committing my soul into the hands of that Holy Being who gave it
          me, I dispose of my worldly estate in the following way. First,
          I desire that all my just debts be paid. Secondly in order to
          pay those debts my will is that the debts due me by Hinchey Pet-
          way for the balance of land conveyed to me by the said Hinchey,
          be applied to this purpose and if these Hinchey should refuse or
          neglect to pay for sd. land at the rate of twenty-five dollars
          per acre my desire is that the land to be reconveyed to me by
          the sd. Hinchey, together with so much of the Tract of land on
          which I now live as lies East of the Mill Creek running through
          it (or as much of either or both as may be necessary sold by my
          Executors to pay my sd. debts). Thirdly my further will is that
          after my last debt be paid, the remainder of my Estate both real
          and personal remain with my wife Susannah during her natural life
          or widowhood or until my children come of age or marry and as they
          come of age or marry I desire that they have two-thirds of their
          equal properties of my estate both real and personal to be given
          and assessed to them by my Executors. If my sd. wife Susannah
          should marry after my death, I then will or desire that she should
          have only a child's part of my estate. After all my just debts
          shall be paid and when Hinchey Petway shall at the rate of twenty-
          five dollars per acre have payed for the land which I sold him
          adjoining the Town of Franklin and which I executed to him a deed
          of conveyance, or in case of failing to pay for the whole or any
          part thereof shall reconvey to me or my heirs, so much thereof as
          shall remain unpaid for, then my Will and Desire is that my Daugh-
Page   ter Caroline, who is married to the said Hinchey be entitled to
(273)   an equaly portion of my estate both real and personal, with the

rest of my children as before mentioned. My Will is, if my sd. wife
should die that my estate be equally divided by my Executors among
my children; if she should marry, then my will is that my estate
be equally divided by my ds. Executors bewteen my sd. wife and my
children.

Nov. 27th 1811. The within having been read to Joel Parrish,
he averred it to contain all of his will and declared it to have
always been his intention, but suggested some embarrassments as to
the appointment of Executors.

Signed A. Maury, Senior
C. White.

27th Nov. 1811. Then read the within to Joel Parrish and he
assented to the correctness of the whole of it, except that sentence
which gives to his wife in case of her marrying only a child's part.

Signed John Reed.

Which Nuncupative will as before recited was duly proven in Open
Court January Session 1812 by the oaths of Abram Maury Senr. and
Chapman White to be the Nuncupative Will of Joel Parrish, deceased,
and the same was ordered to be recorded and Susannah Parrish, widow
and relict of the said Joel Parrish , deceased, came into Court and
relinquished her right of Administration on the estate of sd. Joel
Parrish, deceased, whereupon it was ordered by the Court that letters of Administration on said estate open to Abram Maury Senr. and
Chapman White in due form who gave bond with Hinchey Petway and
Daniel Perkins their Securities in the sum of Ten Thousand Dollars
and qualified according to law.

N. P. Hardeman, C. W. C.

Page
(274)

Inventory of the Goods and Chattels rights and credits of
Joel Parrish, deceased: 14 negroes, viz. Amos, Molly Bobb, Clary,
William, Nancy, Tom, Micharl, Mariah, Frank, Milly, Israel, Dulcy,
and Julia, 1 note on John Sappington due 8th December next for $110,
5 head horses, 19 ditto cattle, 40 ditto hogs, 11 ditto sheep, 1
still, 1 ox cart, 3 beds and furniture, 3 tubs, 3 trunks, 1 chest,
1 case and bottles, 2 looking glasses, 42 china dishes, 1½ ditto
plates, 2 doz. sallad dishes, 4 glass bottles, 2 ditto tumblers, 1
pr. Salt Setts, 5 pewter basons, 1½ ditto plates, 2 tin coffee
potts, 1 tea pott, 9 sitting chairs, 2 stone butter pots, 1 doz.
reading books, 2 spinning wheels, 2 pr. cards, 1 flax wheel, 1 clock
real, 2 doz. spools, 1 hand-saw, 1 drawing knife, 2 augers, 1 foot
ledge, 1 spade, 3 axes, 3 weeding hoes, 2 plows, and geers, 3 sickles,
one hooks, 2 pr. andirons, 1 pr. shovel and tongs, 1 set knives and
forks, 1 coffee mill, 1 pr. candle moulds, 3 pots, 1 oven, 1 kettle,
4 pails, 2 churns, 1 frying pan, 10 barrels.

Signed Abram Maury
Chapman White, Admrs.
13th April 1812

Returned to April Session 1812.

N. P. Hardeman, C. W. C.

Nuncupative Will of WILLIAM HIGGINS, deceased - Last Will and
Testament of William Higgins, deceased, verbally made immediately
before his death. Sworn to by William Halbert and Martha Barnett
they the said Halbert and Barnett depose that the said William Higgins declared to them, his will was that his wife Phoebe should have
His black mare and all the household furniture together with as much

corn and meat as would be sufficient to support her until she could
go to her friends or words to this effect. He then said Higgins
further declared that he wished his land containing about sixty
acres lying on the head of the Harpeth, together with all the residence of his property to be sold to pay the Doctor and his other
debts.

                    Signed William Halbert
                              x his mark
                         Martha Barnett
Session 1812   x her mark
                         N. P. Hardeman, Clk.

age
275)   Which Nuncupative will as before recited was duly proven in
Open Court, January Session of 1812 by the oaths of William Halbert
and Martha Barnett to be the Nuncupative Will of William Higgins,
deceased, and the same was ordered to be Recorded, whereupon it was
ordered by the Court that Letters of Administrators on the estate of
the said William Higgins, deceased, issue to John Higgins according
to law who gave bond with William Halbert and John Hill, his securities in the sum of five hundred dollars, and qualified according
to law.
                         N. P. Hardeman, C. W. C.
        Inventory of the property both real and personal of William
Higgins, deceased: 60 acres of land head of Harpeth, 1 bay filly
2 years old, 1 cow and 2 yearlings, 2 sows, and pigs, 2 spinning
wheels, 1 sett of slea tools, 4 chair frames, 4 pails, 1 oven and
hook, 2 pewter plates, 3 tin cups, 4 dollars cash, 1 axe, 1 mans
saddle, 1 churn, 1 black mare, household furniture.
                    Signed John Higgins, Admr.
                              x his mark
Returned to January Session 1812.
                         N. P. Hardeman, C. W. C.
        Account of Sales of the Estate of William Higgins, deceased:
William Ray knives and forks $1.36, John Pigg 3 tin cups .25, John
Windrow 1 bucket .43, John Patterson 1 oven and lid $3.50, Thomas
Hendrix pot hooks .75, Mariman Landrum sow and piggs $3, William
Halbert sow and pigs $3.6¼, William Powell 1 cow and yearlings $12.27,
William Halbert 1 yearling $1.25, James Hefflin 1 mare $10.25,
John Windrow 1 pail .32, James Higgins 1 piggin .12½, John Webb
60 acres land $99, Jarvis Jones 1 mans saddle $2, William Page 1
churn .75, John Lamb 5 chairs $2.6¼, James Ray 1 wheel $2.18, John
Windrow coopers crow and round .25, James Higgins slay makers tools
$1.62½, Halbert Higgins 1 weeding hoe $1.7¼, John Higgins 1 barrel
age
276) .50, William Taylor shovel plough $1.90, John Webb chains swingle
tree $3.6¼, William Powell 1 ax $1.38, William Ray 1 bridle .56,
Beverly Harris pewter $2.51, Thomas Carson 1 cotton wheel $2.43¼,
Thomas Heflin 2 bushels corn .58¼. Total $158.68.
        Returned to April Session 1812.
        Signed John Higgins - x his mark. N. P. Hardeman, C. W. C.

        JOHN SEAY'S Will - In the name of God amen I John Seay of Wil-
liamson County, State of Tennessee, being weak of body but of perfect
mind and memory and knowing the certainty of death and the uncertainty
of life, do make this my last Will and Testament, which is as follows,
to wit: I lend to my beloved wife Jenny Seay the land whereon I now
live consisting of one hundred and fifty-eight acres and all my
household and kitchen furniture during her natural life or widowhood
and in case my wife should remarry or decease this life, then for all

of the above property to be sold and equally divided between my four
children Ed A. Seay, Martha A. Seay, Elizabeth W. Seay, and Polly
Ann Seay, to them and their heirs forever, and also my part of my
father's estate which is coming to me. I wish as soon as convenient
for it to be collected and put out on interest until my above named
children come of age, them to be also equally divided among them.
I constitute and appraise my beloved friends, John Windrow and Henry Windrow my lawful Executors to this my last Will and Testament.
In witness whereof I have set my hand and seal this 24th day of
March in the year of our Lord one thousand eight hundred and eleven.
Signed, sealed and acknowledged in the presence of Ben Carr.
                                        Lieut. Brown. *LENT*

       Which Will and Testament as before recited was duly proved
in open court January Session 1812 by the oaths of Benjamin Carr
and Lieut. Brown, the Subscribing witnesses, thereto, to be the act
and deed of John Seay and the same was ordered to be recorded and
John Windrow and Henry Windrow the Executors therein named came
       into Court and qualified as Executors thereto and received let-
ters testamentary.
                  N. P. Hardeman, C. W. C.

       An Inventory of the personal Estate of JOSEPH POTTS, de-
ceased, returned to October term of Williamson County Court by
Samuel Crockett, administrator, viz., 1 negro man named Peter,
1 negro woman named Sarah, 3 negro children, 1 wagon and geer, 5
head of horse, 5 beds, and furniture, 3 head of cattle, 15 head of
hogs, 1 sett of carpenter's tools, 1 cross cut saw, 4 axes, 2
plows, 2 hoes, 4 pots and other cooking utencils, 2 wheels, 1 reel
2 saddles, 6 stocks of fodder, 1 field of corn, 10 chairs, cupboard and table furniture.
                  Signed Samuel Crockett.

       ANN STEWART'S Will - In the name of God amen I Ann Stewart
of the County of Williamson and State of Tennessee being in a weak
and low state of health but in perfect mind and memory calling to
mindtthe mortality of my body do make and ordain this to be my last
Will and Testament. I do give and bequeath unto Jinea Kee one
chest. I likewise give to Nancy Lee my spinning wheel and check
reel. I Likewise give and bequeath to my loving daughter Jinea
Kee my cloke not made up. I likewise give a satton bonnet to
Margaret Stewart not made. I likewise give and bequeth to Joseph
Edwards a certain bay horse. I likewise give to Sarah Stewart one
satten gown, to the rest of my wearing apparel I give my daughter
Jinney Kee all and every part thereof. I likewise give Joseph Alexander a bed and furniture belonging to it. I likewise give
and bequeth Nancy Kee and Joseph Alexander all and every part of
my property, including hogs, cattle, and horses and cows and all
the rest of my property together I leave them the whole to be put
up and sold at twelve months credit with bond and Security for
said money to be equally divided between them, Nancy Lee and
Joseph Alexander, which money is to be put at interest for Nancy
Kee and paid to her when she comes of age, or at the day of her
marriage. Joseph Alexander's money is to be put in Dannold Par-
kings' hands and for him to pay the said Joseph the yearly interest for his part of said estate until he thinks he can take

Page
(277)

Page
(278)

care of it himself. And I do by these presents constitute and
appoint Charles Brown my whole and sole executor with full power
to sell either at or prevent sale such part of my Estate as is not
willed to my children with full power to execute Lawfull deeds of
conveyance of property which I now possess of stock and household
furniture and I do acknowledge this to be my last Will and Testament
and revoking all others. In witness whereof I hereunto set my hand
and offer my seal this third day of November eighteen hundred and
three. Signed, sealed, publixhed, and pronounced in the presence of
Ephraim Brown, John Johnson, Charles Brown.
        Signed Ann Stewart x her mark   (SEal)
        State of Tennessee, Williamson County - Charles Brown came
into open Court January Session 1812 and brings with him the last
Will and Testament of Ann Stewart, deceased, and it appearing from
said Will that the said Charles Brown was in said Will appointed Sole
Executor of said Will and he the said Charles Brown, renounces taking upon himself the Execution of said Will, whereupon came Ephraim
Brown, John Johnson and Charles Brown and proved the Executor and
publishing thereof by the said Ann Stewart, deceased, and the same
was ordered to be recorded and came also Thomas Stewart who on mo-
tion is appointed Administrator of the goods and chattels rights and
credits of the said Ann Stewart, deceased, with the Will annexed
who gave bond with Charles Brown and John Johnstone his Securities in
the sum of five hundred dollars conditioned for the Execution of
said Administration, who took the oath of an Administrator, and it
is ordered that Letters of Administration with said Will annexed
issue to said Thomas Stewart accordingly.
            N. P. Hardeman, C. W. C.

(Page 279)

        An Inventory of the Goods and Chattels rights and credits
of Ann Stewart, deceased: 1 spinning wheel, 1 reel, 1 table, 1
bedstead and furniture to wit, 2 sheets, a pair of blankets, 2
coverlets, 2 pillows, feathers for a boulster, 1 calico counterpaine,
1 bedstead, bed and furniture, to wit, a coverlet and quilt, 2 blankets, a pillow called Joe's bed, 1 feather bed said to have been
given to Nancy Key, 1 feather bed, 1 chest, 1 barrel, 5 pails, 1
bucket, 1 keeler, 1 pot rack, 1 Dutch oven, 1 large kettle and pot-
hook, 1 big pot, 1 little box of pot hooks, 1 keg, 1 trap hackle,
1 middle sized pewter dish, 8 small pewter plates, 1 tin strainer,
6 pewter spoons, 1 pr. of iron tongs, 1 bag, 1 bread tray, 1 sett
of plow irons, 1 pair of iron traces, 1 clevis and tweisted link,
1 pair of iron traces, 1 horse, swingle tree, 1 hand saw, 1 old
trunk, 1 hair sifter, 1 falling ax, 1 vol. of Allan's Album Family Instructor, Doolittle on Sacrament, 1 dozen old books, 2 weeding
hoes, 4 bunches of broken flax, a pair of steelyards, 1 small tin
coffee pot, 1 bay horse, 1 bay mare, 1 sow and 5 shoats, 6 fat
hogs killed since her Decease by Joseph Alexander, 1 heifer with
a star, a red and white bull, a brindle steer, a red heifer calf,
4 geese, 1 dozen chicken fowls, 1 crib of Indian Corn, 1 tin lamp,
1 woman's saddle, 1 scarlet cloak, 1 flat iron, 1 shoe of upper
leather, 2 salting barrels, 4 hanks of cotton yarn, wearing apparel,
3 dollars cash, Robert Smith's bond for $4.62½, Robert Bettick's
and Thomas Berry's bond for $4.00½, Jonathan Cooper and Thomas Ber-
ry's bond for $10.12½, Henry Stuart and Samuel McCutchan's bond for
$14.50, William Sneed and Samuel McCutchan's bond for $37. Nathan
Snæed and William Sneed's bond for $11.25, William Carpenter and
Henry Stuart's bond for $10.25. Jan'y. 18,1812.

Signed Thomas Stewart, Admr. with the Will annexed of Anne
Stewart. Returned to January Session 1812. N. P. Hardeman, C.W.C.

(age
280)
        An Account of Sales of Estate of Ann Stewart, deceased:
Joseph Alexander 1 bay horse $42, Nancy Kee 1 bay mare $22, John
Porter 1 sample of corn $12, Joseph Alexander 1 large kettle
$6.12½, Ezekial Dawson, 1 large pot $2.75, Nancy Lee 1 small pot
$2.25, Hugh Barr 1 little pot $1.52, Vincin Greer 1 Dutch oven
$2, Nancy Kee 1 bag, 1 churn .62½, Nancy Lee 2 potts .31¼, Nancy
Lee ditto ditto, Nancy Lee lppale and tray, Ezekiel Dawson 1 bed
without clothes $6., John Porter 1 bed, bedstead, and furniture
$25., Joseph Alexander 1 lot plow, geer, clevis, and singletree
$10.25, Barnet Markem 1 hoe .75, Thomas Berry 1 pot zinc tub .62½,
John S. Campbell 1 axe $1.25, Joseph Alexander 2 chairs $1.37½,
Lorene Young 2 chairs, $1.25, Nancy Lee 1 strainer .25, John Hull
1 qt. coffee, irons, 1 pot, spoons, cups $1., Joseph Alexander 1
potrack $2.62½, Thomas Malone 1 pair tongs $2.25, Joseph Alexander 1 table .50, Joseph Alexander 1 lantern .87½, Jacob Garret 1 bell and collar $1, Nancy Lee 1 trap hackel .81¼, Jacob
Garrett 1 pr. stillards $1.81¼, Joseph Aldxlrside upper leather
$2.37½, m Joseph Alex'r. 1 bag .37½, Nancy Lee cauler .6¼, Andrew
Jameson 1 dish six plates $4.10, Nancy Lee 1 sifter .6¼, Jacob
Garrett 1 saw $1.25, John Dilling 1 lot of flax $2, John S.
Campbell 1 flat iron .87½, Joseph Alexander 1 barrel .12½, Lau-
rence Young 1 yearling calf, Nancy Lee 1 book .25, John Mayfield 1 Bible .31¼, John Mayfield 1 Bible .25, Charles Brown
1 side sadale .75, Nancy Lee 1 lot of spun cotton $1.18½,
Joshua Burnam 4 ganders $1.25, Joseph Alexander 1 dozen fowls
.31¼, ditto Alexander five shotes $2.33¼, ditto 1 sow and pigs
$1.62½, Cornelius Mackfadin 1 heffere $3.50, Jacob Garrett 1
Bridle steer $1.50, Joseph Alexander 1 trunk .12½.
        Williamson County to wit - This day personally appeared be-
fore me, David Mason, a Justice of the Peace, for the county aforesaid, Thomas Stewart, Administrator of all and singular the goods
and chattels rights and credits of Anne Stewart, deceased, with
her will annexed and made oath that the within account of sales
contains a true account of sales at a credit of 12 months of the
goods and chattels of the Estate of said Anne Stewart made by
said Anne Stewart made by said Administrator on the second day
of April 1811 to the best of his knowledge and belief in which
Stephen Childress was auctioneer and that and that this account
of Sales is intended to be returned to next County Court for
Williamson County.
        Signed Thomas Stuart.
    Sworn to and Subscribed before me this 11th day of April
1812. N. P. Hardeman, C. W. C.

(age
281)
        A list of the Sales of the property of CHARLES TAYLOR, de-
ceased: 1 bay horse $27.25, 15 yards of linen $5.40 - total
$32.65. All sold on 6 months credit.
        17th October 1811. Signed Henry H. Jackson, Admr. Returned
to October Session 1811. N. P. Hardeman, C. W. C.

(Page 282)
        Inventory of the Property of MARTHA EVANS, deceased: 1 wag-
gon, 5 head of horses, 10 head of cattle, 25 head of hogs, 1 crib
of corn, 1 do. with some corn, 2 sows, 1 pair fire dogs, 1 flax-
wheel, 1 cotten wheel, 1 chest, 1 table, 2 bedsteads, some flax, 1

woman's saddle, 3 pair harnesses for a loom, two hogs, 3 chairs,
1 pair stretchers, 4 tin cups, a lease of land for one year, 1
churn, 1 keeler, 1 pot, 1 negro man.

Returned to January Session 1812 by Thomas Clark and John
Evans, the Administrators.

N. P. Hardeman, C. W. C.

Account of Sales of the Estate of Martha Evans, deceased,-
Sold 12th February 1812: 1 plough $1.70, one pr. Stretchers .50,
1 shovel .33, 2 chairs $1.2, 1 chair .50, 1 pot .80, 1 pot rack
and hand-saw $1.78, 1 pr. fire dogs $3.76, one waggon $30, 1
flax wheel $3.75, one cotton wheel $2.75, 65 barrels of corn $88.13,
one cotton wheel $2.75, one cow $9, one steer $8.25, one cow and
calf $7.50, 1 steer $5.30, one keeper $3.87½, one do. $4.6¼, 1
heifer yearling $1.75, 1 steer $3.25, 1 sow and pigs $.14, one negro
fellow $201, 1 black mare $16.25, one grey ditto $24, 1 table $2.75,
1 pale .16, 1 churn and keeler $1.1, 1 tub .27, harness for loom
.20, 1 barrel .25, 1 hog and some wheat $1, one woman sold at $8.1,
1 chest $2, fine hogs $9.12, fine ditto $7.76, 5 hogs $5.4, 7 ditto
$7.1, 1 filly $20.50, one ditto $14.2, one colt $8.3, 2 geese, 5
ducks $2.25, one bed and cord, 1 bed and furniture $15.26, 1 ditto
ditto $11, 1 bedstead and cord $2.75, 1 ditto ditto $1.66, 1 lease
of land for one year $11. Total $575.22¾

Returned to April Session 1812. N. P. Hardeman, C. W. C.

age
283)

Inventory of the estate of John Dowd, deceased; 4 head of horses, 22 head of cattle, 35 head of hogs, 1 mattock, 1 oven, 1 pot,
1 skillet, 1 kettle, 1 comb, 4 axes, 1 saddle, 1 iron wedge, 1
plow, 2 pr. of bedsteads, corn and cotton quantity not known, 6
pewter plates, 1 dish do., 2 augers, 1 handsaw and drawing knife,
some cooper's ware, knives and forks, 1 gun in by us undersigned.

Signed Jane Dowd

Returned to January Session 1812 - Charley Dowd - James Wilkins
N. P. Hardeman, C. W. C.

An Account of Sales of the Estate of JOHN DOWD, deceased -
Sold 24th January 1812: James Wilkins 1 book title Buchan $2.,
1 mattock .50, 1 fine quarter auger .6¼, Isaiah White 1 plow $1.6¼,
Jean Dowd saw auger and drawing knife $2.6¼, 1 log chain $1.6¼, one
bell $1.6¼, settle wheel $2.50, one saddle $6, one curry comb .37½,
1 plow $1.6¼, one axe .56¼, 1 do. $2.1, Thomas McEwen 1 axe $3,
Jean Dowd big wheel $1, one kettle $3.12½, Little oven $.32½, big
oven $3.75, one pot .81¼, 1 skillet .62½m k rack 2 hooks $1.18¾,
1 horsehare plow $4.75, Charles Dowd 1 axe $1.18¾, Jean Dowd 2
pan gears $5, one for double trees $1.65, Isaiah White 1 fodder
stack $2, Thomas Gillespie 1 ditto $2.80, Clem Wall 1 fodder stack
$2.6¼, Jean Dowd 1 washing tub .50, coopers ware $1., 1 pail .50,
1 bason and 5 plates $1.50, 1 bason and dresser ware $1.75, knives
and forks .50, 1 bottle .12½, 1 cooking glass .18¼, Anderson
Powell 1 shot gun $6.20, James Wilkins 1 pistol .97, Charles Dowd
1 bag $1, Andrew McCorkle 1 slay .12½, Jean Dowd 1 slay .37½, 2
ditto $1, 1 chest .25, 1 do. .25, bedstead and furniture $12, 1
do. $12.6¼, 1 mare $11.26, 1 horse $30, one bay colt $10, one filley $20.25, candle stick and fork .50, Anderson Powell 4 books,
Jean Dowd 1 loom $1, one side saddle $2.50, old vessels $1, four
hoes $5, one iron wedge .94¾, Andrew McCorkle 1 red steer $12.97¾,
Clem Wall 1 cow $8.6¼, Isaiah White 1 lot of corn 5 bar'ls no. 1
$6.31¼, Thomas McEwen 1 ditto 5 bar'ls no. 2 $6.30, ditto 1 ditto

Page
(284)

5 bar'ls no. 3 $6.25, William Carson 1ditto 5 bar'ls. no. 4 $6.6¼,
ditto 1 ditto 5 bar'ls no. 5 $5.66, Jean Dowd 1 cow $8, one do.
$6.62½, one do. $9.25, one do. $10., Anderson Powell 1 heifer
$6.12½, James Wilkins $5.50, one do. $4, Jean Dowd 4 yearlings
$8, two do. $4, 1 heifer and steer $6, one heifer $3.12½, 1 bull
$7.50, James Wilkins 1 steer $6.50, Jane Dowd 1 do. $2, Anderson
Powell 1 slate .25, Jean Dowd 1 smoothing iron $1, 1 pr. pinchers
.50, 3 chairs $1, two sows and 16 pigs $7, Isaiah White 1 white
sow $3.12½, one spotted sow, $1.12½, Charles Dowd 5 pigs $2.51,
Nelson Chapman 6 hogs $11.37½. Charles Dowd 2 piggs $1, David Gillespie 1 white sow $1.50, Jean Dowd 1 cage $1, one bow hide $2,
James Wilkins 12 ducks $1.12½, Jean Dowd 1 bridle .25, Polly Powell
12 chickens .12½, Granberry Dean 1 lancet .27, Jean Dowd 1 bridle
.25, Polly Powell 12 chickens .12½, Anderson Powell 4 horse shoes
.51, Jean Dowd cotton .12½.
     One year allowance for Jean Dowd and family allowed to them
by Dowd Gillespie and David Crisman, 8 head of the best hogs, 150
bushels of corn and 1 fodder stack, 2 dollars paid to Nelson Chapman for crying the vendue. Returned to April Session 1812.
          N. P. Hardeman, C. W. C.

     An Inventory of the Estate of GEORGE HUDLOW, deceased, taken
11th January 1812: 1 note of hand on Charles Boyles for $116.62 2/3,
four beds and furniture, 12 pounds of feathers in each bed, 4 common chairs, 1 walnut chest, 4 ovens, 2 potts, 3 skillets, 1 griddle, 1 coffee pot, ½ doz. plates, ½ doz. knives, 1 doz. spoons, 2
 tin pans, 1 pewter dish, 1 pewter bason, 1 qt. bottle, 1 coffee
mill, 1 flat iron, 2 rifles, 1 shot-gun, 1 shot pouch, 4 tin cups,
5 tin tumblers, 1 flax wheel, 1 cotton wheel, 4 plows, parcel of
old hoes and axes, 5 pair of geers, 1 waggon, 7 horses, 2 yearlings,
1 sow and 5 shoats, 1 three square harrow, a parcel of hemp not
broke, 2½ small cribs of corn the quantity not known, 1 hand saw,
3 chizels, 1 barrel, auger, 2 screw augers, 1 foot adze, 1 pair
steelyards, 1churn, 4 pails, 1 cutting box, some flax, 7 stacks
of fodder, 3 bulls, 1 pitch fork, 1 fish geg, 1 good axe, some
hemp seed and some flax seed, 1 frying pan, a parcel of old horse
shoes, 1 pr. of cotton cards, 1 note $33. of Jack Camden, 2 pair of
pot hooks, 60 lbs. of cotton, 6 books,
               Signed Barbara Hudlow
                         x - her mark
Returned to January Session 1812. N. P. Hardeman, C. W. C.

     An Inventory of the Estate of WILLIAM STONE, Senr., deceased,
taken by us the 9th day of Jan'y. 1812 - 7 negroes, viz. Cloe,
Ben, Milley, Harry, Lewis, Season and Manuel, 1 waggon and four
pair of geers, 1 feeding trough, 6 head of horses, 10 head of cattle, 6 head of hogs, 3 feather beds and furniture, 2 bedsteads,
1 table, 2 trunks, 2 plank boxes, 1 flax wheel, 1 cotton wheel, 1
pr. cotton cards, 4 water pails, 1 churn, 1 tubb and half bushel,
7 pewter plates, 2 pewter dishes, 2 basons, 5 cups, 5 saucers, 1
tea pot, 1 tea canister, 1 tin coffee pot, 4 tin cups, 6 knives,
6 forks, 1 carving knife, one white earthern mug, 1 sail boat, 2
earthern crocks, 1 bowl, 1 tin waiter, 1 Server, 1 black bottle
1 glass tumbler, 1 glass gobbler, small butter plate, 1 cream pot,
1 pepper box, 1 candle stick and candle mold, 11 books, 1 flat
iron, 1 coffee mill, 1 mans saddle and bridle, 1 pr. dog irons, 3

Salt barrels, 2 sitting chairs, 200 weight of ginned cotton, 2 pots,
1 Dutch oven, 1 skillet and spider, 1 pr. of pot hooks and pot
racks, 3 ploughs, 4 weeding hoes, 2 iron wedges, 2 augers, 1 handsaw, 1 drawing knife, 1 mattock, 2 claw hammers, 1 hatchet, 1 foot
addze, 2 cliveses, 1 weaver's loom and 1 seven hundred reed one, 1
inch chizel, 3 gimblets, a crop of hemp in the stalk, some hemp seed,
1 iron bound keg, some corn, 1 log chain, 1 bell and coller, 2 narrow axes, 122 acres of land, 35 dollars in cash.
                    Signed Jane Stone
                              x her mark - Administrators
                        William Stone
Returned to January Session 1812 - N. P. Hardeman, C. W. C.
     An Account of the property sold on the 14th day of February
1812 at the sale of William Stone, deceased: John McCutchen 1 basket
with iron in it $1.50, G. L. Nolen 2 hammers and 3 gimblets .90,
David Lovet 1 foot adze $1, Rowley Stone 1 mattock $1.18¾, E. Riggs
1 pair of harnes .12½, E Riggs 1 handsaw $1.89½, Robert Carothers
1 iron wedge $1, James Fulton 1 iron wedge $1.6¼, Caleb Willis 2
augers .36¼, John Holt 1 spider $1.68¾, Ambrose Owen 1 pail and half
bushel .37½, Edw. Stone 1 large bell $1.62½, one mans saddle and
bridle $10.50, John L. Fielder 1 lot of hemp seed $2, Edw. Stone
1 plow and stock $1, Sam Stone 1 plow and stock $2.75, John Hill 1
lot of cotton $5.50, Thomas Balew 2 do. of cotton $4.31¼, James
Tobe 3 do. of cotton $4.25, John Carothers 4 do. of cotton $4.31¼.
Thomas Simmons 1 lot of corn 5 barrels $6.50, S. B. Morton 2 lots
of corn $6.50, Sam Stone a parcel of hemp $6, James Tobe 1 black and
white heifer $5, Izrael M. Carrel 1 red and white heifer $3.25,
William Nolen 1 red and white heifer $2.62½, Gursom Hunt 1 red and
white heifer $2.62½, Jabez Owen 2 red and white heifers $2.62½,
William Nolen 1 bull $2, James Fulton 1 bay horse $17.50, William
McEnters 1 sorrel horse $5.31¼, William Stone 1 sorrel filley $23.37½,
John McCutchen 1 waggon and hand geer $60, Agnes Stone 1 loom $5,
Agnes Stone 1 sorrel mare and colt $40, John Mayfield 1 empty bar-
rel .25, John McCutchen 1 iron bound kegg $1, Total $234.29¼.
N. P. Hardeman, C. W. C.

     Inventory of the Estate of DUDLEY PORTER, deceased: 1 waggon,
4 pair of geers, collars and bridle and 6 head of horses, 3 feather
beds, furniture and 2 bedsteads, 200 weight of cotton, 1 trunk, 1
table, 2 bridles, 1 handsaw, 2 axes, 1 iron wedge, 1 log chain, 2
plough hoes, 2 smoothing irons, 1 iron coffee mill, 1 brass coffee
pot, 1 box of old irons, 2 hoes, 2 skillets, 1 oven lid, 1 hammer,
1 drawing knife, 1 chizel, 5 pair of pot hooks, 1 jug, 2 bottles,
3 pewter dishes, 3 pewter basons, 5 pewter plates, 9 pewter spoons,
6 deep plates, cups and saucers, 1 set knives and forks, 1 tin
bason, 1 bread basket, 1 mug and pitcher, 1 server, 6 tins, sugar
box, half gallon, 6 veals, 1 tin strainer, iron table, flesh fork,
1 iron spoon, 1 pepper box, 2 glass tumblers, 9 wooden vessels, 3
hogs, 1 calf, one book case, 4 books, 1 set of kegs, 2 pair of cotton cards, 1 sifter, 3 chairs, 2 candle sticks, 2 bells, 2 pair nippers, 2 pair scissors, 2 flax, 2 saddles, 1 padlock, 1 cream jug,
Mr. Duncan due $5, William Wilson fifty gallons of Whiskey, due
David McCord $9, due Kazey Shinold $10,. The above is a true Inventory of the Chattel Estate of Dudley Porter, deceased.
                    Signed Sarah Porter, Admr.
                              x her mark
Returned to April Session 1812.   N. P. Hardeman, C. W. C.

Page
(288)
Inventory of the Goods and Chattels of PETER REEVES, deceased:
1 waggon and geers, 4 horses, 1 mare and 2 colts, 1 bed and furniture, 1 spinning wheel, 1 cradle, 1 skillet, 1 bread hoe, shovel
and tongs, 1 coffee pot, 1 tea pot, half dozen earthern plates,
1 dish and bason, 1 hoe and 2 axes, 2 trunks, 1 iron kettle, a
pair of smoothing irons, 1 slate, a parcel of books, pickling tub,
a washing tub, 1 piggin, 3 decanters, 2 butter pots, 2 iron wedges,
umbrella and drawing knife, 3 bells and a small negro boy. 16th
April 1812.
          Signed James Owen, Admr.
Returned to April Session 1812. N. P. Hardeman, C. W. C.

Inventory of the Estate of LITTLEBERRY EPPERSON, deceased,
taken 30th day of March 1812: 1 bay mare called Fan and colt, 1
sorrel filley called Fly, 1 brown mare and colt called Mill, 1 bay
horse called Hornet, 1 bay horse called Jim Crack, 1 bay horse
called Dick, 1 cow and calf called White Face, 1 cow and calf called
Brindle, 1 heifer, 2 years old, 1 heifer and steer 1 year old,
some hogs supposed to be 20 head, 1 waggon and hind geer, 1 barshare plow, 2 hoes, 1 mattock, 1 axe, 2 small pots, 1 large oven,
3 pair pot-hooks, 2 feather beds and furniture, 2 bedsteads and
cords, 1 coffee mill, 2 chairs, 1 flat iron, 1 pewter dish, 1 large
spinning wheel, 1 table, 1 chest, 1 looking glass, 1 womans saddle,
3 portk barrels, 1 pail, 2 piggins, 2 churns, 1 pair of stilliards,
3 horse bells.
          Returned to April Session 1812. N. P. Hardeman, C. W. C.

Page
(289)
Inventory of the Estate of JAMES BUFORD, deceased: 4 head of
horses, 28 ditto of cattle, 63 ditto of hogs or thereabouts, young
and old, 1 cupboard, 1 bureau, 1 folding table, 2 looking glasses,
2 axes, 5 hoes, 1 plow, 1 pair stilliards, 1 drawing knife, 1 hand
saw, 1 cross cut and whip saw, 1 waggon and 3 pair chains, 1 log
chain, 2 feather beds and furniture, 1 pair cart wheels, 3 large
kettles and 1 pott, 1 Dutch oven and 2 skillets, 2 pr. fire dogs,
12 rush cotton chairs, 1 coffee mill, 4 glass tumblers, 4 white
bowls and plates, one earthern dish, 1 water pail, 1 pewter dish,
2 basons, 1 washing tub, 1 reel, 1 flax wheel, 3 cotton do., 1 set
razors and case, 2 bottles and two salt sellers, 1 pepper box, 1
saddle, 1 stone jug, 2 candle sticks, 1 pair flat irons, 1 spice
mortar, 3 reep hooks, 1 loom, 1 coopreads, 2 pair iron wedges,
2 barreled augers, 8 volumes Stern's works, 1 large Bible, Burkett's
Translation and others (notes due the Estate, the one on Nicholas
Lavendar $25.60, 1 on Peter Edwards $20., 1 on Richard Rooks $5.70,
1 on John House $18, 1 on Joseph Feat $17.10, 1 on Benny Goodman
$17, 1 on Samuel Braddon $10., 1 on George Glascock $25., 1 on
Bud Lavender $3., 1 on George Crow $7.33 2/3, 1 on Neil Johnson
$7., 1 on Thomas Kelly $4.25, 1 on Samuel Bond $5.12½, 1 on James
Fitzgerald $1.82½, 1 on William Sa Allen $5.66, 1 on Robert Alex-
ander .83¼, 1 on Joshua Barnes $14.16¼, notes due to the estate:
1809 Samuel Dotson Dr. $3.72, 1809 William Pepper .90, David
Long $23.40, James Alexander $3.95, 1808: Andrew Cuff, Dr. $10.83,
Peter Ragsdale $13.16, William Wells $1.95, 1805: Hugh Smiley
Page
(290)
Dr. $5.8 1/3, 1811 William Fisher $5.80, Richard Barnes $3.80,
Charles Kelsey $7.80, John Whealy $10.35, Accounts in James
Hewey's hands of Collection: James McCraven $6.30, Henry Davis
$10, Armistead Mays $2, Thomas McElwell note $2.62½, 400 lbs.

second rate gined cotton, $503\frac{1}{4}$ first rate ditto, Money now on hand 78.16\frac{1}{2}$.

Signed Spencer Buford, Charles Buford, James Buford, Edward Buford.

Returned to October Session 1811. N. P. Hardeman, C. W. C.

Account of Sales of the Estate of James Buford, deceased:
William Gurley 1 Dutch oven $1.25, Edward Buford 1 skillet $1.25, do. do. 1 pot rack $1.75, Spencer Buford 1 kettle $4.25, Caleb Manley 1 flat skillet $1, S. Buford 1 kettle 5.6\frac{1}{4}$, George Mebane 1 do. 5.37\frac{1}{2}$, Edward Buford 1 pot $5.25, Spencer Buford 1 pr. pot hooks .43$\frac{3}{4}$, Edwd. Buford 1 churn .75, George Mebane 1 pail and nogin .25, Charles Buford 1 hackle 2.6\frac{1}{4}$, do. do. 1 spice mortar 1.18\frac{3}{4}$, George Mebane 1 coffee mill 2.37\frac{1}{2}$, S. Buford 1 pr. wedges 1.56\frac{1}{4}$, Charles Buford 1 pr. sheep shares .56$\frac{1}{4}$, Elisha Hassell 1 drawing knife and plow 1.12\frac{1}{2}$, Ezekial McKearley and candlesticks .50, Edward Buford 1 pair wedges $1.50, William Gurley 1 ax 1.81\frac{1}{4}$,

(page 291)

Somerset Moore 1 reep hook .31$\frac{1}{4}$, do. do. do. .43$\frac{3}{4}$, Charles Buford do. do. .37$\frac{1}{2}$, Edward Buford 1 plow 2.6\frac{1}{4}$, Charles Buford 1 bell $1, Alexander Clark 1 auger .50, George Mebane 1 bason 1.31\frac{1}{4}$, Edward Buford 1 do. 1.18\frac{3}{4}$, Somerset Moore 1 dish $2.75, Spencer Buford 1 do. .31$\frac{1}{4}$, William Gurley 1 hand saw 1.81\frac{1}{4}$, Edward Buford 1 howel 1.66\frac{1}{4}$S, Spencer Buford 1 crop cord saw 8.18\frac{3}{4}$, Edw. Buford 2 sifters .36$\frac{1}{4}$, Daniel Derryberry 1 augur .12$\frac{1}{2}$, Edwd. Ragsdale 1 pail .31$\frac{1}{4}$, James Giddens 1 half bushel .50, George Mebane 1 hoe .50, ditto 1 ditto .50, James Giddens 1 do. .93$\frac{3}{4}$, Caleb Manley $1, Cornelius Mathis 1 do. $1, James Giddens 1 ax and hoe $1, Charles Buford 1 jug 1.62\frac{1}{2}$, William Gurley 1 real 1.12\frac{1}{2}$, Elisha Dodson 1 sett of spools .75, Spencer Buford 1 hoe 1.6\frac{1}{4}$, do. do. 1 wheel $1.25, George Mebane 1 f. Wheel 3.12\frac{1}{2}$, Edward Buford 1 Bible $3.50, James Buford 1 pr. flat irons $1.25, Charles Buford 1 Burkette's Exp. 5.37\frac{1}{2}$, Edward Ragsdale Stern's Works $8, Charles Buford Telleson's Works 12.12\frac{1}{2}$, George Mebane 3 hooks .50, Caleb Manley 1 table $4.50, George Mebane 1 lot of cookery ware $1.50, James Buford 2 salt stands 1.1\frac{1}{4}$, Amos Duncan knives and forks .50, S.

(page 292)

Buford 3 tumblers .75, Thomas Slags 2 razors and case 1.12\frac{1}{2}$, William Gurley 12 checo 3.12\frac{1}{2}$, do. do. one bed stead $1.51, George Mebane 6 slays $2.50, Malachi Nicholson 1 andiron $4.50, George Mebane 6 slays $2.50, Somerset Moore 1 Beauro, $12.75, James Davis 1 cupboard $12.25, Spencer Buford 1 waggon $31, Edw. Buford 1 pr. cart-wheels $10, Alexander Mebane 1 pair old wheels $3.50, Alexander Clarke 1 log chain $6., Edward Buford 1 sow and 8 pigs 1.54\frac{1}{4}$, William Gurley 1 sow $3, Ezekial McEarley 5 hogs 1st choice $15., George Mebane 5 do. do. 12.62\frac{1}{2}$, Bluff Lavendar 5 do. do. 2nd choice $8.25, Jeremiah Brady 5 do. do. 3rd choice $8., Edward Buford 5 do. do. 5th 6.12\frac{1}{2}$, do. do. 5th do. 6th do. 3.31\frac{1}{4}$, do. do. 5 do. 7 do., do. do. 12, do. do. 12 do., Spencer Buford 1 steer $12, James Buford 1 steer $10, Charles Boyles 2 steers 20.62\frac{1}{2}$, Edw. Buford 2 steers 11.12\frac{1}{2}$, Thomas Slags 1 cow and calf 11.12\frac{1}{2}$, Archibald Beasley 1 cow and calf $12, William Blakely 1 cow and calf $7.50, Cornelius Wilson 1 heffer $5.50, do. do. $5.50, William Blakely 1 heffer $2.50, do. do. 1 heffer and steer $6.50, Charles Hulsey 1 cow and calf 7.37\frac{1}{2}$, George Glascock 1 bull $6,

(page 293)

James Giddens 1 cow and calf $1, Somerset Moore one cow and calf $8, Spencer Buford 1 steer $5.25, Edward Ragsdale 1 steer $5, Edward Ragsdale 1 steer $4.60, Spencer Buford 1 pot rack 2.56\frac{1}{4}$, do. do. 1 clevis .43$\frac{3}{4}$, Edward Buford 1 bedstead .31$\frac{1}{4}$, Beverly Reese 2 cans .75, James Giddens 1 side board and candle s tand .12$\frac{1}{2}$, Malachia Nicholson 1 bottle .30, do. do. 1 pr. stilliards $2.75, George Mebane 1 loom $5, James Giddens 1 pr. of scissors .87½, Somerset Moore 1 butter pot .18¾, George Mebane 1 candle box and canister .50, James Giddens 1 pr. of scissors .25, Allen Hill 100 lbs. of ginned cotten $4.87½, Elisha Dodson 100 lbs of ginned cotten, Edward Buford 58 lbs. of ginned cotten $2.61, Samuel Harris 50 do. do. $2.50, Archibald Beasley 1 cotton rect. $22.¾, William Blakely 1 cotton receipt $2.31, Elisha Dotson 1 cotton receipt $2.10½, Edward Buford 1 hogshead .62½, James Giddens 1 do. .18¾, Edward Bufored 1 do. .18¾, Allen Hill sugar box .50, James Giddens 1 pr. of tongs .27, Charles Boyles 1 ox yoke .37½, Spencer Buford 1 waist coat and pattern $1.93¾, Charles Buford 1 table cloth .37½, Somerset Moore 1 do. .37½, Edward Buford 1 saddle $4.43¾, James Buford 1 rope .12½, George Mebane 1 bed and furniture $15, do. do. do. .50, Daniel Carter 1 sorrel horse $40.25, Cornelius Wilson 1 old horse $10.50, William Blakely 1 bay mare $72.25, Charles Buford phials .25, Peter Edwards 25 barrels corn $25.25, George Mebane 110 do. $110, Elisha Dodson 75 do. $74.93¾, Thomas Old 75 bar'ls corn $74.93¾, Edward Buford 1 bee hive $1.25, do. do. do. .31¼, James Giddens 1 gun .63, Spencer Buford 1 stack of oats $4, Peter Edwards 500 lbs of fodder $2.6¼, do. do. 500 do. $1.62½. Signed Spencer Buford, Charlie Buford, James Buford, Edw. Buford. Returned to January Session 1812. N. P. Hardeman, C. W. C.

We, Richard Puckett and Nicholas Scales, Commissioners appointed by the worshipful Court of Williamson County to settle with David Craig and Alexander Miller, Adm. on the estate of Michael Waran, deceased, have done the same as follows to wit, we find the Admrs. charged with amt. of Sales. The above administrators are allowed for Vouchers and necessary expenses attending their Administration, $322.75.

Given under our hands this 3rd day of Nov. 1811. Signed Richard Puckett. Returned to January Session 1812. N.P.Hardeman,C.W.C.

October 14th 1811. We, Richard Puckett and Samuel Davis being appointed by the worshipful court of Williamson County to settle with Stephen Childress, Administrator of Robert Carlile, deceased, do find that all the property that appears on the inventory to be sold, and the total amount is $277.63 and that the amount of Debts and costs that Mr. Childress produced receipts for is $54.70½ and that we have also allowed Mr. Childress for maintaining of the widow and children to the present day $120 and the balance is $102.93, one third of which is the widow's dowry and after deducting the Widow's Dowry off, leaves to the orphans $68.66 2/3.

Signed Richard Puckett, J.P. and James Davis, J. P. Returned to October Session 1811. N. P. Hardeman, C. W. C.

William Parham, Guardian in acc't. with orphans of William C. HILL,dec'd., 1813, Jan'y. 1st. To the hire of a negro man Bromfield for 1811 $40, ditto ditto Isham for 1811 $96,ditto ditto Toby $70, ditto Negro woman Ester and child $20, ditto man Lewis $70, ditto boy Jerry $45, ditto ditto Phil $17.50. Total $348.50.

Cr. 1812 Jan'y 1st. By a deduction on consequence of Lewis'S. Summers boarding Martha Hill for 1811 $35., Cash pd. pr.receipt No.1 $20, do. No. 2 $9,do.No.3 $14.62½. Boarding J.G. Hill for 1811 $35, Cash pd. pr. rec. No.1 $20, no. 2 $9, no. 3 $14.62½. Boarding Jas. G. Hill $35. Balance due the orphans of W. C. Hill $195.25.

N. P. Hardeman, C. W. C.

Page
(297)
State of Tennessee, Williamson County. In obedience of an order
from the worshippful court of the County aforesaid at October Session 1811 to us directed to settle with Amos Davis, relative to
the estate of Jonathan Davis, deceased, have done the same as
follows, to wit: we find from Clerk's Certificates that Amos
Davis is charged with amount of Sales $684.1¼. Amos Davis pro-
duced the following receipts of vouchers of money paid: Rec't. No.
1 from Clerk $3.45, No. 2 Proven Act $8.75, No. 3 ditto $6, No.
4 ditto $23., No. 5 ditto $2, No. 6 ditto $2.45, No. 7 ditto $6.75,
No. 8 ditto $9, no. 9 Voucher $18.67, No. 10 proven Act $1.12½,
No. 11 ditto $4.25, No. 12 ditto .50, No. 13 ditto $5, No. 14 ditto
$1.50, No. 15 ditto $9.
　　　Amos Davis' troubles and expenses relative to the Admrs. above,
the above Statement is estimated at $135.51¾. Balance due $548.49½
Given under our hands this 19th December 1811.
　　　　　　　Signed Nicholas Scales, J. P.
　　　　　　　　　　Archer Jordan, J. P.
　　　　　　Returned to January Session 1812. N. P. Hardeman, C. W. C.

Page
(298)
　　　Lawrence Bass Admr. of the Estate of J. Patton, deceased - Dr.
　　　The amount of monies rec'd. for sales of the Estate - $659.48¾
Cash rec'd. of John and Thomas Williamson $1632.
Interest   16.
Am't. received of James Wilson   112.50
Am't.   do.   do.   do.   27.00
Received of David Cummins   70.87½
"   David McGavock   2.00
"   John Nichols   .78
By cash pd. as the Voucher's herewith   2520.64½
By allowances for expences necessarily   423.64
　　incurred in conducting the business

                                                             2097.00
                                                              100.00
                                                             1997.00

John Weatherspoon and Hinchey Petway appointed by the County
Court of Williamson for selling and adjusting the accounts of
Lawrence Bass, admr. of the Estate of John Patton, dec'd., do
make report and say that we find in the hands of said Bass in
cash $1997 in notes on persons supposed to be solvent.
　　　　　　　　　　　　　　　　John Witherspoon
Returned to January Session   H. Pettway
1812   N. P. Hardeman, C. W. C.

　　　A list of all the property that came into my hands as Guar-
dian for the heirs for Sarah Clark, deceased, namely negro Wat,
Frank, Jude, Anne, Molley, Mary, Allen, Caroline, their children,
born since, namely, Jacob, Ruth.
　　　The above is a true statement given under my hand, this 1st
of January 1812.
　　　　　　　　　　Signed S. Green, Guardian.
Page
(299)
　　　Also the hire of the negroes for the year 1810 $221.
One-fifth part deducted for widow's part as will appear from a
Settlement with the Court $44.20
Also the sum of $176.80
                            78.41¼
Which the Add's. fell in debt to said Heirs on a settlement with

the Court which sum is fully accounted for in the within Settlement. Signed S. Green, Guardian. Dtr. in account with the heirs of Sam'l. Clark, deceased. 1810 Jan'y. To Ballance due the heirs from the Adrs. as will appear by a settlement with the Court $78.41¾. 1811 Jan'y. To the hire of Negroes for the year 1810. For the hire of negroes for the year 1811 $251.62½. 1812 April 14th To balance due as contra. In obedience to an order from the worshipful Court of Williamson County, we have proceeded to examine the above account and find the balance due the heirs of Samuel Clark to be one hundred and ninety-four dollars and eighty two cents, now in the hands of Sherwood Green, Guardian. C. H. McAlister and David Mason.

Credit - By one fifty part of the hire of negroes for year 1810 which was the widow's equal share on the division of said Estate $44.20 By the maintenance of sd. heirs for the year 1810-$100., by cash pd. Fields to cry negroes 1.75, Cash paid for books and paper for Salley and Martin $2,- Sept. 1st96th by cash paid merchandize for Salley Clark $7.15.

By cash paid William Martin for Samuel Clark's note payable to Richard Hopkins for $80 with interest from the year 1804 till paid $84.50, by cash paid N. Wyche for the schooling of Salley and Martin $10.25, by the maintenance of the heirs for the year 1811 $100, by cash paid J. Sawyer for extra charges as rec'd. $6.37½, by balance as per contra $194.82. Total $551.4½

Returned to April Session 1812. N. P. Hardeman, C. W. C.

D   Dr.-William Parham, Guardian, in account with the orphans of William C. Hill, deceased: To ballance due the orphans for the year 1808 $334.72 1/3, to interest on ditto from 1st Jan'y. 1809 till 1st of Jan'y. 1812, say 3 years $60.24 - ($394.96 1/3), to interest on ditto from 1st Jan'y. 1810 till 1st Jany. 1812, say 2 years $2.34, to the ballance due the orphans for year 1809 $19,52, to ballance due the orphans for the year 1810 $127.84 2/3. Interest on ditto from 1st Jany. 1811 till 1st Jany. 1812, say one year 135.5 2/3 To ballance due the orphans for the year 1811 $195.25

Cr. By the Guardian Commissions on $500.4½ reference being had to and acc't. returned to Court 1st of Jan'y. 1809 $25.

By the Guardian's Commission on $177.76, reference being had to an acc't. returned to January Session 1810 $8.25.

By the Guardian's Commission on $339, reference being to an account returned to January Session 1811 $16.95,

By the Guardian's Commission on $348.50 reference being had to an account returned to Jan'y. 1812, $17.42, By paid Henry W. Hill account against William Parham, Guardian $99.31. By paid Doct. Crockett account $5.87½, by paid Clerk's fees $2.65, by balance due the orphans the 1st Jan'y. 1812 $591.59. Total $747.59.

Pursuant to an order of Williamson Court, January Session 1812, which made it our duty to divide the negroes belonging to the orphans of William G. Hill, deceased, according to the Term of his last will, we have proceeded to make a division of said negroes and also to examine the Guardians acc't. and find a balance in the hands of the Guardian of $591.50. Given under our hands this 30th March 1812. Signed T. Saunders, D. Dunn, G. Hill D. Dickerson, J. Reese. N. P. Hardeman, C. W. C.

The full amount of the valuation of the negroes and money in the hands of the Guardian - Child's Share - Martha Hill No. 2 $3660, James Hill no. 3 $591.50.

Each child's proportion of the negroes: Martha Hill $1262, James Hill $1147, Henry W. Hill $1251.

Each child's proportion of money in the guardian's hands:
Martha Hill $155.16 2/3, James Hill $270.

Total amount of each child's part: Martha Hill $1417.16,
James Hill $1417, Henry W. Hill $1417.16

'age
302)
Martha Hill no. 2 drew Lewis $600, and Phill $437. and Bromfield $225. Total $1262.

James Hill no. 3 drew Toby $500, drew Terry $500, drew Mouring
$147. Total $1157.

Henry W. Hill no. 1 drew Isham $750, drew Esther and child
$500, and Chloe $1, Total $1251.

Martha Hill's proportion of money now in the hands of her
Guardian W. P. $155.16 2/3, James Hill's proportion of ditto in the
hands of his Guardian W. Parham $270.16 2/3, Henry W. Hill's pro-
portion of ditto in the hands of his guardian W. Parham $166.16 2/3
Total $4251.50.

In pursuance to an Order of the County Court of Williamson
January Session 1812, we have divided the estate of William C.
Hill agreeable to the above statement this 30th day of March 1812.

Signed G. Hill, T. Launders, D. Dickinson, D. Dunn, J. Reese.
Returned to April Session 1812. N. P. Hardeman, C. W. C.

PETER PRYOR and GREEN PRYOR, Orphans of JOHN PRYOR, deceased,
to Hendley Stone, Guardian of said orphans. January 1811 - To
surveying land in Wilson County and serches to get a Duplicate
Warrant as per rec'ts ₤3. 15, to two quires paper, the best kind
at 2/7½ 5 shillings, 3 pence, to one book for surveying ₤1.4 -
February 1811 - to two quires of paper at 2/3 4 shillings 6 pence,
to 2 pr. cotton socks at 3/9 7 Sh. 6 P., March 1811 - to 5¼ pr.
cotton socks at 3/9 7 sh.6 p., to Making the two shirts at 1/6
3 Shillings, to 5½ yds. the same sort for coats at 3/ 16 sh.6p.
to making the two coats at 3/ 6 sh., to 2 pr. shoes lined and
age
303)
bound at 7/6 15 sh., to Latin book Vergil $4.75 or ₤1.8-6,
to 2 do. books Mars' Interduction at $1.42 or 16 sh., June 1811 -
1 1 do. book Vitrey 4 sh.6 p. , to 2 pocket handkerchiefs at 2/
4¾, To one pair cotton socks for Green 3¾, to 2¼ yds mixt. for
Green's panterloons 3¾, to cash pd. Sion Hunt for board and schooling for two months as per rec't. ₤5-8, to making mixt. panterloons 1/6, July 1811 - to 4½ yds. flax linnen for panterloons, 10/6,
to makeing two pr. panterloons at 3/, to makeing two pr. panterloons at 1/6 3/, to 2 pr. shoes at 6/ - 12/.

October 1811 - To old woman's fee for Sukey at Hobs 12/,
to Sugar, sperrits, clothes for little one 4/6, to 2 pr. fine shoes
at 7/7, 15/, to 2 Greek grammers at Currens at 6/ - 12/, to 1
quire of paper at do. 1/6, to 2 Greek books at do. 30/ and 21/ -
₤2-11, to 5½ yds fine chex cloth for 2 coats at 4/6, 4/9, to making the 2 coats at 4/6 4/9, to 2¼ yds fine chex cloth for Peter's
panterloons 10/1½, to making do. 1/6, to 2¼ yds. fine chex cloth
for Green's panterloons 10/1½, to makeing the same 1/6,

November 1811 - to 3 yds. baise to cover Books at Pettway's
₤26 1/3, 3/9, to 2 pr. fine mixed socks at 4/6 9/, to 2 Sharns
worked, ruffled and made at 6/ 12/, to one square for crevats 6/,
Dec. 1811 - to 2¼ yds cloth to make Green a sutood coat at Stewart's at 15/ ₤1-13-9, to 1 dozen buttons for the same 3/, to 1½
yds. binding for do. 3/, to makeing do. 6/, to 4¼ yds. mixt. cloth
for pantaloons at 3/, to makeing do. two pair at 1/6 3 sh., to
5½ yds. for shirts at 3/ and 2 shirts at 1/6 19/6, to taxes in
Wilson County for land 1812 7/6, to taxes for land in Virginia
1811 ₤1-18-½, to cash for Mr. Blackburn for schooling per rec't.
₤6.

age
304)

To do. pd. Mr. Hamilton in part for boarding Ŀ18-17-3, to washing, mending, candles, paper, etc. for 1811 Ŀ6, to my trouble
and expense as Guardian for 1811 Ŀ13-10, February 1812 - To a
Greek book for Green at Petway's $9 - Ŀ2-14, to 2 pr. shoes at
6/ - 12/, to 1 pr. yarn socks for Green 3/9, to 1 pr. cotton do.
for Peter 3/9, to cash pd. the clerk of Williamson County for
recording Settlement as per rec't. 11/3, to 7 yds. coduroy at
Stewart's at 7/6 Ŀ2,12,6, to 2 Hawk's silks 1/6, to 20 buttons
at 3/per dozen 5/, to 1 yds. cloth for binding 2/, to making 2
pair pantaloons of the same 3/, to 1 pr. cotton socks for Green
3/9, March 1812 - to E. for fine shoes made by Oakes at 10/6
Ŀ1-1, to cash pd. Blackburn for schooling per rec't. Ŀ6, to do.
pd. Hambleton for boarding in full Ŀ1-5-3, to Expence at Curren's
for Sack for rooming scholars 1/10½. Total Ŀ94-15-1½

Credit

January 1811 - By hire of Sukey and 3 children to Hob's 23/25,
by hire of Frank to Col. Perkins 34/, by do. Jude and 3 children to
do. 30/, by do. Hannah and 3 children to Corder 17/25, by do. Sam
to Dan Dunn 78/87½, by do. Cloe to Dan Witherspoon 25/75, by do.
Joe to Dan'l. Perkins 76/, by do. Jessee to do. do. 76/, by do.
George to James Hews 10/25, by the rent of your part of Land in
Virginia, say the river plantation 66/66½, by balance of last year's
settlement which is returned and recorded $12, the amount of the
bill brought forward, balance due the Orphans 120/44 - Bill brought
forward-Ŀ436/29, Balance due the orphans 315/44 - 120/44

age
305)

Agreeable to a Commission to us directed from the worshipful
Court of Williamson County, Tennessee, to settle the account current with Hendley Stone, Guardian for Peter and Green Pryor,
orphans of John Pryor, deceased, we have assembled ourselves together this 30th day of March 1812, report as follows (viz.) when
examining the vouchers tendered to us up to the date above mentioned we find due the orphans of the said deceased $120.44, given
under our hands.

Returned to April Session 1812. Signed N. Perkins, Senr.,
Daniel Perkins, Edw. Warren, Robert McLemore -

SAMUEL WILSON'S Will - State of Tennessee, Williamson County -
I, Samuel Wilson, being weak in body but of sound mind and memory
through the mercies of Almighty God and calling to mind the mortality of my body and the uncertainty of life I do constitute and
appoint this my last Will and Testament as to the distribution of
my temporal estate to be divided in the manner and form following -
I will and bequethe to my wife Martha a bed and bedstead and furniture and a suitable maintenance of my farm and the privilege of
the House in thich I now live during her widowhood - also her
wheel. I will and bequeath to my oldest daughter Margaret three
cows and calves, a bed and furniture called her own, the above
cows called Rigg, Blacky and Flower, also her spinning wheel and
saddle. I will and bequeath to my two sons Robert and Josiah my
plantation on which I live, to be equally divided between quantity
and quality all things to be taken into consideration, the Division
to be made when Robert comes of age also what farming utensels
shall be remaining when Robert and Josiah come of age, to be equally
divided between them. I will that all my children be maintained
out of the profits of my farm and the increase of the stock and
that Polley, Betsy, Rispeh, and Sally be schooled out of the same

comes that said maintainance be till they severally come of age if
the live in a family capacity which is my sincere wish. 5 - I will
that all my household and kitchen furniture be kept for the use of
the family till the youngest child comes of age but if a division
becomes necessary before then it is to be equally divided betwixt
my wife and daughters. 6 - I will that all my stock and other property not yet mentioned except what my executors may think most
convenient to dispose of to defray debts to be kept together un-
less necessity call for a division to be equally for the use of my
heirs. I appoint and nominate Robert Wilson, Martha Wilson, and
Zacheus Wilson Executors of the within Will, being my last Will
and Testament done and made in presence of Zacheus Wilson, Aaron
Wilson, Moses Wilson.
     Samuel Wilson - (Seal) July 30, 1804.
     Which foregoing last Will and Testament of Samuel Wilson, de-
ceased, was presented in Court July Session 1812 and proven by the
oaths of Zacheus Wilson and Martha Wilson, qualified as executors
thereto and received letters testamentary. N. P. Hardeman, Clerk
of Williamson County Court.

     JOHN SHEPHERD'S Will - In the name of God amen, I John Shep-
herd of the State of Tennessee and County of Williamson, being
very weak in body and of perfect mind and memory, thanks be to
God, calling unto mind the mortality off my body and knowing that
it is appointed for all men once to die, do make and ordain this
my last Will and Testament, that is to say, principally, and first
of all, I give and recommend my soul into the hands of Almighty God
that gave it and my body I recommend to the Earth to be buried in decent Christian burial at the discretion of my executors, nothing
doubting but at the general resurrection I shall receive the same
again by the mighty power of God and as touching such worldly estate,
wherewith it has pleased God to bless in this life I give, demise,
and dispose of the same in the following manner and form: first,
I give and bequethe to Jane, my dearly beloved wife, one mare and
colt, two cows, and calves, two beds and every article or piece
of property whereof I am possessed or is in any way belonging to me
this and no other to be my last Will and Testament. In witness
whereof I have hereunto set my hand and seal this twenty-sixth day
of August in the year of our Lord one thousand eight hundred and
eleven. Signed, sealed, published, pronounced and declaimed by the
said John Shepherd as his last will and Testament in the presence
of us who in his presence and the presence of each other have
hereunto inscribed our names.
                    John Shepherd x his mark (SEAL)
Teste. J. B. Thompson - William Hunter
     Which foregoing last Will and Testament of John Shepherd, de-
ceased, was duly proven in open Court July Session 1812, by the
oaths of James B. Thompson and William Hunter, the Subscribing witnesses thereto, to be the act and deed of the said John Shepherd
and the same was ordered to be recorded.
                    N. P. Hardeman, Clerk of Williamson
                         County Court

     PATRICK McCUTCHEN'S Will - In the name of God, amen, I Patrick
McCutchen of Williamson County and State of Tennessee, having all
the faculties of my mind in their usual vigor and preparing for
that event which is the common lot of all human beings in order that
no dispute may arise about what it has pleased the Almighty to

age
306)

grant to my industry and in order to make such a sisposition of all my worldly affairs as shall be most consistant with my feeling do make and ordain this my last Will and Testament hereby revoking all others heretofore made. In the first place it is my will and desire that my executors hereafter mentioned shall pay all my just debts with the greatest punctuality as I have hitherto endeavored to make myself that no one can tax me with injustice. Secondly, I will and bequeath to my brother James McCutchen , to my brother Samuel McCutchen, to the legal heirs of my brother John McCutchen, deceased, to the legal heirs of my brother William McCutchen, deceased, the legal heirs of my sister Sarah McNutt, deceased, to the legal heirs of my sister Margaret Buchanan, deceased, the several sums following, (to wit): to my brother James three dollars, to my brother Samuel three dollars, to the heirs of my brother John, deceased, jointly, two dollars, to the heirs of my brother William, deceased, jointly, one dollar and fifty cents, to the heirs of my sister Sarah, deceased, jointly, one dollar, to the heirs of my sister Elizabeth, deceased, jointly, one dollar, to be paid by my executors, whenever called for after twelve months from the time of my decease. Thirdly, I will and bequeath to my beloved wife Hannah dureing her natural life the Tract of land on which I now live with all its appurtenances together with all the residue of my personal property of every kind including the slaves which shall remain after the payment of my just debts mentioned in the first article and the several legatees mentioned in the second amounting to twelve dollars and fifty cents and a contingency which shall be hereafter mentioned to be used as she may think p roper, the slaves nevertheless to be subject to the arrangement to be made in a subsequent article of the Testament. Fourthly, I will and bequeath to Patrick McCutchen, fourth son of my brother Samuel, all my right, interest, and claim to an undivided part of a Tract of land for which Matthew Talbot gave his obligation to James McCutchen and to which I have together with the said James and Samuel McCutchen a claim for a certain portion not now recollected to be expended and laid out by Samuel McCutchen on the education of the said Patrick but if the claim which is now litigating in law should not amount to two hundred dollars it is my will that the same shall be made equal to the sum of two hundred dollars out of my personal property which is the contingency mentioned in the third article. Fifthly, I will and bequeath to the said Patrick McCutchen, fourth son of my brother Samuel McCutchen and to Elizabeth Larkins, daughter of John Larkins by his first wife Margaret, jointly and equally, the land on which I now live with all its appurtenances together with all the residue of my personal property (slaves excepted) which shall remain after the payment of my just debts and the several legacies mentioned in the second article and after making good the deficiency of two hundred dollars mentioned as a contingency in the fourth article to Patrick McCutchen or severally to take effect at the death of my beloved wife Hannah to when the same property is given dureing her natural life as mentioned in the third article. Sixthly, it is my will and desire that my negroe man slave named Jack aged about twenty-four years, also my negro man slave named Ben aged about nineteen years, also my my negroe woman slave named Rose aged about twenty-six years together with what children she may hereafter have (if any) before the death of my wife Hannah, also my negroe girl slave named Elisa, aged abbut eleven years, also my negro girl slave named Scinthia, aged about seven years, also my negroe boy slave named Thomas aged about four

years, also my negro girl slave named Harriet aged about two years,
also my negro girl slave named Maria aged about two months, the four
last named slaves being the children of the above named Rose shall
all and each at the time of the death of my beloved wife Hannah
to whom they are given during her natural life as mentioned in the
third article be liberated from slavery and forever and entirely
set free, provided those who are not now of age or shall not have
arrived at the age of twenty-one years at the happening of the
death of my beloved wife Hannah shall be subject to the following
disposition (viz.), Elisa shall at the contract and under the direction of my brother Samuel McCutchen until her arrival at the age
of twenty-one years and then be set free. Scinthia, Ben, Thomas,
Harriet, and Maria shall be at the contract and under the direction
of James Marshall, my wife's brother, until they shall each respectively arrive at the age of twenty-one years and then be set free.
Scinthia, Ben, Thomas, Harriet and Maria shall be at the contract
and under the direction of James Marshall, my wife's brother, until
they shall each respectively arrive at the age of twenty-one years,
at which time or times they are to be each respectively liberated and
forever set free. Lastly, I do hereby nominate and appoint my beloved wife Hannah my trustee and well-beloved brother Samuel McCutchen and my trusted friend James Marshall executors of this my last
Will and Testament. In witness whereof I have hereunto set my hand
and seal this twenty-ninth day of April in the year of our Lord one
thousand eight hundred and twelve.
        Signed Patrick McCutchen.
        Signed, sealed in presence of us: John Hardeman, William Marshall.
        It is my will and desire I do hereby make as a part of my will
and which shall be of equal validity, the following additional and
explanatory article, whereas some debts may be entertained respect-
ing the construction of the fifth article and as I find upon review
of the subject I have not expressed my meaning with sufficient
prespicuity, I declare this to be my will and meaning of the said
fifth article Patrick McCutchen named in that article is to be joint
Legatee with Elizabeth Larkins of the land only, and Elizabeth Larkins sole residue or legatee of the personal property, which shall
remain at the death of my wife. In witness whereof I have hereunto
set my hand and seal the day and date above written. Signed
Patrick McCutchen...Witness: John Hardeman and William Marshall
        Which last Will and Testament as before recited was presented
in open Court July Session 1812 and proven by the Oaths of John
Hardeman and William Marshall, the Subscribing witnesses thereto, to
be the act and deed of Patrick McCutchen and the same was ordered
to be recorded whereupon Hannah McCutchen, Samuel McCutchen and
James Marshall, the Executrex and Executors, therein named came
into court and took the oath of Execution and received Letters
Testamentary.
        N. P. Hardeman, Clerk of Williamson County Court.

PETER PERKINS' Will - In the name of God, amen, I Peter Perkins of Williamson County, Tennessee, being weak in body but of a
sound mind and memory do make and publish this my last Will and
Testament in manner and form following, that is to say, first I
wish my Executors hereafter to be named shall pay all of my just
debts out of my property. Second - I give and bequeath to my
grand-daughter Agnes Stone, half dozen silver tea-spoons, one

silver soup spoon and sugar tongs and silver bowls for scissors,
all my wife's wearing apparel that she may want and one bed and
furniture. I also give and bequeath to my said grand-daughter
Agnes Stone and my grand-daughters Polly and Ruth Stone all my
other beds and furniture and household goods to be equally divided
between them. My will and desire is that my four favorite negroes,
Bob, Esther, Charles and Hannah shall at my death be free and I
further give and bequeth to them one good horse, two cows and calvesm,
two sows and pigs, eight head of killing hogs, twenty barrels of
corn and my blacksmith's tools, and further my will and desire is
that my Executors shall pay particular attention to the aforesaid
free negroes so that they shall be under no encumbrance whatever,
and whereas there is long and old existing accounts between my son
Nicholas and myself and my brother Harden and myself which is now
out of date and our recollection and whereas I hold mu son Nicholas'
bond for considerable money and my brother Harden holds my bond,
which last bond I want discharged out of the first and not otherwise and after all my last debts is paid as aforesaid I wish all
the rest, residue, and remainder of my Estate of what kind or nature whatsoever to be sold for the best price that can be had. Be
it remembered that Pater Hairston of Stokes County, No. Carolina,
has a power authorizing him to sell the Snow Creek Iron Works
and lands appertaining thereto and transmit me the money which
proceeds if sold or when hereafter sold. I give and bequeath one
third part to Nicholas Scales. Should there be any surplus after
paying my just claims I wish my Executors to divide between Hand-
ley Stone's children, had by my daughter Betsy, equally. I hereby
constitute and appoint my son Nicholas Perkins, my nephew Nicholas
Scales my Executors of this my last Will and Testament, hereby revoking all other Will and Testament, by me made. In Testimony whereof I have hereunto set my hand and Seal this 26th day of January
in the year of our Lord 1813. Signed, sealed and acknowledged in
the presence of us who were called upon to be witnesses.
          Signed Peter Perkins (Seal)
Witnesses: Anne. P. Scales, Thomas H. P. Scales, John Bostick
          Which last Will and Testament as before recited was duly
proven in Open Court April Session 1813 by the othes of Thomas
H. P. Scales and John Bostick, the subscribing witnesses, is
thereto to be the Act and Deed of Peter Perkins and the same was
ordered to be recorded and Nicholas Perkins and Nicholas Scales
the Executors therein named came into Court and qualified as
Executors thereto and received Letters Testamentary.
          N. P. Hardeman, C. W. C.
          An Inventory of the Estate of Colonel Peter Perkins taken this
9th day of February 1813: 1.10 gallon pot, 1.6 do. kettle, 1 pot,
1 ductch oven, 2 skillets and 1 led frying pan, 1 gridiron, 1 potrack, 1 spice morter, 1 bakeing iron, 1 brass skilled, 3 pareppot-
hooks, 1 washing tub, 2 water packs, 3 piggins, 6 pewter dishes,
5 basons, 6 pewter plates, ten spoons, 2 coffee potsm p pewter
pint, 1 old funnel, 2 flat irons, 1 pewter tanquid, devised 3
salt sellors, 1 glass pitcher, 1 silver soup spoon and do. tea-
spoons, 1 pr. do. sugar tongs, 1 earthern tea pot, 1 do. pitcher,
4 small holes, 4 cannisters, 1 tin sugar dish, 1 pr. candle muf-
fers, 13 saucers and 9 cups, 1 candle stick, 5 bottels, 3 vials,
1 cream pot, 12 earthen plates, 1 pepper box, 1 glass ruct., 1 do.
gar., 3 butter pots, 3 jugs, 1 wooden sugar box, 1 sallad dish, 2
old waters, 1 tram glass, 1 knife box, 13 knife's, and 18 forks, 2
tin cups, 4 feather beds, 2 coverlids, 4 bedsteads and cords, 4

Page
(311)
P
(

Page
(312)

bolsters, 1 under bed, 1 hide, 10 sheets, 6 counterpins, 7 bed
quilts, 3 pillows, 3 tables, 8 old chears, 3 table cloths, 1 old
umbrella, 2 old trunks, 1 brass warming pan, 2 good trunks, 13
old books, 1 pare of fire tongs, 1 slay, 1 set bed curtains, 1
coffee mill, devised 1 bareshin, 1 pr. steel rods, 1 box wafers,
4 yds. of bailing, 7½ yds. country cloth, remnant of leather, 6
yds. of bailing, 1 bee-stand, 2 cotton wheels, 1 flax do., 1 pr.
of brass scales, 5 axes, 3 barespeer plows, 1 mattock, 5 old plows,
1 clock reel, 3 swingletrees ironed. Devised 1 blacksmith bellows,
1 stake anville, 1 iron horn for anvil, 2 smithshammers, 2 pr.
tongs, 1 nail machine, sundry scraps of iron, 10 iron bands for
tubbs, 1 tub of fat, 1 churn of do., 1 tub with some soap, 65 lbs.
of bar iron, parcel of tobacco, old waggon and geer, 1 empty whis-
ky barrel, 3 new leather collars, 1 stage and harness, 1 handsaw,
1 drawing knife, 3 augers, 3 clevises, 1 iron wedge, 2 bells, 1
pr. old hamers, 1 churn, 1 old shot gun, 4 meel bags and a quantity
of bacon, a small do. of cotton, parcel of corn, some wheet, 6
hed of horses, 23 head of cattle, head hogs, 4 negroes, to wit:
Hannah, Bob, Esther, and Charles willed to be free, 1½ yds. of
flannel, 1 trunk with papers, 4 turkeys, 27 ducks, 11 chickens,
cash $7.62½, 1 gold watch, 1 waggon cloth, 1 fifth chain for wag-
gon, 1 old acc't. book, 1 Dutch plow.
    Signed Nicholas Perkins and Nicholas Scales, Excrs.
    Returned to April Session 1813. N. P. Hardeman, C. W. C.

Page
(313)
    WILLIAM OGILVIE'S Will - In the name of God amen, I William
Ogilvie of the County of Williamson and State of Tennessee, being in perfect sence and memory but calling to mind the mortality
of man, that it is appointed all men once to die, do make and
ordain this my last will and Testament, disannuling and revoking
all other wills heretofore by me made. First and principally I
give and bequeth my Soul into the hands of Almighty God who gave
it me and my body to the earth to be buried in a Christian manner
at the discretion of my Executors hereafter named and all the
worldly goods it hath pleased God to bless me with, I give, devise and dispose of manner and form following:
    Imprimus, I give and bequeth to my son Richard Ogilvie the
land and plantation whereon I now live containing by estimation
three hundred and fifteen acres of land be the same more or less,
also one still and one shot gun, to him and his heirs forever. Item
I give and bequeth to my Daughter Nancy Allison my negro man
named Pompey and my negro woman named Juniper, also all my stock
of horses, cattle, and sheep, that I have at home, also all my
household and kitchen furniture to her and her heirs forever.
Item I also give and bequeath to my son Richard Ogilvie all my
stock of cattle that is in the care of Henry Arthur in Rutherford
County. Also all my stock of hogs that I have at home to him and
his heirs forever with my share of grain made on the plantation.
Item - I give and bequeath to the remainder of my children what I
put into their hands at their departure from me (viz.),: Harris,
Smith, Kimbrough, William, John, Sally, Patty, Manire and Nancy -
also all my money and money debts either by bond, bill, book
or open account with my shear of the whiskey that is made at the
distillery on the farm for this season to be equally divided between them. Lastly I appoint, constitute, and ordain my son-in-
law James Allison and my son Richard Ogilvie tto be the Executors
of this my last will and Testament in witness whereof I have here-

age
314)

unto set my hand and Seal this 2nd day of March 1811.
Signed, Published, and declared in presence of William
Ogilvie (Seal) John Manire, John White, Jacob Boring.
Which last Will and Testament as before recited was duly pro-
ven in Open Court April Session 1813 by the othes of John White
and the subscribing witnesses thereto to be the Act and Deed of
William Ogilvie and the same was ordered to be recorded and James
Allison and Richard Ogilvie the Executors therein named came into
Court and qualified as Executors therefore and received Letters
testamentary.
N. P. Hardeman, C. W. C.
An Inventory of the Estate of William Ogilvie, deceased,
excep such as are by special legacies bequeathed, to wit: one
note on Richard Ogilvie for $70, one third part of the wry after
paying the stiller, one foot ads, some books, one scythe blade,
9 still tubs, 1 pr. of corn traces, 1 saddle, 1 grubbing hoe, 5
wagon boxes, 1 pr. money scales, 1 pr. sled.
James Allison, Exec'r. Returned to April Session 1813.
N. P. Hardeman, C. W. C.

Page
(315)

JORDAN REESE'S Will - In the name of God amen, I Jordan Reese of
the County of Williamson and State of Tennessee, being in toler-
able health of body and of sound mind and memory and knowing that
it is appointed unto all men once to die and in order to prevent
disputes about the worldly goods with which I am blessed after my
disease do ordain this to be my last Will and Testament in manner
and form following: First, I direct all my just debts shall be
paid. Items, I lend unto my beloved wife Sally Reese during her
natural life the use of five hundred acres of land whereon I now
live, also the following negroes (to wit): Aaron, which come by
my said wife, Daniel, my Gardiner, old Dulcy, Maria, Betty, Little
Daniel, Hanibal, Rusey and Terey, four horses of her own choice.
except my stud horses, ten choice cattle, one half my stock of
sheep, half my stock of hogs, my riding carriage and plantation
utencils, sufficient for her negroes to work with and four feather
beds and furniture also one half the crop, growing or on hand not
otherwise disposed of at the time of my decease.
Item, I give and bequeath unto my Elizabeth Old the negroes,
stock, and household furniture which I have heretofore lent her
now in her possession, also five hundred acres of land lying in
said County of Williamson, which I have already made her Thomas Old
a deed for all which I give unto her and her heirs forever. Item -
I give and bequeath unto my three grand-children Sally, Ann and
Hartwell Hobbs, three negroes in the following manner (to wit): to
Sally Hobbs a negro girl named little Judea, to Ann Hobbs a negro
girl named Hannah and to Hartwell Hobbs a negro boy named Sam, all
which I give to them and their heirs forever, provided they all
be living at my decease, otherwise it is my will and desire that

Page
(316)

the survivor or survivors shall have wholly or equally the negro
or negroes devised with their increase to the deceased to them and
their heirs forever. Item, I give and bequeath to my son Herbert
Reese the land and plantation which I gave to him in Dinwiddie
County, Virginia, and which he has sold since to Dr. Hardaway, also
the negroes heretofore given by me to him together with their increase, also the household furniture and stock of every kind left in

his possession by me at the time of my removal to the western
country. Also the thousand pounds which I lent him to begin business
with all of which I give to him and his heirs forever. Further it is
expressly to be understood that theaabove-mentioned stock was that
left in his possession at the store and no more. Item, I give and
bequeath to my son Beverly Reese all my land lying between White Oak
Creek and Cox road exdept what I have before given reserving one
acre to the meeting house thereon containing fourteen hundred acres
be the same more or less. Also eight negroes and their increase
if any (to wit): Charles, Ceasar, Big Bob, Little Bob, Charlotte,
Winney, Reuben and David, also one feather bed and furniture. Six
head of cattle and six head of sheep and twenty head of hogs to
him and his heirs forever. Item. I give and bequeath to my daughter Matilda Reese one feather bed and furniture, also such other
articles of household furniture as are called hers also five hundred acres of land lying in said County of Williamson on West Harpeth, beginning where Patton's road crosses West Harpeth where said
road crosses with said road to the cross road east with said cross
road to Allens Hill line, thence north to West Harpeth, thence down
West Harpeth with it meanders to the beginning containing five
hundred acres as aforesaid be the same more or less. Also eight
negroes (to wit) Little Dulcy, Moses, Terry, Merika, Salina, Brister,
George and Chelsey all which I give to her and her heirs fore-ver
Also one sorrel filly now at my other plantation to her and her heirs
forever.

Item - I give and bequeath to my daughter Jane Watson five
hundred acres of land in said County of Williamson which I have
made her husband John Watson a deed for, also the negroes and furniture which I have heretofore lent her now in her possession all
which I give to her and her heirs forever. Item - I give to my son
Patrick Reese twelve hundred acres of land in said County of Williamson including the houses and plantation whereon I now live
reserving five hundred acres including said improvements for the
use of my wife Sally Reese during her natural life as herein before mentioned, also twelve negroes (to wit): Sam, Peter, Edmund,
Little Aaron, Ben, Lew, Jim, Fanny, Gillum, Sook, Lewis, and Tom -
also one roan mare commonly called his roan filly, also at the
decease of my wife it is my will and desire that he should have
all my household and kitchen furniture, also the plantation utensils
lent to my wife as herein before mentioned to him and his heirs
forever. Item - it is my will and desire that all my Estate both
real and personal not herein before mentioned or disposed of be
equally divided between my children (to wit): Elizabeth Old, Jane
Watson, Matilda, Beverly and Patrick Reese to them and their heirs
forever. It is also my desire that the nine negroes herein before
mentioned as lent to my wife with their increase at her decease be
equally divided between my five children last above mentioned to
them and their heirs forever. Item - I give to my daughter Nancy
Hobbs one dollar in cash to her and her heirs forever. Lastly, I
nominate Thomas Old and John Watson my sons in Law and my friend
Abraham North Executors to this my last will and Testament utterly revoking and making void all wills by me heretofore made. In
Testimony whereof I have hereunto set my hand and affixed my Seal
this Eighteenth day of January in the year of our Lord Eighteen
Hundred and Thirteen.
Signed, Sealed, published and declared in presence of us -
James Hicks Q Leonard Dunn Avent, Fendall Crump.
Jordan Reese (Seal)

'age
316)
Which last **Will and** Testament as before recited was proven
in Open Court April Session 1813 by the orders of James Hicks,
Leonard Dunnavan and Fendall Crump, the Subscribing witnesses
thereto to be the Act and Deed of Jordan Reese and the same was
ordered to be recorded, whereupon came John Watson, the Executor,
therein named, and took the oath of Executor and received Letters Testamentary.
          N. P. Hardeman, C. W. C.
     An Inventory of the Estate of Jordan Reese, deceased, (to wit)
slaves devised to the widow for life, Aaron, Daniel the Guardian,
Old Dilly, Maria, Betty, little Daniel, Hannabald, Rusey and Ty-
ree. Four head of hogs, eleven head of sheep, five axes, six hilling hoes, three grubbing hoes, two pair Iron Wedges, five ploughs,
two spades, and one hand-saw, one drawing knife, 1 x cut saw, one
waggon and geer, one riding carriage and harness, four feather
beds and furniture, five hundred acres land, one desk and book-
case, one bufat, two folding tables, one chest of drawers, one
candle stand, fourteen rush bottom chairs, eight different sets of
trunks, one dozen table spoons silver, one ladle, fifteen tea-
spoons and one sugar tong, four bed steads, one looking glass,
two dozen knives and forks, one tea board and five waiters, four
brass candle sticks and twenty-nine china cups and two doz. sawsers
one glass pitcher, three quart decanters, one half-pint decanter,
two casters, three china tea-pots, three china sugar dishes, two
china cream pots, ten caster cups, one goblet, sixteen wine glasses,
two slop boles and plates, thirteen dishes, 2 bake plates, twenty-
six earthern plates, three mugs and one pitcher, four salt sel-
larsm nine tumblers, two sugar cannisters, one gallon bottle, one
tin tea cannister, one half gallon bottle, three earthern butter
plates, four tin pans, four earthern boles, two baking pans, four
dishes, nine butter pots, two tin buckets, three iron pots, one
bell mettle, skillet, one iron kettle, one copper kettle, one tea
kettle, two tubs, one loom, ten pictures, one pair iron dogs, 1
pair tongs and shovel, one large tin tea canister, one water Earn
two sawse boats, safe, four flat-irons, four cotton wheels, six
table cloths, six towels.

'age
317)
     Property not specifically divised (to wit) slaves, Gardiner,
Frank, Will Stephen, John, Miles, Jinner and her child Ursey, Biddy, Jim, Ventu, Judy, Jack, Billy, Oliver and Isaac. Six horses
and two colts, two beds and furniture, one gig and harness, two
shot guns, twenty-one head of cattle, thirty-one head of hogs, 1
whip saw, two cartwheels, one odd Waggon, a parcel corn, hemp and
whiskey, one set blacksmith tools, 6 axes, 4 hilling hoes, 2 pr.
iron wedges, 5 ploughs, 1 hand saw, debts due the estate (to wit):
one promisory note, one Young Gray, four hundred dollars, one
ditto on Turner Sanders, three hundred dollars, one ditto on
Isham R. Trotter, four hundred and twenty-one dollars, one ditto
on Herbert Reese and Stephen Shaw, one hundred six dollars forty
two cents, one do. William C. Wills thirteen pounds three shillings, one ditto on Robert and Leonard Dunavant twenty-seven dollars and fity cents, one ditto on Herbert Reese six hundred and one
pounds two shillings and nine pence, one ditto Lawrence Jones and
William Wills twenty-one pounds twelve shillings, one ditto William French and Brook Dunavant thirty-one pounds and nineteen shillings, one ditton Benjamin Bevell and William Wills five pounds
two shillings, done ditto on Gabriel Baugh and Clements Old nine

pounds two shillings, one do. on William Good and Herbert Reese
nine pounds twelve shillings, one do. William Featherstone and
Daniel Beachy fifteen pounds seventeen shillings and four pence,
one ditto Patrick Boyles and Tim Woodard seven pounds fifteen shillings, and sixpence, one do. John Allen, Labone Epps, nine pounds
eleven shillings, one do. Tim Woodard, Patrick Boyles fourteen pounds
three shillings.
      Open acc't. one on Abraham North eight hundred and thirty-one
dollars fifty cents, one one John Watson two hundred dollars for
cotton on Herbert Reese, one hundred and thirty-nine pounds thirteen
shillings and three pence. A list of bonds and accounts put in the
hands of Herbert Reese by the testation in his life time to collect
or return as pd. Receipts (to wit): John Tally one pound fifteen
shillings and one penny farthing, Nelson Jones two pounds eleven
shillings and halfpenny, George R. Claibourne sixteen pounds seven
shillings and nine pence, William Wills one hundred thirty-one pounds
thirteen shillings and six pence, one ditto on William Wills one
hundred and thirty one pounds thirteen shillings and six pence, one
ditto David Jones two hundred nine pounds ten shillings on John
Allen seven pounds ten shillings, on John Wills eight pounds six
shillings and three pence, on Eligah Old thirty-six pounds five
shillings and eight pence, on Thomas Worsham three pounds eight
shillings and eleven pence, on George Smith nine pounds, on Robert
Ritcher one hundred and one pounds, seven shillings and seven pence,
One note on Joseph Moore for one hundred pounds, one do. one William French for one hundred and sixty dollars, one receipt given
by Beverly Reese to Herbert Reese for seven hundred dollars rec'd
for Jordan Reese to Herbert Reese for seven hundred dollars rec'd.
for Jordan Reese one note on Thomas Woodard for thirteen dollars
twenty cents. Slaves devised to Patrick Reese a minor, to wit: Sam,
Peter, Edmund, Little Aaron, Ben, Lew, Jim, Fanny, Gillum, Sook,
Lewis and Tom.
      Signed John Watson, acting Executor of Jordan Reese, deceased.
April 13, 1813, then returned.
      N. P. Hardeman, C. W. C.

BENJAMIN BUGG'S Inventory returned April Session 1813 -
Household (to wit): 5 feather beds, steads and furniture, 2 chests,
and trunks, one of them small, one beaufat or cupboard, and sundry
earthern and glass, furniture, two tables, one walnut the other
poplar, 11 chairs, one looking glass, 6 pewter basons, one pair
fire dogs, 2 smoothing irons, 5 puter dishes, 11 ditto plates, one
candle stand, 5 baking tin pans, one bread basket and one bail
bucket, 1 large stone butter pot, 1 tin ditto, 1 small ditto, one
stand pitcher, one copper coffee pot, 1 tin do., parcel of knives
and forks, 1 loom, 5 slays, 5 pair weaving gears, temples, shuttles,
1 candlestick, 1 pewter candle mould, books (viz,) 2 Bibles, 2 dic-
tionaries and sundry other books, 1 grid iron, iron poker and shovel,
one stone chamber pot, 1 pair stilliards, 3 guns (viz.) 2 rifles
and one shot gun or musket, 1 doz tablespoons, 4 cotton wheels, 1
flax ditto, 5 pair cotton, 2 pair wool, ditto one flax hackle, 3
sides soal leather, and parcel of upper leather, 6 bells and parcel
of tobacco, a box of old lumber iron, kitchen furniture, two large
kettles, 3 ovens, 2 small pots, 5 pr. pothooks, 2 iron pothangers,
1 iron morter cast, one iron coffee mill, 1 small skillet, 1 frying
pan, 2 washing tubs, 1 pail, 3 piggins, 1 watering bucket, one half

bushel and parcel of salt and other lumber barrels, one keg, farming utensils and other tools, 6 axes, 3 weading hoes, 2 hilling hoes, 1 garden ditto, 1 grubbing ditto, 2 bar spear plows, 2 pr. iron chains, traces, collers and haims, 1 log chain, swingletrees and clevises and 1 cross cut saw, 2 hand ditto, 2 drawing knives, 5 augers, 5 chissels, 1 gouge, 4 gimblets, 2 iron wedges, 1 foot adze, coopers adze and trowel, coopers compass, 1 carpenter's do., 1 coopers crows and pointer, parcel of shoemaker tools, 1 claw hammer, 1 pair of spoon moulds and nippers, 4 sickles, 1 mowing scythe, 1 round shaver, one grind-stone, one mans saddle, 1 wire seive, 2 wheat riddles, a parcel of baskets, 1 pr. saddle bags, parcel of bridles, grain forage, a parcel of corn, 2 hogsheads full of wheat, 2 haystacks, parcel of fodder and corn shucks, a parcel of undressed flax, parcel of seed cotton, a parcel of pickled pork, stock - horses 7 head (viz.) 2 geldings, 3 mares and two colts, cattle 13 head sheep, 14 head out hogs, 34 head fat hogs, 8 head, 16 head of geese, 16 ducks, Due twenty-eight dollars by note of Jesse Bugg per note twenty-five dollars and twenty five cents from Lucy Bugg by note two dollars 13¾ cents; John Williamson. Slaves, 13 negroes (viz), Charles, Allen, Peter, Jacob, Terry, Warreck, Doreas, Luch, Elenor, Rachel, Jinny, Viney and Dulcy. All of which is submitted.
       David Pinkston.
    Recorded April 13th 1813 - Ephraim M. Bugg.
N. P. Hardeman , C. W. C.

An Inventory of the Estate of Patrick McCutchen, deceased: 17 head of horses, 25 head of horned cattle, 23 head of sheep, 34 head of geese, 16 bee hives, a quantity of small grain in the field, 4 feather beds with their bedsteads, 16 sheets, also 3 woolen blankets, 4 double bed covers, also 5 suits of mans clothes, 3 chests, 1 table, 2 cupboards with the furniture, also 8 chairs, 2 candlestands, 1 cotton, flax wheel, also one check reel, also a quantity of linnen and cotton thread, one rifle gun and shot bag, one looking glass, one case of razors, 2 pare of cotton cards, one hat and 2 pare of shoes, a quantity of bacon, also a quantity of tallow and beeswax, 4 glass bottles about 70 lbs. of wool, also about 500 weight of flour, one loom, 2 sets of harness and one slay, one saddle and bridle, one kettle and 2 pots and hooks and one oven, one flatiron, 2 axes and three weeding hoes, 2 mattocks, a small quantity of Dry corn, one pot rack, 2 plows, with harness, a quantity sope, also one cutting box and knife, one sickle, one Iron Wedge and drawing knife and handsaw, also one set of shew tools, one grind stone, also about 70 head of hoggs, sundry other small articles too tedious to mention of a small kind.
   Hannah McCutchen -her mark- Sam'l. McCutchen, James Martial.
   Recorded 6th June 1813. Returned July 1812.
   N. P. Hardeman, C. W. C.

Account of the sale of Littleberry Epperson, deceased, and a Supplementary Inventory: One young colt, 2 young calves, Bible, 1 Testament, 1 slay, 1 set knives and forks, 1 canister, 1 smoothing iron, 1 bell, 1 keg. James Joyce, Admr. Recorded 6th June, 1813. Also two notes of $90. N.P. Hardeman, C. W. C.
   May 25, 1812   James Joyce, Administrator
   Amount of sale (to wit) Anne Epperson to one horse colt $14.50. Ann Edison to one mare $45, do. do. $34.25, do to one plow $2.50, to

Page
(320)

Page
(321)

one pot $4.25, to one pare of hooks .37½, to one ax .95, to one
half bushel .50, to one oven and hooks $2.75, to two barrels .75,
to one table $2.50, to one churn .65, to one coffee mill $1.12,
to one wheel $1.50, to one bed and furniture $18, to one bedstead
$1.40, to one bed and bedstead $20.37½, to one chest $2, to one
slay .65½, to knives and forks .66, to one pair steelyards $1.50,
to two chairs .54, to one looking glass .62, to one dish .56, to
one saddle $7, to one canister 12½, to one piggin .16, to one pail
.30, to one heifer and calf $9.7, to one cow and calf $9.58¼, to
one heifer $4.95¼, to hogs $6.35, James Joyce one horse colt $9,
James Joyce one colt $21.25, James Armstrong one waggon and hind
geer $30, James Joyce one hoe .5, William Dickson iron and bell
.7, Frances Smith one steer $5, James Joyce one steer $1.89, James
Joyce one heifer $2.11, Sally Allen one cow and calf $10, Signed
James Joyce, Administrator.
        Returned to July Session 1812. N. P. Hardeman, C. W. C.

        JAMES SULLARD'S Will - Whereas the same James Sullard do make
this my will and Testament and that the same James Sullard is weak
in body but in sound mind, memory and understanding blest be God
for the same. Those Executors that I make choice of is L. W. Mansker and Henry Flowers, the said James Sullards. Do wish to give
to my Brother Samuel Sullard nine hundred dollars in a note on
Joseph Johnson, the rest of my goods and chattels I leave to L. W.
Mansker this I leave as my last will and Testament, this 20th March
1812.
        James Sullards - R. W. Shannon, David Kaigler,
James Davis.
        The foregoing recited Will and Testament was duly proven in
Open Court October Session 1812 by the othes of R. W. Shannon and
David Kaigler to be the Act and Deed of James Sullard for the use
and purposes therein expressed and the same was ordered to be re-
corded.

Page
(322)

        JANE WHEATON'S Will - I, Jane Wheaton of Williamson County,
Tennessee, being indisposed in body but of sound disposing mind do
make and ordain this to be my last Will and Testament in manner
following (viz.): after all my just debts are paid it is my will
and desire that all my property and estate whether real, personal,
or mixed, be divided between my two sons Sterling Wheaton and John
Lord Wheaton, by my Executors hereinafter named when my son Sterling shall arrive at legal age. It is also my desire that the profits
of my estate, rents, hires of negros and in trust of money be applied to the support and education of my aforesaid sons and the surplus (if any) with the money in hand due me on notes, bond, or
open account and what my personal estate may sell for be disposed
of by my Executors in the purchase of Bank stock or other Source
and productive stock or property for the profits, advantages, and
increase of their estates. And lastly I appoint my friend John
Lord of Wilmington and Dr. Sterling Wheaton of Raleigh, North Carolina, Executors of this my last will and Testament but it is my
particular desire that both my sons be educated at Raleigh under
the care and superintendence of their uncle Dr. Sterling Wheaton
aforesaid. In witness whereof I have hereunto affixed my hand and
seal this twenty second day of April Eighteen hundred and twelve.
        Signed Jane Wheaton (Seal)
Whose names a re signed as witnesses: James Shannon, William Black,
T. Bruce, Eliza Bruss ⊖ Returned April Session 1812.

  The foregoing recited Will and Testament was duly proven in
Open Court, July Session 1812 by the othes of James Shannon and
William Black to be the act and Deed of Jane Wheaton for the use
and purposes therein expressed and the same was ordered to be
recorded.

  JOHN MANIRE'S Will - In the name of God amen, I John Manire
of the County of Garrard and Stateeof Kentucky being in perfect
sense and memory but calling to mind the mortality of man, that it
is appointed for all men once to die, do make and ordain this my
last will and Testament, disanuling all other wills heretofore by
me made, first and principally I give and bequeath my Soul into
the hands of Almighty God who gave it me, and my body to the Earth
to be buried in Christian manner at the directions of my Executors
hereafter named and all the worldly goods it hath pleased God to
bless me with. I give, devisee, and dispose of in manner and form
following. Imprimus, after my just debts and funeral Expenses are
paid, I give and bequeath the remainder of my Estate unto my beloved wife, to be disposed of at her discretion to her and her heirs
forever.
  Lastly I appoint, constitute, and ordain my loving wife, Betty
Manire, and my son in law, Daniel Hubbard, to be the Executrix and
Executor of this my last Will and Testament. In testimony whereof
I have hereunto set my hand and affixed my seal this 30th day of
April 1808. Signed, published and declared in presence of Achilles
Finnell, James Finnell, John Hubbard - John Manire (Seal)
  I hereby certify that I have removed and settled myself
in Williamson County in the Stateoof Tennessee and do not see cause
to alter this my last will and Testament, given under my hand and
seal this 9th day of Dec. 1807.
      John Manire (Seal)
In Witness of us: Thomas Wilson, James Ridley, John Walter.
  Returned October Session 1812.

  The foregoing recited Will and Testament was duly proven
in Open Court October Session 1812 by the othes of Thomas Wilson
and John Walker to be the Act and Deed of John Manire for the use
and purposes therein expressed and the same was ordered to be recorded.

  ROBERT WINSETT'S Will - In the name of God amen, I Robert
Winsett of the State of Tennessee and Williamson County being sick
and weak in body but of a sound and disposing mind, memory and understanding, thanks be to God, calling to mind the mortality of
my body and knowing that it is appointed once for all men to die,
do make and ordain this my last will and Testament, that is to
say principally and first of all I give and recommend my soul
into the hands of God that gave it, and my body I recommend to
the earth to be buried in a deasent Christian-like manner at the
discretion of my Executors, nothing doubting but at the General
Resurrection I shall receive the same again by the mighty powers
of God, and as touching such worldly Estate which God hath been
pleased to bless me with in this life I give, devise, and dispose
of in the manner and form folbowing (viz.) that all my Lawful
debts be .. first out of my Estate. In the next place I will and
bequeath unto my beloved wife Miley Winsett and my son Jason the

Land I now live on agreeable to a deed of gift I made them and
confirm the same. I also bequeath unto my wife Miley a negroe woman called Rachel during her life or widowhood. Reserving the two
first children, the said negroe woman may have theffirst I gave
unto my Daughter Silvey Brown and the second child unto my daughter Ann Winsett and in case the said negroe woman should not have
the children above mentioned, then and in that case I allow my
negroe man James to be sold and the sum of two hundred dollars to
be paid to each of my daughters above mentioned in lue of the
children in case the negroe woman has then not the said money to
be paid in the course of five years from the present date. I also
bequeath unto wife Miley Winsett one negroe man by the name of
Jack during her life or widowhood. I also bequeath unto my wife

Page
(·325)

Miley Winsett all my brutil stock of all kind with all my household
furniture and plantation tools furing her life or widowhood and the
disseas of my wife Milley Winsett I allos the property here mentioned be left to her to be sold and equally divided amongst all
my children and as in regard to my negroe man James, I allow him
to be hired out from the present date and the hire thereof to be
divided equally amongst my children yearly. I also will and bequeath
unto my son William Winsett one dollar and the land he now lives
on, confirming the same by a deed of Gift I made to him. I also
will unto my son John Winsett one note of hand I have against him
of a hundred and ten dollars with the interests bearing date the
twentieth day of March 1806, and fifty dollars at the Decease of
my wife Milley Winsett. I also will and bequeath unto my son Amon
Winsett one dollar and the land he now lives on. I also will and
bequeath to my son Silvo Winsett one dollar and the land he now
lives on by a Deed of Gift. I also confirm the same. I also will
and bequeath unto my son Jesse Winsett thirty dolla rs to be paid
at the Deceasee of my wife Milley Winsett and in regard to my negroe man James if he is not sold by the Negro woman Rachel bearing
the children above mentioned, then and in that case at the decease
of my wife Milley Winsett, he is to be sold and equally divided
amongst my children. And I the sd. Robert Winsett do hereby utterly
disallow and revoke all and every other former Testament, Wills,
Legacies. Except the Land I now live on which I give to my son
Jason and Executors by me in any ways beffore mamed wills and bequeaths. Ratifying and confirming this and no other to be my last
Will and that I do appoint, ordain, and authorize to be my Executors my beloved wife Milley Winsett and my son William Winsett and
my son Amos Winsett to execute this my last Will and Testament,
and in witness of the same I have hereunto set my hand and affixed
my seal this thirteenth day of May one thousand eight hundred and
twelve. Signed Robert Winsett (Seal)
    Sealed and Delivered in the presence of us (to wit)
Teste: Daniel Brown x his mark   Robert Winsett (Seal)
       Silas Winsett   Milley Winsett
       James Gillespie   x her mark
    The foregoing recited will and Testament was duly proven in
Open Court by the othes of Daniel Brown and Silas Winsett at October
Court 1812 to be the Act and Deed of Robert Winsett, deceased, for
the purposes therein expressed and the same was ordered to be
recorded.

'age
326)

    ANDREW HARRIS' Will - In the name of God amen, I Andrew Harris,
of Williamson County, State of Tennessee, being weal in body but
in perfect soundness in the Execution of my reason and Judgment
and calling to mind the mortality of my body, do hereby ordain,
appoint and constitute this my last Will and Testament and I do
hereby revoke, make void and disavail, all former wills and Testaments by me made. Imprimus, I commit my soul to God who gave it.
Item - I commit my body to the Earth to be decently-interred. Item
I will that all my just debts be paid. Item, I will that my dear
wife Ede two negroes Hillard and Nancy to be her lawful property,
to be disposed of by her either in her lifetime or at her death
as she may think proper, also I bequeath to her all the plantation
on which I now live with every kind of stock, utensil and household
furniture (except so much as will pay all my just debts which is
to be raised out of the perishable property. The rest is to be
in possession of my dear wife Ede should think proper to marry
in that case she is to have allotted to her one third of all my
personal estate except the negroes which are to remain as above
disposed of, also the new dwelling house with eighty acres of
land, to be laid off in the southwest corner of the tract running
one hundred and sixty poles east from sd. southwest corner, thence
north for compliment, to have said land with all thereon and other
property during her life-time and at her death to be appropriated
to the benefits of my children, the balance of the Land and two
thirds of my personal estate to be appropriated to the benefit
of my children in the way and manner that my Executors shall think
most proper for their support and schooling, and as some of my
children (viz.): Cassandra, Samuel, and Josepphus have already
received of my Estate to the amount of one hundred and eighty dollars each it is my Will that as the rest of my children come of
age or marry (which last case is to be considered as of age in all

Page
(327)

cases with respect to receiving their part) they may have each
of them the same amount that is one hundred and eighty dollars
to be raised out of my personal estate, if my Executors see that
it can be spared from the support of my wife and children if there
should not be property to share then they are to have as much at the
death of my dear wife Ede out of the property or out of the plantation I now live on which I will that at the death of my dear
wife Ede shall be sold or otherwise as my Executors shall think
best and all aforementioned legasies paid the balance to be equally
divided amongst all my child ren (to wit), Casandra, Samuel,
Joseph, Edward, Patsy, Meekezene, Caro and Sidney and if my dear
wife should beare any more children by me in all cases it or
they are to have an equal part, I also will to the aforesaid
children twelve hundred and fifty acres of land left to me by my
father and for which I have his deed of conveyance to be equally
divided amongst them all as soon after it is purchased from the
Indians, as my Executors shall deem it practicable, also all other
lands that I may be entitled to is to be divided equally amongst
all my children. I do hereby constitute and appoint my dear wife
Ede executrix, my son Josephus, Ephraim Sampson and George Bur-
nett Executors of this my last will And Testament in testimony
whereof I have set my hand and affixed my Seal this twenty-eighth
day of April, one thousand eight hundred and twelve. Signed,
sealed, and delivered in the presence of Robert Guthrie, James
House, Andrew House, Andrew Cowsert - Signed Andrew Harris (Seal)
Teste: Glen Owen.

The foregoing recited Will and Testament was duly proven in
Open Court, October Session 1812, by the othes of James House,
Jun'r. and Glen Owen to be the Act and Deed of Andrew Harris,
deceased, for the purposes therein expressed and the same was
ordered to be recorded.

DAVID CRAIG Jun'r. Inventory - One mare and colt, one sorrel
mare, one two yearl old horse colt, one bay horse, one rifle gun and
shot bag, one man's saddle, one woman's saddle, one belt and tomahawk, one oven and pot, one pot rack, one pair of pot bails, one
table, one candle-stand, one pickling tub, one salt barrel, two
beads and furniture, one dozen earthern plates, one set knives and
forks, half dozen cups and saucers, one waiter, three tin pans, one

Page
(328)

coffee pot, one case razors and box, two water pails, one liiking
glass, one cream pot, half-dozen tea spoons, one glass jar, two
bedsteads, one cotton wheel, one flax wheel, three chairs, two
bridles, one pocket book. The foregoing returned to October 1812.

JOHN SHEPPARD Inventory - Two home-spun coats, four cotton
shirts, four pair of white pantaloons, one pair leather, two white
dimity waist-coats, two silk hankerchiefs, two pair of hone knit
socks, three weaving shuttles, one wool hat, two pair half worn
shoes, one pair spectacles, one pair do., one glass, a small striped
bag, three yards of coloured home spun double wove. One scrubing
gauge, one coblers awl, two memorandum books, three dollars and
fifty cents cash. Returned July Session 1812.

DUDLEY PORTER, deceased: Acc't. Saled by Sarah Porter, Exect'r.
Sarah Porter one table .16¾, three pewter dishes $3.25, five pew-
ter plates $1, three pewter basons $2.51, eight spoons .12½, six
plates .50, set cups and saucers .12½, set knives and forks .50,
bred basket and tin pan .25, Mug and pitcher .37½, one server and
six tins .50, one sugar box .32¼, one strainer .6¼, six vials .30½,
spoon ladle and flesh fork .30¼, two glass tumblers, p aper box .43,
one coffee pot .30, one jug $1½26 cents, two bottles $1, one coffee mill $1.83, one cream jug .25½, one hammer .26½, one padlock
.25, one hammer .26½, two books .12½, one candle stick .19, two
bags .51½, two bags .40½, two pare scissors .25½, one ax .75, one
ax e .36½, two hoes .26, one clevis .13, one skillet .75, one pot-

Page
(329)

rack and pot $1.53, eight wooden vessels $1.2, one sifter .8, two
pare of cards .27, one pair of cards .12½, one band and box .12½,
one bed furniture $1.63 cents, two beds and furniture $10.13 cents,
two bedsteads $2, three chairs .25, one woman's saddle .50, one
bridle .16, one horse and bridle $22, one sorrel filly $25.66, two
bells .50, cotton $2.12½, one pare of flat irons $1.25, one plow
hoe.56¼, one sorrel mare .6¼, one saddle $3.70 cents. William Web-
ster one hand saw $2.30, James Berry one half gallon .44½, James
Berry one candle stick .19, James Busby two pair of pinchers .50,
Mordica Pillow one tub old irons and $1.75, David McCord one skil-
let .25, James Berry one set razors and box $1.6¼, James Berry one
shaving glass $1.63, William Walls one mans saddle $5.37½, Robert
McClenen one collar and bridle $2, Robert McClenen one bridle and
collar $2.66, William Walls one pare geers $5, John Brim one pair
geers $3.80, James Miller one set of hip straps, $1.35, William
King one bay horse $11.12½, Mordica Pillow one colt $10.50, Mordica
Pillow one set strechers $1.41, William King forty gallons of whis-
key $14.15, John Porter one waggon $42.25, John Porter one plow hoe
$1, John Porter two books .37½. Returned July Session 1812.

JOHN SEAY'S Inventory - To three head of horses, thirteen head of cattle, twenty one head of hogs, six head of sheep. To three beds and bedsteads with their furniture, to one table, one loom, one trunk, to one chest, eight chears, one kettle, two pots and two pare of hooks, one oven, one skillet, twelve plates of puter, dishes, and 2 puter dishes, and 2 puter basons, eight spoons, six knives, and three forks, five water vessels, two butter pots, one churn, one plow, two hoes, two axes, one coffee pot,to one spinning wheel as as given under my hand this 10th day of May 1810.
        Returned July Session 1812. John Windrow.

(Page 330)

Agreeable to an order from the County Court of Williamson to us, John Witherspoon and C. Boyles, directed, we have proceeded to make a settlement with Lancaster Glover, Guardian, for Nancy Sammons, otherwise Nancy Pate of her part of her father's Estate, Hardy Pate, deceased. For which see the following statement.
        Nancy Sammons. 1807 Feb'y. 10th-To Lancaster Glover, Guardian to 1 5/8 coatin 21/ $5.68½, 2½ Yds. white flannel 4/6 $1.87½, Cash paid for shoes 6/ $1, one handkerchief .42, Cash paid A. Taylor $1, black velvet and silk .35, one doz. buttons..25, April Cash paid Expences from Virginia $17, ½ quire paper .25, one spelling book .37½, 1808: Cash paid for schooling $3.50, do. do. $2, one Yd. Muslin .50, 1 qt. tar 1/6 .25, 1812 April 14th - to paid Currin and Mason $8.12½. To paid Petway and Maury $19.6¼. To services rendered $30, Amount $91.64¼.
        Credit by her part of her father's estate being $139.98¼.
        There appears interest up to this time $41.70. Balance due Nancy Pate $90.04.
        The above appear to be the way the above account stands, this 15th July 1812, John Witherspoon, C. Boyles.

WRIGHT RIGG'S Inventory - Two head of horses, three head of cattle, supposed to be nine or ten head of hogs, one silver watch, one rifle gun and wareing clothes and some books - accompts not known how much one chest returned October Session 1812.
        Signed David Riggs, Administrator.

(Page 331)

JAMES WILKINS' Executor of WILLIAM WILKINS'. Deceased, Settlement To John Sappington,physician, his amt. $13.37½, To William Williams July 1805 $2, to Samuel Dobbins 4th December 1806 $4.96, To Edward Jones 21st Aug. 1806 $6.50, to Joseph Braden 3rd July 1805 $8.41¾, to Edward Swanson May 10th 1805 $11.82½, to James Thompson April 15th 1804 $5, to John N. Hardeman 13th Feb. 1805 $9.50, to Joseph Braden part of note $21.37½, to balance due R. Plurren on note 10th May 1805 - To note John Record 3rd May 1805 $22, To acc't. Mr. Wright $2, to Acc't. Samuel Dobbins $1.66 2/3, to Acc't. James Wilkins $31.50, Total $147.12½ - Persuant to an order of the Worshippful Court of Williamson County made January Session 1812. To David Dunn and John Witherspoon to examine the accounts of James Wilkins, Executor of William Wilkins, deceased, and we report that the above vouchers are just and should be allowed the Executor by the said Court, given under our hands this third day of April 1812.
        Signed D. Dunn and John Witherspoon.

Agreeable to an order of the Worshipful County Court of
Pleas and quarter Sessions of Williamson County to us directed
from their July Session 1812, we have settled with John Crafton and
Daniel Wilkes, Administrators of the Estate of James Crafton, deceased, in the following manner to wit - We find from the face of
the papers produced to us by the Administrators on the settlement
with us that they have sold the Estate of the deceased for the
sum of one hundred and seventy-two dollars, seventy one and two
thirds cents out of which sum they have pd. debts oweing by the
deceased. To Dr. Samuel Crockett as pr. voucher marked .. and
filed here with $3.14 to Nicholas P. Wilbourn for medicine and
attendance on the family before the deceased as pr. Voucher marked
no. 2 and filed herewith, $3 to Jacob Halfacre for a cow killed
by a negroe of the deceased as pr. voucher marked No. 3 and
filed herewith.

Page
(332)
To William P. Harrison, deceased, of Williamson County Court
as per voucher marker No. 4 and filed herewith to Robert Davis for
schooling the children of the deceased as per voucher marked No. 6
and filed herewith $8. Then assumed to pay Robert Davis $13, the
balance of his account for schooling the children of the deceased
to money received by the administrators of the sale of tobacco which
they are chargeable with $6.33 1/3 and there is yet remaining in
the hands of the Administrators the sum of one hundred and thirty-
four dollars and forty-two cents given under our hand this the
first day of October 1812. Signed Oliver Williams.
       Returned October Session 1812. Richard Pucket,
                                   Samuel Shelburne
       Persons Pate Dr. to Lancaster Glover, Guardian, 1813, Ap'l.
13th am't. your acc't. herewith rendered $30.82, making return to
April Court 1812, your part 15¾ cents return to Jan'y. Court.15¾
interest on $30.82 - $10.12 my services as your Guardian 6 years
$25.50¾ - total $67.20 to Balance due $140. Total $67.20 to Balance due $140. Total $207.20. By your part of money in my hands
received from your grand-father's estate $140, by 8 years interest
on said sum $67.20. Total $207.20.
       Ap'l. 13, 1813 - We, George Hulme and Hinchey Pettway, com-
missioners, appointed by the County Court of Williamson to settle
and adjust the accounts between Persons Pate and his guardian, Lancaster Glover, do find the above sum of one hundred and forty
dollars to be due from him, the said Lancaster to Persons Pate
given under our hands this day and date above.
       George Hulm, Hinchey Pettway.
       Person Pate chargeing to Lancaster Glover $207.20.
       L. Glover's charges as Guardian to P. Pate   67.20
       Balance due Person Pate $1.40

Page
(333)
An Account of Sale of the Estate of WILLIAM STONE, deceased -
To James Fulton a small box of hemp seed .6¼, Alexander McDaniel
one flower tub .6¼, Jane Stone one washing tub .37½, do. one pot
$1.25, William Nolin one Dutch oven $3, Jane Stone one skillet
.25, Gurshum Hunt one hatchet and hoe .75, Jane Stone one hoe .77,
John Waters one plow $1.85, Jane Stone one shovel plow $1.25, William Stone one log chain $2.31½, Jane Stone one ax $1, James Fulton one large pot and hooks $3, Gurshom Hunt one ax $1.80, John
L. Fielder one pare dog irons $3.75, Jane Stone a parcel of crock-
ery ware $1, James Fulton one bason $3.6¼, John Roy one waiter .50,

Jane Stone one dish and 4 plates $2, Joh Roy one dish and three plates $3, Jane Stone one lot of tins .75, do. one flat iron .37½, do. two crocks .60, John Roy one candle stick stand .50, Jane Stone knives and forks and box $2.76, William Stone one coffee mill $2.37½, Jane Stone one large bell $2, John Roy one Bible and sermon book $1, William Stone 3 books $3.6¼, Jane Stone one book $1.1, do. two books .75, do. one book .30, do. 2 chears .51, do. one walnut table $4, John Roy one slay .25, Jane Stone one feather bed $10, do. do. $10, do. one flax wheel $2, do. one cotton wheel and cards .50, do. one trunk .12½, do. one cow $6., do. one cow $8, Cubb Willis one sorrel mare $9.50, Jane Stone one cow $10. Returned April Session 1813. Total amount Sales $119.17¾.

Amount of Sale of Green House, deceased; Horse and saddle $34.81½ - Bridle and saddle bags $2.50, Sword $4, clothes $10.25, Total $51.56½. Signed James House, Admr. Total amount of sales of Green House Estate $51.56½.

Page (334)

An Inventory of the Estate of JOSEPHUS, deceased - Returned by Edith Harris, Administratrix, April Session 1813. Property advertised and sold agreeable to law. Viz., one cotton shirt, one pare of pantaloons, one satoot, coat walkers, Dictionary, one grey horse, bid off by the Administratrix, amounting to $85.62½, one saddle and bridle bid off by the same for Zens Harris, an infant, $25., two vests, one broadcloth coat, one home-spun do., one fur hat, one pr. boots, Murrey's Grammer, Duncan's Logick, Morse's

Page (336)

Gazette, one pocket book, one mixed coat, one pr. pantaloons, bid off by Edward Harris for which I have his bond with security for $39.31¼. Property not sold, viz., Morse's Geography - the Patent Right of a certain washing machine for the county of Giles claimed under Eli F. Hill of New York. A note of hand on Cheatham of Columbia, Maury County, for $150. and credited by 4 items, amounting to $46. Returned Ap'l. Session 1813. Edith Harris.
Total amount of Sale $237.18¾

Agreeable to an order of the County Court of Pleas and quarter Sessions held for the County of Williamson at their Ap'l. Session 1812 and to us directed we have proceeded to settle with Lewis Stephens and Michael Kinnard, Administrators of Michael Kinnard, deceased, relative to their administration on the Estate of the Deceased, we find from the face of the papers produced to us by the Administrators that they have sold the Estate of the deceased for the sum of $1384.41¼ cents, out of which sum they have paid to the credit of the Deceased. To Robert Mitchell $11.66 2/3 as pr. Voucher marked No. 2 and filed here with John Sample and Co. $12.70½ as per Voucher marked No. 3 and filed herewith, to Robert McCoy $11.50 as per voucher marked No. 4 and filed herewith. To Robert McCoy 11.50 as per Voucher marked No. 4 and filed herewith, to George Kinnard $34.3½ as per voucher marked No. 5 and filed herewith, to William Tate on a note given to Felix Grundy as per voucher marker No. 6, filed herewith $20.60, George Bennet's rec'd. $15 No. 7 filed, Peter Pinkston rec't. for a judgment obtained by Bennett Smith ag. the deceased $30.25, pr. voucher marked No. 8 filed herewith, Thomas Raleigh $1.37½ pr. voucher marked No. 9 and filed herewith, William Culwell Rec't. for .37½ cents as per voucher marked no. 11 and filed herewith. Given under our hands this the 15th Oct'r. 1812. Signed Oliver Williams and Rich'd. Puckett.

Page (335)

Amount of the Decedent's estate in the hands of the
Adm'rs. $1384.1¼, amount paid by Administrator's on the Estate
of M. C. Kinnard $145.0¼, balance due the Estate $1238.91.
Returned to April Session 1813.

Oliver Williams, Guardian of Nancy Jordan, Dtr. To her pro-
portion of the Estate of John Jordan, deceased $339.50, Interest
6 years and 9 months to 19th $131.50.
April 1812: to Cash received from the Estate of Stephen
Woods, deceased, by sale of negroes in the hands of William Jordan $54.06¼.
Interest from 7th Sept. 1808 to 19th April 1812 $11.89¼.
Total $542.95½.
By Cash for boarding, schooling and clothing for six years
and nine months to the 19th Ap'l. 1812 $137.50.
Balance due the 19th Ap'l, 1812 $405.45½.
We, William Anthony and George Hulm, Commissioners, appointed
by the County Court of Williamson Ap'l. Session 1813, to settle
with Oliver Williams, Guardean of Nancy Jordan, one of the heirs
of John Jordan, deceased, have settled with said Guardean up to
the nineteenth day of Ap'l. eighteen hundred and twelve and find
due said Nancy Jordan from her Guardean Oliver Williams the sum of
four hundred and five dollars and forty-five cents and five mills
at said time given under our hands this 13th day of April 1813.
William Anthony and G. Hulm

Page
(336)

NICHOLAS SCALES, Guardean of Susanna G. Jordan, dr.
To her proportion of the estate of John Jordan $339.50, interest
6 years and nine months to 19th April 1812 $137.50, To cash rec'd,
from the Estate of Stephen Wood, deceased, by sale of negroes in
the hands of William Jordan $54.06¼, interest from 7th Sept. 1808 to
19th Ap'l. 1812 $11.89¼, by cash for boarding, schooling and
clothing $542.95½, (for 6 years and 9 months to the 19th Ap'l.
1812). Balance due on the 19th April 1812 $405.45.
We, William Anthony and George Hulm, commissioners appointed
by the County Court to settle with Nicholas Scales, Guardean of
Susanna G. Jordan, one of the heirs of John Jordan, deceased, have
settled with said Guardean up to the nineteenth of April Eighteen
hundred and twelve and find due said Susanna G. Jordan from her
Guardean Nicholas Scales the sum of four hundred and five dollars
and forty-five cents five mills at said time given under our hands
the 13th April 1813. Signed William Anthony, G. Hulme.

SALLY L. R. GRAY'S Supplemental Inventory: fine old furniture
and suit of curtains, debt on a/c against Rob't. Stockard $110. and
undivided moity of a tract of land of acres in Stewart County.
Returned April Session 1813 by Young A. Gray, Admr.

RICHARD WILLET, deceased, Acc't. of sales of the Estate: four
beads, bead clothes and two steads, Charlotte Willet $20, two chests
and one table, do. $5, a parcel of pewter and tin, one tub, some
piggins, knives and forks and one pot, do. $7, one cotton wheel and
one flax wheel do. $3, one side saddle $3, some castings $4, one
plow hoe, two axes, some augurs, one clevis, weading hoes, drawing
chains and drawing knife $6, a parcel of cards, slays, sifter and
bread tray $2, a parcel of earthern and glass ware and one cooking
glass $2, one chear and two churns $1, one hackle .50, one jug .75,

Page
(337)

sixteen head of hogs $5, one mare and colt $22, five head of
cattle $38.25, two raw hides $5, Samuel Andrews two augurs .25,
John Floyd one grey mare $6.50, Eli Hope one gray horse $49, William
Willet one red heifer $8.75, John Floyd ome cow and calf $9.50,
James Cranshaw one brindle steer $9, do. one pided steer $11.25,
James Pugh one frow $1.6¼, Reuben Huggins one small log chain $1.10,
Edward Russel one mans old saddle .50, Amount of sale Total $221.41¼.
The gun and sheep not got into possession and are not sold, the
geese not sold given under my hand - Charlotte Willet, Administra-
trix to Richard Willet, deceased, returned Ap.'l Session 1813.

Agreeable to an order of the Worshipful County Court of Williamson County to us directed January Session 1813, we met at the
hous e of Federick Davis and examined the accounts of Samuel Wilson, guard'n. of David Page and Jacob Page and John Page, minor
offins of John Page of John Page, deceased, and find said Samuel
Wilson in an account current with said orphans as follows, to
wit: Dr. as Guardian for David Page Toone note on William Stephen payable 1st Jan'y. 1811, $21 to one note on Henty Stephen
payable 10th Nov. 1809 $30.38½ to one note on Robert McClelland
principal and interest $18.6½. Due David Page in the division
of the estate by John Page $134.82, due David Page in the division
of the Estate by Stokely Page $11.64. Credit to the above ac-
count for services rendered $1. To cash paid David Page this re-
ceipt $18.6¼. Balance due David Page $196.34½.
Dr. as Guardean to Jacob Page: to one note on William Stephens payable 12th Aug. 1810 - $61.25½
To one note on William Stephens payable 23rd March 1810
$170.43

To one note on William Stephens payable 11th of November
1809 $12.
To one note on Charles Stephens payable 23rd January 1811
$3
To one note on William Stephens Jnr. payable 10th Nov'r.
1809 $10.35½
To one note on David Craig $87.22½. To one note on Charles
Stephens payalbe 13th June 1812 $57.87½. Total 402.14.
Credit to the above to cash paid for schooling and paper
$3.12½.
To cash paid for Guardean bond .25, to services rendered
in the division of the Estate .66. Total $4.3½.
Balance due Javoy Page $398.12½.
Do. as Guardean for John Page. To one note on William
Stephens, Jnr. payable 25th Dec. 1812 - $80. Total $150.50.
Credit to the above -
To cash paid for Recording Guardian: bond caring negro
ten years $1.75. To cash paid for schooling, paper, and book
$4.62, to services rencered in the division of the estate .60.
Total $6.03.
Balance due John Page $144.47.
Agreeable to the within Statement we find in the hand of
the Guardean of David Page a balance due the ward $196.84½.
As due to Jacob, we find a balance due the ward $144.47
up to the first of January 1813.
                         William Benson
                         Richard Pucket
                         A. Williams.

Agreeable to an order of the worshipful County Court of
Williamson to us directed January Term 1813, we met at the
house of Frederick Davis and examond the accounts of Owen T.
Watkins, Guardean of Frederick Page and Patsey Page, minor orphans of John Page, deceased, and find the said Owen T. Watkins in an account current with Patsey Page as her Guardean
as follows to wit.

25th January 1811 to note on Henry Stephens $111.64.
25th January 1811 to note on Henry Stephens $ 6.50.
25th December 1812 to note on Andrew Johnston 12.50
25th December 1811 to cash received of Frederick Page 28.22

Page (339)

GContra $158.86
To cash paid for Patsey's part of the Guardean bond .37½
Allowed the guardean for his services $3.
                                                      $3.

To cash paid P. Pinkston for crying negroes at hire .37½

                                                      $3.75
Balance due his ward Batsey   ----- ---- $155.11
Do. as guardean for Frederick Page
25th Decr. 1811 one note on Eli McGan   ----   40.18¾
25th Decr. 1812 to note on Isaac Marrs   31.
               Contra $71.18¾
To cash paid for Frederick's part of the
     guardean bond   .37½
To cash paid P. Pinkston for crying negroes at hire --.37½
Allowed the guardean for his services $3.
To cash pd. for pr. of shoes for Milly $2.
To cash paid for Young A. Gray for medicine and
attendance on the negroe Milly $7.75
25th Dcr. 1812 to cash pd. Patsey Page for Frederick
Page in division of the Estate $28.22
     Balance due his ward Fredrick --$29.46¾ $41.46¾
     The above account is settled up to the first day
of January 1813.
     Given under our hands this 25th January 1813.
          William Denson, A. Williams, Rich'd. Puckett

     Agreeable to an order of the Worshipful County Court of
Williamson to us directed January term 1813, we met in the town
of Franklin on the 13th of April 1813 and examond the accounts
of Samuel Crockett, guardian of Stokely Page and Hervey Page,
minor orphans of John Page, deceased, and find the said Samuel
Crockett in an account current with Stokely Page as his guardean as follows to wit:

Page (340)

To judgment obtained against John L. Fielder for hire of
negro $28.41. The 17th January 1813 by cash rec'd. for hire of
negroe $9.62½. To note on Henry Rutherford for hire of negro
Arons, due the 25th December 1812 $31. Total $67.9½, credit to
the above to cash paid Nov'r. 18th 1813 for schooling $3.25,
To cash paid for Stokley's part of the guardean land .37½ cents
to cash paid Peter Pinkston for crying negroes for hire .75,
allowed the guardean for four days services $4, Total $8.37½.
     Balance due his ward Stokley Page $58.62, do. as guardean
of Hervey Page by cash rec'd. the 10th October 1811 $100, credit
the above to cash paid for Hervey's part of the guardean land

.37½. To cash paid November 18th 1812 for schooling $3.25. Al-
lowed the guardean for two days services $2, Total $5.62½.
Balance due his ward Hervey $94.37½. The above accounts is set-
tled up to the first day of January 1813. Given under our hands
this 13th of April 1813. O. Williams, William Denson, Rich'd.
Puckett.

THOMAS BALLOW'S Inventory - 1 negroe woman, 2 horses, 12
head cattle, 41 head hogs, 2 sheep, 8 head geese, 2 beds and furniture, 2 trunks, 1 chest, 1 wheel, 1 clock reel, 2 pots, 1 oven,
8 pewter plates, 1 do. dish, 1 do. bason, 2 water pails, 1 churn,
2 keggs, 2 pair drawing chains, 2 iron wedges, 2 plows, 2
grubbing hoes, 2 weeding hoes, 3 guns, 2 padlocks, 3 axes, 1 grid
iron, 1 pair flatirons, 1 handsaw, 1 cooper adds, 2 drawing knifes,
1 grind-stone, 3 chissels, 1 augur, 1 trow, 1 crows, 1 water
bucket, 1 table, 5 chairs, knifes and forks, 1 case and razors,
1 coffee pot, 1 mans saddle, 1 womans saddle, 3 slays and 2
pr. of geers, corn and meat, quantity not known. This is an Inventory of the Estate of Thomas Ballow, deceased. Signed Ann
Ballow, Alexander Smith. Returned Ap'l. Session 1813.

Page
(341)
     An account of Sale of the Estate of JOHN CRAWFORD, deceased:
James Whooton 1 barshare plow $2.1, Henry Rutherford 1 do. $3,
do. 1 pair traices, $3., do. 1 hoe .35¼, James Whooten 1 pr.
double trees $1.54, Elizabeth Crawford 1 ax $1.37½, John White
one grindstone $1.6¼, Elizabeth Crawford 1 candle stand $3, do.
1 bed and furniture $30., do. 1 table and furniture $10, Henry
Rutherford one bed and furniture $255 Elizabeth Crawford one bu-
reau and cover $16, do. half dozen chairs $1.50, Alexander Crawford, Haywood's revisal and Justice $5, H. Rutherford one slait
and 2 books $2, C. Crawford one looking glass $1, do. two wheels,
1 reel and so forth $5, do. 2 pots, 2 pr. pothooks, 2 potracks,
$6, James Rutherford one mans saddle $20., H. Rutherford 1 pr.
saddle bags $2.50, Nicholas Perkins 1 bay mare $15, Samuel
Crawford 1 sorrel horse $31, Nicholas Perkins one bay mare $16m
do. one brown colt $15, James Rutherford 1 bay horse $46, Nicholas Perkins 1 sorrel filly $40, Elizabeth Crawford 1 sorrel
horse $45, Matthew Johnston one desk $30.50, Samuel Crawford one
negro named Lewis $100, Duncan Robertson 1 negro girl hired
$33, Ryley Slocolm 1 negro girl hired $28.12½, G. W. Rutherford
1 negro boy hired $30.25, Nicholas Perkins 1 black cow and calf
$7.25, John Gray 2 steers $3.12½, Elizabeth Crawford 1 cow and
yearling $6, John West 1 cow and calf $8.25, Nicholas Perkins 1
steer and yearling calf $5.50, Michael Long 28 head of hogs $29,
Elizabeth Crawford 2 head of hogs $3.50, do. 8 head of hogs
$10, Abraham Secress last flock of hogs $6.37½, Elizabeth Crawford one womans saddle $6, James Walker 100 yds. of bailing cloth
$25, 67 different pieces of rope sold to different persons, in
Page
(342)
all $22.95¼. The bailing cloaths and ropes belonging to the firm
of Rutherford and Crawford in two equal parts, the whole amounting to $73.95½. One half $36.97½. Total amount of the Estate as
sold and hired $755.56¼.
     Elizabeth Crawford, Henry Rutherford, Admr.
   Henry Rutherford's surveying instruments and book $30,
James Campbell one case of razors $1.37½, Andrew Ewing one arith-
metick book .75, Tomas Alfred 1 cow and young calf $3.25, -this
belonging to page 341 - returned April Session 1813.

We, the Commissioners, appointed by Court January Session have met according to order this twentieth of January one thousand eight hundred and thirteen and find the valuation of James Crafton's estate to be worth $2400, and have divided the same among the widow of said James Crafton, Richard Crafton, and Daniel Crafton in the following manner to wit: 1st Dennie Crafton draws Mary and Charles $525., widow of James Crafton, deceased, do. Elick $450, George Crafton do. Mariah and Sam $525, Daniel Crafton do. Moses $400, Richard Crafton do. Scinda and Enee $500, and each dificiency to have a renumiration paid by those whoose lots have a surplus $480, being a just demand of legatee of negroes out of the above mentioned of $2400.
Returned April Session 1813.
Jacob Halfacre, Freeman Walker, James Harder, Ellen Alexander, Robert Davis.

End of Book No. 1 through 1800-1812

A

Acuff, Isaac, 97
Adams, Benjamin, 62
   Charles, 117
   Daniel, 132
   Howell, 48, 49
   Thomas, 94, 95
   William, 94
Akins, Moses, 106
Aldridge, Nathaniel, 134
Alen, David, 112
Alexander, David T., 97
   Ellen, 178
   Joseph, 143, 145
   Robert, 149
   William, 99, 117, 128
Alfred, Tomas, 177
Allen, Carr, 113, 114
   George, 117
   George H., 127
   George S., 107
   John, 138, 164
   Sally, 166
   Val., 128
   Valentine, 117
   William S., 149
Allexander, William, 117
Allison, Hugh, 33, 121
   James, 112, 118, 126, 161
   Nancy, 160
   Thomas, 127
Alsap, John, 73
Alsup, John, 81
Anderson, David P., 122
   John, 104, 130
   Willliam P., 139
Andrew, Ann, 25
   Elizabeth, 25
   Ephraim, 25
   ephraim, 25
   George, 25
   James, 117
   Knacy, 25
   Nancy, 25
   Stacy, 25
Andrews, Ann, 27
   Ephraim, 26, 121, 126, 127
   George, 27
   John, 139
   Knacy, 27, 126, 129
   Samuel, 87, 88, 175
   Tapley, 128
Anthony, William, 174
Appleby, Agness, 20
   Daniel, 20

James, 20, 21
John, 20, 22
William, 20, 21
Armstrong, James, 166
   John, 88
   Lancelot, 78
Arthur, Benjamin, 85
   Henry, 160
Arthurs, Benjamin, 90
Asteen, Jesse, 134
   Mr., 134
Atkinson, Henry H., 131
   John, 94
Avent, Leonard Dunn, 162
Aydelott, Thomas, 13

B

Bachman, Samuel, 57
Bailey, Elizabeth, 13
   Henry, 24, 118
   William, 13
Baker, Humphrey, 88
   John, 126, 128
Baldridge, Andrew, 123
   John, 20, 82
   Robert, 123
Balew, Thomas, 148
Ballow, Ann, 177
   Thomas, 177
Banks, William, 117
Barnes, Joshua, 149
   Richard, 149
   Seth, 73
Barnett, Martha, 141, 142
Barnhart, John, 88
Barr, Hugh, 145
Bass, Lawrence, 106, 107, 152
   Nancy, 120
Bateman, Enoch, 76
   Isaac, 51
Battle, Isaac, 140
Baugh, Gabriel, 163
Beachy, Daniel, 164
Beard, William, 95, 96
Beasley, Archibald, 150, 151
Beaver, Elizabeth, 14
Beavers, William, 90
Beet, Barnabas, 76
Bell, H., 134
   Hugh F., 139
   James, 5
   John, 5
   Sally, 5
   Stinson, 5
   Thomas, 5
   William, Jr., 5

   William, Sr., 5
Bells, Isaac, 97
Bennett, George, 132
   William, 99
Benthall, Mathew, 96, 98
Bently, Richard, 93, 94
Benton, Ellizabeth, 112
   Jesse, 16
   Nancy, 16
   Peggy, 16
   Polly, 16
   Samuel, 16
   Susannah, 16
   Thomas H., 16, 17
Berry, Basil, 122
   James, 115, 117, 170
   Martha, 117
   Thomas, 117, 122, 144, 145
   William, 115, 117
Bethell, Carter, 87
Bettick, Robert, 144
Betts, Jonathan, 82
Bevell, Benjamin, 163
Beverly, Matilda, 162
Bevill, Robert, 118
Biller, Abraham, 109
Billingsly, James, 90
Binckley, Adam, 4
Black, Hugh, 106
   James, 108, 124
   John, 93, 94
   Willilam, 166
Blackamore, John, 1
Blackburn, teacher, 155
Blackman, Benjamin, 139
   John, 76
Blackshare, Hannah, 68, 69
   Jesse, 67, 68
   Thomas, 68
Blakely, Saarah, 17
   William, 95, 150, 151
Bond, Samuel, 149
Booker, Peter R., 28, 104, 109
   Suckey, 27
   Sukey, 28
Borin, William, 129
Boring, Jacob, 161
   Willilam, 25
Borland, James, 63
Bostick, John, 117, 159
Bowen, John, 139
Bowers, William, 90
Boyd, Armistead, 31
   H., 16
   Harrison, 17
   James, 53, 54

E

Eaton, John, 98
Edmeston, Sam'l, 2
Edmiston, Sam'l, 86
    T. H., 104
    Thomas, 103
Edmondson, Samuel, 114
    William, 98
Edmonston, Samuel, 113
Edney, Leven, 81
Edwards, Joseph, 143
    Peter, 55, 151
Elam, Edward, 6, 88
Elison, Joseph T., 129
Ellet, Josiah, 90
Ellilson, J. T., 129
Elliot, Barnett, 90
Elliott, John, 94, 95
Ellison, Joseph T., 129
Elliston, J. T., 101, 102, 103
    Joseph T., 102
Epperson, Anne, 165
    Littleberry, 149, 165
Epps, Labone, 164
Evans, Daniel, 10
    Jesse, 9, 10
    John, 10, 146
    Martha, 145, 146
    Mary, 10
    Rachel, 10
    Rebeckah, 10
    Robert, 10
    Robin, 10
Evins, Lewis, 138
Ewin, John, 127
Ewing, Andrew, 177
    Edley, 32, 122
    William, 31

F

Fanney, Abram, 112
    David, 112
    Elizabeth, 112
    Moses, 112
    Rhodey, 112
Fares, James, 73
Farmer, John, 8
    Nathan, 8, 66
Farrar, John, 87
Feat, Joseph, 149
Featherstone, William, 164
Ferrell, Levy, 99
Fielder, J. L., 105
    John L., 116, 124, 148, 176
    Mr., 88

Fields, Nelson, 140
Finnell, Achilles, 167
    James, 167
Finney, James, 48
Fish, Moses, 139
Fishburn, Phillip, 107
Fisher, Frederic, 4
    William, 149
Fitzgerald, James, 95, 149
Fitzpatrick, Andrew, 107
    Morgan, 98
    Samuel, 98
Fleming, Hannah, 98
Flowers, Henry, 166
Floyd, David, 14
    John, 175
Fluallen, Wm., 51
Fly, Jere, 48
Folks, John, 88
Foster, Jesse, 88
Fowlkes, John, 98
Franch, William, 163
Franklin, Robert, 107
Freeman, Arthur, 47, 108
    James, 47
    Miles, 47
    Polly, 47, 108
    Rebecca, 47
Friel, Moses, 90
Frierson, David, 17, 18
    Isaac Edwin, 17
    Moses G., 17, 18
    Sam'l, 18
Fulgum, Arthur, 100
Fuller, Arthur, 90
Fulton, James, 148, 172
Funkhouser, C., 86

G

Gabrills, Benjamin, 110
Gambill, Benjamin, 139
Gamble, Benjamin, 139
    John, 77
Gambling, John, 97
    Polley, 97
Gambrel, Benjamin, 91
Gambrell, Benjamin, 92
Gardner, Dawning, 19
    Hannah, 12, 19
    Jane, 12, 18
    John, 12, 18, 20
    Joseph, 18
    Martha, 18
    Polly, 19
    Richey, 12, 18, 19
    William, 12, 18, 19

Garley, William, 99
Garner, Britain, 76
    John, 79
Garret, Thomas, 82
Garrett, Jacob, 68, 80, 81, 82, 145
    Jenny, 80, 81
    John, 79, 80, 82
    John D., 80, 81, 113, 114
    Thomas, 80, 82
Garrott, Thomas, 63
Gatling, John, 101
Gault, James, 63, 64, 78, 105
Gay, James, 82
Geary, John, 93, 94
Gentry, Sam'l, 79
George, Reuben, 90
German, Stephen, 69, 70
    William, 117
Gibson, James, 93
    John B., 93, 94
    Patrick, 94, 129
Giddens, James, 150, 151
Gillaspie, John, 95, 106
Gillespie, Alex., 95
    David, 147
    Dowd, 147
    James, 168
    John, 94
    Thomas, 146
Given, Edward, 139
Givens, Edward, 48, 49
    Ephraim, 91
Glascock, George, 87, 96, 149, 150
Glover, James, Sr., 60
    Jones, 24, 61, 62
    Lancaster, 62, 128, 129, 130, 171, 172
    William, 52, 59, 61, 93, 94
Gloves, Lancaster, 61
Goff, John, 55, 58
Good, William, 139, 164
Goodman, Benny, 149
Gordon, John, 129
Goslold, Garrot, 139
Gough, Mathew M., 83, 96
Gower, Alexander, 4
Goyne, J., 82
Graves, Alexander, 125
    Hannah, 125
    Keziah, 125
    Martha, 125
    Priscilla, 125
    Sarah, 125
    Thomas, 125
Gray, Henry H., 7
    Henry K., 8, 27, 28

J., 29
James, 7, 27, 28, 46, 47
James , 8
James M., 27, 28
James McK., 7
John, 177
Joseph, 28
M. K., 8
Sally L. R., 174
Sally S., 7
Sarah S. R., 28
Stephen, 21
Suckey, 27
Sukey, 7
William, 49
Young, 163
Young A., 7, 8, 27, 28, 29, 176
Green, John, 139
  Mary, 22
  Nathaniel, 17
  Patsey, 137
  S., 111, 114, 116, 124, 139, 152, 153
  Sherwood, 137, 138, 140, 153
  Thomas, 22
  William, 22, 139
Greenlee, John, 51, 53
Greer, Vincin, 145
Gregory, Edw'd, 138
Grider, William M., 134
Griffin, John, 139
Griggs, Thomas, 140
Grimes, John, 58
Grinder, Robert, 104
Grundy, Felix, 173
Gunter, Frances, 66
Gurley, William, 95, 150
Guthrie, Robert, 66, 169

H

Hafflin, James, 142
Hail, John, 88
Hairston, Peter, 159
Halbert, William, 141, 142
Haley, James, 139
Halfacre, Jacob, 172, 178
Hall, John, 90
  Joseph, 140
  Wm., 77
Hallum, John, Jr., 49
Hamilton, Mr., 155
Hampton, Presley, 88
Hanell, William, 81
Hansley, Gideon, 127
Harademan, N. P., 50
Hardaway, Dr., 161

Hardeman, Garner, 76
  John, 158
  John N., 171
  N. P., 26, 32, 33, 45, 46, 47, 51, 53,
    54, 55, 56, 57, 58, 59, 60,
    61, 62, 64, 65, 67, 68, 69,
    70, 71, 74, 75, 76, 77, 78,
    79, 80, 81, 83, 84, 86, 87,
    88, 89, 90, 91, 92, 93, 94,
    96, 97, 98, 99, 101, 102,
    103, 104, 105, 106, 108,
    109, 110, 111, 112, 113,
    114, 115, 116, 118, 119,
    121, 124, 126, 131, 133,
    134, 136, 138, 140, 141,
    142, 146, 147, 148, 149, 156
Harden, Delilah, 30
  John, 30
Harder, Jacob, 100, 101
  James, 178
Hardgrove, James, 82
Hardin, John, 55
  Presley, 50, 51, 55, 62
Harding, John, 80
Hardy, Murfree, 50
Hargrove, James, 81
Harkins, John, 134
Harness, John, 51
Harney, Thomas, 139
Harrilson, Ezekiel, 87
Harris, Andrew, 169, 170
  Arthur, 138
  Benton, 132
  Caro, 169
  Cassandra, 169
  Ede, 169
  Edith, 173
  Edward, 169
  Josephas, 104
  Josepphus, 169
  Margaret, 23
  Meekezene, 169
  Patsy, 169
  Samuel, 151, 169
  Sarah, 23
  Sidney, 169
  Simpson, 139
Harrison, Edw., 125
  William P., 172
Harrlson, William, 88
Hart, Richard, 121
Hartgrave, James, 80
Hartley, John, 78
Hassell, Elisha, 150
Hay, Ann, 9
  Balaam, 93, 94

  Edith, 93, 94
  John, 132
  Rich'd, 93, 94
Hays, Doctor, 70
  R., 53
  Robert, 104, 107
Haywood, John, 138, 139
Hemphill, William, 122
Henderson, John, 77
  Robert, 123
Hendrix, Thomas, 142
Herbert, Nath'l, 124
Hess, William, 108, 109
Hewey, James, 149
Hickman, William, 117
Hicks, Harrison, 29
  J., 16, 17
  James, 93, 162, 163
  John, 29
Higgins, Albert, 109
  James, 109, 142
  John, 29, 45, 46, 109, 142
  Martha, 29, 46, 109
  Phoebe, 141
  Reuben, 68, 69
  William, 109, 141, 142
Hightower, John, 4, 54
  Polly, 4, 54
  Richard, 123
Hill, Allen, 151
  Dann, 53
  G., 15, 153
  H. M., 109
  H. W., 125
  Henry W., 125, 153, 154
  J. C., 125
  J. G., 151
  James, 153, 154
  James C., 109, 125
  James G., 151
  John, 79, 123, 142, 148
  John D., 47
  Martha, 109, 125, 153, 154
  McAlester, 125
  Nichol, 125
  W. C., 151
  William, 15
  William C., 109, 124
  William G, 153
  Willilam C., 151
Hinds, John, 78
  Simeon, 97, 114
Hines, David, 95
Hobbs, Ann, 161
  Hartwell, 161
  Joel, 72, 95

Sally, 161
Hodge, Francis, 68
Hodges, Edmond, 90
   Elizabeth, 13
   James, 13
   Lydda, 13
   Philip, 13
   Welcom, 13, 14
   Welcome, 89, 90
Holbert, John, 29, 46, 109
Holemane, Thomas, 4
Holland, Gustis, 51
Holliday, Henry, 66
Holmes, Elm, 138
Holt, John, 120, 148
Honoll, Peter, 121
Hood, John, 95
Hooker, William, 92
Hooks, Betty, 132
   Charles, 129
   Curtis, 132
Hope, Eli, 48, 175
   Thomas, 122
Hopkins, Bitha, 1
   Elizabeth, 1, 2
   Hannah, 1
   Heziah, 1
   James, 1, 2
   James Pickering, 1
   Jason, 1, 122
   John, 1
   John Pickering, 2
   Jonathan, 1, 63, 121
   Joseph, 2
   Neal, 122
   Richard, 153
   Winifred, 1
Hotton, Thomas, 75
House, Andrew, 169
   Green, 173
   James, 132, 169, 173
   James, Jr., 90, 170
   James, Sr., 90
   John, 108, 109, 149
   William, 90, 91
Houston, David, 110
   James, 110
   Lydia, 110
   Samuel, 103, 110
   Sidney, 103
Howard, Dawson, 138
   Richard, 138
Howell, Joseph, 100
Hubbard, Daniel, 167
   John, 167
Hudlow, Barbara, 147

George, 147
Hudson, John, 48
Huey, James, 87
Huggins, Reuben, 175
Hughes, Christian, 123
   Henry, 109
Hull, John, 145
Hulm, George, 174
Hulme, G., 54, 63, 76, 83
   Geo., 70
   George, 80, 172
   John, 69
   Patrick, 86
   Rob't, 70
   Robert, 62, 63, 64, 68, 69, 78, 81, 122
   Susanna, 62, 64
   Thomas, 86
   Wm., 68
Hundspeth, David, 51
Hungerford, James, 99
Hunnel, Peter, 33
Hunnell, wife and children - unnamed, 32
   William, 32, 33, 121
Hunt, G., 123
   Gersham, 97
   Gurshum, 172
   Gursom, 148
   O., 129
   S., 129
   Sion, 83, 129
Hunter, Elijah, 11
   Elisha, Sr., 87
   Elizah, 48
   Henry, 82
   William, 156
Hurley, John, 54
Huston, David, 52
Hutcheson, Wm., 97
Hutson, John, 61
Hyde, Hartwell, 98
   Rich'd W., 98
Hynes, Simeon, 98

I

Ingram, Frances, 85
   Henry, 99
   John, 85
   Sam'l, 85
   Susanna, 85
   Thomas, 85
Inman, Henry, 121
Ivey, William, 81
Ivy, William, 80, 81

J

Jackson, Henry H., 145
   James, 80
   Joseph, 98
   Sam'l, 10
   Sarah, 10
Jamison, John, 95
Jarman, Stephen, 69
Johnson, Grace, 105
   James, 105
   John, 3, 144
   Joseph, 166
   Neil, 149
   Thomas, 139
Johnston, Andrew, 176
   John, 76
   Lawn, 95
   Matt, 95
   Matthew, 177
   Robert, 8, 80
   Swanson, 87
Johnstone, Alexander, 128
Jones, David, 164
   Edward, 171
   James, 115
   John, 81, 82, 121, 138
   Lawrence, 163
   Nelson, 164
   Thomas, 132
Jordan, Archer, 152
   Burton, 13, 47, 70
   Henry, 100
   James, 48
   John, 70, 130, 174
   Nancy, 174
   Sally, 70, 71
   Sarah, 71
   Susanna G., 174
   William, 174
   Wiltshire, 98
Joslin, Daniel, 106
Joyce, James, 127, 165, 166

K

Kaigler, David, 166
Kearny, Lucy, 27
Kee, Jinea, 143
   Nancy, 145
Keeth, John, 14
Keigler, Andrew, 96
Kelly, Thomas, 149
Kelsey, Charles, 149
Kenard, George, 132
Kennard, Anthony, 132
   John, 132

Michael, 132
Kennedy, Dempsey, 95
Kenney, John M., 61
Key, Henry, 129
   henry, 129
   William M., 66, 89
Kindrake, William, 11
Kindrick, Olsimus, 94
King, William, 170
Kinnard, Anthony D., 115
   George, 115, 128, 173
   John, 115
   M. C., 174
   Michael, 52, 115, 127, 173
   Nathaniel, 132
   Walter, 134
Knight, William W., 12
Kyle, Rebekah, 25

L

Lamaster, James, 21
Lampkins, Ezekiel, 94
Landrum, Mariman, 142
Lane, Turner, 139
Larkins, Elizabeth, 157
   John, 157
   Margaret, 157
Laton, William, 115
Latta, Thomas, 87, 88
Launders, T., 154
Lavendar, Bluff, 150
   Nicholas, 149
Lavender, Bud, 149
Lawrance, Abraham, 23
   Elizabeth, 22
   John, 22
Lawrence, Jacob, 23
   John, 23
   Polly, 23
Lay, Isaac, 52, 53
Lea, William, 88
Lee, Benjamin, 6, 7
   Braxton, 6
   Jenny, 6
   John, 6
   Mary, 6
   Nancy, 143
Legate, William, 129
Lewis, Joel, 106
   William T., 107
   Wm. T., 106
Lightfoot, Jason, 110
Lindsey, John, 94, 95
Little, Abrm., 69
   Benjamin, 129
   John, 68

Livesy, Jesse, 117
Locke, Charles, 128
   Richard, 121
   Richard S., 129
   William, 99
Logan, William, 84
Long, David, 149
   Michael, 177
Lord, John, 166
Love, Bennora, 32
   David B., 108, 109
   James, 5
   John G., 32, 108
   Joseph, Jr., 32
   Polly, 32
   Rob't, 33
   Susan, 16
   William, 107, 108
   William M., 31
Lovet, David, 148
Luster, James, 131
Lyon, Henry, 139
Lyons, Patrick, 106, 139

M

Macfadin, Cornelius, 145
Mackay, William, 89
Macllin, John, 107
Maginson, William G., 139
Mahan, Andrew, 121
Malone, Miles, 25, 26
   Thomas, 145
Malroy, James, 23
Mandley, Caleb, 7
Maneo, George, 128
Manire, Betty, 167
   John, 161, 167
Manley, Caleb, 150
   John Caleb, 104
Mansker, George, 99, 100
   George, Sr., 134
   L. W., 166
   William, 99, 100
Marcel, Ben'j, 139
Markem, Barnet, 145
Marlin, George, 108
Marr, John, 108, 110
   Josiah, 136
   William Christmas, 136
Marris, Isaac, 176
Marrs, William C, 137
Marshall, James, 158
   William, 158
Martial, James, 165
Martin, George, 63, 69
   Henry, 63, 81

Jonathan, 98
   William, 91, 92, 110, 111, 114, 153
   Zachariah, 97
Mason, Abram, 91
   David, 153
   Isaac, 140
   Isaac, Jr., 91
Masterson, Thomas, 67, 118
   Thos., 8
Matherrin, James, 48
Mathews, Cornellius, 127
   John, 92
   William, 115
Mathis, Cornelius, 150
Matthews, William, 132
Mattocks, William, 82
Maury, A., Sr., 141
   Abraham, 8, 66
   Abram, 18, 113
   Abram, Sr., 141
   Philip, 66, 89
May, John, 106
   William, 132
Mayfield, Elijah, 128
   George, 77
   Izrael, 80
   James, 105
   John, 105, 116, 123, 145
   Thomas, 108
Mays, Armistead, 149
McAfee, John, 69
McAffee, John, 69
Mcaffee, John, 69
McAffee, John, 122
   Miles, 69
McAlister, C. H., 153
McBride, Hugh, 99, 128
   James, 100
McCall, Catren, 106
   Francis, 93, 105
McCalpan, John, 77, 124
   John, Sr., 77
   William, 77
McCandless, James, 104
McClellan, John, 98
McClelland, John, 99
   Robert, 175
McClellen, Robert, 90
McClenen, Robert, 170
McClure, Henry, 140
   William, 139
McCollum, Claud, 87
   Isaac, 87
   John, 81, 86
   Thrasher, 87
McConnico, Ann, 59

Gardner, 50
Garner, 53
Heziah, 59, 60
Jared, 58, 59
McCord, David, 117, 170
McCorkle, Andrew, 146
McCormac, James, 70
McCoy, Robert, 173
McCracken, John, 95
McCraven, James, 149
McCray, Armez, 134
McCrory, Thomas, 106
McCutchen, Sam'l, 63
McCuiston, James, 5
McCurdy, David, 21, 23
   Elizabeth, 20
   Grssy, 21
   Samuel, 21
McCutchan, Hannah, 121, 122
   James, 117, 121, 122
   John, 122
   Samuel, 144
   William, 122
McCutchen, Elizabeth, 157
   Hannah, 157, 158, 165
   James, 63, 69, 157
   John, 69, 113, 148, 157
   Patrick, 156, 157, 165
   Sam'l, 2, 3, 64, 69, 111, 165
   Samuel, 157
   William, 157
McDaniel, Alexander, 172
   John, 96
McDonald, Alex'r, 134
McDowel, William, 4
McEarley, Ezekial, 150
McElwell, Thomas, 149
McEnters, William, 148
McEwen, Thomas, 146
McGan, Eli, 176
McGavock, David, 106, 152
McGimsey, William, 138
McHugh, Jane, 78, 79
   Janes, 77
   Moses, 77, 78, 79
   Nancy, 78
   Polly, 78
McKearley, Ezekial, 150
McKey, John, 18
McKnight, James, 96, 98
   John, 53, 83, 84, 96, 100
   Robert, 96, 100
   Sam'l B., 96
   Samuel, 83
   William, 83
McLain, Robert, 94, 95

William, 94, 95
McLean, Willliam, 94
McLemore, Burrell, 52, 61, 62
   Robert, 104, 155
   Young, 7, 8
McLennon, Robert, 99
McMahon, Andrew, 121
   Daniel, 104
McMahoon, John B., 94
McMin, David, 59
   William, 59
McMullin, Andrew, 57
   James, 58
   Mary, 57, 58
   William, 53
   Wm., 51
McNeal, Edward, 117
McNutt, Sarah, 157
McReynolds, Arch'l, 106
Meachem, P., 139
Mebane, Alexander, 131
   George, 150, 151
Meddleton, Sam'l, 80, 81
Megah, Wm., 51
Merrill, William, 139
Merrit, Sam'l, 51
Michel, Mark, 132
Miles, Thomas, 91
Miller, Alex., 94, 95
   Alexander, 151
   James, 115, 117, 170
   John, 94
   William, 79
Minor, Isaac, 79
Mitchel, Samuel, 106
Mitchell, Charity, 112
   Edward, 139
   Evan, 112, 118
   Hamblen, 112
   John, 95
   Robert, 173
   William, 139
Mobary, Frederick, 87
Molloy, Thomas, 4
Montgomery, Alex., 94
   David, 13
   Hannah, 12
   Jane, 13
   Mary, 13
   Stephen, 139
   Willliam, 139
Moody, Moses, 4
Moore, Alexander, 87, 88
   Betsy, 73, 87
   Catherine, 72, 73, 86
   H., 48

Henry, 48, 49, 87
James, 71, 123
John, 72, 73, 74, 87, 88
Joseph, 164
Robert, 132
Somerset, 150, 151
William, 139
Morgan, Carey, 132
Moser, Christopher, 4
Mullin, Jesse, 129
   Joshua, 102
   Joshus, 129
   Mary, 101, 102, 103
   William, 129
   William S., 101, 102
   William s., 129
   William, Jr., 102, 129
Mullins, William M., 55
Murfree, H., 48
   Hardy, 48
   W. H., 48
Murphey, Ad., 126
   Alex., 126
Murphy, Butler, 125
Murrey, John, 139
   Riley, 90
   William, 64

N

Nash, Dempsey, 80, 81
   John, 4
   Patsy, 10
Neal, James, 85
   John P., 7
   Julilan, 128
   Julis, 26
   Nich., 129
Neelly, George, 62, 133
   J., 13
   James, 52, 72
   James M., 78
   John, 72, 73
   William, 73, 87
Neely, James, 50, 61
   James M., 69
   William, 48
Nelson, William, 139
Newman, Thomas, 103
Newsom, Balaam, 61
Nichols, John, 99
Nicholson, Malachi, 150
   Malachia, 151
Nolan, David, 79
Noland, Easter, 92
   John, 92
Nolen, Allen, 140

Ansalom, 139
G. L., 148
William, 91, 110, 140
Nolin, G. L., 139
William, 172
North, Abraham, 162, 164
Nowlin, Anney, 133
David, 133
Gen'l L., 134
General Lee, 133, 134, 136
Golsbey, 133
John, 133, 134
Littleberry, 133
William, 133, 134
Nully, William, 11, 26

O

Ogilvie, Harris, 160
John, 126, 160
Kimbro, 26, 128
Kimbrough, 118, 160
Manire, 160
Nancy, 160
Patty, 160
Richard, 118, 160, 161
Sally, 160
Smith, 160
William, 160, 161
Wm., 112
Old, Clements, 163
Elizabeth, 162
Thomas, 162
Olive, Robert, 116
Ore, Rob't, 88
Orr, Robert, 90
Orton, David, 95
Rich'd, 51
Richard, 54, 58, 91
William, 5, 79
Oslin, John, 129
Outlaw, William, 139
Overall, Aaron, 68
Overton, John, 139
Owen, Ambrose, 148
Frederick, 123, 124
Glen, 169, 170
James, 79, 149
Owens, Amelia, 9
Elijah, 8, 9
Nancy, 9

P

Page, Hervey, 176
Jacob, 175
Javoy, 175
John, 99, 124, 175, 176

Lovey, 99
Patsey, 176
Robert, 87
Stokely, 175, 176
Page, Lovey, 100
Pailey, Robert, 88
Paisley, Robert, 88
Parham, Dr. William, 109, 124
W., 154
William, 110, 151, 153
Parkers, William, 107
Parking, Dannold, 143
Parks, John, 53
Parmely, Ephraim, 6
Giles, 5, 6
Samuel, 6
Parrish, Joel, 140, 141
Susannah, 140
Parsons, Thomas, 99
Pate, Elizabeth, 130
G., 130
Hardy, 171
Nancy, 171
Persons, 172
Polley, 129
Patterson, Anne, 19
Gilbert, 87, 88
James, 19, 88
Joab, 87
John, 99, 100, 142
Luke, 87
Patton, Betsy, 119, 120
Drucilla, 119
George, 107, 120
J., 152
James, 64, 84, 85, 120
John, 76, 106, 107, 119
Margaret, 84, 85
Nancy, 120
Robert, 84
Sally, 119
Thomas, 120
William, 120
Payton, Joseph, 5
Pearee, A., 15
Arthur, 15
Peck, Jediah, 72, 87
Pepper, William, 149
Perkins, Andrew, 99
Col., 155
Colonel Peter, 159
Dan'l, 3, 89, 111, 123
Daniel, 109, 112, 122, 141, 155
Hardin, 108, 159
John P., 89
Leah, 89

N., 123
Nicholas, 30, 31, 160, 177
Nicholas T., 104
Peter, 89, 104, 158
Samuel, 85, 130
Thomas H., 103, 104, 108
Perry, Darsing, 68
William, 122
Perryman, John, 98
Pettway, Hinchey, 172
Petty, Henry, 62
Petway, Hinchey, 140, 141, 152
Peyton, George Y., 69
Philips, Bennet, 136
Phillips, John C., 106
Jonathan, 89
Pickens, Andrew, 99
Pierce, Arthur, 74
Pigg, John, 29, 142
Pillow, Gideon, 138
John, 98, 128
Mordica, 170
Stines, 139
Pinkerton, David, 122
Pinkly, Fredrick, 73
Pinkston, David, 126, 165
Hugh, 127
P., 176
P. H., 15
Peter, 15, 99, 100, 126, 173, 176
Turner, 99, 100
Polk, William, 110
Pope, J., 13
William B., 138
Porter, Dudley, 148, 170
John, 63, 68, 69, 81, 122, 145, 170
Rus., 11
Sarah, 148, 170
Potts, Joseph, 143
Powell, Anderson, 146, 147
Jean, 11
Polly, 147
William, 142
Pressett, Elisha, 139
Prewitt, John, 86, 122
Robert, 86
Price, William, 134
Prichett, James, 121
Priest, James, 112
Jenney, 112
John, 112, 118
John T., 112, 113
Mary, 112, 113, 119
Moses, 112
Primm, John, 139
Prince, Robert, 139

Adam, 136
Agney, 104
Ailse, 120
Aim, 27
Allen, 90, 114, 152
Alugail, 60
Amey, 127
Amos, 141
Anderson, 27
Andrew, 131
Anne, 152
Annekey, 89
Anthony, 6, 7
Arthur, 61
Beliah, 27
Ben, 6, 7, 47, 49, 64, 67, 108, 147,
    162, 164
Benjamin, 7
Bett, 49
Betty, 161
Beverly, 162
Biddy, 163
Big Bob, 162
Bill, 27
Billy, 163
Bob, 27, 31, 49, 159
Bobb, 141
Boy, 75
Brister, 162
Bromfield, 151, 154
Burrell, 61, 62
Buster, 49
Caroline, 114, 152
Ceasar, 162
Charity, 65
Charles, 27, 49, 109, 132, 159, 162
Charlotte, 49, 162
Cheary, 93
Chelsey, 162
Cherry, 49
Chloe, 154
Clary, 141
Cloe, 109, 147
Cloey, 49
Conkard, 11
Daniel, 22, 161
Darby, 131
Darcas, 27
David, 162
Dick, 27, 114, 116, 127, 131, 136
Dilcey, 125
Dilcy, 127
Dinah, 138
Doll, 27
Dolly, 12, 126
Dorcas, 127

Doreas, 165
Dover, 65
Dred, 49
Dudley, 7
Dulcy, 141, 165
Easter, 124
Edmund, 162, 164
Edy, 49
Elenor, 165
Elisa, 157
Elizabeth, 161
Ellick, 109
Eny, 109
Ephraim, 27
Essex, 7
Ester, 151
Esther, 154, 159
Fanney, 125
Fanny, 103, 104, 131, 162
Frank, 49, 90, 114, 141, 152, 163
Franky, 27
Friday, 17
Furry, 7
Ganny, 164
Gardiner, 161, 163
George, 49, 120, 162
Gillum, 162, 164
Gloster, 131
Godphrey, 65
Hanibal, 161
Hannah, 61, 159, 161
Hanner, 49
Hardy, 7, 27
Harper, 7
Harriet, 158
Harry, 18, 49, 55, 131, 147
Henry, 7
Hester, 7
Hetty, 49
Isaac, 163
Isbel, 125
Ishah, 124
Isham, 31, 49, 151, 154
Israel, 141
Jack, 27, 49, 65, 67, 111, 157, 163,
    168
Jacob, 27, 49, 152
James, 6, 7, 27, 31, 64, 168
Jane, 24
Jeffery, 27
Jeffrey, 127
Jemina, 61
Jeney, 112
Jenney, 127
Jenny, 27, 49, 65, 118
Jerno, 31

Jerry, 121, 124, 126, 151
Jim, 62, 63, 106, 107, 162, 163,
    164
Jinner, 163
Jinney, 7
Jinny, 165
Joan, 27
Joe, 27
John, 126, 163
Joyce, 7
Judah, 90
Jude, 114, 131, 152
Judity, 27
Judy, 11, 163
Julia, 141
Juner, 75
Juniiper, 160
Kissy, 27
Kitty, 49
Labina, 17
Lawson, 104
Lee, 126, 132
Levenia, 31
Lew, 162, 164
Lewis, 90, 114, 116, 147, 151, 154,
    162, 164
Little Aaron, 162, 164
Little Bob, 162
Little Daniel, 161
Little Dulcy, 162
Little Judea, 161
London, 120
Luch, 165
Lucy, 6, 7, 27
Luke, 54
Mahomet, 65
Manuel, 147
Maria, 158, 161
Mariah, 141
Mary, 90, 109, 114, 136, 152
Matt, 64, 114
Melley, 61
Memgo, 61
Meriah, 65, 109
Merika, 162
Micharl, 141
Miles, 163
Milkey, 89
Mill, 49
Milley, 75, 114, 121, 125, 147
Milly, 11, 31, 127, 141, 176
Mingo, 61
Minney, 62
Minty, 27
Molley, 60, 90, 152
Molly, 141

Moses, 49, 109, 162
Mouring, 154
Nan, 7
Nance, 120
Nancy, 31, 49, 75, 141
Naney, 65
Nanny, 17
Napper, 103, 104
Natt, 49
Ned, 17, 64, 134
Nelly, 27
Nelson, 25
Noley, 49
Old Dulcy, 161
Old Frances, 49
Old Lena, 17
Old Lucy, 125
Oliver, 163
Orra, 114
Orrey, 90
Pammey, 89
Pat, 131
Pate, 25
Patsey, 27
Peter, 89, 117, 143, 162, 164
Phil, 124, 151
Philis, 126
Philiss, 12
Phill, 154
Phillis, 125
Philllis, 132
Pompey, 160
Rachel, 125, 127, 165, 168
Rachel Dilse, 27
Reuben, 54, 125, 162
Rose, 157
Ross, 64
Ruben, 132
Rusey, 161
Ruth, 152
Salina, 162
Sally, 49
Sam, 31, 103, 104, 109, 131, 161,
    162
Sarah, 27, 49, 143
Sawyer, 65
Scinthia, 157
Season, 147
Selvy, 49
Silon, 65
Simon, 18
Sindey, 109
Size, 27, 127
Solomon, 64, 67
Sook, 162, 164
Starling, 27

Stephen, 7, 126, 131, 132, 163
Suck, 27
Suckey, 131
Sugar, 154
Sukey, 154
Susan, 127
Sydia, 7
Tempathy, 60
Tempy, 62
Terey, 161
Terry, 64, 154, 162
Thomas, 61, 65, 157
Tillman, 61
Tilman, 62
Toby, 151, 154
Tom, 6, 7, 27, 49, 125, 141, 162,
    164
Treacy, 49
Ursey, 163
Ventu, 163
Venus, 49
Vine, 25
Viney, 165
Warrick, 27, 49
Wat, 152
Watt, 90
Will, 27, 126, 127, 163
William, 89, 141
Willie, 49
Winney, 65, 162
Worick, 127
Young Doll, 27
Young Lucy, 125
Sleeker, George, 133
Slocolm, ryley, 177
Slocumb, Joseph, 76
    Riley, 76
Smiley, Hugh, 149
Smith, Alexander, 5, 177
    Bennett, 173
    Charles, 103
    David, 98
    Frances, 166
    George, 164
    John, 114, 116
    Luke, 29
    Molinde, 30
    Robert, 144
    Senneah, 30
    William, 30
    Wm., 54
Sneed, Nathan, 144
    William, 114, 144
    Wm., 113
Snell, William, 97
Soloman, Jerdan, 132

Solomon, J., 133
    Jordan, 66
Spain, David, 117
Sparkman, Jesse, 87
Speaks, Thomas, 63, 80, 81
Spence, John, 51
Spencer, John, 58, 61, 70
Sprinkle, Moses, 88
Sprinkler, Moses, 87
Spurlin, Eli, 108
Squier, David, 93
Squire, David, 104
Stacy, Eli, 51, 55, 58, 59
Stainback, Drucilla, 119, 120
Stanley, Martin, 69
Stephen, William, 175
Stephens, Charles, 175
    Henry, 176
    Joel, 93, 126
Stepleton, Edward, 75
Stevens, Charles, 49, 128
    Edward, 100
    Joel, 94, 99, 100, 127
    Lewis, 100, 115, 132
    Loammie, 132
    Will, 127
    William, 99, 128
    William, Jr., 100
    William, Sr., 100
Stewart, Ann, 143, 144
    Anne, 145
    B. G., 139
    George, 77
    John, 2
    Thomas, 2, 110, 144
Stockett, Joseph, 113
    Noble, 62, 63
    William, 64
Stone, Agnes, 148
    Edw., 148
    Handley, 155
    Hendley, 104, 123, 154
    Jane, 148, 172, 173
    Polly, 159
    Rowley, 148
    Ruth, 159
    Sam, 148
    William, 147, 148, 172, 173
Stovall, Aggey, 133
    Barthew, 80
    Bartholomew, 91, 133
Stramlar, George, 104, 131
Stramler, George, 80, 81
Stramter, George, 61
Strickland, Thomas, 76
    Tilpha, 76